Unit 8 · Ready, Set, Grow!

Program Authors

Carl Bereiter
Andrew Biemiller
Joe Campione
Iva Carruthers
Doug Fuchs

Lynn Fuchs
Steve Graham
Karen Harris
Jan Hirshberg
Anne McKeough
Peter Pannell

Marsha Roit
Marlene Scardamalia
Marcy Stein
Gerald H. Treadway Jr.
Michael Pressley

Level K

SRA

Columbus, OH

ACKNOWLEDGMENTS

Grateful acknowledgment is given to the following publishers and copyright owners for permissions granted to reprint selections from their publications. All possible care has been taken to trace ownership and secure permission for each selection included. In case of any errors or omissions, the Publisher will be pleased to make suitable acknowledgments in future editions.

READ ALOUD

WHAT'S ALIVE? COPYRIGHT © BY KATHLEEN WEIDNER ZOEHFELD. Used by permission of HarperCollins Publishers.

BIG BOOK

A TREE IS A PLANT by Clyde Robert Bulla. Used by permission of HarperCollins Publishers.

"Trees," from SILVER SEEDS by Paul Paolilli and Dan Brewer, copyright © 2001 by Paul Paolilli and Dan Brewer. Used by permission of Viking Penguin, A Division of Penguin Young Readers Group, A Member of Penguin Group (USA) Inc., 345 Hudson Street, New York, NY 10014. All rights reserved.

BECOMING BUTTERFLIES by Anne Rockwell. Printed by arrangement with Walker & Co.

STORY TIME COLLECTION

ZINNIA'S FLOWER GARDEN by Monica Wellington. Copyright © 2005 by Monica Wellington. All rights reserved including the right of reproduction in whole or in part in any form. This edition published by arrangement with Dutton Children's Books, a member of Penguin Young Readers Group, a division of Penguin Group (USA) Inc.

PICKLED PEPPERS

From ONE HUNGRY MONSTER by Susan Heyboer O'Keefe. Copyright © 1989 by Susan Heyboer O'Keefe (text); copyright © 1989 by Lynn Munsinger (illustrations). By permission of Little, Brown and Company (Inc.).

"Rope Rhyme" from HONEY, I LOVE by Eloise Greenfield. Used by permission of HarperCollins Publishers.

From WHO SAID RED? By Mary Serfozo, illustrated by Keiko Narahashi. Text copyright © 1988 by Mary Serfozo, Illustrations Copyright © 1988 by Keiko Narahashi. Reprinted by arrangement with Margaret K. McElderry Books, an Imprint of Simon & Schuster Children's Publishing Division. All rights reserved.

"Rhyme," by Elizabeth Coatsworth. Reprinted with permission of Elizabeth Gartner. All rights reserved.

"Tent" from BALLOONS AND OTHER POEMS by Deborah Chandra. Reprinted by permission of Farrar, Straus & Giroux, LLC.

"Little Pine" from MAPLES IN THE MIST, Text copyright © 1996 by Minfong Ho. Reprinted with permission of McIntosh & Otis. "Little Pine" illustration: Jean & Mou-sien Tseng. Used by permission.

"Houses/Casitas" text, from MY MEXICO/MEXICO MIO by Tony Johnston, copyright © 1996 by Roger D. Johnson and Susan T. Johnson as Trustees of the Johnson Family Trust, text. Used by permission of G.P. Putnam's Sons, A Division of Penguin Young Readers Group, A Member of Penguin Group (USA) Inc., 345 Hudson Street, New York, NY 10014. All rights reserved. "Houses/Casitas," illustrations by F. John Sierra, from MY MEXICO/MEXICO MIO by Tony Johnston, Illustrated by F. John Sierra, copyright © 1996 by F. John Sierra, illustrations. Used by permission of G.P. Putnam's Sons, A Division of Penguin Young Readers Group, A Member of Penguin Group (USA) Inc., 345 Hudson Street, New York, NY 10014. All rights reserved.

"Keep a Poem in Your Pocket" From SOMETHING SPECIAL by Beatrice Schenk de Regniers. Copyright © 1958 Beatrice Schenk de Regniers. © Renewed 1986. All rights reserved. Reprinted by permission of Marian Reiner.

Meet the Imagine It! Authors

Carl Bereiter, Ph.D.
A professor emeritus and special advisor on learning technology at the Ontario Institute for Studies in Education, University of Toronto, Dr. Bereiter also invented Computer Supported Intentional Learning Environments, the first networked system for collaborative learning, with Dr. Marlene Scardamalia.

Andrew Biemiller, Ph.D.
A coordinator of elementary teacher education programs at the University of Toronto for thirty-six years, Dr. Biemiller's research on vocabulary development and instruction has had a significant effect on the shape of vocabulary instruction for elementary education in the twenty-first century.

Joe Campione, Ph.D.
A leading researcher on cognitive development, individual differences, assessment, and the design of innovative learning environments, Dr. Campione is a professor emeritus in the School of Education at University of California, Berkeley.

Iva Carruthers, Ph.D.
Equipped with both hands-on and academic experience, Dr. Carruthers serves as a consultant and lecturer in educational technology and matters of multicultural inclusion.

Doug Fuchs Ph.D.
Dr. Fuchs, the Nicholas Hobbs Professor of Special Education and Human Development at Vanderbilt University, has conducted programmatic research on response-to-intervention as a method for preventing and identifying children with learning disabilities and on reading instructional methods for improving outcomes for students with learning disabilities.

Lynn Fuchs, Ph.D.
A co-director of the Kennedy Center Reading clinic at Vanderbilt University, Dr. Fuchs also conducted research on assessment methods for enhancing instructional planning and instructional methods for improving reading and math outcomes for students with learning disabilities.

Steve Graham, Ph.D.
A professor of literacy at Vanderbilt University, Dr. Graham's research focuses on identifying the factors that contribute to writing development and writing difficulties.

Karen Harris, Ph.D.
The Currey-Ingram Professor of Special Education and Literacy at Vanderbilt University, Dr. Harris's research focuses on theoretical and intervention issues in the development of academic and self-regulation strategies among students who are at risk.

Jan Hirshberg, Ed.D.
Focusing on how children learn to read and write and the logistics of teaching reading and writing in the early grades, Dr. Hirshberg works as a language arts resource coordinator and consultant in Alexandria, Virginia.

Anne McKeough, Ph.D.
A professor in the Division of Applied Psychology at the University of Calgary, Dr. McKeough teaches graduate courses in cognitive development and educational assessment, as well as teacher preparation courses to undergraduates.

Peter Pannell, MA

Principal of Longfellow Elementary School in Pasadena, California, Mr. Pannell has worked to develop the literacy of countless students. To help accomplish this goal, he wrote and implemented a writing project that allowed his students to make great strides in their writing performance.

Marsha Roit, Ed.D.

The Director of Professional Development for SRA/McGraw-Hill, Dr. Roit spends considerable time in classrooms developing reading curricula and working with teachers and administrators in effective instructional practices.

Marlene Scardamalia, Ph.D.

Dr. Scardamalia is the Presidents' Chair in Education and Knowledge Technologies at the University of Toronto and is also the Director of the Institute for Knowledge Innovation and Technology. She received the 2006 World Award of Education from the World Cultural Council for outstanding work in education.

Marcy Stein, Ph.D.

Professor and founding faculty member of the education program at the University of Washington, Tacoma, Dr. Stein teaches At-Risk and Special Education graduate and teacher certification programs.

Gerald H. Treadway Jr, Ph.D.

Chair of the Literacy Education Program and professor of education at San Diego State University, Dr. Treadway teaches classes on reading methods, English Language Learner methods, balanced reading programs, assessment, and reading comprehension. He is also a consultant for the California Reading and Literature Project.

In memoriam

Michael Pressley, Ph.D.
1951–2006

Dr. Pressley was a tireless supporter of education. He championed the rights of all children to a quality education, made seminal contributions in research and practice, and nurtured the development of a host of beginning teachers, young scholars, and editors. While his work and spirit lives on in those he influenced and inspired, there is no substitute for the real thing. We will all miss his wisdom and friendship every day.

Table of Contents

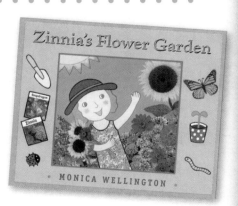
Additional Reading

You may wish to provide some of the following titles to students for additional theme-related reading.

Plant Packages: A Book About Seeds
by Susan Blackaby

Big Sarah's Little Boots
by Paulette Bourgeois

The Very Hungry Caterpillar
by Eric Carle

Growing Vegetable Soup
by Lois Ehlert

One Little Seed
by Elaine Greenstein

From Tadpole to Frog
by Jan Kottke

Leo the Late Bloomer
by Robert Kraus

Once I Was…
by Niki Clark Leopold

What's This?
by Caroline Mockford

Two Blue Jays
by Anne Rockwell

Note: You should preview any trade books and videos for appropriateness before recommending them to students.

OVERVIEW

Ready, Set, Grow!

Have you ever tried to watch something grow? What did you see? Living things need time to grow. They also need a few other important things. What do you need to get bigger and stronger?

Fine Art

Theme Connection

Look at the painting *Sunflowers, Provence* by Josephine Trotter. What do you see? How do you think this painting relates to Ready, Set, Grow? How did these sunflowers get so big?

Josephine Trotter. *Sunflowers, Provence*. Oil on canvas. Private Collection.

T3

Launching the Theme

Setting Up the Theme

Children have a natural curiosity for living, growing things—perhaps because they know that they are growing too. In this unit, students will read a variety of selections that teaches them what it means to be alive and how different living things grow. Through their own investigations, students will explore the plant life in their classroom and learn to understand and appreciate how plants grow and change.

To get students excited about Ready, Set, Grow! try one or more of the following ideas:

- Fill your classroom with an assortment of growing things.
- Wear clothes with a plant, insect, bird, or animal pattern.
- Use the Unit 8 *eBackground Builders* video to give students additional background information about the theme.

Inquiry Students will decide on a unit investigation about growing things and will determine together how to share the results of their research. Students will use the **Concept/Question Board** as a tool to ask questions and to share ideas about growing things.

Concept/Question Board

Using the **Concept/Question Board** as a tool, students will explore concepts and develop inquiry questions. Resources from the classroom as well as from home can be posted on the **Concept/Question Board.** Referring to the **Concept/Question Board** daily as part of your routine is a good way to emphasize to students the importance of this learning tool.

To learn more about the theme Ready, Set, Grow! display a **Concept/ Question Board** in your classroom. This will be a place you and students post questions about the theme and anything related to the concept of growth.

The following materials will encourage students to post their ideas and questions on the **Concept/Question Board:**

- Books and poems about growing things
- Cut-out shapes of flowers, insects, birds, and animals
- Packets of seeds

After discussing the Big Idea question, discuss with students the following questions. These questions can be used to begin the inquiry process.

- What does it mean to grow?
- How do you know you are growing?
- What do plants need to grow?

Using the Inquiry Planner

Students will research the theme Ready, Set, Grow! using the steps below.

BIG Idea

What makes living things grow?

Read the Big Idea question to students. Then discuss what living things need to grow. Students might point out that living things need food and water to grow.

	Steps	Models
Week 1	**STEP 1** Begin discussing and sharing ideas.	**MODEL 1** *How does a seed sprout? What does a plant need to grow? What do animals need to grow?*
	STEP 2 Think about a question for the **Concept/Question Board**.	**MODEL 2** *What are some things that grow?*
Week 2	**STEP 3** Begin investigating and collecting information.	**MODEL 3** *Observe plants growing in different environments, and record observations on a chart with drawings to show change over time.*
	STEP 4 Generate a question or idea for the **Concept/Question Board**.	**MODEL 4** *What would happen if this plant got no sunlight?*
Week 3	**STEP 5** Share your findings with others.	**MODEL 5** *I will show my chart with the drawings of the plant I was observing.*
	STEP 6 Do you have more questions?	**MODEL 6** *What do you need to grow?*

About the
Authors and Illustrators

What's Alive?

What's Alive?

Zinnia's Flower Garden

Author of *What's Alive?*

Kathleen Weidner Zoehfeld

Zoehfeld grew up loving science and nature. She spent a lot of time as a child hiking and looking for fossils in the mountains of New York. Now Zoehfeld writes books explaining science and natural history. She travels a lot to research her books.

Author of *A Tree Is a Plant*

Clyde Robert Bulla

When Bulla was young, his father told him that he needed to experience life so that he could tell good stories. Bulla continued to write, but his stories were rejected. A teacher friend gave him a story idea, which became Bulla's first children's book. His books have won several awards including an ALA Notable Children's Book.

Illustrator of *A Tree Is a Plant*

Stacey Schuett

Schuett enjoys the way that illustrations bring stories to life. When she was young, she dreamed about drawing pictures for books. Schuett then studied art in college. She is always surprised that drawing pictures for books is now her real job.

Author of *Becoming Butterflies*

Anne Rockwell

Rockwell likes to write nonfiction because she believes that nonfiction helps children to find their way in the world. She began writing stories while illustrating her husband's children's books. Their daughter is an author and illustrator of children's books as well.

Illustrator of *Becoming Butterflies*

Megan Halsey

Halsey knew she had found the perfect career when she took a class in college on drawing for children's books. Since then, her illustrations have received many honors including a gold award from the National Parenting Publication Awards. She now teaches others to draw pictures for children's books.

Author of *Zinnia's Flower Garden*

Monica Wellington

Wellington was born in London and then moved to both Germany and Switzerland. Her family traveled a lot before settling in the United States when she was seven. Many of her drawings are inspired by her childhood memories of the European countryside.

Unit Skills

Week 1

Sounds and Letters

✓Phonics ★
- Final Phoneme Blending
- Initial, Medial, and Final Phoneme Matching
- High-Frequency Words *said, that*

Alphabetic Knowledge ★
Long *Aa*

Reading and Responding

Comprehension ★
  Strategies
   • Asking Questions
   • Clarifying
  Skills
   ✓Classify and Categorize

Print and Book Awareness

Selection Vocabulary ★

Inquiry

Language Arts

Writing
Dialogue

Grammar
Pronouns

Week 2

Sounds and Letters

✓Phonics ★
- Medial Phoneme Matching
- Medial Phoneme Manipulation
- Initial Phoneme Blending
- High-Frequency Words *down, they*

Alphabetic Knowledge ★
Long *Ii*

Reading and Responding

Comprehension ★
  Strategies
   • Visualizing
   • Making Connections
   • Predicting
  Skills
  Sequence

Print and Book Awareness

✓Selection Vocabulary ★

Inquiry

Language Arts

Writing
- How-To Instructions
- Revising

Grammar
- Verb Tense
- ✓Action Words

Week 3

Sounds and Letters

B ✓Phonics ★
- Medial Phoneme Manipulation
- Phoneme Segmentation
- Word Order
- Initial Phoneme Blending
- Phoneme Replacement
- High-Frequency Words *some, there*

B ✓Alphabetic Knowledge ★
- Long *Aa*
- Long *Ii*

Reading and Responding

Comprehension ★
  Strategies
   • Clarifying
   • Making Connections
   • Asking Questions
   • Predicting
  Skills
   • Cause and Effect

B Print and Book Awareness

B ✓Selection Vocabulary ★

Inquiry

Language Arts

Writing
- Revising
- Developing Characters and Plots

Grammar
B ✓Verb Tense

Key: ★ = five components of Reading   ✓ = Lesson Assessment   B = Benchmark Assessment   **T7**

Assessment Plan for Making AYP

 is an ongoing cycle.

1 Screen

Administer the initial Benchmark Assessment as a screener to target students who are at risk for failing end-of-year measures.

2 Diagnose and Differentiate

Diagnose students' strengths and weaknesses, and **differentiate** instruction according to their abilities.

Diagnosing, differentiating instruction, and monitoring progress is an ongoing cycle.

3 Monitor Progress

Monitor progress weekly, monthly, or anytime as needed with both formal and informal assessments.

4 Measure Outcomes

Administer summative assessments, such as Lesson, Benchmark, or state assessments, to measure student outcomes.

Screen

At the beginning of the year or for students entering class after the school year has begun, administer the initial *Benchmark Assessment*, Benchmark 1, to target students at risk for reading failure.

Diagnose and Differentiate

Use the results from the *Lesson Assessments, Benchmark Assessments,* and informal observation measures to diagnose students' strengths and weaknesses and to differentiate instructions individually and in small groups.

	Approaching Level	On Level	English Learner	Above Level

Leveled Practice	• *Reteach*
	• *Workshop Kit*
	  - Activities
	  - Games
	• *Intervention Guide*
		• *Skills Practice 2*
		• *Workshop Kit*
		  - Activities
		  - Games
		• *Intervention Guide*
			• *English Learner Support Activities*
			• *Workshop Kit*
			  - Activities
			  - Games
				• *Challenge Activities*
				• *Workshop Kit*
				  - Activities
				  - Games

Technology	• *eSkills & eGames* • *eDecodables*	• *eSkills & eGames* • *eDecodables* • *eGames*	• *eSkills & eGames* • *eDecodables*	• *eSkills & eGames*

Monitor Progress

Between *Benchmark Assessments,* use the following to monitor student progress. Regroup students daily or as needed, based on these formative assessment results.

Formal Assessment

- *Lesson Assessments*
- *Online Assessments*
- Comprehension Observation Log
- *Skills Practice 2*

Measure Outcomes

Assess student understanding and mastery of skills by using the *Lesson Assessments*.

Unit 8

Resources to **Monitor Progress** AYP

Week 1

Skills Practice 2

Letter and Sound Identification, pp. 51, 54
Penmanship, p. 52
Pronouns, pp. 53, 56, 58
Numeral Identification, pp. 55, 57

Reteach

Pronouns, pp. 113, 146
Letter and Sound Identification, pp. 145, 147, 150
Phoneme Matching, p. 148
Numeral Identification, p. 151

Challenge Activities

Letter and Sound Identification, p. 110
Pronouns, pp. 111, 149
Phoneme Matching, p. 112
Numeral Identification, p. 114

Decodables

Decodable 14: *Jake Plants Grapes*

Lesson Assessments

Lessons 4–5, pp. 74–75

Benchmark Assessments

Technology e-Suite

e Skills

Unit 8 Phonics

e Decodables

eDecodable 14: *Jake Plants Grapes*

e Games

Skill: Consonant Sounds Review

e Assess

Lesson Assessment, Unit 8, Lessons 4–5

Week 2

Penmanship, pp. 59, 61, 65
Letter and Sound Identification, pp. 60, 62
Past and Present Tenses, pp. 63–64, 66

Letter and Sound Identification, pp. 152, 155
Past and Present Tenses, pp. 153, 157
Syllable Segmentation, p. 154
Penmanship, p. 156

Penmanship, pp. 115, 118
Letter and Sound Identification, p. 116
Past and Present Tenses, p. 117

Decodable 15: *Mike and Spike*

Lessons 7–8, 10, pp. 76–78

Unit 8 Phonics

eDecodable 15: *Mike and Spike*

Skill: Vowel Sounds Review

Lesson Assessment, Unit 8, Lessons 7–8, 10

Week 3

Numeral Identification, pp. 67, 71, 73
Blending, pp. 68, 72
Past, Present, and Future Tenses, pp. 69–70, 74

Blending, p. 158
Past, Present, and Future Tenses, p. 159
Numeral Review, p. 160

Blending, p. 119
Numeral Identification, p. 120
Numeral Review, p. 121
Past, Present, and Future Tenses, p. 122

Decodable 16: *A Nut Pile*

Lessons 12–15, pp. 79A–83

Benchmark 5

Unit 8 Phonics

eDecodable 16: *A Nut Pile*

Skill: Vowel Sounds Review

Lesson Assessment, Unit 8, Lessons 12–15
Benchmark 5

Lesson Planner

Day 1

Day 2

Sounds and Letters

- *Alphabet Letter Card:* Aa
- Routines 1, 2, 4
- *Skills Practice 2,* pp. 51–52, 54–55, 57
- *Pickled Peppers Big Book,* pp. 10–11, 40–41
- *Pocket Chart Picture Cards*
- *Decodable* 14

Day 1

Warming Up, pp. T24–T25
Phonemic Awareness
Phoneme Blending: Final Sounds, p. T25
Alphabetic Principle
- Introducing Long-Vowel Sounds, p. T26
- Introducing the Sound of Long *Aa,* p. T26
- Listening for /ā/, p. T26
- Penmanship, p. T27

Day 2

Warming Up, pp. T32–T33
Phonemic Awareness
Phoneme Blending: Final Sounds, p. T33
Alphabetic Principle
- Reviewing the Sound of Long *Aa,* p. T34
- Listening for Initial /ā/, p. T34
- Listening for Medial /ā/, p. T34
- *Pickled Peppers Big Book,* p. T35

Reading and Responding

- *Ready, Set, Grow! Big Book,* pp. 4–29
- *Home Connection,* pp. 59–62
- *Read Aloud Collection: What's Alive?*
- Routines 5–7

Preview
- Browsing the Unit, p. T28
- Setting Reading Goals, p. T28
Inquiry, p. T29

Read Aloud Collection: What's Alive?
- Activate Prior Knowledge, p. T36
- Preview the Selection, p. T36
- **Vocabulary,** p. T36
Discuss the Read Aloud, p. T39
Vocabulary Review, p. T39

Language Arts

- *Language Arts Big Book,* pp. 11, 23
- *Ready, Set, Grow! Big Book,* p. 62
- *Skills Practice 2,* pp. 53, 56, 58
- *Willy the Wisher,* p. 78
- *Story Lines Big Book,* pp. 16–17
- Ball Diamond Game Mats
- *Alphabet Letter Cards*

Writing Process
Prewrite: Brainstorming Ideas for Characters, p. T30
Fine Art
Discussing Fine Art, p. T31

Writing Process
Model: Creating Dialogue, p. T40
Grammar, Usage, and Mechanics, pp. T40–T41
Willy the Wisher, p. T41

Monitor Progress

✔ = Formal Assessment

Ⓑ = Benchmark Assessment

✔ Letter and Sound Identification, p. T26
✔ Penmanship, p. T27

✔ Pronouns, p. T41

★ Phonemic Awareness ★ Phonics ★ Fluency ★ Vocabulary ★ Comprehension

Day 3

Warming Up, pp. T42–T43
Phonemic Awareness
- Phoneme Matching: Initial Sounds, p. T43
- Phoneme Matching: Final Sounds, p. T43

Alphabetic Principle
- Reviewing the Sound of Long *Aa*, p. T44
- Listening for Medial /ā/, p. T44
- Linking the Sound to the Letter, p. T44
- Penmanship, p. T45

Preview and Prepare, p. T46
Vocabulary, p. T47
Read the Selection, p. T47 1st READ
Comprehension Strategies, pp. T48, T50, T52, T54
Print and Book Awareness, pp. T49, T51, T53, T55
Discussing the Selection, p. T55
Vocabulary Review, p. T55

Writing Process
Draft: Using Speech Bubbles, p. T56
Story Crafting
Story Lines Big Book, p. T57

✔ Phoneme Matching, p. T43
✔ Letter and Sound Identification, p. T44
✔ Numeral Identification, p. T45
✔ Vocabulary, p. T47

Day 4

Warming Up, pp. T58–T59
Phonemic Awareness
- Phoneme Matching: Initial Sounds, p. T59
- Phoneme Matching: Final Sounds, p. T59

Alphabetic Principle
- Reviewing the Sound of Long *Aa*, p. T60
- Listening for Medial /ā/, p. T60
- Linking the Sound to the Letter, p. T60
- *Pickled Peppers Big Book,* p. T61

Preview and Prepare, p. T62
Vocabulary, p. T62
Read the Selection, p. T63 2nd READ
Comprehension Strategies, pp. T64, T66, T68, T70
Comprehension Skills, pp. T65, T67, T69
Reading with a Writer's Eye, pp. T65, T67, T69, T71
Discussing the Selection, p. T71
Vocabulary Review, p. T71

Writing Process
Draft: Drawing Pictures to Illustrate Dialogue, p. T72
Grammar, Usage, and Mechanics, pp. T72–T73
Story Crafting
Story Lines Big Book, p. T73

✔ *Lesson Assessment Book,* p. 74
✔ Phoneme Matching, p. T59
✔ Pronouns, p. T73

Day 5

Warming Up, pp. T74–T75
Phonemic Awareness
Phoneme Matching: Medial Sounds, p. T75
Alphabetic Principle
- Blending with the Sound of Long *Aa*, p. T76
- Penmanship, p. T77
Reading a *Decodable*
Decodable 14: *Jake Plants Grapes,* pp. T78–T79

Inquiry
- Whole-Group Time, p. T80
- Small-Group Time, p. T81
- Concept Vocabulary, p. T81

Writing Process
Present: Sharing Pictures, p. T82
Grammar, Usage, and Mechanics, pp. T82–T83
Game Day
Ball Diamond Game, p. T83

✔ *Lesson Assessment Book,* p. 75
 Comprehension Observation Log
✔ Letter and Sound Identification, p. T76
✔ Numeral Identification, p. T77
✔ Pronouns, p. T83

Student Resources

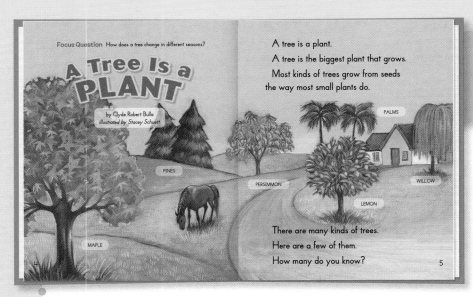

Big Books

Audio CD

Big Book Selection

***Ready, Set, Grow!* Big Book**

A Tree Is a Plant by
Clyde Robert Bulla, pp. 4–29

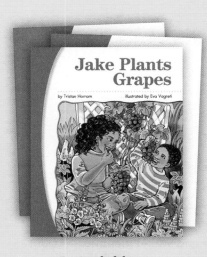

***Decodable* 14:**
Jake Plants Grapes

Teacher Support

Language Arts Big Book

**Teacher's
Resource Book**

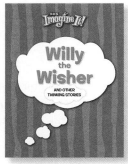

Willy the Wisher

Curriculum Connections

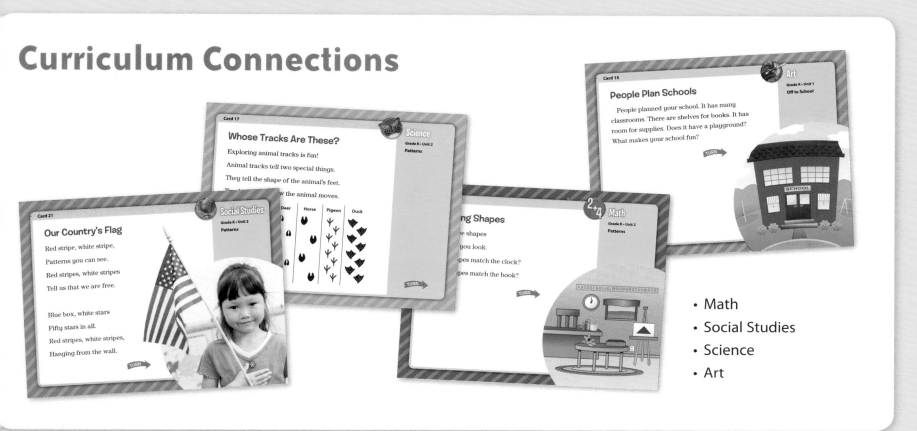

Card 17

Whose Tracks Are These?

Science
Grade K • Unit 2
Patterns

Exploring animal tracks is fun!

Animal tracks tell two special things.

They tell the shape of the animal's feet.

| Deer | Horse | Pigeon | Duck |

Card 21

Our Country's Flag

Social Studies
Grade K • Unit 2
Patterns

Red stripe, white stripe,
Patterns you can see.
Red stripes, white stripes
Tell us that we are free.

Blue box, white stars
Fifty stars in all.
Red stripes, white stripes,
Hanging from the wall.

Card 15

People Plan Schools

Art
Grade K • Unit 1
Off to School

People planned your school. It has many classrooms. There are shelves for books. It has room for supplies. Does it have a playground? What makes your school fun?

ng Shapes

Math
Grade K • Unit 2
Patterns

e shapes
you look.
pes match the clock?
pes match the book?

- Math
- Social Studies
- Science
- Art

Additional Skills Practice

Approaching Level	On Level	English Learner	Above Level
Reteach	**Skills Practice 2**	**English Learner Support Activities**	**Challenge Activities**
Letter and Sound Identification, pp. 145, 147, 150	Letter and Sound Identification, pp. 51, 54	Lessons 1–5	Letter and Sound Identification, p. 110
Numeral Identification, p. 151	Numeral Identification, pp. 55, 57		Numeral Identification, p. 114
Phoneme Matching, p. 148	Penmanship, p. 52		Phoneme Matching, p. 112
Pronouns, pp. 113, 146	Pronouns, pp. 53, 56, 58		Pronouns, pp. 111, 149

Differentiating Instruction
for Workshop

Lessons 1-5 Overview

AYP

Day 1

Approaching Level	On Level	English Learner	Above Level
Sounds and Letters			
Alphabetic Principle: Students use the *Listening Library CD* to listen for the /ā/ sound in a rhyme of your choice.	**Alphabetic Principle:** Have students use the *eGames* activity for this unit to review consonant sounds.	**Alphabetic Principle:** Refer to Unit 8 Lesson 1 of the *English Learner Support Guide.*	**Alphabetic Principle:** Students work independently to complete *Challenge Activities* page 110.
Reading and Responding			
Preview: Students listen to *What's Alive?* on the *Listening Library CD.*	**Preview:** Students draw any questions they have about things that grow and post them on the **Concept/Question Board.**	**Preview:** Preview the selection *What's Alive?*, and have students discuss anything that confuses them.	**Preview:** Students draw any questions they have about things that grow and post them on the **Concept/Question Board.**
Language Arts			
Writing: Discuss with students what they remember about developing a character.	**Writing:** Students share what characters they liked in the reading selections.	**Writing:** Discuss with students the aspects of memorable characters from stories they have read so far in the year.	**Writing:** Students share their favorite character from a reading selection with partners.

Day 2

Approaching Level	On Level	English Learner	Above Level

Sounds and Letters

Alphabetic Principle: Use an activity from Unit 8 Lesson 2 of the **Intervention Guide** for additional help with the /ā/ sound.

Alphabetic Principle: Students use the **Listening Library CD** to listen to "Little Boy Blue" and identify the /ā/ sound.

Alphabetic Principle: Refer to Unit 8 Lesson 2 of the **English Learner Support Guide.**

Alphabetic Principle: Have students use **eSkills** to review the /ā/ sound.

Reading and Responding

Vocabulary: Students browse the selection and point to any words they recognize or wonder about.

Vocabulary: Have students use the selection vocabulary words *seedling, exploring, sorting,* and *separate* in complete sentences.

Vocabulary: Preview the selection "A Tree Is a Plant" with students, and have them point out any words or illustrations that puzzle them or they wonder about.

Vocabulary: Students draw pictures to illustrate the selection vocabulary words.

Language Arts

Writing: Discuss with students characters they remember from the stories the class has read.

Grammar: Have students complete **Reteach** page 146.

Writing: With your help, students make lists of characteristics for those characters.

Grammar: Review pronouns with students.

Writing: Help students make a list of three characters from these stories.

Grammar: Refer to Unit 8 Lesson 2 of the **English Learner Support Guide.**

Writing: Students tell partners why these characters are their favorites.

Grammar: Have students complete **Challenge Activities** page 111.

Differentiating Instruction
for Workshop

Day 3

Approaching Level	On Level	English Learner	Above Level
Sounds and Letters			
Alphabetic Principle: Have students draw pictures of an object beginning with the /ā/ sound.	**Alphabetic Principle:** Students match **Alphabet Letter Card** *Aa* to objects in the classroom beginning with the /ā/ sound and the letter *Aa*.	**Alphabetic Principle:** Refer to Unit 8 Lesson 3 of the **English Learner Support Guide.**	**Alphabetic Principle:** Browse **Ready, Set, Grow! Little Big Book** for words with the letter *Aa* and the /ā/ sound
Reading and Responding			
Comprehension: Browse the selection with students, and have them point out illustrations that puzzle them.	**Comprehension:** Invite students to discuss the selection and make connections to their own lives.	**Comprehension:** Refer to Unit 8 Lesson 3 of the **English Learner Support Guide.**	**Comprehension:** Have students research things that grow on the Internet and post their findings and questions on the **Concept/Question Board.**
Language Arts			
Writing: Students help you create lists of characters they would like to include in a story.	**Writing:** Students choose two characteristics and create two original characters.	**Writing:** Discuss with students the common traits of characters, and help them to generate a list of characteristics for each of the three characters.	**Writing:** Students choose one more character from a selection and share it with partners.

Day 4

Approaching Level	On Level	English Learner	Above Level
Sounds and Letters			
Phonemic Awareness: Help students complete the activities on page 148 of *Reteach.*	**Phonemic Awareness:** Have students use *eSkills* to review the /ā/ sound.	**Phonemic Awareness:** Refer to Unit 8 Lesson 4 of the *English Learner Support Guide.*	**Phonemic Awareness:** Students draw pictures of three objects with the same beginning or ending sound.
Reading and Responding			
Comprehension: Invite students to discuss any connections they see between the selection and their own lives.	**Comprehension:** Have students draw the sequence of how an apple seed grows into a tree.	**Comprehension:** Refer to Unit 8 Lesson 4 of the *English Learner Support Guide.*	**Comprehension:** Students visit the school library, choose books related to the unit theme, and share their questions and wonderings with you.
Language Arts			
Writing: Students discuss and choose two of the characters from their lists. **Grammar:** Help students complete *Reteach* page 149.	**Writing:** Students draw pictures of their main character. **Grammar:** Students help you create a list of pronouns.	**Writing:** Students discuss and choose two of the characters from their lists. **Grammar:** Refer to Unit 8 Lesson 4 of the *English Learner Support Guide.*	**Writing:** Students tell partners what they like about this character. **Grammar:** Have students work independently to complete *Challenge Activities* page 113.

Differentiating Instruction
for Workshop

Day 5

Approaching Level	On Level	English Learner	Above Level
Sounds and Letters			
Reading a *Decodable*: Reread **Decodable** 14 with students, reviewing what is happening in the illustrations.	**Reading a *Decodable*:** Have students reread, using **eDecodable** *Jake Plants Grapes*.	**Reading a *Decodable*:** Review **Decodable** 14 with students, pointing to the high-frequency words *said* and *that* as you read aloud to them.	**Reading a *Decodable*:** Students reread **Decodable** 14 with partners.
Reading and Responding			
Inquiry: Students draw pictures of questions or wonderings about growing things and post them on the **Concept/Question Board.**	**Inquiry:** Students research plant growth on the Internet with partners and generate questions or wonderings to post on the **Concept/Question Board.**	**Inquiry:** Review the selection "A Tree Is a Plant" with students, and have them ask any questions or share wonderings about the selection with you.	**Inquiry:** Students research various things that grow like plants and animals and post any questions or wonderings on the **Concept/Question Board.**
Language Arts			
Writing: Discuss with students what they think their characters should be like. **Grammar:** Refer to Unit 8 Lesson 5 of the **Intervention Guide** for additional support for this Grammar activity.	**Writing:** Students draw pictures of their second character. **Grammar:** With your help, students make simple sentences with each pronoun.	**Writing:** Discuss with students what they think their characters should be like. Prompt them with yes-no and either-or questions as needed. **Grammar:** Refer to Unit 8 Lesson 5 of the **English Learner Support Guide.**	**Writing:** Each student draws a picture of the two characters. **Grammar:** As a group, students create a list of pronouns and say aloud one sentence using each.

T20   Theme: Ready, Set, Grow!

Resources for Differentiating Instruction

English Learner

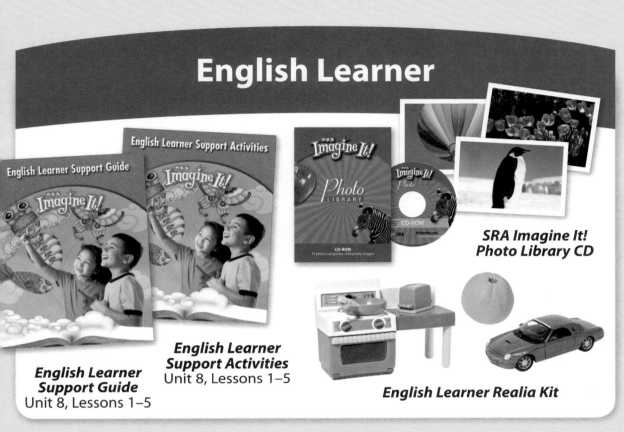

English Learner Support Guide
Unit 8, Lessons 1–5

English Learner Support Activities
Unit 8, Lessons 1–5

**SRA Imagine It!
Photo Library CD**

English Learner Realia Kit

Approaching Level

Intervention

Intervention Guide

Intervention Workbook

Workshop Kits

- High Frequency Words
- Letter Recognition
- Phonemic Awareness
- Print and Book Awareness
- Sequencing

Technology

eDecodable Jake Plants Grapes
eSkills & eGames
Listening Library CD

Listening Library Unit 8

Lesson Assessment

Monitor Progress to Differentiate Instruction

Use these summative assessments along with your informal observations to assess student mastery.

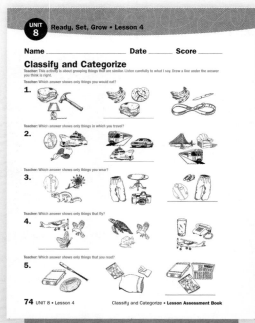

Lesson Assessment Book, p. 74

Lesson Assessment Book, p. 75

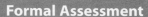

Lesson Assessment Book

Comprehension Observation Log

Student _____ Date _____

Unit _____ Lesson _____ Selection Title _____

General Comprehension
Concepts discussed: _____

Behavior Within a Group
Articulates, expresses ideas: _____

Joins discussions: _____

Collaborates (such as works well with other students, works alone): _____

Role in Group
Role (such as leader, summarizer, questioner, critic, observer, non-participant): _____

Flexibility (changes roles when necessary): _____

Use of Reading Strategies
Uses strategies when needed (either those taught or student's choice of strategy)/Describes strategies used:
_____

Changes strategies when appropriate: _____

Changes Since Last Observation

110   Comprehension Observation Log • Lesson Assessment Book

Lesson Assessment Annotated Teacher's Edition, p. 110

The Comprehension Observation Log, found in the *Lesson Assessment Annotated Teacher's Edition,* is a vehicle for recording anecdotal information about individual student performance on an ongoing basis. Information such as students' strengths and weaknesses can be recorded at any time the occasion warrants. It is recommended that you maintain a folder for each student where you can store the logs for purposes of comparison and analysis as the school year progresses. You will gradually build up a comprehensive file that reveals which students are progressing smoothly and which students need additional help.

Sounds and Letters

Students will

✦ review the letters of the alphabet and their sounds.

✦ blend final phonemes to make words.

✦ identify the /ā/ sound and attach it to the letter *Aa*.

✦ practice writing the numeral *0*.

✦ *Alphabet Letter Card* *Aa* for each student

✦ Routine 1

✦ *Skills Practice 2,* pp. 51–52

✦ Supply Icons

Calendar

Su	M	T	W	Th	F	S
		1	2	3	4	5
6	7	8	9	10	11	12
13	14	15	16	17	18	19
20	21	22	23	24	25	26
27	28	29	30	31		

Point to the box that represents today. Take this opportunity to identify any important events that will happen during the coming weeks, such as students' birthdays, school functions, and national holidays, and discuss each one.

Warming Up

MORNING MESSAGE

Today's date is _____.

The weather is _____ outside.

Today we will learn more about the letter _____.

Kindergarten News

✦ Copy the text above on the board or on chart paper.

✦ Ask students to look out the window and to tell what kind of weather it is today. Have the class decide on the appropriate Weather Icon.

✦ Tell students they will learn more about the letter *Aa* today. Have a volunteer come to the board and write the letter *Aa* (both capital and small) in the blank. Congratulate the student on the writing. Ask the student to proofread his or her writing, and help the student rewrite the letter if necessary.

✦ Ask students to find a letter *a* somewhere in the Morning Message. Ask volunteers to come up and circle each letter *a* they see. *Today, date, weather, learn, about*

✦ Remind students of how they clapped out the words in sentences before. Guide them in clapping out the words in the Morning Message sentences.

Letter Search

✦ To begin this new unit with a general alphabet review, have students participate in a brief letter/sound identification game.

✦ Have the class form two teams. Give one group small letters and the other group the matching capital letters you have prepared ahead.

✦ Tell students to go around the room looking at others' letters until they find their partners. Ask one partner in each pair to say his or her letter's name and the other partner to say its sound. Focus on reviewing the short-vowel sounds when you come to each vowel.

✦ Have students sit in a circle with you until everyone finds his or her partner. When everyone has his or her partner, have each pair of students say aloud its letter's name and sound in alphabetical order.

Phonemic Awareness

Phoneme Blending: Final Sounds

✦ Tell students the *Lion Puppet* is ready to play another blending game. Explain that the puppet will say a word except for the ending sound. You will say the final sound. When the puppet asks what the word is, students should put together the parts and say the word.

✦ Practice with the following word:

Puppet:	*afternoo . . .*
Teacher:	*/n/* (Emphasize the /n/ sound.)
Everyone:	*/n/*
Puppet:	*What's the word?*
Everyone:	*afternoon*

✦ Continue with the following words:

tra . . . /k/ /k/, track	*bubb . . . /l/ /l/, bubble*
blosso . . . /m/ /m/, blossom	*snee . . . /z/ /z/, sneeze*
col . . . /d/ /d/, cold	*baske . . . /t/ /t/, basket*

 Teacher Tip

VARYING TECHNIQUES Remember to use different techniques during the phoneme-blending activities. For example, sometimes you may say both parts of the word, and sometimes you might have the *Lion Puppet* say a part. Also switch between individual and whole-class response, a technique that will require students to be more attentive.

Teacher Tip

ALPHABET SOUND WALL CARDS This lesson introduces the first long-vowel sound and spellings. The picture on each long-vowel *Alphabet Sound Wall Card* is an elongated (or long) version of the letter. The picture and the yellow background are to remind students that the long-vowel sound is the same as the vowel's name.

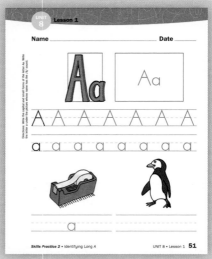

Skills Practice 2, p. 51

Monitor Progress ✓

to Differentiate Instruction
Formal Assessment

Letter and Sound Identification Note how quickly students identify the /ā/ sound.

APPROACHING LEVEL

| IF ... students are having difficulty, | THEN ... guide them in completing **Reteach** page 145. |

ON LEVEL

| IF ... students need more practice, | THEN ... use **Skills Practice 2** page 51. |

ABOVE LEVEL

| IF ... students are comfortable, | THEN ... have them work independently to complete page 110 in **Challenge Activities.** |

ROUTINE 1

Alphabetic Principle 🕐

Introducing Long-Vowel Sounds

✦ Remind students that some special letters of the alphabet are called vowels. Ask volunteers to say the names of the vowels they remember learning. *a, e, i, o, u* Then review the sounds students have learned to attach to the vowels. /a/, /e/, /i/, /o/, /u/ Remind them that these vowels are called short and that the green background helps us remember these short vowels. Explain that sometimes you can hear the names of the vowels in words such as *acorn, eat, island, over,* and *unicorn.*

✦ Tell students they will hear a vowel song. Sing the song, pointing to the *Alphabet Sound Wall Cards* for *Aa, Ee, Ii, Oo,* and *Uu* as you sing the letters. The "Vowel Song" is sung to the familiar tune of "B-I-N-G-O." (See the Appendix.) Sing the song together several times.

Alphabet Sound Wall Card 1

Introducing the Sound of Long *Aa*

✦ Point to *Alphabet Sound Wall Card* Long *Aa*, and remind students the letters called vowels are special because every word or syllable in English needs a vowel. Say to students *When the* a *says its name,* /ā/, *it is called long* a. Point to it on the card, reminding students that the letter is red because it is a vowel. Tell them the yellow background helps us remember the long vowel.

✦ Share with students the following rhyme to help them remember the sounds of *Aa,* and point to the cards for short *Aa* and long *Aa* as you say:

A's my name.

Two sounds I make:

Short a in lamb,

Long a in cake.

Listening for /ā/

Give each student an *Alphabet Letter Card Aa.* Ask students to raise the cards and say /ā/ when they hear a word that has the /ā/ sound. Try the following words:

| **ape** | trap | *Adam* |
| apple | **April** | **ache** |

Penmanship

✦ Distribute a sheet of writing paper to each student, or have each student use a **White Board.** Place the Supply Icon for *pencil* on the board or in the **Pocket Chart.**

✦ Use the procedure established for writing letters to illustrate how to form the numeral *0:* Place your pen or chalk at the starting point on the overhead or board, and ask students to place their fingers in the air. As you write the numeral, say *Begin here. Then curve to the left and all the way back around to the starting point.* Zero.

✦ Now invite students to practice writing numeral *0*s from left to right across the top row of the paper or **White Board.**

✦ Remind students the numeral *0* shows we have none of something.

Guided Practice

✦ Have students complete **Skills Practice 2** page 52 for additional practice with the numeral *0.*

✦ Draw students' attention to the first penmanship line. Ask them to trace the *0*s outlined across the row. Then ask students to write a row of *0*s across the next line.

✦ Then ask students to look at the word *zero* written on the line. Tell students this is how you write the word that names the number *0.*

✦ Invite four volunteers to identify the letters that make up the word *zero,* and have the class practice writing the word by tracing the letters. *z, e, r, o* Then have them try writing the word on their own on the next line.

✦ After students have finished, help students proofread their work using the established procedure. They should use a colored pencil to star their best numerals and then to circle and correct the numeral(s) they would like to make better.

Teacher Tips

ZERO AND Oo Discuss with students how the number *0* looks similar to the letter *Oo.* Explain that while both look like circles, the letter *Oo* is rounder than the number *0.* Write a rotund capital *O* on the board, and say *This is the letter O.* Then write a narrower *0* next to or beneath it, and say *This is a zero.*

NUMERAL-FORMATION PROCEDURES If you have a prescribed writing system that is standard in your school, use those number-formation procedures. However, you may also reference the Appendix, which has specific instructions for the formation of each number *0* to *10.*

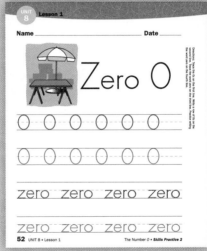

Skills Practice 2, p. 52

Monitor Progress to Differentiate Instruction

Penmanship Note how easily students write the numeral *0.*

APPROACHING LEVEL	IF ... students are having difficulty,	THEN ... have them practice the strokes on the board or on chart paper using a paintbrush and water.
ON LEVEL	IF ... students need more practice,	THEN ... have them write the number in shaving cream on their desks or vinyl placemats.
ABOVE LEVEL	IF ... students would enjoy a challenging activity,	THEN ... have them work independently to cut the letters for the word *zero* out of a magazine or catalog and paste them in order. Then have them write the word *zero* below the pasted version.

Reading and Responding

Students will

✦ locate the Table of Contents and the title of the *Big Book.*

✦ discuss the concept of growing things.

✦ set goals for reading each selection.

✦ generate questions and statements about the unit theme.

✦ *Ready, Set, Grow! Big Book*

✦ *Home Connection,* pp. 59–60

Ready, Set, Grow! Big Book

Give each student a copy of *Home Connection* page 59. This same information is also available in Spanish on *Home Connection* page 60. Encourage students to discuss the unit with their families and complete the activity provided.

Preview

Browsing the Unit

✦ In the Ready, Set, Grow! unit, students will think about plants, animals, and people and how they grow. Students also need to think about their personal growth—how they can grow in knowledge. During this year, the class's understanding of school and friendship has grown; their knowledge of shadows, patterns, and the sea has increased; and their ability to read and write has developed. In these lessons not only will students ask questions and make conjectures, but they will also chronicle their observations about growth using charts and diaries.

✦ Display the *Ready, Set, Grow! Big Book.* Have a volunteer identify the front and back covers. Focus attention on the front cover illustration, and invite students to talk about what they see. Identify the title, and read it aloud. Then ask students to say the title with you. Turn to the Table of Contents, and explain what information it contains. Tell students one of the selections tells how an apple tree grows and changes across the seasons. Share that another selection is a story about how caterpillars grow and change into butterflies, and two selections are poems about growing things. Explain that at the end of the unit, you will also read them a story about a character who plants and tends her own flower garden. Browse the *Big Book* selections with students, and encourage them to make predictions about what each selection might say.

Setting Reading Goals

✦ Tell students in this unit they will be reading selections about growing things. Explain that the goals for reading these selections may include listening for lessons taught in the selections, listening for ideas for answering their questions about growing things, and learning more about print and reading. Ask students to think of reasons for reading the first selection, "A Tree Is a Plant."

✦ Remind students that readers are always thinking when they read. Tell them readers get into the habit of setting reading goals for themselves.

Inquiry

✦ Tell students in addition to reading stories and poems about growing things, they will be investigating how things grow. They will use their skills as scientists. Ask students what they remember about Inquiry and what new inquiry words they learned, such as *investigate, ask questions, make conjectures,* and *observe.* Students may remember that they took a survey, that they made charts of what they observed, and that they began to evaluate their Inquiry in the last unit. If necessary, remind students to check the inquiry word cards they have been creating during the year.

✦ While Inquiry in this unit will focus on physical growth, help students connect the concept of growth to learning and to their time in kindergarten. Examples of personal growth are expanding knowledge by learning new things, reading and writing numerous words, and developing friendships.

Concept/Question Board

• Share the plants, seeds, tadpoles, or any other living things that will allow students to see growth over the next few weeks. Ask students what questions they have about how these things grow. Use the following samples to model questions:

  • What are some things that grow?

  • What does a plant need to grow?

  • What do animals need to grow?

  • What kind of changes might you see in the tadpoles as they grow?

• During the week, have students plant the soaked seeds. Take a bottle or glass with a wide mouth opening, and line it with blotter paper or some other stiff but porous paper. Stuff the bottom only with a paper towel. Then take a few of the same type of seeds, and place them between the paper and the glass. Thoroughly moisten the bottom. The students will be able to see the seeds sprouting. Be sure that the lining paper absorbs the water and that it is kept moist. Have students label their gardens and write what kind of seeds they planted. Keep the gardens in a warm, well-lit area, and have students check them every day.

• Remind students to observe or look at the plants, the tadpoles, and their gardens during the week. They can write about what they see, write new questions, and put them on the **Concept/Question Board.**

Teacher Tips

INQUIRY Write the key inquiry words on cards: *investigate, science, wonder, ask questions,* and *conjecture.* You may want to add icons to help students connect to these words. Keep these simple. You may want to have the class make suggestions about what might be good icons for these words. The goal is to have a visual reminder of the language of inquiry so the class will begin to use these words themselves.

PLAN AHEAD You may want to make the following preparations in your classroom for the inquiry in this unit: Have a variety of plants for students to observe; presoak several different kinds of seeds, such as corn, beans, and radishes, to promote faster germination; and obtain tadpoles that are getting ready to grow frog legs. Tadpoles will need a home—an aquarium or terrarium—and fish food. You will not need to clean the water because tadpoles eat algae.

Research in Action

At this point in the year, students should be comfortable posting pictures, articles, and questions on the **Concept/Question Board.** Some children are ready to write their own questions and label their contributions to the **Concept/Question Board.** You may still need to support some students by having them dictate their questions or comments as you transcribe them onto paper. Always read what you have written, write the student's name on it, and have the student post it on the **Concept/Question Board.** In order to help students appreciate the value of the **Concept/Question Board,** take time regularly to have students share their contributions and questions.

(Marsha Roit)

Language Arts

OBJECTIVES

Students will

✦ brainstorm ideas for another character.

✦ view, appreciate, and react to fine art.

MATERIALS

✦ *Language Arts Big Book,* p. 23

✦ *Ready, Set, Grow! Big Book,* p. 62

Language Arts Big Book, p. 23

Writing Process 🕐

Prewrite: Brainstorming Ideas for Characters

Teach

✦ Pointing to the Listening Icons, remind students to listen carefully.

✦ Tell students they will work as a class to write a story.

✦ Ask students to think about two characters they would like to have in the story. With students' help, create a list of possible names for the characters in their story.

✦ Ask the class to vote for the name they like best for the main character.

Guided Practice

✦ Display page 23 of the *Language Arts Big Book,* and discuss the pictures of Doodle. Be sure to talk about what Doodle looks like, how Doodle acts, and what Doodle likes to do. Tell students to create another character for the story. Students need to think about what that character will look like, act like, and like to do.

✦ Help students create a new character for the story. Begin by having students decide the major traits for the character, such as human or animal, boy or girl, and so on.

✦ Then invite students to brainstorm details about the character, and write their ideas on the board.

✦ Before the end of class, have students vote on the traits they want the character to have. Make a list of the chosen traits, and keep it until the next lesson when you will resume the writing process.

🍎 Teacher Tip

PLAN AHEAD In preparation for the following activity, have drawing paper and art supplies on hand.

Traits of Good Writing

Ideas and Voice Writers often consider possible personality traits when creating a character.

Fine Art

Fine
Art

Steve Kroop. *Robin with Eggs.*

Discussing Fine Art

✦ Turn to page 62 in the ***Ready, Set, Grow! Big Book.*** Focus students' attention on *Robin with Eggs* by Steve Kroop.

✦ Discuss the painting. Use questions such as the following:

- *What do you see in this picture?*
- *Where is the nest? How can you tell?*
- *What does this painting have to do with the unit theme Ready, Set, Grow?*

✦ Discuss the colors the artist uses in this painting. Ask the following questions:

- *What colors do you see? Which one do you see the most?*
- *Are the colors bright or dull? Are they like the colors you see in real life? Are they brighter or duller than real-life colors?*

✦ If time permits, ask students to make their own drawings of birds they have seen. To offer inspiration, you might lead them outside or to the classroom windows to observe nearby birds for a few moments.

 **Teacher Tip**

FOR FURTHER STUDY Students might enjoy comparing and contrasting *Robin with Eggs* with other paintings and photos of birds. For artistic representations of specific birds, see any of John Audubon's bird paintings.

Background Information

Birds have been a popular subject of artists for centuries. From Chinese Song Dynasty silken scrolls (1000s) to Aztec ceramic pottery (1400s) to American folk art quilts (1800s), the bird has been admired and presented as a symbol of freedom and beauty. In more modern times, contemporary artists such as Steve Kroop continue the art world's infatuation with the avian world.

Sounds and Letters

OBJECTIVES

Students will
+ identify and produce rhyming words.
+ blend final phonemes to make words.
+ identify the /ā/ sound.

MATERIALS

+ *Alphabet Letter Card Aa* for each student
+ *Pickled Peppers Big Book,* pp. 10–11

Calendar

Su	M	T	W	Th	F	S
		1	2	3	4	5
6	7	8	9	10	11	12
13	14	15	16	17	18	19
20	21	22	23	24	25	26
27	28	29	30	31		

Point to the box that represents today. Have a volunteer point to the number *0* on the calendar to review what students learned in the previous lesson.

Warming Up

MORNING MESSAGE

Today is _____.

It is in the season called _____.

(Child's name)'s favorite season is _____.

Kindergarten News

+ Copy the text above on the board or on chart paper.

+ Have students tell what their favorite seasons are and why. Discuss their favorite activities to do during their favorite seasons.

+ Use prompts such as the following to discuss the letters and words in the message:

  • *Can someone find the letter Vv in the message?* favorite *Come underline it.*

  • *How many letters make up the name (child's name)? What are they?*

  • *What is the name of the mark at the ends of the sentences?* period *Come circle them.*

Oral Language

+ Sing the song "Down by the Bay" with students. (See the Appendix.)

+ Sing the song with students again, this time ending it with the following:

  Did you ever see a yak carrying a _____ *?* sack

* Tell students to supply rhyming words to complete the following:

a *weasel* painting at an _____ *easel*

a *shark* walking through the _____ *park, dark*

an *eel* spinning a _____ *wheel, deal, peel, reel*

* When a student has supplied a rhyming word, have other students join in as you sing the song again.

Phonemic Awareness

Phoneme Blending: Final Sounds

* Tell students the **Lion Puppet** wants to play a blending game. Tell them the puppet will say a word except for the ending sound. You will say the final sound. When the puppet asks what the word is, students should put together the parts and say the word.

* Practice with the following word:

Puppet: *foun ...*

Teacher: */d/ (Emphasize the /d/ sound.)*

Everyone: */d/*

Puppet: *What is the word?*

Everyone: *found*

* Continue with the following words:

lan ... /d/ /d/, land   *chipmun ... /k/ /k/, chipmunk*

dra ... /g/ /g/, drag   *canno ... /t/ /t/, cannot*

mysel ... /f/ /f/, myself   *distur ... /b/ /b/, disturb*

 Teacher Tip

ALPHABET REVIEW Have students sing "Alphabet Song" or perform "Alphabet Cheer" as a quick review before the phoneme-blending activity.

Differentiating Instruction **English Learners**

IF ... students have difficulty with the phonemic awareness activity, **THEN ...** refer to Unit 8 Lesson 2 of the **English Learner Support Guide.**

Teacher Tip

BODY MOVEMENT While repeating the /ā/ sound, have students make their bodies tall like the long *a*. Model for students how to put their arms above their heads while saying /ā/. You might have students stoop down low when they say the short *a* sound to illustrate the contrast.

English Learners

IF ... students are native speakers of Spanish or of certain other languages, **THEN ...** they may associate the letter name *a* with the letter *e* because in their native languages, *e* represents a sound similar to English long *a*. These students will need extra practice associating the letter *a* with its English name and with the long *a* sound.

Technology

Have students use the **eSkills** activity for a review of the /ā/ sound.

Audio CD

Alphabetic Principle

Reviewing the Sound of Long *Aa*

✦ Point to **Alphabet Sound Wall Card** Long *Aa*, and ask a volunteer to say the name of the letter. Remind students vowels are special because every syllable or word needs a vowel.

✦ Have students recite the rhyme for the sounds of *Aa*. Reread the rhyme for students if they have trouble remembering it from the previous lesson.

A's my name.

Two sounds I make:

Short a in lamb,

Long a in cake.

Listening for Initial /ā/

Give each student an **Alphabet Letter Card** *Aa*. Ask students to raise their cards and say the /ā/ sound when they hear a word that begins with the /ā/ sound. Try the following words:

apron	*ice*	**able**	*action*
under	**April**	*offer*	*enter*
acorn	*useful*	*Anna*	**Amy**

Listening for Medial /ā/

Give each student an **Alphabet Letter Card** *Aa*. Ask students to raise their cards and say /ā/ when they hear a word that has the /ā/ sound in the middle. Try the following words:

bake	*hope*	*duck*	**tape**
hat	**sale**	*black*	*ramp*
cave	**name**	**grape**	**grate**

Alphabet Sound Wall Card 1

Pickled Peppers Big Book

✦ Display the **Pickled Peppers Big Book.** Ask a volunteer to come up to the book and to point to the front cover. Now ask the student to point to the back cover. Remind students a book's cover helps protect the pages inside.

✦ Turn to pages 10–11, "Little Boy Blue." Point to the title, and read it aloud. Invite students to share anything they remember about the rhyme.

✦ Tell students you will read the rhyme aloud and you would like them to listen for the words that have the /ā/ sound. Ask students to close their eyes as they listen. Refer to the Listening Icons.

✦ Invite students to say any /ā/ words they noticed while you read the rhyme aloud.

✦ Reread the rhyme, pointing to each word as you say it. Ask students to stop you each time you point to a word that has the letter *a* in it. *meadow, after, a, haystack, Fast, asleep, wake* When you pause, work with students to evaluate the sound the letter *a* makes in each word. When you find a word with the /ā/ sound, have students make their bodies tall like the long *a*. *haystack, wake*

Pickled Peppers Big Book, pp. 10–11

Teacher Tip

PRINT AND BOOK AWARENESS Throughout *SRA Imagine It!* various activities are dedicated to teaching students print and book awareness. However, any activity that has students interacting with books and print can be a teaching opportunity. Remember to have students identify print features each time you use a **Big Book** or a trade book.

Technology

Use the **Listening Library CD** to support the **Pickled Peppers** lessons.

Audio CD

Students will

+ locate the title and the names of the author and the illustrator.
+ connect their own life experiences to the text.
+ develop an understanding of vocabulary words.
+ become familiar with the unit theme Ready, Set, Grow!

MATERIALS

+ **Read Aloud Collection:** *What's Alive?*
+ Routines 5–7
+ **Home Connection,** pp. 61–62

Read Aloud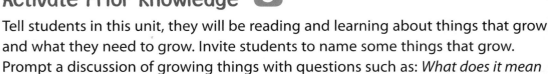

Activate Prior Knowledge ROUTINE 5

Tell students in this unit, they will be reading and learning about things that grow and what they need to grow. Invite students to name some things that grow. Prompt a discussion of growing things with questions such as: *What does it mean to grow?*

Preview the Selection ROUTINE 5 ROUTINE 7

+ Display the cover of *What's Alive?* Follow Routine 5, the previewing the selection routine, as you introduce the title and the names of the author and the illustrator. Ask students what an author and an illustrator do.

+ Prepare to read the story. Ask students to look at the illustrations for clues as to what the selection might tell them.

+ Follow Routine 7, the reading the selection routine, and read the Focus Question printed above the **Read Aloud Collection** selection. Encourage students to listen carefully as you read to find the answer to the question. Have students identify the living and nonliving things in each illustration. As you read, stop to ask and answer questions about *What's Alive?*

Vocabulary ROUTINE 6

+ Follow Routine 6, the selection vocabulary routine, as you introduce the vocabulary words for this selection.

+ Explain to students that the word *seedling* means "a young plant." Use the following sentence to illustrate: *Before long, the flower seeds had sprouted and become little seedlings.*

+ Tell students the word *exploring* means "finding or discovering." Ask if they have ever gone exploring for shells, rocks, or animal homes.

+ Explain that the word *sorting* means "putting into groups." Remind students they have been sorting objects into groups in the classroom.

+ Point out to students when they *separate* objects they move apart the objects. Have two students stand together, and then separate them.

Vocabulary

seedling	sorting
exploring	separate

Technology

To promote independent reading, encourage students to use Workshop to listen to the recording of the selection on the **Listening Library CD.** Invite them to follow along and to say the words whenever they can.

Audio CD

Focus Question How can you tell if something is alive?

What's Alive?

by Kathleen Weidner Zoehfeld

Are you like a cat? You don't look like a cat. A cat is furry. It has a long tail and four legs. You have two legs and no fur. But you can run and jump like a cat.

Are you like a flower or a tree? You don't look like a flower or a tree. A tree is tall. Its green leaves grow high up in the air, and its roots grow deep underground.

A flower can have petals of pink or yellow or red. You have no petals, and you won't grow as tall as a tree. But, like a flower and a tree, you are growing.

Are you like a bird? You don't look like a bird. A bird flies on feathered wings. You have no feathers and cannot fly. But a bird, a flower, a cat, a tree, and you are all alike in one important way. You are all alive.

Many things are not alive. A stone is not alive. Your tricycle, a book, the swing set, a doll—none of these is alive.

Do you know how to tell if something is a living thing or not?

All living things are alike in certain ways. All living things need water and food and air.

Living things use water and food and air to give them energy. They need this energy to grow and move.

Ask: *Why is a stone not alive?*

When a cat is born it is small. It is called a kitten. A kitten gets food from its mother. As the kitten grows bigger, it begins to lap up water and nibble on food from a bowl. It breathes air in and out through its nose. The kitten is alive and growing. Kittens and cats need food, water, and air to give them energy so they can run and jump and play.

What's Alive?

A baby bird hatches from an egg. It is called a chick. The chick's mother and father feed it. It breathes air in and out through small holes in its beak. The chick is alive and growing.

Chicks and birds use the energy from food and water and air to fly or hop along the ground.

Birds and cats are animals. You are an animal, too. All animals are living things.

Trees and flowers are also living things. But they are not animals. Trees and flowers are living things called plants.

Plants cannot run or jump or fly. They do not eat or drink or breathe the way you do, or the way a cat does. But they do need water, air, and food. And they can move and grow.

Ask *How are plants and animals different?*

Trees and flowers begin as seeds. When they are still small, trees and flowers are called seedlings.

The seedlings grow roots. Roots take in water and nutrients from the soil.

The seedlings grow leaves. Leaves help plants to breathe in a special way. If you look at the underside of a leaf with a magnifying glass, you will see tiny holes. Plants take in air through these tiny holes.

Green leaves also help plants to catch sunlight. Plants use the power of sunlight to make food out of air, water, and nutrients from the soil.

Plants use the food they make to give them energy. The energy helps them move. They do not run or jump, but they do grow and grow. They bend their stems and leaves to follow the sun.

Ask *How do plants move on their own?*

All animals and all plants are living things.

Anything that never needs food or water or air is not a living thing.

Now you can go exploring!

Walk through your house slowly, then through your backyard or the park. Look carefully at everything you see. Draw pictures of each different thing.

When you are finished exploring, look at your pictures and see if you can tell which are living things and which are nonliving. For each picture, ask yourself these questions: Does this thing need food? Does it need water? Does it need air? Can it grow or move all by itself? If the answer to these questions is yes, then that is a living thing.

But what if you find a plant that is brown and dry? It will not grow anymore. It cannot take in water or air. It cannot move, except to blow in the wind. Is that a living thing?

A stone, or other nonliving things, can never eat or grow. It can never run and jump and play. A nonliving thing cannot die, because it has never been alive.

Ask *Why can't a nonliving thing, like a stone or bicycle, die?*

When you've looked through your pictures, try sorting them into piles of living things and nonliving things. Then separate the pictures of living things into piles for plants and animals.

You can hang the pictures on your wall or bulletin board. Whenever you find anything new, you can ask yourself: Does it need food? Does it need water? Does it need air? Can it grow or move all by itself? Then you can add its picture to your collection.

You will always be able to tell what's alive, and what's not.

Discuss the Read Aloud

✦ After you have finished reading *What's Alive?* invite students to ask questions about what they have heard. Turn through the pages again, and encourage students to discuss what they see in the illustrations.

✦ Review the Focus Question with students: How can you tell if something is alive? *It needs food, water, and air and can grow or move by itself.*

✦ Have students discuss what they learned about growing things from listening to this selection. Ask them the following questions about the unit theme:

- *How do plants breathe? They take in air through tiny holes on the undersides of their leaves.*

- *How do plants make food? Their leaves catch sunlight and use it to make food out of air, water, and nutrients from the soil.*

- *How are you like a flower or a tree? I need food, water, and air to grow.*

Vocabulary Review

Review with students the selection vocabulary words *seedling, exploring, sorting,* and *separate.* Ask students the following questions:

- *What kinds of living things start out as seedlings?*
- *When was a time you went exploring?*
- *What are we doing when we are sorting things?*
- *What do we do when we separate something?*

Research in Action

During the primary years, average students add an average of at least 840 root word meanings per year. Students in the lowest quartile add an average of 570 meanings per year during the same period.

(Andy Biemiller)

Give each student a copy of *Home Connection* page 61. This same information is also available in Spanish on *Home Connection* page 62. Encourage students to discuss the selection "A Tree Is a Plant" with their families and complete the activity provided.

OBJECTIVES

Students will
✦ create dialogue between story characters.
✦ learn about the pronouns *he, she,* and *it.*
✦ participate in a Thinking Story.

MATERIALS

✦ *Language Arts Big Book,* p. 11
✦ *Skills Practice 2,* p. 53
✦ *Willy the Wisher,* p. 78

Writing Process 🕐

Model: Creating Dialogue

Teach

✦ Display page 11 of the *Language Arts Big Book,* and point to the speech bubbles. Tell students *Mike and Tanisha are talking to each other. That's what these bubbles show.*

✦ Explain to students that in many stories, the characters talk to one another. Remind them of "Swimmy," the story they read in the last unit, and how Swimmy talked to the other fish.

✦ Tell students the characters in the story they are writing should talk to each other as well.

Guided Practice

✦ Draw two stick figures on the board. Tell students that they are the two characters in the class story.

✦ Create a simple dialogue exchange between the two characters, presenting their words in speech bubbles. Keep the exchange to one speech bubble per character for the purpose of this model.

✦ Remind students that this is an easy way to show (in a drawing) what characters in a story are saying to each other. Tell them they will work on more dialogue for the characters in the next lesson.

Grammar, Usage, and Mechanics 🕐

Teach

✦ Ask a female student to stand up. Tell the class *(girl's name) is standing.* Then say *She is standing.* Explain that *she* can be used instead of a girl's name. Help students understand that the meaning in the sentence does not change.

✦ Have a male student take out a pencil. Say *(Boy's name) has a pencil.* Then say *He has a pencil.* Explain that *he* can be used instead of a boy's name. Remind students the sentence's meaning does not change.

✦ Write on the board *The clock is broken.* Read the sentence aloud, and then write *It is broken.* Explain that like *he* and *she,* *it* replaces *The clock* and that the sentence's meaning does not change. Explain that because the clock is not a boy or a girl, we use the pronoun *it.*

✦ Tell students the words *he, she,* and *it* are also called pronouns. (You may remind students of *I* and *you.*) *He* replaces a boy's name, *she* replaces a girl's name, and *it* replaces a noun that is neither a boy nor a girl.

Language Arts Big Book, p. 11

Grammar, Usage, and Mechanics continued

Guided Practice

✦ Have students open their **Skills Practice 2** to page 53.

✦ Work through the page with students, and review their answers as a class when you finish.

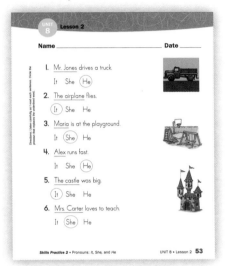

Skills Practice 2, p. 53

Monitor Progress

Formal Assessment ✓

to Differentiate Instruction

Grammar Note how quickly students understand the concept of pronouns.

APPROACHING LEVEL

IF ... students are having difficulty,

THEN ... have students complete **Reteach** page 146.

ON LEVEL

IF ... students need more practice,

THEN ... with your help have them create a list of pronouns they see in the selection "Becoming a Butterfly."

ABOVE LEVEL

IF ... students are comfortable,

THEN ... have them complete **Challenge Activities** page 111.

Teacher Tip

SECONDARY SKILL: DESCRIPTIVE WORDS Make sure students understand that Mr. Breezy tried to offer important details about what he wanted. For example, he talked about a car's wheels, windows, motor, and steering wheel. However, the details he talked about did not offer enough information to specify what he wanted. Suggest to students that Mr. Breezy should have used words that describe, such as *small* and *red,* to get better results.

Willy the Wisher

✦ Display the book **Willy the Wisher.** Turn to "How to Get Exactly What You Want" on page 78 of the book.

✦ Before reading the story to students, ask them to tell you what they know about Mr. Breezy and Mark. In this story, Mr. Breezy often omits important pieces of information when he talks to people.

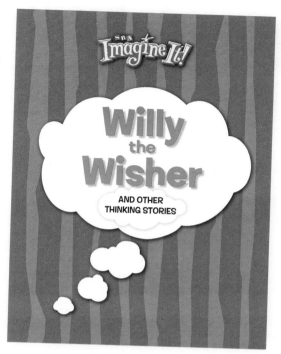

Willy the Wisher, p. 78

✦ Read the story, pausing at the red text to ask students the questions and encourage them to share their thinking.

✦ After reading the story, review each shopping scenario, and have students explain why Mr. Breezy's explanations were unclear. Use questions such as the following:

- *What could Mr. Breezy have said to the car saleswoman immediately to get the exact car he wanted?*

- *Whose pet description was better—Mark's or Mr. Breezy's? Why do you think so?*

- *Have you ever asked for something but didn't get exactly what you wanted? Tell us about it.*

Sounds and Letters

OBJECTIVES

Students will
✦ blend initial phonemes to make words.
✦ identify and match initial and final phonemes.
✦ attach the /ā/ sound to the letter *Aa*.
✦ practice writing the numeral *1*.

MATERIALS

✦ *Alphabet Letter Card Aa* for each student
✦ Supply Icons
✦ *Skills Practice 2,* pp. 54–55
✦ *Pocket Chart Picture Card* 2

Calendar

Su	M	T	W	Th	F	S
		1	2	3	4	5
6	7	8	9	10	11	12
13	14	15	16	17	18	19
20	21	22	23	24	25	26
27	28	29	30	31		

Walk to the class calendar, and point to the box that represents today. Ask students to tell the name of the current season. Then invite students to talk about their favorite seasons and what they like about them. Remind them they could talk about the weather during a season or some activities associated with it, for example, raking leaves in the fall.

Warming Up 🕐

MORNING MESSAGE

Good morning, boys and girls!

Today is _____.

Who has a birthday in April?

Who has a baby brother or sister?

Kindergarten News

✦ Copy the text above on the board or on chart paper; however, make a few errors when you write the sentences today. For example, use periods or exclamation points in place of the question marks, or write a letter *s* backward.

✦ Ask students to check your writing to make sure you have not made any mistakes. Have students proofread your errors and come to the board to correct them by circling the error and making it better.

✦ Use prompts such as the following to discuss the letters and words in the message: *Which word in the message has a capital* A? *April Come circle it. Does that* A *make the short* a *sound or the long* a *sound? long a Which word in the last sentence has the long* a *sound? baby Come underline it.*

✦ End by asking a volunteer to come point to the number *1* on the classroom calendar. Tell students they will learn how to write the number *1* today.

Phoneme Blending: Initial Sounds

✦ Tell students the **Lion Puppet** wants to play a blending game again. Tell them you will say the beginning sound of a word and they should repeat after you. Then the puppet will say the rest. When the puppet asks what the word is, students should put together the parts and say the word.

◆ Use the following words:

/f/ /f/ . . . *inger* finger	/t/ /t/ . . . *unnel* tunnel
/s/ /s/ . . . *tep* step	/n/ /n/ . . . *ibble* nibble
/h/ /h/ . . . *undred* hundred	/j/ /j/ . . . *umper* jumper
/r/ /r/ . . . *abbit* rabbit	/z/ /z/ . . . *ipper* zipper
/c/ /c/ . . . *limb* climb	

Phonemic Awareness

Phoneme Matching: Initial Sounds

◆ Bring out the **Lion Puppet,** and tell students he wants to play a sound-matching game. Tell students you will say three words and they should listen closely to find the two words that begin with the same sound.

◆ Say three words, with two of the words beginning with the same phoneme. For example:

Teacher:	*dust, dark, pink*
Puppet:	*Which words begin the same?*
Everyone:	*dust, dark*

◆ Continue with these words:

gate	*join*	*June*
moth	*nose*	*main*
cone	*tail*	*cake*
fail	*love*	*line*

Phoneme Matching: Final Sounds

Tell students you will continue the game but this time the puppet will ask which two words end in the same sound. Use these words:

jump	*wrap*	*wand*
way	*wax*	*six*
train	*storm*	*green*
brown	*faint*	*beat*

 Teacher Tip

PROGRESSION OF SKILLS The Phonemic Awareness activities that begin Unit 8 review several skills students have been practicing in previous units. It may be tempting to skip these review activities, especially if students are comfortable with the skills, but their placement serves to lead students gently into the new phonemic-awareness skills introduced in Unit 8. Instead of skipping the activities, proceed through them quickly, limiting students' practice to only a few of the suggested words.

Monitor Progress
to Differentiate Instruction
Formal Assessment

Phonemic Awareness Note how readily students can match phonemes.

APPROACHING LEVEL

IF . . . students are having difficulty, THEN . . . help them think of two objects beginning with the same sound, and have them draw pictures of those objects side by side.

ON LEVEL

IF . . . students need more practice, THEN . . . choose an assortment of **Pocket Chart Picture Cards** beginning with several of the same sounds, and have students match the cards.

ABOVE LEVEL

IF . . . students would enjoy a challenging activity, THEN . . . have them work independently to complete **Challenge Activities** page 112.

UNIT 8 Lesson 3

Name _____ Date _____

Directions: Write the letter a under each picture whose name has the /ā/ sound.

54 UNIT 8 • Lesson 3   Identifying Long A • *Skills Practice 2*

Skills Practice 2, p. 54

Monitor Progress

to Differentiate Instruction
Formal Assessment

Letter and Sound Identification Note how quickly students identify the /ā/ sound.

APPROACHING LEVEL

| IF ... students are having difficulty, | THEN ... guide them in completing the activities on **Reteach** page 147. |

ON LEVEL

| IF ... students need more practice, | THEN ... have them draw pictures of someone they know who has the /ā/ sound in his or her name. |

ABOVE LEVEL

| IF ... students are comfortable, | THEN ... have them work independently to name objects in the room or in classroom books whose names begin with /ā/. |

Alphabetic Principle 🕐

Reviewing the Sound of Long *Aa*

Point to **Alphabet Sound Wall Card** Long Aa, and have students recite the rhyme for the sounds of *Aa*:

A's my name.

Two sounds I make:

Short a *in* lamb,

Long a *in* cake.

Listening for Medial /ā/

Give each student **Alphabet Letter Card** Aa. Ask students to raise the cards and say the /ā/ sound when they hear a word that has the /ā/ sound. Try the following words:

date	lamp	**wave**
cute	**late**	nose
blank	**flame**	front
brave	**table**	planted

Linking the Sound to the Letter

✦ Write a pair of words on the board, one with the /ā/ sound and one with a different vowel sound. For each pair, say the word with the /ā/ sound, point to each of the words, and have students identify the correct word by signaling thumbs-up when you point to it. After the student answers correctly, ask him or her how he or she knows the correct word. *The word begins with long* a. Try these word pairs:

| *April* ... uncle | *age* ... egg | *age* ... egg |
| *apron* ... onion | inch ... *ache* | Eve ... *Amy* |

✦ Finish the activity by helping students complete **Skills Practice 2** page 54.

Penmanship

✦ Distribute a sheet of writing paper to each student, or use **White Boards** turned to the sides with writing lines.

✦ Place the Supply Icon for *pencil* on the board or in the **Pocket Chart.**

✦ Using the established procedure, review with students how to form the numeral *1*: Say *Begin here. Go straight down to make a vertical line, and stop. One.*

✦ Now invite students to practice writing numeral *1*s across the top row of the paper or **White Boards** from left to right.

✦ Remind students the number *1* means we have one of something. Draw one star on the board as a visual if necessary.

Guided Practice

✦ Have students complete **Skills Practice 2** page 55 for additional practice with the numeral *1*.

✦ Draw students' attention to the first penmanship line. Ask them to trace the *1*s outlined across the row. Then ask students to write a row of *1*s across the next line.

✦ Then ask students to look at the word *one* written on the line. Tell students this is how you write the word that names the number *1*.

✦ Invite three volunteers to identify the letters that make up the word *one,* and have the class practice writing the word by tracing the letters. Then have them try writing the word on their own on the next line.

✦ After students have finished, help them proofread using the established procedure. They should use a colored pencil to star their best numerals and circle and correct those they would like to make better.

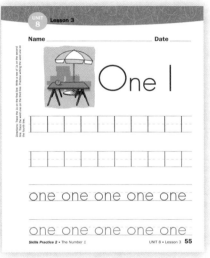

Skills Practice 2, p. 55

Teacher Tip

USING PROGRAM MATERIALS Use *Pocket Chart Picture Card* 2 to help you review the shape of the numeral *1*.

Monitor Progress
to Differentiate Instruction
Formal Assessment

Numeral Identification Note how easily students identify the numeral *1*.

APPROACHING LEVEL

| IF ... students are having difficulty, | THEN ... have them look for and cut out 1s in old magazines. |

ON LEVEL

| IF ... students need more practice, | THEN ... have them look through the **Ready, Set, Grow! Big Book** to find *1*s on the pages. |

ABOVE LEVEL

| IF ... students would enjoy a challenging activity, | THEN ... have them make a drawing using only the number. |

Reading and Responding

OBJECTIVES

Students will

✦ locate the title and the names of the author and the illustrator.

✦ develop an understanding of vocabulary words.

✦ use the comprehension strategies Asking Questions and Clarifying.

✦ identify print and book features.

MATERIALS

✦ *Ready, Set, Grow! Big Book,* pp. 4–29
✦ Routines 5–7

Focus Question How does a tree change in different seasons?

A Tree Is a PLANT
by Clyde Robert Bulla
illustrated by Stacey Schuett

PINES
MAPLE

Ready, Set, Grow! Big Book, p. 4

Technology

To promote independent reading, encourage students to use Workshop to listen to the recording of the selection on the *Listening Library CD.* Invite them to follow along and say the words whenever they can.

Audio CD

1st READ

Preview and Prepare

ROUTINE **5**

Activate Prior Knowledge

✦ "A Tree Is a Plant" is a nonfiction selection that explains how an apple tree grows from a seed to a mature tree and then changes from season to season. The selection discusses the different parts of a tree and explains how a tree stays alive and produces apples. As you read the selection aloud, relate what you already know to what you are reading, and encourage students to do the same.

✦ Invite students to describe the trees in their neighborhoods and to share all they know about trees and how they grow. Tell students some trees produce fruit. Ask students if they have ever picked fruit from a tree and what that was like. Let students know they will be learning about apple trees and how they grow and change as they listen to this selection.

✦ Encourage students to discuss what they are learning about the unit theme as they listen to "A Tree Is a Plant." Key concepts include the following:

• Trees need soil, air, water, and sunshine to grow.

• The roots of a tree serve many purposes.

• The apples on a tree begin as blossoms.

• The leaves of a tree make food for it to grow.

• Apple trees change in appearance from season to season.

Preview the Selection

✦ Open the *Ready, Set, Grow! Big Book* to pages 4–5, the opening pages of "A Tree Is a Plant." Follow Routine 5 as you introduce the title and the names of the author and the illustrator. Ask students what an author and an illustrator do.

✦ Prepare to read the selection. Turn through the pages, focusing students' attention on the illustrations. Tell them to look for clues as to what the selection might tell them. Encourage students to comment on anything they find interesting or puzzling.

✦ Encourage students to think of reasons to read "A Tree Is a Plant." Ask students to consider what they might learn about the unit theme Ready, Set, Grow!

Vocabulary

ROUTINE **6**

Vocabulary

soil	blossoms
branches	during

✦ Follow Routine 6, the selection vocabulary routine, as you introduce the vocabulary words for this selection.

✦ Explain to students that *soil* is the dirt the trees grow in.

✦ Tell students *branches* are stems growing out of the main stem of a tree. Ask students if they have ever climbed on the branches of a tree.

✦ Tell them *blossoms* are flowers. Use the following sentence to illustrate: *Pink blossoms appeared just days after the rain.*

✦ Explain that the word *during* means "while something is going on." Ask students what games they play during recess.

Read the Selection

ROUTINE **7**

✦ Before beginning the selection, read the Focus Question at the top of the first page. Tell students to keep this question in mind as they listen to the story.

✦ Follow Routine 7, the reading the selection routine, and read the entire selection.

✦ Before, during, and after the first reading, encourage students to ask questions and to think aloud about the selection. In this way, you prepare them for the kind of thinking they will need to become independent, enthusiastic readers.

Comprehension Strategies

✦ You will introduce and model the following comprehension strategies:

- Asking Questions
- Clarifying

✦ Think aloud through each strategy, and encourage students to share their ideas as well.

 Monitor Progress

to Differentiate Instruction
Formal Assessment

Vocabulary Note how easily students understand vocabulary.

APPROACHING LEVEL

IF ... students need help with the vocabulary words,	THEN ... refer to Unit 8 Lesson 3 of the *Intervention Guide.*

ON LEVEL

IF ... students need to practice the vocabulary words,	THEN ... have them play Password with other students.

ABOVE LEVEL

IF ... students understand the vocabulary words,	THEN ... have them work in a small group to think of as many words as possible that relate to each vocabulary word.

Comprehension Strategies

Teacher Modeling

1 Clarifying *Wait a second! We need to think about what a plant is. We know most plants grow in the ground. They are living things, but they're different from animals because they can't move around on their own. So I guess a tree is a plant, and I can't really think of a larger plant than a tree.*

2 Asking Questions *The apple seed in the picture is changing. I wonder what makes that happen. I'll read the words to find the answer. The words say the rain falls and the sun warms the earth. Then the seed begins to grow. Part of the seed is growing up, and part is growing down.*

3 Asking Questions *What is this? Could it be a little apple tree? If it is, when does it start looking like an apple tree and making apples? I'll read this page to see if it answers our questions. Yes, it is a little apple tree, but it won't have apples on it for a long time. It has to grow up first, and the story says that can take seven years.*

Focus Question How does a tree change in different seasons?

A Tree Is a PLANT

by Clyde Robert Bulla
illustrated by Stacey Schuett

PINES
MAPLE
PERSIMMON
PALMS
LEMON
WILLOW

A tree is a plant.
A tree is the biggest plant that grows. **1**
Most kinds of trees grow from seeds the way most small plants do.

There are many kinds of trees.
Here are a few of them.
How many do you know?

4

5

This tree grows in the country.
It might grow in your yard, too.
Do you know what kind it is?
This is an apple tree.

This apple tree came from a seed.
The seed was small.
It grew inside an apple.
Have you ever seen an apple seed?

Ask an adult to help you cut an apple in two.
The seeds are in the center.
They look like this.

6

7

 Teacher Tip

GLOSSARY The words *soil, branches* and *blossoms* can be found in the Glossary of the *Ready, Set, Grow! Big Book.*

Most apple trees come from seeds that are planted.

Sometimes an apple tree grows from a seed that falls to the ground.

The wind blows leaves over the seed.
The wind blows soil over the seed.

8

All winter the seed lies under the leaves and the soil.

All winter the seed lies under ice and snow and is pushed into the ground.

2

Spring comes.
Rain falls.
The sun comes out and warms the earth.
The seed begins to grow.

9

At first the young plant does not look like a tree.

The tree is very small.

It is only a stem with two leaves.

It has no apples on it.

A tree must grow up before it has apples on it.

Each year the tree grows. It grows tall.

3

In seven years it is so tall that you can stand under its branches.

In the spring there are blossoms on the tree.

Spring is apple-blossom time.

10

11

Ready, Set, Grow! Big Book, pp. 4–11

Print and Book Awareness

Question Marks

Have volunteers find and point to the question marks on pages 5–7 of the **Big Book.** Ask students what this mark means. If necessary, tell them it means a question has been asked. Demonstrate how a question sounds by rereading the three questions. Then invite students to read the questions with you.

Sentences: Periods

Display page 9 of the **Big Book,** and have volunteers point to the first and last word of each sentence. *All, soil; All, ground; Spring, comes; Rain, falls; The, earth; The, grow* Have them point to the periods at the ends of sentences and say *This is a period.*

High-Frequency Words

Display pages 10–11, and have students point to and read any high-frequency words they have learned. Words they might find include *a, at, you, in, is, the, with, look,* and *on.*

Comprehension Strategies

Teacher Modeling

4 Clarifying *It says a little apple appears in each place that had a blossom. I wonder if the blossoms help make the little apples. What do you think? The story doesn't say. Let's see if we can find any little green apples in the picture.*

5 Clarifying *How can roots grow like branches under the ground? Let's look at the picture to clarify, or figure out, what this means. Wow! The roots look just like an underground tree. I didn't know so many roots were under a tree.*

6 Clarifying *How do the roots do all this? I don't understand. Maybe the picture will explain. The roots of these trees spread deep and wide. Can you see how this would make the tree strong and keep it from falling over? Can you see how the roots might hold it in place?*

7 Clarifying *When I hear the word* food, *I think of what we eat—bread, milk, eggs, and so on. But the food that leaves make must be very different. It sounds like sunshine, water, and air are the ingredients for the food that leaves make. The leaves make the food for the tree just like your family prepares your food.*

The blossoms last only a few days. Then they fall to the ground.

12

Now there are green leaves on the tree. Among the leaves there are small apples. The apples are where the blossoms were before. **4**

The apples are green, and they are almost too small for you to see.

The apples grow slowly.

13

They grow all during the spring and the summer.

In the fall they are large and ripe. They are ready to eat.

We can see the apples and the leaves on the branches.

14

We can see the branches growing out of the trunk.

We can see the trunk growing out of the ground.

We can see the bark of the tree.

The bark covers the branches and the trunk like a coat.

But there is a part of the tree that we cannot see.

15

 Teacher Tip

CLARIFYING Remind students that readers stop reading when some part of the text does not make sense. Model for students the various ways readers clarify difficult ideas or passages. These include rereading, using charts and other graphic organizers, thinking of other comprehension strategies that might help, and asking someone for help.

We cannot see the root .
They are under the ground.
Some of the roots are large.
Some of them are as small as hairs.
The roots grow like branches under **5**
the ground.
A tree could not live without roots.

16

Roots hold the trunk in the ground.
Roots keep the tree from falling
when the wind blows.
Roots keep the rain from washing
the tree out of the ground. **6**

17

Roots do something more. They take water
from the ground.

They carry the water into the trunk of the tree.
The trunk carries the water to the branches.
The branches carry the water to the leaves.

18

Hundreds and hundreds of leaves
grow on the branches. The leaves make
food from water and air. They make **7**
food when the sun shines.
The food goes into the branches.
It goes into the trunk and roots.
It goes to every part of the tree.

19

Ready, Set, Grow! Big Book, pp. 12–19

Print and Book Awareness

Sentences, Directionality

Display page 15 of the **Big Book,** and have volunteers show where to start reading each sentence and where to stop. Remind students we read from left to right, a sentence begins with a capital letter, and some sentences end with periods. Have each volunteer run his or her hand under each line of print.

Picture-Text Relationship

Reread the text on pages 16–17 and 18–19, and have students comment about the illustration on each page. For each illustration, ask *What does the picture tell you that the story does not?* Tell students the pictures and words work together to tell the whole story.

Comprehension Strategies

Teacher Modeling

8 Asking Questions *When the leaves die, won't the tree die too? The tree won't have food if the leaves aren't there to make it. I'll see if the next page answers my questions. The tree certainly looks dead. But the words say that under the bark, the tree is alive. Maybe it has stored food for the winter like some animals do.*

9 Asking Questions *What makes an apple tree live? Do you remember what it needs to grow and make food?*

10 Asking Questions *Let's think about this question. Do you like apple trees best in the summer? The picture reminds me I do like the shade of the apple tree. It's a good place to keep cool. But let's think about what the apple tree is like at other times. Maybe then we can decide when we like it best.*

Differentiating Instruction **English Learners**

IF ... students need additional help with the comprehension strategy Asking Questions, **THEN ...** refer to Unit 8 Lesson 3 of the *English Learner Support Guide.*

Fall comes and winter is near.
The work of the leaves is over.

The leaves turn yellow and brown.
The leaves die and fall to the ground. **8**

20

Now the tree is bare.
All winter it looks dead.

But the tree is not dead.
Under its coat of bark, the tree is alive.

21

Spring comes again. Rain falls.

22   23

 Teacher Tip

ASKING QUESTIONS Inform students they should keep asking questions and trying to answer them as they read.

The sun warms the earth.
The tree blossoms, and new leaves grow.
As long as it lives, the apple tree grows.

As long as it lives, the apple tree blossoms
in the spring, and apples grow on it. **9**

24   25

When do you like apple trees best?

In spring when they are covered
with blossoms?

In summer when they are covered
with leaves? **10**

26   27

Ready, Set, Grow! Big Book, pp. 20–27

Print and Book Awareness

Alphabetic Knowledge

Have volunteers come to the **Big Book** and point to and say the names of any letters and words they recognize.

Letter Shapes

Have volunteers point to and identify letters with rounded shapes. Then have volunteers point to letters with straight lines.

Capital Letters

Invite a volunteer to point to the first word in the first sentence on page 20. Ask *What kind of letter do we use at the beginning of a sentence?* Then say *This sentence begins with a capital* F. Have volunteers point to and say the beginning capital letter of each sentence on pages 20–21. *F, T (three times), N, A, B, U*

Comprehension Strategies

Teacher Modeling

11 Asking Questions *Do you like an apple tree best in winter? The picture reminds me of how pretty it looks covered with snow. Birds and animals use the tree branches. We need to think carefully about our answer. When do you like an apple tree best?*

In winter when they are bare? **11**

28

Or in fall when they are covered with apples?

29

Ready, Set, Grow! Big Book, pp. 28–29

Concept/Question Board

Tell students readers keep thinking about any questions that are generated as they are reading. As they read, tell them to keep in mind the questions on the **Concept/Question Board.** Tell them readers are always thinking about what is important in selections and they try to remember this important information.

Print and Book Awareness

Question Marks

Have a volunteer point to the question marks on pages 28–29 of the **Big Book.** Ask students what this mark means. If necessary, tell them it means a question has been asked. Demonstrate how a question sounds by rereading the question. Then invite students to read the question with you.

Discussing the Selection

✦ Review the Focus Question with students: How does a tree change in different seasons? *An apple tree has blossoms in the spring, leaves in the summer, apples in the fall, and bare branches in the winter.*

✦ Have students visit the school library and select other non-fiction selections about things that grow.

✦ Have students discuss the purpose of informational text and text read for pleasure.

Vocabulary Review

Review with students the selection vocabulary words *soil, branches, blossoms* and *during.* Ask students the following questions:

• *What can we plant in the soil?*
• *What kinds of animals live in tree branches?*
• *Where can we see blossoms?*
• *What happens during lunchtime?*

Language Arts

OBJECTIVES

Students will
✦ create dialogue, using speech bubbles.
✦ identify, draw, and describe details missing from illustrations.

MATERIALS
✦ *Language Arts Big Book,* p. 11
✦ *Story Lines Big Book,* pp. 16–17

Language Arts Big Book, p. 11

Research in Action

Skilled writing does not take place in a vacuum. What and how well students write is influenced by a host of social factors, including the amount of time devoted to writing, the creation of a supportive writing environment, and interactions with peers and teachers.

(Steve Graham and Karen Harris)

Writing Process

Draft: Using Speech Bubbles

Teach

✦ Display page 11 of the *Language Arts Big Book,* and ask students what they remember about the bubbles above Mike's and Tanisha's heads. If necessary, remind them these are speech bubbles and we can use speech bubbles to show what two characters in a story say to each other.

✦ Talk about the dialogue model you created for students in the previous lesson. Have students recall what the dialogue was. If possible, re-create the dialogue on the board, drawing the two characters as stick figures again.

✦ Tell students it is their turn to decide what the characters are talking about.

Apply

Guide students in creating dialogue that reflects the class plans for the story. Use the method of drawing stick figures on the board. Or use chart paper so you can refer to today's work when you resume the writing process in the next lesson.

Story Crafting ✦

Story Lines

✦ Pointing to the Listening Icons, remind students to listen carefully.

✦ Display the ***Story Lines Big Book,*** and open it to pages 16–17, "Plants Move! I Can Prove It."

✦ Ask students to look at the story frames as you read the story. Tell them to listen to the story and to think about what is missing from the picture frames.

✦ As you read the captions, point to each corresponding frame.

✦ Next tell students you are going to read the story again but this time you will pause at certain frames so they can help you fill in what is missing in those frames.

✦ When you reach Frame 2, point out to students that the boy's speech bubble is empty. Invite a volunteer to suggest what word or words should be in the speech bubble. Reread the frame caption if necessary.

✦ After the class has decided what belongs in the bubble, write it in for them.

✦ Continue this procedure through Frame 6. Before moving to the next frame, discuss the clues in the story text that helped students know what belongs in the empty spaces.

✦ Tell students they will continue working with the story in the next lesson.

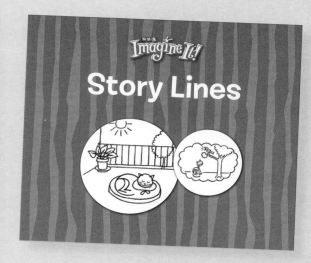

Story Lines Big Book, pp. 16–17

 **Teacher Tip**

INTERACTIVE FRAMES Note that the illustrations for several frames have pieces missing from the "Plants Move! I Can Prove It" story. Use these frames to help students interact with the story, taking cues from the text you read and explaining what you should draw to complete each frame.

Differentiating Instruction **English Learners**

IF ... students have limited proficiency, **THEN ...** help them participate in discussions by asking them questions that can be answered by nodding, by saying *yes* or *no*, or with one or two words.

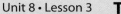

Students will

+ understand and follow multi-step oral directions.
+ identify and match initial and final phonemes.
+ attach the /ā/ sound to the letter Aa.

+ *Alphabet Letter Card Aa* for each student
+ *Pickled Peppers Big Book,* pp. 40–41

Calendar

Su	M	T	W	Th	F	S
			1	2	3	4	5
6	7	8	9	10	11	12
13	14	15	16	17	18	19
20	21	22	23	24	25	26
27	28	29	30	31		

Point to the box that represents today. Refer students to the Weather Icons, and ask a volunteer to describe today's weather. Review the differences among various types of weather.

Warming Up

MORNING MESSAGE

Today is _____ .

There is _____ flag in the room.

There are _____ alligators in the room.

Kindergarten News

+ Copy the text above on the board or on chart paper.

+ Have students help you fill in the blanks for the sentences. Invite students to write the number words *one* and *zero* in the blanks. You might write the words first in dotted lines and have students trace them. Or you could help them write the words hand over hand.

+ Use prompts such as the following to discuss the letters and words in the message:

  • *Can someone find a word that appears two times in the message? is, there, in, the, room Come point to it.*

  • *How many letters are in the word* alligators? *ten Let's count them.*

  • *How many syllables are in the word* alligators? *four Let's clap them out.*

Following Directions

+ Call on volunteers to stand in front of the class and to follow the directions you give. Tell the other students to listen and to watch the student to see that he or she does what you say in the right order. Tell them to signal thumbs-up or thumbs-down to show whether the student has followed directions.

Differentiating Instruction — English Learners

IF ... students have difficulty following directions, **THEN ...** perform the command as you give it, and have students mimic both your actions and the command. This will help students build vocabulary.

✦ Say a sequence of three simple directions. For example:

Pat your nose. Touch your right ear. Wiggle your fingers.

Hop on one foot. Turn around. Say "Hey!"

✦ Have several students serve as volunteers to perform the actions.

Phonemic Awareness

Phoneme Matching: Initial Sounds

✦ Bring out the **Lion Puppet,** and tell students he wants to play a sound-matching game. Tell students you will say three words and they should listen closely to find the two words that begin with the same sound.

✦ Say three words, with two of the words beginning with the same phoneme. For example:

Teacher:	*told, flat, folk*
Puppet:	*Which words begin the same?*
Everyone:	*flat, folk*

✦ Continue with these words:

mint	*mall*	*nail*
pick	*date*	*drip*
belt	*have*	*help*
rake	*runt*	*wait*

Phoneme Matching: Final Sounds

Tell students you will continue the game but this time the puppet will ask which two words end the same. Use these words:

late	*cart*	*made*
cliff	*ring*	*off*
bread	*scrub*	*grab*
fizz	*grass*	*squeeze*

 Teacher Tip

PHONEMIC AWARENESS Remember to move quickly through these activities. Students are often provided with several opportunities to practice each skill. Continued drilling on the same activity will bore students who already grasp the concept and frustrate those who do not. Plan to work with struggling students individually during Workshop.

Monitor Progress

to Differentiate Instruction
Formal Assessment

Phonemic Awareness Note how easily students match initial phonemes.

APPROACHING LEVEL

IF ... students are having difficulty, THEN ... guide them in completing **Reteach** page 148.

ON LEVEL

IF ... students need more practice, THEN ... use **Alphabet Flash Cards** of letters and sounds students have learned, and have them say the beginning sound as you come to each letter.

ABOVE LEVEL

IF ... students are comfortable, THEN ... have them work with partners to identify objects and their initial sounds in a **Little Big Book** or classroom book.

Teacher Tip

SPELLINGS FOR LONG Aa In kindergarten, **SRA Imagine It!** teaches two ways to write the long *a* sound: *a* and *a_e*. Any activities in which students interact visually with words that have the /ā/ sound, such as the Linking the Sound to the Letter activity in this lesson, will feature only these two spellings. (Other spellings for the long *a* sound are taught in later grades.) When choosing your own words to illustrate the /ā/ sound, remember to also limit your choices to the *a* or *a_e* spelling for consistency.

Alphabetic Principle

Reviewing the Sound of Long *Aa*

Point to **Alphabet Sound Wall Card** Long *Aa*. Review with students the rhyme for the sounds of *Aa*:

A*'s my name.*

Two sounds I make:

Short a *in* lamb,

Long a *in* cake.

Listening for Medial /ā/

Give each student an **Alphabet Letter Card** *Aa*. Ask students to raise the cards and say */ā/* when they hear a word that has the /ā/ sound. Try the following words:

tale	beat	crack	**state**
back	**game**	**shape**	must
fast	**lazy**	**label**	strong

Linking the Sound to the Letter

✦ Write the word *at* on the board. Help students blend the word.

✦ Now write the word *ate* next to *at*. Pronounce the new word, and explain to students that sometimes the letter *e* can be a "signal." In the word *ate,* the letter *e* signals that the vowel *a* says its name or is long.

✦ Write a pair of words on the board, one with the /ā/ sound spelled *a_e* and one with the /a/ sound.

✦ Read each pair of words, then ask students to identify the word with the /ā/ sound by signaling thumbs-up when you point to it.

✦ Have students come to the board and underline the letters that together make the /ā/ sound. Assist them as necessary. Remind students to look for the signal *e* at the end of the word.

cap ... **cape**	**made** ... mad	**pane** ... pan
tape ... tap	mat ... **mate**	**Jane** ... Jan

Pickled Peppers Big Book

✦ Display the **Pickled Peppers Big Book.** Ask a volunteer to come up to the book and identify the book's Table of Contents. After the student has identified the Table of Contents, have him or her help you find the poem "Rhyme" on page 40.

✦ Turn to pages 40–41, "Rhyme." Point to the title, and read it aloud. Invite students to share anything they remember about the rhyme.

✦ Tell students you will read the rhyme aloud and you would like them to listen for the words that have the /ā/ sound. Ask students to close their eyes as they listen.

✦ Invite students to say any /ā/ words they noticed while you read the rhyme aloud.

✦ Reread the rhyme, pointing to each word as you say it. Ask students to stop you each time you point to a word that has the letter *a* in it. *a, black, and, at, shake* When you pause, work with students to evaluate the sound the letter *a* makes in each word. Point out the *a_e* in *shake*. When you find a word with the /ā/ sound, have students make their bodies tall like the long *a*.

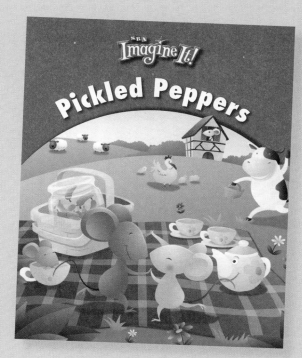

Pickled Peppers Big Book, pp. 40–41

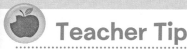 **Teacher Tip**

TRACKING Create opportunities to have students come to the **Big Book** and track the text from top to bottom and from left to right. Using a ruler or a pointer, read and track the text with students.

Technology

Use the **Listening Library CD** to support the **Pickled Peppers** lessons.

Audio CD

OBJECTIVES

Students will
+ review the comprehension strategies Asking Questions and Clarifying.
+ use the comprehension skill Classify and Categorize.
+ analyze the text structure of the selection.

MATERIALS

+ *Ready, Set, Grow! Big Book,* pp. 4–29
+ Routines 5, 6

Preview and Prepare

2nd READ

Preview the Selection ROUTINE 5

+ Display the *Ready, Set, Grow! Big Book,* opened to the Table of Contents page. Use Routine 5, the previewing the selection routine, to guide students in understanding and using the Table of Contents. Then turn to the selection, and say the title and the names of the author and the illustrator.

+ Prepare to reread the selection. As you turn through the pages, have students use the illustrations to retell important facts from the selection.

Vocabulary ROUTINE 6

+ Follow Routine 6, the selection vocabulary routine, as you introduce the vocabulary words for this selection.

+ Explain to students that the word *trunk* has several meanings but that in this selection it means "the main part where all the branches grow from." Use the following sentence to illustrate: *We ran around the tree trunk.*

+ Tell students the word *bark* also has several meanings, but in this selection it means "the outer covering of a tree." Explain to students that not all bark looks or feels the same. The color can be white or shades of brown or gray. The texture can be smooth, shaggy, or rough with deep grooves.

+ Explain to students that the word *roots* refers to another part of the tree. The roots of a plant are the parts of a plant under the ground.

+ Tell students in this selection, the word *washing* means "pushing." Use the following sentence to illustrate: *The waves are washing the boat out to sea.*

Focus Question How does a tree change in different seasons?

A Tree Is a PLANT

by Clyde Robert Bulla
illustrated by Stacey Schuett

PINES

MAPLE

Ready, Set, Grow! Big Book, p. 4

Vocabulary

trunk	roots
bark	washing

Read the Selection

Comprehension Strategies

✦ During the first reading of "A Tree Is a Plant," you introduced and modeled the following comprehension strategies:

- Asking Questions
- Clarifying

✦ In this second reading of the selection, you will revisit each comprehension strategy model from the first reading.

Comprehension Skills

In this lesson of "A Tree Is a Plant," students will use the comprehension skill Classify and Categorize.

Reading with a Writer's Eye

✦ In this rereading of "A Tree Is a Plant," you will discuss with students how the author structures the text to make the information more understandable.

✦ As students analyze the author's writing techniques, they become more aware of ways to improve their own writing.

Concept/Question Board

Tell students readers keep thinking about any questions generated as they are reading. As they read, tell them to keep in mind the questions on the **Concept/Question Board.** Tell them readers are always thinking about what is important in selections and they try to remember this important information.

Technology

To promote independent reading, encourage students to use Workshop to listen to the recording of the selection on the *Listening Library CD.* Invite them to follow along and to say the words whenever they can.

Audio CD

Comprehension Strategies

Teacher Modeling

1 Clarifying *Here we needed to stop and think about what a plant really is. We had to think about what we knew about plants and if we believed that a tree is the biggest plant. We realized that we agreed with what the selection says.*

2 Asking Questions *When we saw how the apple seed in the picture was changing, we wondered what made this happen. When we read the words, we found out the rain and the sun make the seed grow.*

3 Asking Questions *When we saw this picture of a young plant, we thought it was probably a little apple tree. But we wondered when it would start looking like an apple tree. The words answered our question. They told us it would take seven years for the tree to grow up and make apples.*

Focus Question How does a tree change in different seasons?

A Tree Is a PLANT

by Clyde Robert Bulla
illustrated by Stacey Schuett

PINES

MAPLE

PERSIMMON

PALMS

WILLOW

LEMON

A tree is a plant.
A tree is the biggest plant that grows. **1**
Most kinds of trees grow from seeds
the way most small plants do.

There are many kinds of trees.
Here are a few of them.
How many do you know?

4

5

This tree grows in the country.
It might grow in your yard, too.
Do you know what kind it is?
This is an apple tree.

This apple tree came from a seed.
The seed was small.
It grew inside an apple.
Have you ever seen an apple seed?

Ask an adult to help you cut an apple in two.
The seeds are in the center.
They look like this.

6

7

🍎 Teacher Tip

GLOSSARY The words *trunk, bark,* and *roots* can be found in the Glossary of the *Ready, Set Grow! Big Book.*

Most apple trees come from seeds that are planted.

Sometimes an apple tree grows from a seed that falls to the ground.

The wind blows leaves over the seed.
The wind blows soil over the seed.

8

All winter the seed lies under the leaves and the soil.

All winter the seed lies under ice and snow and is pushed into the ground.

Spring comes.
Rain falls.
The sun comes out and warms the earth.
The seed begins to grow.

2

9

At first the young plant does not look like a tree.

The tree is very small.

It is only a stem with two leaves.

It has no apples on it.

A tree must grow up before it has apples on it.

Each year the tree grows.
It grows tall.

3

10

In seven years it is so tall that you can stand under its branches.

In the spring there are blossoms on the tree.

Spring is apple-blossom time.

11

Ready, Set, Grow! Big Book, pp. 4–11

Differentiating Instruction | **English Learners**

IF . . . students have difficulty understanding the text, **THEN . . .** tell them to use the illustrations to help them understand the selection.

Comprehension Skills

Classify and Categorize

✦ Point out that "A Tree Is a Plant" shares lots of information about trees, especially apple trees. Help students realize we can group things according to how they are alike, the kinds of things they do, or other characteristics.

✦ Ask students the following questions to help them understand how the information on these pages is grouped:

- *Where does an apple tree come from?*
- *How does an apple seed that falls to the ground get its start?*
- *What happens to the young plant after it pushes through the soil?*

Reading with a Writer's Eye

Text Structure: Technique

✦ The author uses illustrations to explain the information about apple trees that he shares. Explain that the illustrations and words work together to tell the whole story.

✦ Show students the illustrations on pages 4–11, and discuss how they help explain the information on these pages.

Reading and Responding

2nd READ

Comprehension Strategies

Teacher Modeling

4 Clarifying *When we read a little green apple appears each place there was a blossom, we wondered if the blossoms help make the apples. The story doesn't say, but we knew we could find out by checking other books.*

5 Clarifying *We were confused about how roots could grow like branches under the ground. But when we looked at the picture, we saw that the roots look just like an underground tree. We didn't know so many roots were under a tree. The picture helped us clarify how roots grow.*

6 Clarifying *We were surprised that roots do all these things. The picture helped us figure out how roots help a tree. We could see how deep and wide the roots spread. We knew this would make the tree strong and hold it in place. We could also see how the roots would hold the soil in place and not let the tree wash away. The pictures helped us understand the words.*

7 Clarifying *Here we were confused about the word* food. *We had to think about the food that leaves make in a different way than we think about our food. So we figured out sunshine, water, and air are the ingredients for the food leaves make. That helped us understand better.*

The blossoms last only a few days. Then they fall to the ground.

12

Now there are green leaves on the tree. Among the leaves there are small apples. The apples are where the blossoms were before. **4**

The apples are green, and they are almost too small for you to see.

The apples grow slowly.

13

They grow all during the spring and the summer.

In the fall they are large and ripe. They are ready to eat.

We can see the apples and the leaves on the branches.

14

We can see the branches growing out of the trunk.

We can see the trunk growing out of the ground.

We can see the bark of the tree.

The bark covers the branches and the trunk like a coat.

But there is a part of the tree that we cannot see.

15

Vocabulary Tip

Review the meanings of the words *trunk* and *bark*. Then have students use the words in sentences.

We cannot see the roots.
They are under the ground.
Some of the roots are large.
Some of them are as small as hairs.
The roots grow like branches under ⑤
the ground.
A tree could not live without roots.

16

Roots hold the trunk in the ground.
Roots keep the tree from falling
when the wind blows.
Roots keep the rain from washing
the tree out of the ground. ⑥

17

Roots do something more. They take water
from the ground.

They carry the water into the trunk of the tree.
The trunk carries the water to the branches.
The branches carry the water to the leaves.

18

Hundreds and hundreds of leaves
grow on the branches. The leaves make
food from water and air. They make ⑦
food when the sun shines.
The food goes into the branches.
It goes into the trunk and roots.
It goes to every part of the tree.

19

Ready, Set, Grow! Big Book, pp. 12–19

Vocabulary Tip

Review the meanings of the words *roots* and
washing. Then have students use the words in
sentences.

Comprehension Skills

Classify and Categorize

Ask students the following questions to help
them understand how the information on
these pages is grouped:

* *How does an apple tree make apples?*
* *What are the different parts of an apple tree?*
* *How do the roots help an apple tree grow?*
* *How do the leaves help an apple tree grow?*

Reading with a Writer's Eye

Text Structure: Technique

✦ Show students the illustration on pages
  12–13, and discuss how it helps explain
  how apple blossoms turn into apples.

✦ Show students the illustration on
  pages 16–17, and discuss how it helps
  explain the appearance and benefits of a
  tree's roots.

✦ Show students the diagrams on
  pages 18–19, and discuss how the
  diagrams help explain the purpose of a
  tree's roots and leaves.

Comprehension Strategies

Teacher Modeling

8 Asking Questions *Here we were worried if the leaves died, the tree would die too. We knew the tree needed the leaves to make food. So we read on to find an answer. Then we found out that under the bark, the tree stays alive. We thought maybe the tree stored food for the winter like some animals do.*

9 Asking Questions *We wondered what makes an apple tree live. So we thought about what it needs to make food and grow. We remembered it needs soil, sunshine, rain, and air.*

10 Asking Questions *Here we wanted to think about the question "When do I like apple trees best?" The picture reminded us we like the shade of the apple tree in the summer. We knew it was a good place to keep cool. But we wanted to think about what the apple tree was like at other times. Then we'd be able to decide when we like it best.*

Fall comes and winter is near.
The work of the leaves is over.

The leaves turn yellow and brown.
The leaves die and fall to the ground. **8**

20

Now the tree is bare.
All winter it looks dead.

But the tree is not dead.
Under its coat of bark, the tree is alive.

21

Spring comes again. Rain falls.

22

23

The sun warms the earth.
The tree blossoms, and new leaves grow.
As long as it lives, the apple tree grows.

As long as it lives, the apple tree blossoms
in the spring, and apples grow on it. **9**

24

25

When do you like apple trees best?

In spring when they are covered
with blossoms?

In summer when they are covered
with leaves? **10**

26

27

Ready, Set, Grow! Big Book, pp. 20–27

Comprehension Skills

Classify and Categorize

Ask students the following questions to help them understand how the information on these pages is grouped:

- *What happens to the apple tree in the fall?*
- *What happens to the apple tree in the winter?*
- *What happens to the apple tree in the spring?*

Reading with a Writer's Eye

Text Structure: Technique

Show students the illustrations on pages 20–27, and discuss how the illustrations help explain how an apple tree changes across the seasons.

 **Teacher Tip**

CLASSIFY AND CATEGORIZE Help students understand classifying and categorizing by having them classify/categorize familiar things.

Comprehension Strategies

Teacher Modeling

11 **Asking Questions** *Here we had to think about whether we like an apple tree in winter. The picture helped by showing us the pretty snow-covered branches. But we decided we didn't know yet about the winter apple tree. We wanted to keep thinking.*

In winter when they are bare? **11**

28

Or in fall when they are covered with apples?

29

Ready, Set, Grow! Big Book, pp. 28–29

Concept/Question Board

Tell students readers keep thinking about any questions that are generated as they are reading. As they read, tell them to keep in mind the questions on the **Concept/Question Board.** Tell them readers are always thinking about what is important in selections and they try to remember this important information.

Reading with a Writer's Eye

Text Structure: Technique

✦ Show students the illustrations on pages 26–29, and ask them how the illustrations help them decide when they like apple trees best.

✦ Ask students how the illustrations in "A Tree Is a Plant" help them understand the information about trees.

Discussing the Selection

✦ Ask students to explain how an apple seed grows into an apple tree that produces apples. Write on chart paper the sequence of steps students share.

✦ Encourage students to share when they would like apple trees best and why.

Purposes for Reading

✦ Remind students they listened to this selection to learn more about growing things. Then ask them what new information they learned.

✦ Ask students to share what they liked best about "A Tree Is a Plant."

Vocabulary Review

Review with students the selection vocabulary words *trunk, bark, roots,* and *washing.* Ask students the following questions:

• *What kind of plant has a trunk?*

• *Where would we find bark on a tree?*

• *What do the roots of a tree do?*

• *What keeps the tree from washing out of the ground?*

BIG Idea

What makes living things grow?

Write the Big Idea question on the board or on chart paper. Ask students what they learned about things that grow. Ask which selections added something new to their understanding about growth.

Language Arts

Students will

✦ draw pictures to illustrate dialogue between characters.

✦ learn about the pronouns *we* and *they*.

✦ identify, draw, and describe details missing from illustrations.

✦ *Skills Practice 2,* p. 56

✦ *Story Lines Big Book,* p. 16

Writing Process

Draft: Drawing Pictures to Illustrate Dialogue

Teach

✦ Ask students to think about the characters in the story they are writing. Display some of the pictures they drew of the main character. Have students recall the ideas they brainstormed about the other character in the story.

✦ Display the dialogue the class collaborated to create in the previous lesson, and review the words with students.

✦ Tell them today they will make drawings to show the characters and the things they say to each other.

Apply

✦ Distribute to each student a clean sheet of drawing paper, and make sure they have access to the class art supplies.

✦ Tell students to draw the story characters and the dialogue they have. Invite students to look at the words you are displaying from the dialogue the class wrote in the previous lesson.

✦ Ask students to raise their hands if they need help with any of the letters or words. Walk around the room, and make sure students are able to copy the dialogue for their own drawings.

✦ When they are finished, ask students to sign their names on their drawings. Collect students' drawings, and store them until you resume the writing process.

Grammar, Usage, and Mechanics

Teach

✦ Tell students what color your eyes are. Ask students with the same color eyes to raise their hands. Say *We have green eyes.* Explain that *we* refers to everyone with green eyes in the class, including yourself. Write the sentence on the board to help students recognize the word *we.*

✦ Ask students who do not have the same color eyes as you to raise their hands. Say *They do not have green eyes.* Explain that *they* refers to everyone in the class with brown, blue, or hazel eyes. Write the sentence on the board to help students recognize the word *they.*

✦ Explain to students how important it is to use pronouns correctly so other people know to whom you are referring and who or what is or is not included.

✦ Explain that the words *we* and *they* are also called pronouns. *We* and *they* can substitute for names, a group of people, animals, objects, and/or things.

Differentiating Instruction **English Learners**

IF ... students have difficulty with penmanship, **THEN ...** keep in mind that some students may be more familiar with other writing systems than with the Roman alphabet (for example, students whose native language is Khmer). Be alert for students who need extra help with penmanship.

Grammar, Usage, and Mechanics continued

Guided Practice

✦ Have students open their *Skills Practice 2* to page 56.

✦ Guide students in completing the page. When finished, review students' work carefully.

Skills Practice 2, p. 56

Monitor Progress

Formal Assessment ✓

to Differentiate Instruction

Grammar Note how quickly students understand the concept of pronouns.

APPROACHING LEVEL

IF ... students are having difficulty,

THEN ... have students complete *Reteach* page 149.

ON LEVEL

IF ... students need more practice,

THEN ... talk with them about the pronoun *they* in the selection "A Tree Is a Plant."

ABOVE LEVEL

IF ... students are comfortable,

THEN ... have them complete *Challenge Activities* page 113.

 Teacher Tip

SKILL REVIEW If time permits, use this *Story Lines Big Book* story to review the skill of Working with Problem/Resolution Plots. To do so, help students identify the story's problem, the idea to fix it, and the resolution. *The girl wants to prove her brother wrong; consulting Aunt Laura; The brother admits he does not know everything.*

Story Crafting 🕐

Story Lines

✦ Display the *Story Lines Big Book,* and open it to page 16, "Plants Move! I Can Prove It."

Story Lines Big Book, p. 16

✦ Reread the story frame by frame, and point out to students the words and drawings they added to the story in the previous lesson.

✦ When you reach Frame 7, tell students something is missing from this frame. Reread the story text, and point to each photo as you describe it. In other words, point to the first photo as you read the words *at nine o'clock in the morning* and the second photo as you say *at noon.*

✦ Ask students what is missing from the third photo. Invite a volunteer to come up and draw a sunflower in the space.

✦ Continue this procedure with the rest of the story frames. Remember to discuss the clues in the story text that reveal what belongs in the empty spaces.

✦ Close the lesson with a discussion of the importance of details in a story.

Sounds and Letters

Students will
+ produce words with the same initial phoneme.
+ identify and match medial phonemes in groups of words.
+ review how to write the numerals *0* and *1*.
+ read and respond to a **Decodable**.

+ Routines 2, 4
+ Supply Icons
+ **Skills Practice 2,** p. 57
+ **Pocket Chart Picture Cards** *1, 2*
+ **Decodable** 14

Calendar

Su	M	T	W	Th	F	S
		1	2	3	4	5
6	7	8	9	10	11	12
13	14	15	16	17	18	19
20	21	22	23	24	25	26
27	28	29	30	31		

Point to the box that represents today. Refer students to the Weather Icons, and ask a volunteer to describe today's weather. Have another volunteer tell about yesterday's weather. Discuss the similarities and differences between the weather of the two days.

Differentiating Instruction   English Learners

IF ... students have difficulty naming *0* and *1*, **THEN ...** keep in mind that many languages use Arabic numbers but that their names vary. In addition, /z/ as in *zero* and /w/ as in *one* do not occur in many languages and are challenging sounds for many English Learners to produce.

Warming Up

MORNING MESSAGE

Today is _____.

This week, we learned about _____ and _____.

Some words with the long a sound are _____, _____, and _____.

Kindergarten News

+ Copy the text above on the board or on chart paper.

+ Ask students to talk about some of the new things they learned about this week. Remind them of learning about the /ā/ sound, about writing the numbers *0* and *1*, and about anything they learned in other subject areas.

+ As a review, invite students to think of words that have the /ā/ sound. You might suggest words such as *make* and *rate* and ask students to produce rhyming words.

Oral Language

+ Have students stand in a circle, and tell them they are going to play the Word Braids game again. Tell them you want them to think of words that start with the /d/ sound. Remind them everyone who says a /d/ word gets "braided" into the circle.

Teacher: *Now we will make a /d/ braid. Connor, can you say a word that starts with the /d/ sound?*

Connor: *Dish!*

✦ Tell the student to cross his arms and to take the hand of the student on either side of him.

✦ Continue with other students and other /d/ words.

✦ When everyone has been "braided," have students "unbraid" the circle by twisting around and going under their upper arms to uncross all the arms.

✦ If time permits, make a new braid, using words that begin with a different sound.

Phonemic Awareness

Phoneme Matching: Medial Sounds

✦ Bring out the **Lion Puppet,** and tell students he wants to play another sound-matching game. Tell students you will say three words and they should listen closely to find the two words that have the same sound in the middle.

✦ Say three words, with two of the words having the same vowel sound. For example:

Teacher: *hat, lip, man*

Puppet: *Which words have the same middle sound?*

Everyone: *hat, man*

✦ Continue with these words:

tip	**dim**	*mud*
bad	**pot**	**dog**
fun	*nod*	**nut**
bet	**red**	*beg*

Teacher Tips

MEDIAL SOUNDS This is students' first practice with medial sounds. Hearing the middle vowel sound in words is more difficult than hearing the initial or final phoneme in words. Help students learn the skill by stretching the middle vowel sounds in the words: /h/ /a-a-a-a/ /t/.

SUPPLEMENTAL WORDS If additional words are needed for the lesson activity, see the Appendix for a supplemental word list.

Teacher Tip

BLENDING During these early lessons of blending long vowels, you may need to support students by blending with them. Gradually reduce your voice, and let students take more responsibility for the blending.

Monitor Progress ✓

to Differentiate Instruction
Formal Assessment

Letter and Sound Identification Note how quickly students identify the /ā/ sound.

APPROACHING LEVEL

IF . . . students are having difficulty,	THEN . . . guide them in completing **Reteach** page 150.

ON LEVEL

IF . . . students need more practice,	THEN . . . have them walk around the room with partners matching **Alphabet Letter Cards** *Aa* to objects with the long-vowel sound.

ABOVE LEVEL

IF . . . students would enjoy a challenging activity,	THEN . . . have them look through the **Ready, Set, Grow! Little Big Book** to find a word with the /ā/ sound, and then write the word on a sheet of paper.

Alphabetic Principle

Blending with the Sound of Long *Aa*

✦ Tell students today they are going to begin blending with the /ā/ sound written *a_e*. Write *a_e* on the board.

✦ To begin blending, first write on the board and blend the word *cap*, using the sound-by-sound blending routine. /k/ /a/ /p/

✦ Then next to *cap*, write the letter *c*, and ask students to say the letter's sound. /k/ Write *a_e*, making sure to underscore the blank between the letters *a* and *e*. Ask the class for the sound of *a_e*. /ā/ If necessary, remind students that a_e says /ā/. Then blend the sounds with students. /k/ /ā/

✦ Point to the blank between *a* and *e*, and tell students we need to have another sound and letter to make a word. Then write the letter *p* in the blank to make the word *cape*. Have students give the sound /p/, and then have students blend the word. /k/ /ā/ /p/

✦ Ask students to read both words on the board. *cap, cape* Help them blend if necessary.

✦ Reread the words, and ask students to say the vowel sound in *cap* and the vowel sound in *cape*. Then ask volunteers to point to the letter or letters that make the vowel sounds.

✦ Continue this blending procedure using the following word pairs. After blending each pair, have students reread the words naturally as they would speak them.

rat . . . rate	*fad . . . fade*
can . . . cane	*man . . . mane*

✦ When the blending is completed, choose a couple of words, and have students use them in sentences. Encourage students to extend the sentences by asking them to tell where, why, how, or when. Have them answer in complete sentences.

Penmanship

✦ Distribute a sheet of writing paper to each student, or use **White Boards** turned to the sides with writing lines.

✦ Place the Supply Icon for *pencil* on the board or in the **Pocket Chart.**

✦ Review with students the procedure for forming the numeral *0* while they make the strokes in the air with their fingers.

✦ Repeat the review for the numeral *1*.

✦ Ask students to write one row of numeral *0*s and one row of numeral *1*s on the writing paper. Remind them to write from top to bottom and left to right.

Guided Practice

✦ Have students complete **Skills Practice 2** page 57 for additional practice writing the numerals *0* and *1*.

✦ Have students practice writing the numerals *0* and *1* on the lines.

✦ Then guide students in identifying the number of apples on each tree. Have them write *0* and *1* on the appropriate lines.

✦ After students have finished, be sure to review their work. Have them proofread, guiding them through the established procedure.

 Teacher Tips

USING PROGRAM MATERIALS Use the *Pocket Chart Picture Cards* 1 and 2 to help you review the shapes of the numerals *0* and *1*.

PENCIL PRESSURE Remind students it is important not to press too softly when writing letters and numbers. When writers do not press hard enough, their writing is difficult to read.

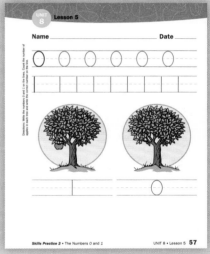

Skills Practice 2, p. 57

Monitor Progress Formal Assessment **to Differentiate Instruction**

Numeral Identification Note how quickly students identify the numerals *0* and *1*.

APPROACHING LEVEL

IF ... students are having difficulty identifying the numerals *0* and *1*,

THEN ... help them complete **Reteach** page 151.

ON LEVEL

IF ... students need more practice identifying the numerals *0* and *1*,

THEN ... have them sort through **Pocket Chart Picture Cards** 1–11 to find them.

ABOVE LEVEL

IF ... students would enjoy a challenging activity identifying the numerals *0 and 1*,

THEN ... have them work independently to complete **Challenge Activities** page 114.

Sounds and Letters

Decodable 14

 Teacher Tips

HOMEWORK After sharing the copy of *Decodable* 14 with family, encourage students to work with one family member to draw a picture of an activity they completed together. For example, they might illustrate a time they baked cookies or completed a puzzle together. Have students bring their drawings to class tomorrow. Remind them to sign their names to their work.

BLENDING SUPPORT If sudents have difficulty reading any of the words in the *Decodables* independently, then stop to write the words on the board as you blend them sound by sound with the whole class.

Technology

Use *eDecodable* Jake Plants Grapes to reinforce high-frequency words *said* and *that* and the /ā/ sound.

Audio CD

Reading a Decodable ROUTINE **2** ROUTINE **4**

> **Decodable 14: Jake Plants Grapes**

High-Frequency Words: *said, that*

✦ The high-frequency words introduced are *said* and *that*. Write *said* on the board, and read it aloud. Have students repeat it aloud with you. Then have students say the word on their own. Repeat the process with *that*.

✦ Offer students a few examples of sentences that use *said* and *that*. You might say *Jim said hello to me* or *Don't touch that bug!*

✦ Point again to *said* written on the board, and have students read the word independently. Do the same with *that*. Have students work with partners to create their own sentences using the words *said* and *that*.

✦ Tell students they will see the words *said* and *that* very often in books, on posters, and in other print. Ask them to find and point to examples on any classroom posters, bulletin boards, or covers of any books.

✦ Review the high-frequency words introduced in previous lessons.

Blending

Before reading *Decodable* 14, review the blending procedure with students. Choose words with the /ā/ sound written *a* and *a_e*, such as *fate, bake,* and *same*. After blending, have students make and extend sentences for each word.

Reading Recommendations

✦ Distribute copies of *Decodable* 14. Invite students to browse the books and look at the pictures, commenting on what they see and making predictions about what they think the story will be about.

✦ Point to the high-frequency words *said* and *that* in the text, and pronounce them. Then have students point to the words and read them aloud.

✦ Hold up your book, and read the title, pointing to each word. Read the names of the author and the illustrator aloud, pointing to each name as you say it. Ask students to explain the jobs of author and illustrator.

✦ Read the *Decodable*, following the established procedure. (See Routine 4 for a detailed description.) After you have read the story, reread the title, and have students repeat after you. Then have students read it chorally with you.

Jake Plants Grapes

by Tristan Horrom   Illustrated by Eva Vagreti

"You can plant grapes," said Mom.

3

"Jake, take that and dig."

4

"Plant that grape bud, Jake."

5

Jake did not see grapes.

6

"Jake, do you see big red grapes?" said Mom.

7

Mom and Jake ate big red grapes!

8

Responding

✦ Display the **High-Frequency Flash Cards** for *said* and *that*. Have students find and point to these high-frequency words in the story. Ask students to identify in the story any of the previously introduced high-frequency words.

✦ Discuss the book with students. Encourage them to talk about the people (characters) they see in the pictures and the events that the pictures illustrate. You might use questions such as the following:

- *How does Jake plant grapes? Name the steps he takes, and point to them in the book.*
- *Who helps Jake plant grapes?*
- *Do you like grapes? Why or why not?*
- *Have you ever planted anything? Tell us about it.*

✦ Conduct a general review of high-frequency words. Hold up **High-Frequency Flash Cards,** and call on volunteers to read the words on the cards and use them in sentences.

✦ Make copies of the story for the students to take home. A black-and-white version of the story is available in **Pre-Decodable and Decodable Takehomes Blackline Masters.**

Decodable 14, inside back cover

Reading and Responding

Students will
✦ experiment with growing things.
✦ describe their observations orally.
✦ record their observations with drawings.
✦ develop an understanding of vocabulary words.

✦ *Read Aloud Collection: What's Alive?*
✦ *Ready, Set, Grow! Big Book*

INQUIRY PLANNER

WEEK 1	✦ Begin discussing and sharing ideas. ✦ Think about a question for the **Concept/ Question Board.**
WEEK 2	✦ Begin investigating and collecting information. ✦ Generate a question and/or idea for the **Concept/Question Board.**
WEEK 3	✦ Share your findings with others. ✦ Do you have **more questions?**

Differentiating Instruction **English Learners**

IF ... students need encouragement to participate in the discussion, **THEN ...** ask them questions that can be answered with *yes, no,* or one or two words.

Inquiry

✦ Discuss with students what new things they learned about growing things from *What's Alive?* and "A Tree Is a Plant."

  • *What did we learn about what living things need in What's Alive?*

  • *What did you learn about trees in "A Tree Is a Plant"?*

✦ Take time to read new questions on the **Concept/Question Board.**

Whole-Group Time Whole Group

✦ Ask students what changes, if any, they have seen in their gardens, in the plants, or in the tadpoles.

  • *What do you notice about these plants?*

  • *How are their leaves the same or different?*

✦ Now discuss the students' gardens.

  • *What do you notice about all the seeds in your gardens?* Some may look bigger because they are absorbing water.

  • *How are the seeds getting food?*

✦ Hold a similar discussion about the tadpoles.

  • *How have the tadpoles changed?*

  • *What will the tadpoles look like when they grow?*

✦ Take any of the above questions or ones that the students have asked, and turn them into conjectures. Write these and any other conjectures the students have on chart paper. Remind students that scientists not only develop conjectures but observe and record information to see if their conjectures are supported. For the next two weeks, the students are going to be observing and recording how things grow. Remind students of the previous unit on Teamwork and how working together helps us achieve our goals.

Small-Group Time Small Group

✦ Assign each group a conjecture. (More than one group can observe and collect information on the same conjecture.) Give each group a large piece of chart paper, and have them write at the top: We are observing ————.

✦ Then have each group make a chart. Model this for the groups by creating a table with one column labeled Days of the Week and the other What We Observed. Have each group create a comparable chart and begin observing and writing down what they see each day. Remind them that scientists look very carefully for changes. Students can write comments such as *No change, The seeds are fatter, The plant in the dark looks sick,* or *The tadpoles are getting strange bumps.* Students should also be encouraged to draw what they are observing and to label and date their drawings. The drawings should be kept in chronological order.

Concept Vocabulary

The first concept vocabulary word for Unit 8, Ready, Set, Grow! is *alive.* Write the word on an index card, and post it in your room. Tell students the word *alive* means "having life or the ability to grow and change." Discuss how the word *alive* relates to the concept of growing things. Use the word in a sentence, and have students repeat the word after you. Tell students you will use this word every day, and encourage them to do the same. The more students hear you using the word, the more they will want to use it too. Invite students to bring in pictures or drawings that show something *alive* to post on the **Concept/Question Board.**

Concept/Question Board

Remind students the **Concept/Question Board** is a place they can post ideas, questions, drawings, and photographs about growing things. Possibilities include the following:

- Student conjectures about growing things
- Student drawings of animals, insects, plants, and people showing growth
- Pictures of growing things from old magazines

Research in Action

In **SRA Imagine It!** students model the behavior of expert learners and researchers. Opportunities for students, individually and in groups, to explore, to write about, and to discuss key concepts in a specific area lead to improved critical thinking and reading skills. Students become independent, intentional, self-directed learners. *(Carl Bereiter)*

Concept/Question Board

You may want students either to take turns recording what is happening each day or to record these observations individually on self-sticking notes and place them in the appropriate columns. Take time to share observations periodically and to talk about how the class's knowledge is growing.

 ### Teacher Tip

RECREATIONAL READING Because it is important to read daily to your students, choose a book from the Additional Reading listed in the Unit Overview, and find a time during the day to read the book aloud to your students.

Language Arts

Students will
+ share pictures with classmates.
+ review the pronouns *you, he, it, we,* and *they.*
+ review letters and sounds through game play.

+ *Skills Practice 2,* p. 58
+ Ball Diamond Game Mats
+ *Alphabet Letter Cards*
+ Game markers
+ Number cubes

Writing Process

Present: Sharing Pictures

Teach

+ Tell students today they will share their story drawings with the class.

+ Distribute students' drawings. Ask them to look closely at the pictures and to think about what they want to tell their classmates about the drawings.

Apply

+ Have students take turns presenting their drawings. Ask the first few presenters specific questions to call attention to the details in their drawings.

+ After each presenter, call on an audience member to say one thing they like about their classmate's drawing.

+ After all students have shared their drawings, collect them, and display them on a class bulletin board.

🍎 Teacher Tip

HIGH-FREQUENCY WORDS Ask students to point out the high-frequency word *said* in the story "Becoming Butterflies." After students have identified the word, encourage them to use the word in their presentations.

Grammar, Usage, and Mechanics

Teach

+ Write the following sentences on the board:

    Tom is hungry. _____ eats an apple. *He*

    The frog and toad are in a cage.

    _____ are hopping. *They*

    (Insert your name) and the students learn about pronouns.

    _____ learn about pronouns. *We*

    The apple is green. _____ is sour. *It*

    I gave (insert student's name) a crayon.

    I gave _____ a crayon. *you*

+ Read each sentence aloud. Ask students which pronoun should be used for each sentence. Read the new versions aloud.

Research in Action

To make grammar, usage, and mechanics effective, follow these five principles:

(1) Define grammar, usage, and mechanics skills in a functional and concrete manner.

(2) After the skill is functionally described or defined, establish why it is important.

(3) Show students how to use the skill when writing.

(4) Provide students with guided practice in applying the skill when writing.

(5) Ask students to apply the skill in their composition.

(Steve Graham and Karen Harris)

Grammar, Usage, and Mechanics continued

Guided Practice

✦ Have students open their **Skills Practice 2** to page 58.

✦ Guide students in completing the page. When finished, review students' work carefully.

Skills Practice 2, p. 58

Monitor Progress
Formal Assessment

to Differentiate Instruction

Grammar Note how quickly students understand the concept of pronouns.

APPROACHING LEVEL

IF ... students are having difficulty,

THEN ... refer to Unit 8 Lesson 5 of the **Intervention Guide** for additional support of this Grammar activity.

ON LEVEL

IF ... students need more practice,

THEN ... have students identify the people in the school, using pronouns.

ABOVE LEVEL

IF ... students are comfortable,

THEN ... ask students to work with a familiar story and circle the pronouns.

Differentiating Instruction **English Learners**

IF ... students have difficulty naming letter sounds, **THEN** ... provide extra practice with the appropriate letters.

GAME Day

Ball Diamond Game

✦ Tell students they will play the Ball Diamond game. Take out the Ball Diamond Game Mats and the **Alphabet Letter Cards.**

✦ Organize the class into several groups, and set up game stations around the room.

✦ Review the rules before students begin playing: To play the game, a player rolls the number cube and moves a marker the correct number of spaces. When a player lands on a space, he or she must draw a card from the pack and identify the letter on the card and the sound the letter makes. If a player cannot correctly identify the letter or sound on the card, the player loses his or her next turn.

✦ If you have adapted the game rules to better suit your class's needs, review these rules instead. Note, however, that students should be required to identify both the letters and the sounds of the cards they choose.

✦ While they play, circulate around the room to make sure students are playing the game properly and to answer any questions that arise.

Lesson Planner

Sounds and Letters

MATERIALS

- *Pickled Peppers Big Book,* pp. 15, 42
- *Ready, Set, Grow! Big Book*
- *High-Frequency Flash Cards*
- *Alphabet Letter Card: Ii*
- Routines 1, 2, 4
- *Skills Practice 2,* pp. 59–62, 65
- *Pocket Chart Picture Cards*
- *Decodable* 15

Warming Up, pp. T96–T97
Phonemic Awareness
Phoneme Matching: Medial Sounds, p. T97
Alphabetic Principle
- Introducing the Sound of Long *Ii,* p. T98
- Listening for /ī/, p. T98
- Penmanship, p. T99

Warming Up, pp. T106–T107
Phonemic Awareness
Phoneme Matching: Medial Sounds, p. T107
Alphabetic Principle
- Reviewing the Sound of Long *Ii,* p. T108
- Listening for Initial /ī/, p. T108
- Listening for Medial /ī/, p. T108
- *Pickled Peppers Big Book,* p. T109

Reading and Responding

MATERIALS

- *Ready, Set, Grow! Big Book,* pp. 30–61
- Routines 5–7
- *Home Connection,* pp. 63–64

Poetry
- Activate Prior Knowledge, p. T100
- Preview the Poem, p. T100
Vocabulary, p. T101
Read the Poem, p. T101
Comprehension Strategies, p. T102
Discussing the Poem, p. T103
Vocabulary Review, p. T103

Preview and Prepare, p. T110
Vocabulary, p. T111
Read the Selection, p. T111
Comprehension Strategies, pp. T112, T114, T116, T118
Print and Book Awareness, pp. T113, T115, T117, T119
Discussing the Selection, p. T119
Vocabulary Review, p. T119

1st READ

Language Arts

MATERIALS

- *Language Arts Big Book,* pp. 7, 9, 38, 54
- *Transparency* 46
- *Ready, Set, Grow! Big Book,* p. 62
- *Willy the Wisher,* p. 81
- *Story Lines Big Book,* pp. 16–23
- *Skills Practice 2,* pp. 63–64, 66

Writing Process
Prewrite: Selecting Topic and Generating Ideas, p. T104
Fine Art
Discussing Fine Art, p. T105

Writing Process
Draft: Making a List of Instructions, p. T120
Grammar, Usage, and Mechanics, pp. T120–T121
Willy the Wisher, p. T121

Monitor Progress

- ✓ = Formal Assessment
- B = Benchmark Assessment

✓ Penmanship, p. T99
✓ Visualizing, p. T102

✓ *Lesson Assessment Book,* pp. 76–77
✓ Letter and Sound Identification, p. T108
✓ Present Tense, p. T121

Day 3

Warming Up, pp. T122–T123
Phonemic Awareness
Phoneme Manipulation: Medial Sounds, p. T123
Alphabetic Principle
• Reviewing the Sound of Long *Ii,* p. T124
• Listening for Medial /ī/, p. T124
• Linking the Sound to the Letter, p. T124
• Penmanship, p. T125

Preview and Prepare, p. T126
Vocabulary, p. T126
Read the Selection, p. T127
Comprehension Strategies, pp. T128, T130, T132, T134
Comprehension Skills, pp. T129, T131, T133, T135
Reading with a Writer's Eye, pp. T129, T131, T133, T135
Discussing the Selection, p. T135
Vocabulary Review, p. T135

Writing Process
Model: Moving Text to Clarify Instructions, p. T136
Story Crafting
Story Lines Big Book, p. T137

✔ *Lesson Assessment Book,* p. 77
✔ Syllable Segmentation, p. T123
✔ Penmanship, p. T125

Day 4

Warming Up, pp. T138–T139
Phonemic Awareness
Phoneme Manipulation: Medial Sounds, p. T139
Alphabetic Principle
• Reviewing the Sound of Long *Ii,* p. T140
• Listening for Medial /ī/, p. T140
• Linking the Sound to the Letter, p. T140
• *Pickled Peppers Big Book,* p. T141

Poetry
• Activate Prior Knowledge, p. T142
• Preview the Poem, p. T142
Vocabulary, p. T143
Read the Poem, p. T143
Comprehension Strategies, p. T144
Discussing the Poem, p. T145
Vocabulary Review, p. T145

Writing Process
Revise: Revising Text, p. T146
Grammar, Usage, and Mechanics, pp. T146–T147
Story Crafting
Story Lines Big Book, p. T147

✔ Letter and Sound Identification, p. T140
✔ Making Connections, p. T145
✔ Action Words, p. T147

Day 5

Warming Up, pp. T148–T149
Phonemic Awareness
Phoneme Manipulation: Medial Sounds, p. T149
Alphabetic Principle
• Blending with the Sound of Long *Ii,* p. T150
• Penmanship, p. T151
Reading a Decodable
Decodable 15: *Mike and Spike,* pp. T152–T153

Inquiry
• Small-Group Time, p. T154
• Whole-Group Time, p. T155
• Concept Vocabulary, p. T155

Writing Process
Draft: Drawing Pictures to Illustrate Instructions, p. T156
Grammar, Usage, and Mechanics, pp. T156–T157
Game Day
Action Words Charades, p. T157

✔ *Lesson Assessment Book,* p. 78
  Comprehension Observation Log
✔ Penmanship, p. T151
✔ Past and Present Tenses, p. T157

Student Resources

Focus Question Why do the students watch the caterpillars every day?

BECOMING BUTTERFLIES
by Anne Rockwell
illustrated by Megan Halsey

One day Miss Dana brought a surprise to school—three striped caterpillars and a flowerpot.

← milkweed plant

cardboard mailing box

Styrofoam box

insect house

caterpillars inside

32

A green plant called a milkweed was growing in the flowerpot.

33

Big Books

Audio CD

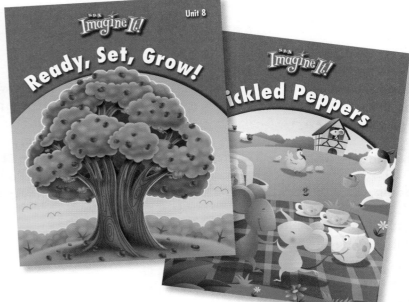

Big Book Selection

Ready, Set, Grow! Big Book

Becoming Butterflies by Anne Rockwell, pp. 32–59

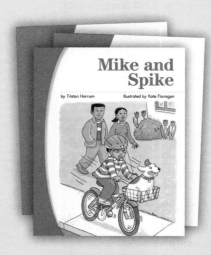

Decodable 15:
Mike and Spike

Teacher Support

Language Arts Big Book

Willy the Wisher

Story Lines Big Book

Curriculum Connections

Card 17

Whose Tracks Are These?

Exploring animal tracks is fun!

Animal tracks tell two special things.

They tell the shape of the animal's feet.

Th... ...w the animal moves.

Science
Grade K • Unit 2
Patterns

	Deer	Horse	Pigeon	Duck

Card 21

Our Country's Flag

Red stripe, white stripe,

Patterns you can see.

Red stripes, white stripes

Tell us that we are free.

Blue box, white stars

Fifty stars in all.

Red stripes, white stripes,

Hanging from the wall.

Social Studies
Grade K • Unit 2
Patterns

Card 15

People Plan Schools

People planned your school. It has many classrooms. There are shelves for books. It has room for supplies. Does it have a playground? What makes your school fun?

Art
Grade K • Unit 1
Off to School

...ng Shapes

...e shapes

...you look.

...pes match the clock?

...pes match the book?

Math
Grade K • Unit 2
Patterns

- Math
- Social Studies
- Science
- Art

Additional Skills Practice

Approaching Level

Reteach

Letter and Sound Identification, pp. 152, 155

Past and Present Tenses, pp. 153, 157

Penmanship, p. 156

Syllable Segmentation, p. 154

On Level

Skills Practice 2

Letter and Sound Identification, pp. 60, 62

Past and Present Tenses, pp. 63–64, 66

Penmanship, pp. 59, 61, 65

English Learner

English Learner Support Activities

Lessons 6–10

Above Level

Challenge Activities

Letter and Sound Identification, p. 116

Past and Present Tenses, p. 117

Penmanship, pp. 115, 118

Differentiating Instruction
for Workshop

Day 1

Approaching Level	On Level	English Learner	Above Level
Sounds and Letters			
Alphabetic Principle: Using *Alphabet Sound Card Long Ii,* students walk around the classroom, matching the letter with classroom labels, posters, or books and saying the /ī/ sound.	**Alphabetic Principle:** Students browse the *Ready, Set, Grow! Little Big Book* for the letter *Ii.*	**Alphabetic Principle:** Refer to Unit 8 Lesson 6 of the *English Learner Support Guide.*	**Alphabetic Principle:** Have students draw pictures of a person or object whose name begins with /ī/.
Reading and Responding			
Comprehension: Have students review the poem and point to and say the words they recognize.	**Comprehension:** Describe a scene to students, and have them visualize and draw what you describe.	**Comprehension:** Preview the selection "Becoming Butterflies" with students, and have them point out anything about the story that confuses or puzzles them.	**Comprehension:** Have students dictate their own poetry about things that grow.
Language Arts			
Writing: Help students create lists of possible characteristics for their characters.	**Writing:** With your help, students discuss topics for their characters' conversation.	**Writing:** Help students list possible characteristics for their characters.	**Writing:** Students discuss with partners possible conversations for the characters.

Day 2

Approaching Level	On Level	English Learner	Above Level

Sounds and Letters

Alphabetic Principle: Work with students to complete *Reteach* page 152 to practice identifying the /ī/ sound.

Alphabetic Principle: Students listen to "Peter Piper" on the *Listening Library CD.*

Alphabetic Principle: Refer to Unit 8 Lesson 7 of the *English Learner Support Guide.*

Alphabetic Principle: Have students work independently to complete *Challenge Activities* page 116.

Reading and Responding

Comprehension: Students browse the selection and discuss what they think they might learn about teamwork based on the illustrations.

Comprehension: Have students retell the story "Becoming Butterflies" in their own words.

Comprehension: Refer to Unit 8 Lesson 7 of the *English Learner Support Guide.*

Comprehension: Have students discuss the process of caterpillars becoming butterflies and draw the sequence of events that take place.

Language Arts

Writing: Students discuss and choose two characteristics for each character.

Grammar: Have students complete *Reteach* page 153.

Writing: Students practice and draw speech bubbles for each character.

Grammar: With your help, students create lists of action words.

Writing: Students discuss and choose two characteristics for each character. Prompt them with yes-no and either-or questions as needed.

Grammar: Refer to Unit 8 Lesson 7 of the *English Learner Support Guide.*

Writing: Students create dialogue for the two characters.

Grammar: Students create lists of pronouns.

Differentiating Instruction
for Workshop

Day 3

Approaching Level	On Level	English Learner	Above Level
Sounds and Letters			
Alphabetic Principle: Refer to Unit 8 Lesson 8 of the ***Intervention Guide*** for additional support activities.	**Alphabetic Principle:** Look through ***Alphabet Book Little Big Book*** with partners to find the letter *Ii* and identify the /ī/ sound.	**Alphabetic Principle:** Refer to Unit 8 Lesson 8 of the ***English Learner Support Guide.***	**Alphabetic Principle:** Students work independently to use the ***eSkills*** activity for practice with the /ī/ sound.
Reading and Responding			
Comprehension: Have students draw pictures of butterflies and dictate any questions they have about how caterpillars become butterflies and post them on the ***Concept/ Question Board.***	**Comprehension:** Have students each draw a section of a caterpillar. Then connect all of the pieces together to help explain how the caterpillar grows. After the pieces are attached, hang the completed caterpillar in the classroom.	**Comprehension:** Refer to Unit 8 Lesson 8 of the ***English Learner Support Guide.***	**Comprehension:** Students review what makes living things grow and post their ideas on the ***Concept/Question Board.***
Language Arts			
Writing: With your help, students draw their characters on the board.	**Writing:** With your help, students create conversations and write them in the speech bubbles.	**Writing:** Students draw their characters on the board. Help them add details to describe the characteristics they chose, if necessary.	**Writing:** Students revise dialogues.

Day 4

Approaching Level	On Level	English Learner	Above Level

Sounds and Letters

Alphabetic Principle: Refer to Unit 8 Lesson 9 of the *Intervention Guide* for activities to help students.

Alphabetic Principle: Students use the *eSkills* activity for practice with the /ī/ sound.

Alphabetic Principle: Refer to Unit 8 Lesson 9 of the *English Learner Support Guide.*

Alphabetic Principle: Students write words that begin with /ī/.

Reading and Responding

Preview: Read the poem "Something About Me" to students and have them ask questions about anything that puzzles them or they wonder about.

Preview: Have students discuss how the poem "Something About Me" connects with the unit theme.

Preview: Review the selection "Becoming Butterflies" with students, and have them share any wonderings or questions about the selection with you.

Preview: Have students dictate their own poems about growing.

Language Arts

Writing: With your help, students draw speech bubbles and create dialogues for each character.

Grammar: With your help, students discuss and create lists of action words.

Writing: With your help, students revise their drawings and conversations.

Grammar: Help students create sentences using action words.

Writing: With your help, students discuss possible things each character might say.

Grammar: Refer to Unit 8 Lesson 9 of the *English Learner Support Guide.*

Writing: Students write dialogue in the speech bubbles.

Grammar: Have students complete *Challenge Activities* page 117.

Differentiating Instruction
for Workshop

Day 5

Approaching Level	On Level	English Learner	Above Level
Sounds and Letters			
Reading a *Decodable:* Have students read at least a few pages of **Decodable** 15 to you.	**Reading a *Decodable:*** Review high-frequency words *down* and *they* with students. Students reread **Decodable** 15 to partners.	**Reading a *Decodable:*** Reread **Decodable** 15 with students, reviewing the high-frequency words *down* and *they*.	**Reading a *Decodable:*** Browse the ***Ready, Set, Grow! Little Big Book*** for high-frequency words *down* and *they*.
Reading and Responding			
Inquiry: Review previous selections with students, and have them discuss what they have learned so far about living things and how they grow.	**Inquiry:** Have students work in small groups on the class project they have chosen.	**Inquiry:** Refer to Unit 8 Lesson 10 of the ***English Learner Support Guide.***	**Inquiry:** Have students work in groups on their class project.
Language Arts			
Writing: Discuss with students how this activity made them feel. **Grammar:** Have students complete **Reteach** page 157.	**Writing:** Students discuss with partners how this activity made them feel. **Grammar:** Help students create another sentence using both an action word and a pronoun.	**Writing:** With your help, students decide on speech bubble dialogue for each character. **Grammar:** Refer to Unit 8 Lesson 10 of the ***English Learner Support Guide.***	**Writing:** Students share their drawings with the group. **Grammar:** Students write sentences using pronouns.

Resources for Differentiating Instruction

English Learner

English Learner Support Guide
Unit 8, Lessons 6–10

English Learner Support Activities
Unit 8, Lessons 6–10

SRA Imagine It! Photo Library CD

English Learner Realia Kit

Approaching Level

Intervention

Intervention Guide

Intervention Workbook

Workshop Kits

- High Frequency Words
- Letter Recognition
- Phonemic Awareness
- Print and Book Awareness
- Sequencing

Technology

eDecodable Mike and Spike
eSkills & eGames
Listening Library CD

Listening Library Unit 8

Lesson Assessment

Lessons 6-10 Overview

Monitor Progress
to Differentiate Instruction

Use these summative assessments along with your informal observations to assess student mastery.

Lesson Assessment Book, p. 76

Lesson Assessment Book, p. 77

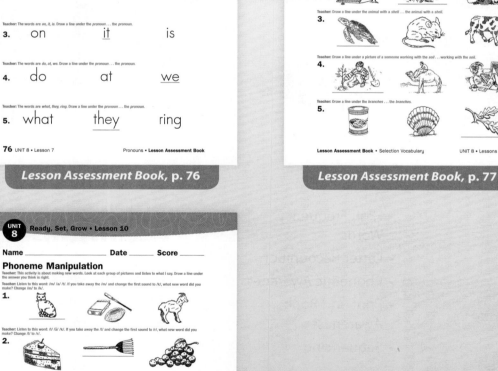

Lesson Assessment Book, p. 78

T94   Theme: Ready, Set, Grow!

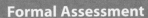

Lesson Assessment Book

Comprehension Observation Log

Student _____ Date _____

Unit _____ Lesson _____ Selection Title _____

General Comprehension
Concepts discussed: _____

Behavior Within a Group
Articulates, expresses ideas: _____

Joins discussions: _____

Collaborates (such as works well with other students, works alone): _____

Role in Group
Role (such as leader, summarizer, questioner, critic, observer, non-participant): _____

Flexibility (changes roles when necessary): _____

Use of Reading Strategies
Uses strategies when needed (either those taught or student's choice of strategy)/Describes strategies used:
_____

Changes strategies when appropriate: _____

Changes Since Last Observation

110   Comprehension Observation Log • Lesson Assessment Book

Lesson Assessment Annotated Teacher's Edition, p. 110

The Comprehension Observation Log, found in the **Lesson Assessment Annotated Teacher's Edition,** is a vehicle for recording anecdotal information about individual student performance on an ongoing basis. Information such as students' strengths and weaknesses can be recorded at any time the occasion warrants. It is recommended that you maintain a folder for each student where you can store the logs for purposes of comparison and analysis as the school year progresses. You will gradually build up a comprehensive file that reveals which students are progressing smoothly and which students need additional help.

Day 6 — Sounds and Letters

OBJECTIVES

Students will

✦ identify high-frequency words in print.
✦ identify and match medial sounds.
✦ identify the /ī/ sound.
✦ practice writing the numeral 2.

MATERIALS

✦ **Pickled Peppers Big Book**
✦ **Ready, Set, Grow! Big Book**
✦ **High-Frequency Flash Cards**
✦ **Alphabet Letter Card** *Ii* for each student
✦ **Alphabet Flash Cards**
✦ Routine 1
✦ Supply Icons
✦ **Skills Practice 2,** p. 59
✦ **Pocket Chart Picture Card** 3

Calendar

Su	M	T	W	Th	F	S
		1	2	3	4	5
6	7	8	9	10	11	12
13	14	15	16	17	18	19
20	21	22	23	24	25	26
27	28	29	30	31		

Point to the box that represents today. Take this opportunity to identify any important events that will happen during the coming week, such as students' birthdays, school functions, and national holidays.

Warming Up

MORNING MESSAGE

Today is _____.

The name of our state is _____.

The color of a banana is yellow.

Kindergarten News

✦ Copy the text above on the board or on chart paper. Create a Secret Word by covering the word *yellow* in the last sentence with a self-sticking note.

✦ Tell students there is a Secret Word today. Ask volunteers to listen for clues as you reread the last sentence. When a student answers correctly, ask how he or she knew. Point out the rest of the sentence is a clue as to what the Secret Word is.

✦ Use prompts such as the following to discuss the letters and words in the message:

  • *Can you find a word that has the long* a *sound?* name, state *Come circle the letters that make the sound.*

  • *What letters make up the word* banana? *b, a, n, a, n, a* What about the word *yellow?* y, e, l, l, o, w

  • *Which sentence has the most words?* second and third *Which has the least words?* first Let's count them.

High-Frequency Word Review

✦ Display the **Pickled Peppers Big Book** and the **Ready, Set, Grow! Big Book.** Use the **High-Frequency Flash Cards** to review those words you think are most appropriate for your class. Refer to the inside back cover of **Decodable 14** for a comprehensive list of words students have learned so far.

✦ Hold up the cards one at a time, and call on students to read the words and to use them in complete sentences.

✦ Have volunteers flip through one of the **Big Books** to see how many of the words they can find.

Phonemic Awareness

Phoneme Matching: Medial Sounds

✦ Bring out the **Lion Puppet,** and tell students he wants to play the middle-sound matching game. Remind students that you will say three words and that they should listen for the two words with the same middle sound.

✦ Say three words, with two of the words having the same middle vowel sound. For example:

Teacher: *dot, lid, pin*

Puppet: *Which words have the same middle sound? What is the sound?*

Everyone: *lid, pin /i/*

✦ Continue with these words:

met	**bed**	*cap*	/e/
sad	not	**can**	/a/
hot	rip	**rod**	/o/
mop	**hug**	**run**	/u/

> ### Teacher Tip
>
> **MEDIAL PHONEMES** Remember that working with medial sounds is often more difficult for students than working with initial or final phonemes. Help students learn the skill by voicing great emphasis on the medial sound in each word.

Teacher Tip

ALPHABET REVIEW Once again, have students review the alphabet by using the **Alphabet Flash Cards.** For each flash card, have them say the letter's name and sound, identify the corresponding **Alphabet Sound Wall Card,** and name the picture.

Differentiating Instruction English Learners

IF ... students are native speakers of Spanish or certain other languages, **THEN ...** they may associate the letter *i* with the letter name *e* because in their native languages, *i* represents a sound similar to English long *e*. These students will need extra practice associating the letter *i* with its English name and with the long *i* sound.

Alphabetic Principle

ROUTINE
1

Introducing the Sound of Long *Ii*

✦ Lead students in a few rounds of the "Vowel Song" while you point to the **Alphabet Sound Wall Cards** for *Aa, Ee, Ii, Oo,* and *Uu*. (See the Appendix.)

✦ Focus students' attention on **Alphabet Sound Wall Card** Long *Ii*, and ask students what they remember about cards that look like this one. If necessary, remind them the picture of the long, thin *I* helps us remember this card is the long *i* vowel card. Remind students that vowels are special because every word or syllable in English needs a vowel.

✦ Share with students the following rhyme to help them remember the sounds of *Ii*:

I's my name.

Two sounds have I:

Short i *in* pig,

Long i *in* pie.

Alphabet Sound Wall Card 9

✦ Repeat the rhyme several times until students can easily recite it with you.

Listening for /ī/

Give each student an **Alphabet Letter Card** *Ii*. Ask students to raise the cards and say the /ī/ sound when they hear a word that has the /ī/ sound. Try the following words:

ice	*idea*	*Irish*	*Ivan*
into	*bit*	*hid*	*inch*
item	*bait*	*ivory*	*Iowa*

Penmanship

+ Distribute a sheet of writing paper to each student, or use **White Boards** turned to the sides with writing lines. Place the Supply Icon for *pencil* on the board or in the **Pocket Chart.**

+ Use the procedure established for writing letters to illustrate how to form the numeral *2*: Place your pen or chalk at the starting point on the overhead or board, and ask students to place their fingers in the air. As you write the number, say *Begin here. Then curve up to the right, slant back to the left, and then straight across to the right. Two.*

+ Now invite students to practice writing numeral *2*s across the top row of the paper or board from left to right.

+ Remind students the number *2* shows we have two of something. You might illustrate the total by drawing two stars on the board.

Guided Practice

+ Have students complete **Skills Practice 2** page 59 for additional practice with the numeral *2*.

+ Draw students' attention to the first penmanship line. Ask them to trace the *2*s outlined across the row. Then ask students to write a row of *2*s across the next line.

+ Then ask students to look at the word *two* written on the line. Tell students this is how you write the word that names the number *2*.

+ Invite volunteers to identify the letters that make up the word *two,* and have the class practice writing the word by tracing the letters. Then have students try writing the word on their own on the next line.

+ After students have finished, have them proofread using the established procedure.

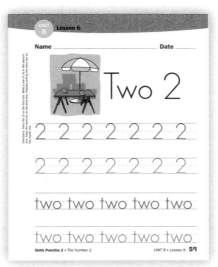

Skills Practice 2, p. 59

 Teacher Tip

USING PROGRAM MATERIALS Use *Pocket Chart Picture Card* 3 to help you review the shape of the numeral *2*.

Monitor Progress
to Differentiate Instruction
Formal Assessment

Penmanship Note how easily students write the numeral *2*.

APPROACHING LEVEL

IF ... students are having difficulty,

THEN ... provide dot-to-dot numeral *2*s for students to trace.

ON LEVEL

IF ... students need more practice,

THEN ... have them write the numerals in shaving cream on a flat surface.

ABOVE LEVEL

IF ... students are comfortable,

THEN ... have them work independently to complete **Challenge Activities** page 115.

OBJECTIVES

Students will
+ locate the title of the poem and the names of the poets and the illustrator.
+ connect their own life experiences to the text.
+ develop an understanding of vocabulary words.
+ use the comprehension strategy Visualizing.

MATERIALS
+ *Ready, Set, Grow! Big Book,* pp. 30–31
+ Routines 5–7
+ *Home Connection,* pp. 63–64

Focus Question
How are tree branches like a person's hands?

TREES
by Paul Paolilli and Dan Brewer
illustrated by Richard Torrey

Tiny hands
Reaching up from the
Earth, tickling an
Enormous
Sky.

30

Ready, Set, Grow! Big Book, pp. 30–31

Technology

To promote independent reading, encourage students to use Workshop to listen to the recording of the selection on the *Listening Library CD.* Invite them to follow along and say the words whenever they can.

Audio CD

Poetry

Activate Prior Knowledge ROUTINE 5

+ "Trees" is a simple five-line poem celebrating the growth of trees. Put together, the first letter of the first word in each line spells the word *trees.* As you read the poem, relate what you already know to what you are reading, and encourage students to do the same.

+ Invite students to discuss what it would be like to be a tree. Ask them what human qualities a tree might have. Are its trunk and limbs like human parts? How might it show that it is happy or sad?

+ Encourage students to make pictures in their heads of the words in the poem you will read. Invite them to perform the lines of the poem as you read them.

+ Have students discuss the knowledge they are building about growing things as they listen to the poem. Ask them how this knowledge might help them appreciate trees.

Preview the Poem ROUTINE 5

+ Display the **Ready, Set, Grow! Big Book** opened to pages 30–31. Follow Routine 5, the previewing the selection routine, as you introduce the poem's title and the names of the poets and the illustrator. Ask students what a poet and an illustrator do.

+ Prepare to read the poem. Invite students to examine the picture and to share what they see. Ask them what the boy in the picture seems to be doing. Remind students that pictures can give readers clues as to what a poem or story is about.

Vocabulary

ROUTINE **6**

- ✦ Follow Routine 6, the selection vocabulary routine, as you introduce the vocabulary words for this selection.

- ✦ Explain to students the word *enormous* means "very big." Ask them what animals are enormous.

- ✦ Tell students *tickling* means "touching lightly to make laugh." Have two volunteers demonstrate the word tickling.

Read the Poem

ROUTINE **7**

- ✦ Before reading the poem, read the Focus Question above it. Tell students to keep this question in mind as they listen to the poem.

- ✦ Follow Routine 7, the reading the selection routine, as you read aloud "Trees." Identify the boldfaced letter at the beginning of each line. Explain that these letters begin the first word in each line. Then say the word that these letters spell—*TREES*.

- ✦ Invite students to ask questions or to think aloud about anything in the poem that interests or puzzles them.

Comprehension Strategies

For this poem, model the comprehension strategy Visualizing to help students make mental pictures of settings, characters, and actions.

Vocabulary

enormous   tickling

 **Teacher Tip**

WRITING POETRY Some students may enjoy dictating poems about trees.

Differentiating Instruction **English Learners**

IF ... students are native speakers of Vietnamese, Hmong, or Cantonese, **THEN ...** they may need extra practice understanding multisyllabic words. In these languages, all words are monosyllabic.

Reading and Responding

Focus Question
How are tree branches like a person's hands?

TREES

by Paul Paolilli and Dan Brewer
illustrated by Richard Torrey

Tiny hands

Reaching up from the

Earth, tickling an

Enormous

Sky. ❶

30

31

Ready, Set, Grow! Big Book, pp. 30–31

 Teacher Tip

GLOSSARY The word *enormous* can be found in the Glossary of the *Ready, Set, Grow! Big Book.*

Comprehension Strategies

Teacher Modeling

❶ **Visualizing** *Let's make pictures in our heads as we pretend to be growing trees. Crouch, and curl into a little ball as if you were a tiny seed. Then slowly stretch one hand and then the other as the seed begins to sprout and reach toward the sky. Slowly stand as you keep reaching upward. You are growing taller and taller like the tree. Then stand as tall as you can, and reach as high as you can. Move your arms and fingers back and forth, swaying in the breeze, as you tickle the sky.*

Monitor Progress

to Differentiate Instruction

Formal Assessment

Visualizing Note how easily students can visualize.

APPROACHING LEVEL	**IF ...** students still need help visualizing,	**THEN ...** refer to Unit 8 Lesson 6 of the *Intervention Guide.*
ON LEVEL	**IF ...** students need to practice visualizing,	**THEN ...** have them play the guessing game I'm Thinking of Something ... with partners.
ABOVE LEVEL	**IF ...** students understand visualizing,	**THEN ...** ask them to visualize a tree's human qualities, and have them draw what they see.

Discussing the Poem

✦ Review the Focus Question with students: How are tree branches like a person's hands? *They can stretch far out. Larger branches break into smaller branches like the fingers of a hand.*

✦ Invite students to share their thoughts and ideas about the poem. Ask students if the poem has helped them think differently about trees. Encourage them to share how their ideas about trees have changed after listening to this poem.

Purposes for Reading

✦ Remind students they were listening to discover what the poem says about growing things. Invite students to share what they learned about trees.

✦ Ask students what they liked best about the poem and why they liked it, and what the differences are between informational text and poetry.

Vocabulary Review

Review with students the selection vocabulary words *enormous* and *tickling*. Ask students the following questions:

• *What kinds of plants and animals are enormous?*
• *What does tickling feel like?*

Give each student a copy of *Home Connection* page 63. This same information is also available in Spanish on *Home Connection* page 64. Encourage students to discuss the selection "Becoming Butterflies" with their families and complete the activity provided.

OBJECTIVES

Students will

✦ select a topic for writing.

✦ generate ideas to tell how to do something.

✦ view, appreciate, and react to fine art.

MATERIALS

✦ *Language Arts Big Book,* p. 7

✦ *Transparency* 46

✦ *Ready, Set, Grow! Big Book,* p. 62

Language Arts Big Book, p. 7

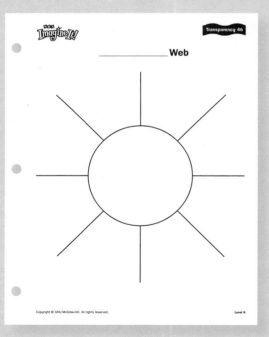

Transparency 46

Writing Process 🕐

Prewrite: Selecting Topic and Generating Ideas

Teach

✦ Display the *Language Arts Big Book* page 7, and read aloud the title *What Will I Write?* as you point to each word. Remind students that writers have to choose a topic, or something to write about, before they begin writing. Point out how Peta, Doodle, and Mr. Lopez are talking about plants, and remind students they too, are learning about how things grow.

✦ Tell students for their next writing assignment they are going to tell how to do something. To narrow students' options and to relate the writing to the unit theme, suggest the class write about plants.

✦ This writing activity will span two weeks throughout the unit. Be prepared to collect, assess, store, and reuse students' drawings and writing as you go.

Guided Practice

✦ Display *Transparency* 46. Remind students that an idea web can help a writer keep track of his or her ideas.

✦ Invite volunteers to offer ideas on a topic for writing a "how to" about plants. Write students' ideas in the idea web, and then have the class vote for its favorite.

✦ After the class topic is chosen, guide the class in generating ideas for the steps in the instructions. For example, if the class chose "How to Grow a Garden" as a topic, you might ask students *What is the first thing someone should do if he or she wants to grow a garden?*

✦ Collect students' ideas on chart paper, or record them in your notes so you can display and discuss them when you resume the writing process.

Fine Art

Josephine Trotter. *Sunflowers, Provence.*

Discussing Fine Art

✦ Turn to page 62 in the ***Ready, Set, Grow! Big Book.*** Focus students' attention on *Sunflowers, Provence* by Josephine Trotter. Have students give their initial impressions of the painting, saying what they like and do not like about it. Have students discuss what they think it has to do with the unit theme.

✦ Guide students in discussing what they see in the painting. Use questions such as the following:

   • *What items are in the picture? Where are they?*

   • *What colors are used? Are they bright or dull?*

   • *How would you describe the sunflowers? Do they look just like sunflowers look in real life? If not, how are they different?*

✦ Invite students to show their reactions to the art by making their own drawings of flowers with which they are familiar. Allow time for students to show their drawings to their classmates, either in pairs or in small groups.

Teacher Tip

FOR FURTHER STUDY Students might enjoy comparing and contrasting *Sunflowers, Provence* with other paintings of the region.

Background Information

Provence is a region in southeastern France, near the Mediterranean Sea and the Alps mountain range. Provence is known throughout the world for its natural beauty, temperate climate, and peaceful lifestyle. For centuries, the Provence region has beckoned artists to capture its landscape, as Josephine Trotter (1940–) does in this painting, *Sunflowers, Provence.*

Sounds and Letters

Students will
✦ produce rhyming words.
✦ review letters and sounds.
✦ identify and match medial sounds.
✦ identify the /ī/ sound.

✦ ***Alphabet Letter Card*** *Ii* for each student
✦ ***Pickled Peppers Big Book,*** p. 15
✦ ***Skills Practice 2,*** p. 60

Calendar

Su	M	T	W	Th	F	S
		1	2	3	4	5
6	7	8	9	10	11	12
13	14	15	16	17	18	19
20	21	22	23	24	25	26
27	28	29	30	31		

Point to the box that represents today. Ask a volunteer to say today's name, and then have the class segment the syllables of the name by clapping. Continue with the names of the other days of the week.

Warming Up

MORNING MESSAGE

Today is _____.

Yesterday in class we read about _____.

I'm afraid of giant spiders!

Kindergarten News

✦ Copy the text above on the board or on chart paper. As you read, have students raise their hands and say *Ii* when they hear a word with the /ī/ sound.

✦ Invite students to tell what they remember about reading yesterday. Have them tell things they liked about what they read. Encourage them to also tell why they liked something.

✦ Discuss the letters and words in the message: *Can someone find the exclamation point in the message? third sentence Come draw a box around it. What is the longest word in the message today? How many letters does it have?*

Oral Language

✦ Have students sit in a circle. Give a student something to toss, such as a beanbag.

✦ Tell students to say a word and then to toss the beanbag. Help the student who catches the beanbag say a word that rhymes with the first word and then toss the beanbag to another student, who says another rhyming word.

+ You may want to review easy-to-rhyme words with students before playing the game.

+ Start another activity. Tell students they can make silly sentences with the letter of their choice. Ask a student to say a letter, and have the class work together to brainstorm words that begin with the letter. Make a list on the board, and then have students mix up the words to create silly sentences.

Phonemic Awareness

Phoneme Matching: Medial Sounds

+ Bring out the **Lion Puppet,** and tell students he wants to play the middle-sound matching game. Remind students you will say three words and they should listen for the two words that have the same middle sound.

+ Say three words, with two of the words having the same middle vowel sound. For example:

Teacher:	*hen, nest, can*
Puppet:	*Which words have the same middle sound? What is the sound?*
Everyone:	*hen, nest /e/*

+ Continue with these words:

tub	back	**duck**	/u/
fish	**wig**	net	/i/
cut	**van**	**bat**	/a/
dock	**lot**	rack	/o/

 Teacher Tip

ACTIVITY VARIETY To vary students' practice with the same skills, you might ask them to identify the word with a different middle sound from the rest. Students are essentially practicing the same identification skills but in the opposite way.

Differentiating Instruction **English Learners**

IF ... students are native speakers of Spanish, Tagalog (Pilipino), or certain other languages, **THEN ...** they may need extra practice saying /u/ and associating it with the letter *u*. These languages lack the short *u* sound found in English.

Teacher Tip

BODY MOVEMENT While repeating the /ī/ sound, have students make their bodies tall like the long *i*. Model for students how to put their arms straight and stiff against their sides while saying /ī/.

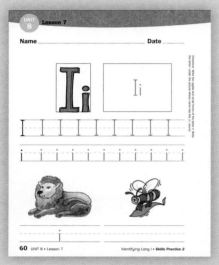

Skills Practice 2, p. 60

Monitor Progress ✓

to Differentiate Instruction
Formal Assessment

Letter and Sound Identification Note how easily students identify the /ī/ sound.

APPROACHING LEVEL

IF ... students are having difficulty,	**THEN ...** help them complete *Reteach* page 152.

ON LEVEL

IF ... students need more practice,	**THEN ...** have them complete *Skills Practice 2* page 60.

ABOVE LEVEL

IF ... students would enjoy a challenging activity,	**THEN ...** have them work independently to complete *Challenge Activities* page 116.

Alphabetic Principle 🕐

Reviewing the Sound of Long *Ii*

✦ Point to *Alphabet Sound Wall Card* Long *Ii*, and ask a volunteer to say the name of the letter. Remind students vowels sometimes say their names in words.

✦ Have students recite the rhyme for the sounds of *Ii*. Review the rhyme if students need a reminder from the previous lesson.

I's my name.

Two sounds have I:

Short i *in* pig,

Long i *in* pie.

Listening for Initial /ī/

Give each student an *Alphabet Letter Card Ii*. Ask students to raise the cards and say /ī/ when they hear a word that begins with the /ī/ sound. Try the following words:

iron	*until*	*envy*	**icicles**
extra	**ivy**	*apple*	*oatmeal*
idea	*instead*	**Ike**	**icon**

Listening for Medial /ī/

Give each student an *Alphabet Letter Card Ii*. Ask students to raise the cards and say the /ī/ sound when they hear a word that has the /ī/ sound in the middle. Try the following words:

fine	**fire**	**nine**	*spell*
fit	*fear*	**drive**	**write**
like	*girl*	*wheat*	*still*

Alphabet Sound Wall Card 9

Pickled Peppers Big Book

✦ Display the **Pickled Peppers Big Book,** and turn to page 15, "Peter Piper."

✦ Ask a volunteer to come to the book and to point to the title. Ask students how many words make up the title. *two* Then ask how many spaces are in the title. *one* Invite a volunteer to read the title aloud. *Peter Piper* Invite students to share anything they remember about the rhyme.

✦ Tell students you will read the rhyme aloud and you would like them to listen for the words with the /ī/ sound. Remind them of the Listening Icons. Ask students to close their eyes as they listen.

✦ Invite students to say any /ī/ words they noticed while you read the rhyme aloud. *Piper*

✦ Work through the rhyme word by word with students. Have them tell you when you come to a word with the letter *Ii* in it. Remind students that they are listening for the /ī/ or /i/ sounds. Write the words on the board, and have volunteers underline the letter that makes the /ī/ or /i/ sound. Have students identify whether the letter *Ii* in each word makes the /ī/ sound or the /i/ sound.

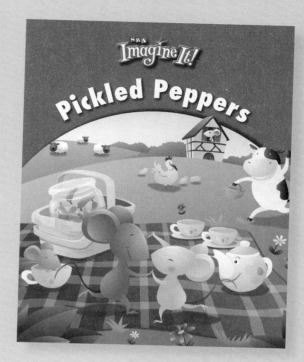

Pickled Peppers Big Book, p. 15

Technology

Use the **Listening Library CD** to support the **Pickled Peppers** lessons.

Audio CD

OBJECTIVES

Students will
- ✦ locate the title and the names of the author and the illustrator.
- ✦ develop an understanding of vocabulary words.
- ✦ use the comprehension strategies Making Connections and Predicting.
- ✦ identify print and book features.

MATERIALS
- ✦ *Ready, Set, Grow! Big Book,* pp. 32–59
- ✦ Routines 5–7

Ready, Set, Grow! Big Book, p. 32

Technology

To promote independent reading, encourage students to use Workshop to listen to the recording of the selection on the *Listening Library CD.* Invite them to follow along and say the words whenever they can.

1st READ

Preview and Prepare

ROUTINE 5

Activate Prior Knowledge

✦ "Becoming Butterflies" is a fictional selection about a classroom of students who eagerly watch three caterpillars turn into butterflies. The students record the caterpillars' progress as they watch them eat and grow, shed their skin, build chrysalises, and fly away. As you read the selection aloud, relate what you already know to what you are reading, and encourage students to do the same.

✦ Ask students what they know about caterpillars. Have them to describe any they have seen and tell where they saw them. Ask students how caterpillars and butterflies are related. Have them tell about butterflies they have noticed. Tell students you are going to read them a story about how caterpillars grow and change and finally turn into butterflies.

✦ Encourage students to think about the knowledge they are building about the unit theme as they listen to the selection. Tell them to listen for how caterpillars grow into butterflies. Key concepts include the following:

- Caterpillars eat the leaves of plants such as milkweed.
- As caterpillars grow, they shed their old skins.
- Caterpillars hang from silk threads and form chrysalises around their bodies.
- Caterpillars live as chrysalises for ten days. Then they turn into butterflies.

Preview the Selection

✦ Open the *Ready, Set, Grow! Big Book* to pages 32–33, the opening pages of "Becoming Butterflies." Follow Routine 5, the previewing the selection routine, as you introduce the title and the names of the author and the illustrator. Ask students what an author and an illustrator do. Ask students if they know what kind of butterfly is on the cover. Explain that it is a monarch butterfly.

✦ Ask students if the pictures give them any clues as to what the story might be about. Encourage them to comment on anything they find interesting or puzzling.

✦ Help students think about what they might learn from the story before they read it. Encourage students to listen for information about how things grow as you read "Becoming Butterflies."

Vocabulary

ROUTINE **6**

- Follow Routine 6, the selection vocabulary routine, as you introduce the vocabulary words for this selection.

- Explain that when something is *striped,* it has stripes on it. Use the following sentence to illustrate: *My father put up the striped wallpaper.*

- Explain that the word *hatch* means "an egg breaks, and the bird or animal comes out." Use the following sentence to illustrate: *The eggs will soon hatch into baby robins.*

- Tell students if they are *becoming* sleepy, they are getting to be sleepy.

- Point out the word *underneath* means the same as "below." Ask students to look underneath their desks or chairs.

Read the Selection

ROUTINE **7**

- Before beginning the selection, read the Focus Question at the top of the first page. Tell students to keep this question in mind as they listen to the story.

- Follow Routine 7, the reading the selection routine, and read the entire selection.

- Before, during, and after the first reading, invite students to ask questions and to think aloud about anything in the selection. In this way, you prepare students for the kind of thinking they will use to become independent, enthusiastic readers.

Comprehension Strategies

- During the reading of "Becoming Butterflies," you will model the following comprehension strategies:
  - Making Connections
  - Predicting

- Think aloud through each strategy, and encourage students to share their ideas as well.

Vocabulary

striped	becoming
hatch	underneath

 Teacher Tip

WORD FLUENCY Have students practice using each of the vocabulary words from the selection in context in a sentence. If students have trouble at first, give them an example. For instance, if the word is *striped,* say *The zebra is striped.*

Comprehension Strategies

Teacher Modeling

❶ Predicting *I think Miss Dana's class is going to raise butterflies. She tells her students how caterpillars become butterflies. Then she says, "You'll see," and puts the caterpillars in a box. I think they will see. What do you think? Let's read on to see if our prediction is confirmed.*

❷ Making Connections *This picture reminds me I've seen caterpillars before. Our garden has lots of them. Some of them have stripes, some have spots, and some have fur.*

❸ Making Connections *When my brother brought home a baby snake to raise, he put it in a box with a screen too. That way it got fresh air and didn't get away. Thinking about how my brother raised a snake helps me understand what the students are doing.*

❹ Making Connections *I know how Julianna feels. When I'm excited about something, it's hard to wait for it to happen. It's hard to be patient. When was a time you were excited about something?*

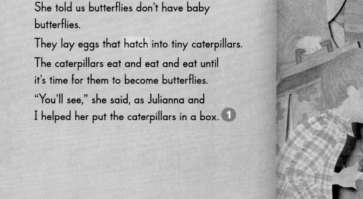

🍎 Teacher Tip

GLOSSARY The words *striped, hatch,* and *underneath* can be found in the Glossary of the *Ready, Set, Grow! Big Book.*

We put some milkweed in the box, and our caterpillars started to eat it.

We put a screened lid over the top of the box so they could get fresh air, but couldn't ❸ crawl away.

Then we drew pictures of them eating the milkweed.

The caterpillar eats a milkweed leaf.

36

37

Our caterpillars ate and ate, and got bigger and bigger.

"But they're not becoming butterflies," Julianna said. "They're just big, fat caterpillars."

"Wait and see," said Miss Dana. ❹

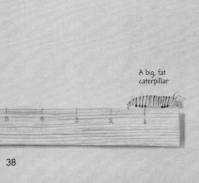

A big, fat caterpillar

38

39

Ready, Set, Grow! Big Book, pp. 32–39

Print and Book Awareness

Sentences: Periods

Display page 36 of the *Big Book,* and have volunteers point to the first and last word of each sentence. *We, it; We, away; Then, milkweed* Have them point to the periods at the ends of sentences and say *This is a period.*

Quotation Marks

Identify the quotation marks on page 38, and ask students what they show. If necessary, explain that quotation marks show the words a person or story character is saying. Have students locate the beginning and the end of each line of dialogue on the page.

Comprehension Strategies

Teacher Modeling

❺ Making Connections *The caterpillar is hanging from a thread of silk that it made. Spiders make silk too. They use it to build their webs. It's cool the way caterpillars and spiders can make what they need.*

❻ Predicting *I think the caterpillar is going to change in a big way. I think the glob of jelly is going to become something really special. What do you think? Miss Dana tells Julianna to watch what happens. Let's read on to see if our prediction is confirmed.*

❼ Predicting *We were right! The jelly changed into a beautiful jewel with gold dots. And look at the picture! Another caterpillar is already hanging from the screen, and the third one is on its way up. I predict these caterpillars will do the same thing. What do you think? Let's read on to see what happens.*

Differentiating Instruction | **English Learners**

IF ... students need additional help with Predicting, **THEN ...** refer to Unit 8 Lesson 7 of the *English Learner Support Guide.*

After three days our caterpillars got so big their skin split.
A new striped skin just the right size was underneath it.
I think caterpillars are always hungry because ours ate their old skins and then more milkweed.
I drew a picture of that.

The caterpillar's skin

40   41

A few days later, their skins split again.
When our caterpillars were about two weeks old one hung upside down from the screened lid from a little thread of black silk it made. ❺
"Hey, look! It's spelling my name!" Julianna said.
She was right.
The caterpillar had made itself into the letter J.

The caterpillar hangs upside down.
 J

42   43

🍎 **Teacher Tip**

PREDICTING Tell students predicting helps keep them involved in the story. Their predictions are not wild guesses. They are based on clues in the story.

Soon that caterpillar's skin split, but we didn't see any new striped skin.

All we saw was a glob of greenish-white jelly.

There wasn't a caterpillar to eat the old skin.

"Ick!" said Julianna. "It looks sort of sick!"

"It's not," Miss Dana said. "Watch what happens." **6**

The caterpillar turns into a chrysalis.

Ick!

44

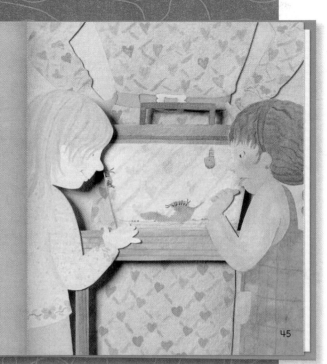

45

We watched the jelly get smoother and greener.

Soon it was hard and smooth with a ring of gold dots. **7**

"Hey! Now it's not icky at all," said Julianna.

"It looks like a beautiful jewel."

"But where did the caterpillar go?" I asked.

"It's becoming a butterfly," said Miss Dana.

"But first it must become a chrysalis. That's what it is now."

The new chrysalis

46

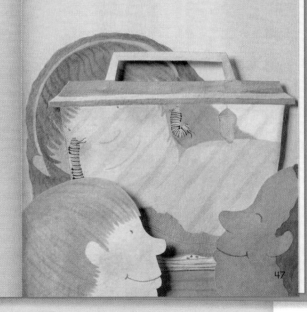

47

Ready, Set, Grow! Big Book, pp. 40–47

Print and Book Awareness

Sentences, Directionality

Display page 40 of the *Big Book,* and have volunteers show where to start reading each sentence and where to stop. Remind students we read from left to right, a sentence begins with a capital letter, and some sentences end with periods. Have each volunteer run his or her hand under each line of print.

Exclamation Points

Have a volunteer point out the exclamation points on pages 42 and 44, and ask students what an exclamation point means. If necessary, remind students an exclamation point means the speaker is excited. Then read the sentences in a normal voice and an excited voice, and invite students to do the same.

Capital Letters

Display page 42, and point to the shape the caterpillar makes with its body. Ask students what letter forms this shape. Then have students make a letter *J* in the air with their index fingers. Ask students why a capital *J* appears in Julianna's name. Then have a volunteer find the capital *J*s on this page.

Picture-Text Relationship

Reread the text on page 46, and have students comment about the illustration on the facing page. Then ask *What does the picture tell you that the story does not?* Tell students pictures and words work together to tell the whole story.

Comprehension Strategies

Teacher Modeling

8 Predicting *We were right! Now three green jewels, or chrysalises, are hanging from the screen. Reading on let us confirm our prediction.*

9 Predicting *The chrysalis has dried up. Miss Dana says it's time. I think a beautiful butterfly will soon crawl out. What do you think?*

10 Predicting *Yes, a beautiful butterfly did crawl out. And look! Another one is on its way. Miss Dana's class did raise butterflies! Reading this confirms a prediction we made early in the story.*

11 Making Connections *I know how Julianna feels. I know how it hurts to raise something and then have to let it go. After our cat's kittens got old enough, we had to find homes for them. It was so sad to say good-bye.*

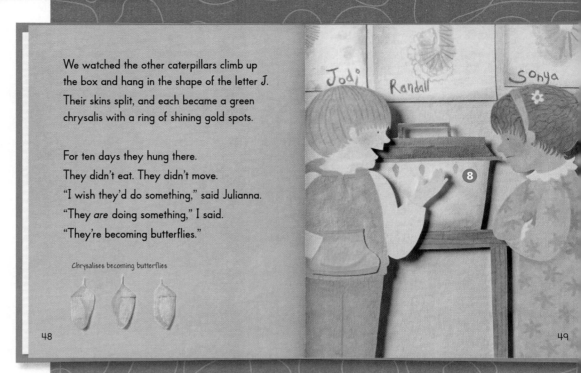

We watched the other caterpillars climb up the box and hang in the shape of the letter J. Their skins split, and each became a green chrysalis with a ring of shining gold spots.

For ten days they hung there.
They didn't eat. They didn't move.
"I wish they'd do something," said Julianna.
"They *are* doing something," I said.
"They're becoming butterflies."

Chrysalises becoming butterflies

48   49

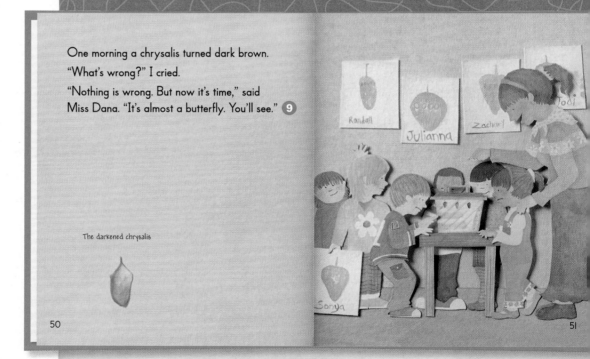

One morning a chrysalis turned dark brown.
"What's wrong?" I cried.
"Nothing is wrong. But now it's time," said Miss Dana. "It's almost a butterfly. You'll see." 9

The darkened chrysalis

50   51

 **Teacher Tip**

CONFIRMING PREDICTIONS Remind students that readers continuously make predictions as they read. They also confirm their predictions and update them as they go along.

We watched as the shell of the chrysalis peeled away. It had turned clear as glass. A butterfly with wet and folded wings hung from it, waiting for its wings to dry. "Wow!" everyone said. "Look at that!" **10**

The shell of the chrysalis

52

53

That afternoon we drew pictures of our beautiful butterflies. When their wings were dry we opened the window. Each one sipped nectar from the flowers outside, then fluttered up to the sky. "But I wanted them to stay!" Julianna looked very sad. **11**

The butterfly sips nectar from a coneflower.

54

Goodbye, butterflies.

55

Ready, Set, Grow! Big Book, pp. 48–55

Print and Book Awareness

Quotation Marks

Have a volunteer point to the quotation marks on page 48, and ask students what they show. If necessary, explain that quotation marks show the words a person or story character is saying. Have students locate the beginning and the end of each line of dialogue on the page.

Question Marks

Have a volunteer point to the question mark on page 50, and ask students what a question mark means. If necessary, remind students a question mark means the speaker is asking a question. Then read the question with the appropriate expression, and invite students to do the same.

Exclamation Points

Have a volunteer point to the exclamation points on page 52, and ask students what an exclamation point means. If necessary, remind students an exclamation point means that the speaker is excited. Then read the sentences in a normal voice and an excited voice, and invite students to do the same.

Comprehension Strategies

Teacher Modeling

⑫ Making Connections *Butterflies must be like the birds that fly south to stay warm. The hummingbirds in our yard fly south at the end of summer. They can't live when it gets too cold outside.*

⑬ Predicting *I think the boys and girls in Chincua, Mexico, will write back to Miss Dana's class. What do you think? Let's read on to find out.*

⑭ Predicting *We were right! The Mexican boys and girls did write back, and they sent a picture. They wanted Miss Dana's class to see where their butterflies were living.*

⑮ Making Connections *I understand how the students in Miss Dana's class feel. They got attached to the three butterflies they raised, just like I got attached to our kittens. You want to know that something you loved will be okay.*

"They'll sip nectar all summer," Miss Dana said. "But they'll fly far south before winter comes. ⑫

Butterflies can only live when the weather is warm."

On the map, she showed us a place in Mexico.

"This is where they will go," she said.

Mexico on the globe

56

We wrote a letter to the boys and girls at a school in Chincua, Mexico. ⑬

"Please take good care of our butterflies," we said.

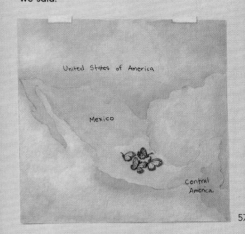
United States of America

Mexico

Central America.

57

One cold winter day we got a letter back from the boys and girls at the school in Mexico.

They sent us a picture of a tree covered ⑭ with butterflies.

All of us looked and looked, wondering which were the three butterflies we hatched in our classroom and set free to fly so far away. ⑮

The letter from Mexico

58

Just some of the millions of butterflies that gather in Mexico

59

Ready, Set, Grow! Big Book, pp. 56–59

 **Teacher Tip**

MAKING CONNECTIONS Tell students that readers are active and make connections as they read. Encourage students to make connections as they read and to share them with the class.

Print and Book Awareness

Tracking Sentences

Display page 58, and have a volunteer find the sentence that begins on the fourth line. Have the volunteer run his or her finger under the sentence as you read it. Point out that the sentence ends at the period, not at the end of the line.

Picture-Text Relationship

Reread the text on pages 56 and 58, and have students comment about the illustration or photograph on the facing page. For each illustration or photo, ask *What does the picture tell you that the story does not?* Tell students the pictures and words work together to tell the whole story.

Discussing the Selection

✦ Review the Focus Question with students: Why do the students watch the caterpillars every day?

✦ Ask students *What did you learn from this story about things that grow and change? Every living thing needs food to grow. It can take a long time for things to grow and change.*

Vocabulary Review

Review with students the selection vocabulary words *striped, hatch, becoming,* and *underneath.* Ask students the following questions:

- *What are some things in the classroom that are striped?*
- *What kinds of animals hatch from eggs?*
- *How are the caterpillars becoming butterflies in the story?*
- *What are items in the classroom that are underneath something?*

OBJECTIVES

Students will

✦ list instructions explaining how to do something.

✦ learn about the present tense of action words.

✦ participate in a Thinking Story experience.

MATERIALS

✦ *Language Arts Big Book,* pp. 38, 54

✦ *Willy the Wisher,* p. 81

Writing Process

Draft: Making a List of Instructions

Teach

✦ Remind students that the class is working together to write instructions on how to do something. Remind students of the topic the class chose in the previous lesson.

✦ Display the *Language Arts Big Book* page 38. Remind students it is important to do things in a special order when you are writing directions.

Guided Practice

✦ Review the ideas the class generated in the previous lesson. Read them to the class, and discuss which ideas would make the best steps in the instructions.

✦ Guide students in creating a complete list of instructions for the "how to" of doing the chosen topic. Try to keep the list short as students will be drawing pictures to illustrate the steps later.

✦ Write the instructions on chart paper, and tell students you will continue working on the list in the next lesson. Write a few items out of order to prepare for the coming lessons on revising and clarifying.

Grammar, Usage, and Mechanics

Teach

✦ Display page 54 of the *Language Arts Big Book.* Remind students words that show action tell us what someone or something is doing. Read each of the sentences on the page, and discuss how each one changes depending on who is doing the action.

✦ Tell students words that show action can tell about something that happens now, in the past, or in the future. These three different categories are called *tenses,* and *tenses* is a word that tells about time.

Language Arts Big Book , p. 38

Language Arts Big Book , p. 54

Grammar, Usage, and Mechanics continued

Guided Practice

✦ Review words that show action by playing a game of Simon says. Use a variety of action words such as *jump, touch, turn, wiggle,* and *shake.*

✦ Point out to students that because they are doing each of these actions right now, the action words are all in the present tense.

Differentiating Instruction **English Learners**

IF ... students need help understanding action words, **THEN ...** have proficient English speakers role-play and say the words before beginning the game.

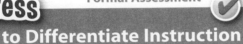

Monitor Progress Formal Assessment ✓

to Differentiate Instruction

Grammar Note how easily students use words in present tense.

APPROACHING LEVEL	
IF ... students are having difficulty,	**THEN ...** have them complete *Reteach* page 153.

ON LEVEL	
IF ... students need more help,	**THEN ...** have them talk about things they see happening when they look outside the classroom windows.

ABOVE LEVEL	
IF ... students are comfortable,	**THEN ...** with your help, have them create three present-tense sentences.

Willy the Wisher 🕐

✦ Display the book ***Willy the Wisher.*** Ask a volunteer to come to the book and to identify its Table of Contents. Together, find the story "Portia's Lost Shoe" on page 81 of the book.

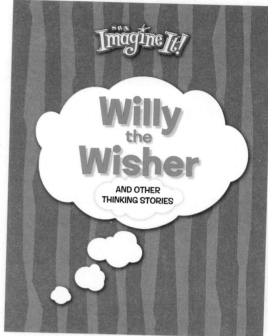

Willy the Wisher, p. 81

✦ Before reading the story to students, ask students to share what they remember about Portia. Have students discuss what they remember about Mark, Mr. Breezy's son.

✦ Read the story, pausing at the red text to ask students the questions.

✦ After reading the story, discuss it in general. Use questions such as the following:

- *Why does Mark ask so many questions about the party Portia went to yesterday?*
- *Do you think the questions Mark asked were good ones? Why or why not?*
- *What questions would you have asked Portia?*
- *Was Loretta correct in thinking Portia's friend sent her the shoe?*

Sounds and Letters

OBJECTIVES

Students will

✦ segment syllables in words by clapping and counting.

✦ substitute medial phonemes to make new words.

✦ attach the /ī/ sound to the letter *Ii*.

✦ practice writing the numeral *3*.

MATERIALS

✦ *Rhyme Poster* "Twinkle, Twinkle, Little Star"
✦ *Alphabet Letter Card* *Ii* for each student
✦ Supply Icons
✦ *Skills Practice 2,* p. 61
✦ *Pocket Chart Picture Card* 4

Calendar

Su	M	T	W	Th	F	S
		1	2	3	4	5
6	7	8	9	10	11	12
13	14	15	16	17	18	19
20	21	22	23	24	25	26
27	28	29	30	31		

Point to the box that represents today. Then ask a volunteer to point to the day that will happen one week from today.

Warming Up

MORNING MESSAGE

Today is _____.

What time is it? Is it five past nine?

(Child's name) likes to ride _____.

Kindergarten News

✦ Copy the text above on the board or on chart paper.

✦ Read each sentence in the Morning Message, pointing to each word. Have a volunteer come and underline a word if he or she hears the /ī/ sound. Then reread the word. *time, five, nine, likes, ride*

✦ Use prompts such as the following to discuss the letters and words in the message:

  • *Let's find words that have two letters.* is, it, to *Who can come up and circle one?*

  • *How can you make the last sentence an exclamation? Come up, and make an exclamation point in the message.*

Syllable Segmentation

✦ Display the **Rhyme Poster** for "Twinkle, Twinkle, Little Star." Have students sing the song:

Twinkle, twinkle, little star,

how I wonder what you are.

Up above the world so high,

like a diamond in the sky.

◆ Say words from the song, and ask students to clap out the syllables of each word and then tell how many syllables they heard. Use these words:

twinkle 2   *little* 2   *star* 1   *you* 1   *up* 1   *world* 1

◆ Say each word again, stressing syllables, and have students repeat the words until they can blend the syllables smoothly.

Phonemic Awareness

Phoneme Manipulation: Medial Sounds

◆ Bring out the **Lion Puppet,** and tell students he wants to play a game in which he changes the sounds in words to make new words.

◆ Say a word, and have students repeat it. Then have the puppet tell students to change the medial phoneme, or vowel sound. Everyone will then say the new word. For example:

Teacher:	*The word is* hat.
Students:	*hat*
Puppet:	*Now change the /a/ to /o/. How do you say the word now?*
Everyone:	*hot*

◆ Continue with these words:

pat pat /i/ pit	*bag* bag /u/ bug	*top* top /i/ tip
rip rip /a/ rap	*rod* rod /e/ red	*men* men /a/ man
lip lip /a/ lap	*not* not /u/ nut	

Teacher Tip

PHONEME SUBSTITUTION The manipulation of medial sounds might pose an extra challenge to some students. If the class is having difficulty identifying the new words after vowel substitution, write the words on the board, erase the middle phoneme, and then write the new one in its place. Help students blend the new word.

Monitor Progress to Differentiate Instruction

Formal Assessment

Syllable Segmentation Note how easily students segment the syllables in the words.

APPROACHING LEVEL

IF ... students are having difficulty,   THEN ... help them to complete **Reteach** page 154.

ON LEVEL

IF ... students need more practice,   THEN ... have students clap the syllables in additional words using another **Rhyme Poster.**

ABOVE LEVEL

IF ... students would enjoy a challenging activity,   THEN ... have them work independently to draw pictures of two-syllable words.

Differentiating Instruction   English Learners

IF ... students have difficulty with the phonemic awareness activity, **THEN ...** refer to Unit 8 Lesson 8, of **English Learner Support Guide.**

Alphabetic Principle

Reviewing the Sound of Long *Ii*

Point to the **Alphabet Sound Wall Card** *Long Ii*, and have students recite the rhyme for the sounds of *Ii*:

I's *my name.*

Two sounds have I:

Short i *in* pig,

Long i *in* pie.

Listening for Medial /ī/

Give each student an **Alphabet Letter Card** *Ii*. Ask students to raise the cards and say /ī/ when they hear a word that has the /ī/ sound. Try the following words:

which	*mass*	**mice**	**hide**
title	**ride**	**life**	*roll*
vine	*beat*	*note*	*plum*

Linking the Sound to the Letter

✦ Write a pair of words on the board, one with the /ī/ sound and one with a different vowel sound. For each pair, say the word with the /ī/ sound, point to each of the words, and have students identify the word you said by signaling thumbs-up when you point to it. Try these word pairs:

Irish ... empty	all ... *island*
idea ... edge	*icy* ... eyes
Iowa ... awe	atom ... *item*

✦ After each student identifies the correct word, ask him or her how he or she knows. *The word begins with long* i.

Technology

Have students use the **eSkills** activity to review the /ī/ sound.

Audio CD

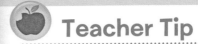
Penmanship

✦ Distribute a sheet of writing paper to each student, or use **White Boards** turned to the sides with writing lines.

✦ Place the Supply Icon for *pencil* on the board or in the **Pocket Chart.**

✦ Using the established procedure, review with students how to form the numeral *3.* Say *Begin here. Curve around to the right, then go in at the middle. Then curve back down to the right and around halfway. Three.*

✦ Now invite students to practice writing numeral *3*s across the top row of the paper or **White Boards.** Make sure they are writing from left to right.

✦ Remind students that the number *3* means we have three of something. Illustrate this concept by drawing three stars on the chalkboard, if necessary.

Guided Practice

✦ Have students complete **Skills Practice 2** page 61 for additional practice with the numeral *3.*

✦ Draw students' attention to the first penmanship line. Ask them to trace the *3*s outlined across the row. Then ask students to write a row of *3*s across the next line.

✦ Then ask students to look at the word *three* written on the line. Tell students this is how you write the word that names the number *3.*

✦ Invite volunteers to identify the letters that make up the word *three,* and have the class practice writing the word by tracing the letters. Then have them try writing the word on their own on the next line.

✦ After students have finished, review their work, and have them proofread using the established procedure.

Teacher Tip

USING PROGRAM MATERIALS Use *Pocket Chart Picture Card* 4 to help you review the shape of the numeral *3.*

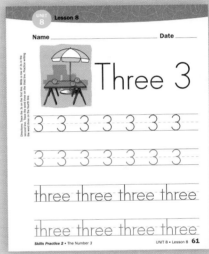

Skills Practice 2, p. 61

Monitor Progress to Differentiate Instruction

Formal Assessment

Penmanship Note how easily students write the numeral 3.

APPROACHING LEVEL	IF ... students are having difficulty,	THEN ... have them write the numeral in shaving cream on their desks or on vinyl placemats.
ON LEVEL	IF ... students need more practice,	THEN ... have them write more rows of numerals using **White Boards.**
ABOVE LEVEL	IF ... students would enjoy a challenging activity,	THEN ... have them work independently to cut the letters for the word *three* from a magazine or catalog and paste them in order. Then have them write the word *three* below the pasted version.

Students will

✦ develop an understanding of vocabulary words.
✦ review the comprehension strategies Making Connections and Predicting.
✦ use the comprehension skill Sequence.
✦ analyze the characteristics of fiction.

✦ *Ready, Set, Grow! Big Book,* pp. 32–59
✦ Routines 5–7

Focus Question Why do the students watch the caterpillars every day?

BECOMING BUTTERFLIES

by Anne Rockwell
illustrated by Megan Halsey

One day Miss Dana brought a surprise to school—three striped caterpillars and a flowerpot.

← milkweed plant

cardboard mailing box

Styrofoam box

insect house

32

caterpillars inside

Ready, Set, Grow! Big Book, p. 32

Vocabulary

shell	sipped
peeled	fluttered

Preview and Prepare

2nd READ

Preview the Selection

ROUTINE 5

✦ Display the **Ready, Set, Grow! Big Book** opened to the Table of Contents page. Use Routine 5, previewing the selection, to guide students in understanding and using the Table of Contents. Then turn to the selection, and state the title and the names of the author and the illustrator.

✦ As you prepare to reread the selection, have students use the illustrations to retell the main events in the story.

Vocabulary

ROUTINE 6

✦ Follow Routine 6, the selection vocabulary routine, as you introduce the vocabulary words for this selection.

✦ Explain that the *shell* of something is its outside cover. Use the following sentence to illustrate: *The shell of the coconut is cracked.*

✦ Explain that the word *peeled* means "came off in layers." Use the following sentence to illustrate: *The skin of the onion peeled away easily.*

✦ Explain to students that the word *sipped* means "drank a little." Use a glass of water to demonstrate.

✦ Tell students the word *fluttered* means "quickly flapped wings." Invite students to pretend their arms and hands are wings and to demonstrate the word *fluttered.*

Read the Selection

ROUTINE **7**

Comprehension Strategies

✦ During the first reading of "Becoming Butterflies," you modeled the following reading comprehension strategies:

- Making Connections
- Predicting

✦ In this second reading of the selection, you will revisit each comprehension strategy model from the first reading.

Comprehension Skills

In this lesson of "Becoming Butterflies," students will use the comprehension skill Sequence.

Reading with a Writer's Eye

✦ In this rereading of "Becoming Butterflies," you will discuss how the author developed the characteristics of fiction—character, setting, and plot.

✦ By discussing the author's writing strategies, students learn how they can be better writers.

 Teacher Tip

VOCABULARY Encourage students to use a variety of sources to build their vocabulary, such as making word banks, discussing characters and events from a story, talking with other people, and thinking about their own life experiences.

Technology

To promote independent reading, encourage students to use Workshop to listen to the recording of the selection on the *Listening Library CD.* Invite them to follow along and to say the words whenever they can.

Audio CD

Reading and Responding

2nd READ

Comprehension Strategies

Teacher Modeling

❶ Predicting *Here we predicted Miss Dana's class was going to raise butterflies. We thought about how Miss Dana explained the way caterpillars become butterflies. Then she said, "You'll see," and put the caterpillars in a box. Those clues helped us make a strong prediction.*

❷ Making Connections *Seeing the picture of this caterpillar reminded me of the caterpillars I've seen in our garden. That helped me remember what caterpillars are like.*

❸ Making Connections *Here I remembered how my brother put a baby snake in a box with a screen so it would get fresh air and not get out. That helped me understand why the students in Miss Dana's class did what they did with the caterpillars.*

❹ Making Connections *When I read Julianna's words, we understood how she felt. Her words reminded me of times we've been excited about something and wanted it to happen fast. Thinking about our own feelings helped us understand Julianna's feelings.*

Focus Question Why do the students watch the caterpillars every day?

BECOMING BUTTERFLIES
by Anne Rockwell
illustrated by Megan Halsey

One day Miss Dana brought a surprise to school—three striped caterpillars and a flowerpot.

← milkweed plant

cardboard mailing box

Styrofoam box

insect house

caterpillars inside

32

A green plant called a milkweed was growing in the flowerpot.

33

She told us butterflies don't have baby butterflies.
They lay eggs that hatch into tiny caterpillars.
The caterpillars eat and eat and eat until it's time for them to become butterflies.
"You'll see," she said, as Julianna and I helped her put the caterpillars in a box. ❶

A tiny caterpillar ❷

34

35

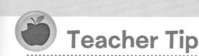

🍎 **Teacher Tip**

GLOSSARY The words *shell* and *peeled* can be found in the Glossary of the ***Ready, Set, Grow! Big Book.***

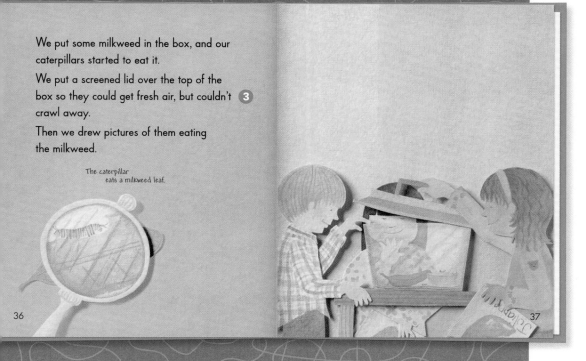

We put some milkweed in the box, and our caterpillars started to eat it.

We put a screened lid over the top of the box so they could get fresh air, but couldn't crawl away. **3**

Then we drew pictures of them eating the milkweed.

The caterpillar eats a milkweed leaf.

36   37

Our caterpillars ate and ate, and got bigger and bigger.

"But they're not becoming butterflies," Julianna said. "They're just big, fat caterpillars."

"Wait and see," said Miss Dana. **4**

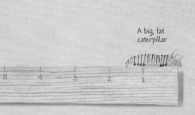

A big, fat caterpillar

38   39

Ready, Set, Grow! Big Book, pp. 32–39

Comprehension Skills

Sequence

✦ Tell students Miss Dana's class learns how caterpillars turn into butterflies as they watch them grow and change. Ask students to list what the class observes on pages 32–39. *The caterpillars ate lots of leaves from the milkweed plants and grew bigger and bigger.*

✦ Start a chart of the story sequence. This will reinforce the step-by-step concept of sequence of events, and it will also serve as an introduction to story plot.

Reading with a Writer's Eye

Genre Knowledge

✦ Tell students "Becoming Butterflies" is a story that did not really happen but could happen. Ask students why this story could happen in real life. *Lots of teachers might want to show their classes how caterpillars turn into butterflies.*

✦ Tell students stories have characters. Ask them which characters appear on these pages. *Miss Dana and Julianna*

✦ Tell students a story also has a setting, or a location where the story takes place. Ask students what the setting of "Becoming Butterflies" is. *Miss Dana's classroom*

✦ Tell students a story also has a plot, or plan that the story follows. Ask students what they think the plot of the story is. *Miss Dana's students will watch three caterpillars turn into butterflies.*

Comprehension Strategies

Teacher Modeling

⑤ Making Connections *We understood how a caterpillar could make a silk thread when we thought about how spiders do the same thing. Thinking about this made us understand them more.*

⑥ Predicting *Here we predicted the caterpillar would change in a big way. We decided the glob of jelly was going to become something really cool. Miss Dana wanted Julianna to watch what would happen because she knew it would be something special.*

⑦ Predicting *Our prediction was confirmed. The jelly turned into something that looks like a beautiful jewel with gold dots. Then we predicted the other caterpillars would do the same thing. We saw that another caterpillar was already hanging from the screen and that the third one was on its way up.*

After three days our caterpillars got so big their skin split.
A new striped skin just the right size was underneath it.
I think caterpillars are always hungry because ours ate their old skins and then more milkweed.
I drew a picture of that.

The caterpillar's skin

40

41

A few days later, their skins split again.
When our caterpillars were about two weeks old one hung upside down from the screened lid from a little thread of black silk it made. ⑤
"Hey, look! It's spelling my name!" Julianna said.
She was right.
The caterpillar had made itself into the letter J.

The caterpillar hangs upside down.

42

43

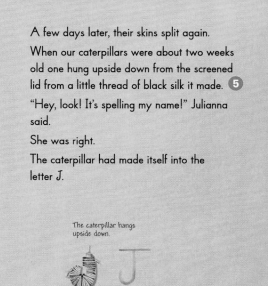

🍎 Teacher Tip

COMPREHENSION Readers constantly evaluate their understanding of what they read. Stop often to make sure students are doing this.

Soon that caterpillar's skin split, but we didn't see any new striped skin.

All we saw was a glob of greenish-white jelly.

There wasn't a caterpillar to eat the old skin.

"Ick!" said Julianna. "It looks sort of sick!"

"It's not," Miss Dana said. "Watch what happens." **6**

The caterpillar turns into a chrysalis.

Ick!

44

45

We watched the jelly get smoother and greener.

Soon it was hard and smooth with a ring of gold dots. **7**

"Hey! Now it's not icky at all," said Julianna. "It looks like a beautiful jewel."

"But where did the caterpillar go?" I asked.

"It's becoming a butterfly," said Miss Dana. "But first it must become a chrysalis. That's what it is now."

The new chrysalis

46

47

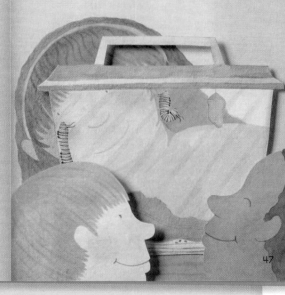

Ready, Set, Grow! Big Book, pp. 40–47

Comprehension Skills

Sequence

✦ Tell students Miss Dana's class continues to watch the caterpillars grow and change. Ask students to list what the class observes on pages 40–47. *The caterpillars ate and ate and split their skins. Their new skins were striped. They ate more leaves and split their skins again. Then they hung upside down from a black thread. Green jelly covered their bodies. The jelly got hard and became chrysalises.*

✦ Add students' responses to the chart of story sequence.

Reading with a Writer's Eye

Genre Knowledge

✦ Ask students to tell what they have learned about the character Julianna. *She is curious and excited to see what happens to the caterpillars. She has a hard time waiting for the caterpillars to change.*

✦ Ask students to tell what they have learned about Miss Dana. *She is patient and understands that her students might have a hard time waiting to see what happens to the caterpillars.*

Comprehension Strategies

Teacher Modeling

8 Predicting *Our prediction was confirmed. Now three green jewels, or chrysalises, were hanging from the screen.*

9 Predicting *The chrysalis had dried up, and Miss Dana had said it was time. These were two strong clues. We predicted a beautiful butterfly was about ready to crawl out.*

10 Predicting *We were right! A beautiful butterfly did crawl out. And the picture shows that another one will soon do the same. This confirmed a prediction we made in the beginning that Miss Dana's class would raise butterflies.*

11 Making Connections *Here I thought about the time when we had to give away kittens we had raised. I was so sad. So I understood how Julianna felt about letting the butterflies go free. When you raise something, you get really attached to it.*

We watched the other caterpillars climb up the box and hang in the shape of the letter J. Their skins split, and each became a green chrysalis with a ring of shining gold spots.

For ten days they hung there.
They didn't eat. They didn't move.
"I wish they'd do something," said Julianna.
"They *are* doing something," I said.
"They're becoming butterflies."

Chrysalises becoming butterflies

48   49

One morning a chrysalis turned dark brown.
"What's wrong?" I cried.
"Nothing is wrong. But now it's time," said Miss Dana. "It's almost a butterfly. You'll see." **9**

The darkened chrysalis

50   51

Teacher Tip

COMPREHENSION Ask students one or more of the following questions to make sure they understand what they are reading: *Is anyone confused? Does this make sense to you?*

We watched as the shell of the chrysalis peeled away. It had turned clear as glass. A butterfly with wet and folded wings hung from it, waiting for its wings to dry. "Wow!" everyone said. "Look at that!" ⑩

The shell of the chrysalis

52

53

That afternoon we drew pictures of our beautiful butterflies. When their wings were dry we opened the window.
Each one sipped nectar from the flowers outside, then fluttered up to the sky.
"But I wanted them to stay!"
Julianna looked very sad. ⑪

The butterfly sips nectar from a coneflower.

Goodbye, butterflies.

54

55

Ready, Set, Grow! Big Book, pp. 48–55

Vocabulary Tip

Review the meanings of the words *shell, peeled, sipped,* and *fluttered.* Then have students use the words in sentences.

Comprehension Skills

Sequence

✦ Tell students Miss Dana's class continues to watch the caterpillars grow and change. Ask students to list what the class observes on pages 48–55. *The caterpillars hung upside down and didn't eat or move. Then their shells turned brown and peeled away. The butterflies crawled out, and after their wings dried, they flew out the window.*

✦ Add students' responses to the chart of story sequence.

Reading with a Writer's Eye

Genre Knowledge

✦ Reread pages 48–51, and ask students who *I* is. Tell students this character is not given a name. Have them look at the illustrations on these pages for clues to this character's identity. *It seems to be the little boy in the picture on pages 49 and 50.*

✦ Ask students if they have learned anything new about the other characters. *Julianna has become very attached to the butterflies and is sad to see them fly away.*

✦ Ask students if the setting of the story has changed at all. *no*

Comprehension Strategies

Teacher Modeling

12 Making Connections *We understood this better when we remembered birds fly south to stay warm too. We thought about the hummingbirds in our yard and how they disappear at the end of every summer.*

13 Predicting *Here we predicted the boys and girls in Chincua, Mexico, would write back to Miss Dana's class.*

14 Predicting *This part confirmed our prediction. The boys and girls from Mexico did write back, and they sent a picture of where the butterflies were living.*

15 Making Connections *I understand how the students in Miss Dana's class felt as they looked at the picture of butterflies. I remembered how attached I had gotten to the kittens my family had raised. Just like Miss Dana's students, I wanted to know they were okay in their new homes.*

"They'll sip nectar all summer," Miss Dana said. "But they'll fly far south before winter comes. **12**
Butterflies can only live when the weather is warm."
On the map, she showed us a place in Mexico.
"This is where they will go," she said.

Mexico on the globe

56

We wrote a letter to the boys and girls at a school in Chincua, Mexico. **13**
"Please take good care of our butterflies," we said.

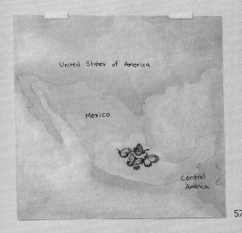

57

One cold winter day we got a letter back from the boys and girls at the school in Mexico.
They sent us a picture of a tree covered **14** with butterflies.
All of us looked and looked, wondering which were the three butterflies we hatched in our classroom and set free to fly so far away. **15**

The letter from Mexico

58

Just some of the millions of butterflies that gather in Mexico

59

Ready, Set, Grow! Big Book, pp. 56–59

Comprehension Skills

Sequence

✦ Ask students to list what the butterflies did after they were set free. *They flew south to Mexico.*

✦ Add students' responses to the chart of story sequence.

Reading with a Writer's Eye

Genre Knowledge

Ask students if the story plot they predicted in the beginning really happened. *yes* Ask them to share any other events that also occurred.

Discussing the Selection

Ask students the following questions about the selection:

- *What steps does a caterpillar take in becoming a butterfly?*
- *What did you like best about the story? Why?*

Purposes for Reading

✦ Ask students what they learned about growing things in "Becoming Butterflies."

✦ Ask students if they would recommend this story to their friends, and encourage them to explain why.

Vocabulary Review

Review with students the selection vocabulary words *shell, peeled, sipped,* and *fluttered*. Ask students the following questions:

- *What kinds of animals have a shell?*
- *What kinds of foods have to be peeled before you can eat them?*
- *When was a time you sipped something to drink?*
- *What would it look like if you fluttered your arms?*

 Teacher Tip

DISCUSSING THE SELECTION Tell students after reading, they should always ask *What did I find interesting? What is important here?* Later remind students again whenever they conclude a reading, they should ask themselves questions about what was in the text.

Language Arts

Students will
✦ move text to clarify instructions.
✦ extend story lines through words and illustrations.

✦ *Language Arts Big Book,* p. 39
✦ *Story Lines Big Book,* p. 16

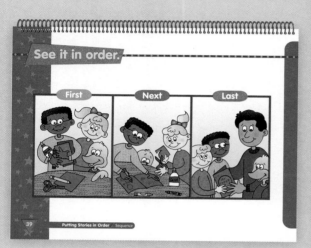

Language Arts Big Book, p. 39

Writing Process

Model: Moving Text to Clarify Instructions

Teach

✦ Display the *Language Arts Big Book* page 39. Invite a volunteer to tell what these pictures show. Discuss why it is important to do some things in a certain order.

✦ Identify the words *first, next,* and *last* on the page. Tell students these words can help readers understand the best order for doing something.

Apply

✦ Display the chart paper with the list of instructions the class created in the previous lesson. Reread what students have written so far.

✦ Take a few moments to talk about each item, and identify one item that is out of order on the list. Turn to a new sheet of chart paper, and read the list aloud. Ask students what to write first, next, and last.

✦ Discuss with students why that change makes the list better. Tell students they will get the chance to help you make the list even better by moving other items to new places in the next lesson.

Traits of Good Writing

Organizing Writers often use lists to help organize their ideas before beginning to write.

Story Crafting

Story Lines

✦ Display the **Story Lines Big Book,** and open it to page 16, "Plants Move! I Can Prove It." Review the story, pointing to each story frame as you read its accompanying text.

✦ Then draw students' attention to the "Tell Me More" extender frames on pages 21–23. Remind students these frames are empty so students can help tell more of the story.

✦ Review Frame 15, and discuss how the existing story ends. Ask students *What do you think happens after the girl's brother admits he doesn't know everything?*

✦ To guide students in continuing the story, use questions such as the following:

   • *Do you think the girl's brother tried to show he knew everything about anything else?*

   • *What could the girl and her brother do together to learn more about plants? How could Aunt Laura help them?*

✦ Choose one of the students' ideas, and make a simple line drawing in the first extender frame to illustrate it. Then ask students to suggest a sentence or two to describe the action in this new frame. Write the sentences in the space provided.

✦ Continue this procedure to complete the extender frames on page 21. When students have completed these frames, you might review the story with the new frames added.

✦ Tell students they will finish the story in the next lesson.

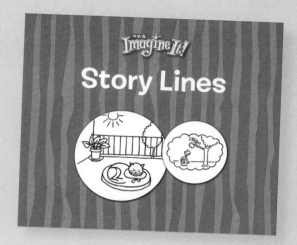

Story Lines Big Book, p. 16

Teacher Tip

THINKING CROWNS Students might enjoy wearing the *Thinking Crowns* while they create an ending for "Plants Move! I Can Prove It."

Sounds and Letters

Students will
+ blend initial phonemes to make words.
+ substitute medial phonemes to make new words.
+ attach the /ī/ sound to the letter *Ii*.
+ identify the /ī/ sound in print.

MATERIALS
+ *Alphabet Letter Card Ii* for each student
+ *Pickled Peppers Big Book,* p. 42
+ *Skills Practice 2,* p. 62

Calendar

Su	M	T	W	Th	F	S
		1	2	3	4	5
6	7	8	9	10	11	12
13	14	15	16	17	18	19
20	21	22	23	24	25	26
27	28	29	30	31		

Point to the box that represents today. Ask a volunteer to point to the next day the class will have a special activity such as art class or a field trip. Have everyone say the date aloud.

Warming Up

MORNING MESSAGE

Good morn____ng, ch____ldren!

Today ____s _____.

Do you l____ke to wr____te letters?

Kindergarten News

+ Copy the text above on the board or on chart paper, leaving out the letter *i* in the blanks. Tell students today a Mystery Letter is in the Morning Message. Explain that the same letter is missing from each letter blank.

+ Read the Morning Message, and then work with students to find what letter is missing. Ask the student who answers correctly to write the letter *i* in each letter blank.

+ Use prompts such as the following to discuss the letters and words in the message:
  + *What is the shortest word in the message?* is, do, to *Does more than one word have that many letters? Come circle them.*
  + *Can you find a word that begins with the /l/ sound?* like, letters *Come underline it.*

+ Read the words again, and have students raise their hands when they hear the /i/ sound. *morning, children, is* Repeat for words with the /ī/ sound. *like, write*

Phoneme Blending: Initial Sounds

+ Tell students the **Lion Puppet** wants to play a blending game again. Tell them you will say the beginning sound of a word and the puppet will say the rest. When the puppet asks what the word is, students should put together the parts and say the word.

✦ Practice with the following word:

Teacher:	/w/ (Emphasize the /w/ sound.)
Everyone:	/w/
Puppet:	. . . *indow. What is the word?*
Everyone:	*window*

✦ Continue with the following words:

/m/ /m/ . . . *ake make*	/b/ /b/ . . . *utter butter*
/n/ /n/ . . . *eedle needle*	/v/ /v/ . . . *isit visit*
/j/ /j/ . . . *elly jelly*	/k/ /k/ . . . *ream cream*
/s/ /s/ . . . *lide slide*	/p/ /p/ . . . *eanut peanut*
/l/ /l/ . . . *ibrary library*	

Phonemic Awareness

Phoneme Manipulation: Medial Sounds

✦ Bring out the **Lion Puppet,** and tell students he wants to play the game in which he changes the sounds in words to make new words.

✦ Say a word, and have students repeat it. Then have the puppet tell students to change the medial phoneme, or vowel sound. Everyone will then say the new word. For example:

Teacher:	*The word is* rug.
Students:	*rug*
Puppet:	*Now change the /u/ to /a/. How do you say the word now?*
Everyone:	*rag*

✦ Continue with these words:

fun fun /i/ fin	*pig pig /e/ peg*	*mop mop /a/ map*
set set /i/ sit	*wig wig /a/ wag*	*cup cup /a/ cap*
bat bat /u/ but	*net net /o/ not*	

Teacher Tip

SPELLINGS FOR LONG *Ii* Remember that only two ways to write the long *i* sound are introduced in kindergarten: *i* and *i_e*. When choosing your own words to illustrate the /ī/ sound, remember to also limit your choices to the *i* and *i_e* spellings for consistency.

Alphabetic Principle

Reviewing the Sound of Long *Ii*

Point to **Alphabet Sound Wall Card** Long *Ii*, and have students recite the rhyme for the sounds of *Ii*:

I's my name.

Two sounds have I:

Short i *in* pig,

Long i *in* pie.

Listening for Medial /ī/

Give each student an **Alphabet Letter Card** *Ii*. Ask students to raise the cards when they hear a word with the /ī/ sound. Try the following words:

four	**ride**	*list*	*trick*
time	**lion**	**rise**	**wide**
last	*milk*	**giant**	*dress*

Linking the Sound to the Letter

✦ Write the word *kit* on the board. Help students blend the word. Now write the word *kite* next to *kit*. Pronounce the new word, and remind students that the letter *e* signals the vowel *i* says its name or is long.

✦ Then write a pair of words on the board, one with the /ī/ sound spelled *i_e* and one with the /i/ sound. Read each pair of words, then ask students to identify the word with the /ī/ sound by signaling thumbs-up when you point to it.

bit ... **bite**	*hid* ... **hide**	**dime** ... *dim*
ride ... *rid*	*lit* ... **lite**	**ripe** ... *rip*

✦ Remind students to look for the *i_e* spelling in the words.

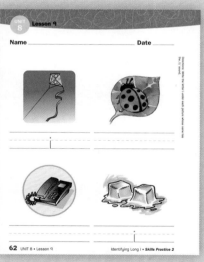

Skills Practice 2, p. 62

Monitor Progress to Differentiate Instruction   Formal Assessment ✓

Letter and Sound Identification Note how easily students identify the /ī/ sound.

APPROACHING LEVEL	**IF** ... students are having difficulty,	**THEN** ... help them complete **Reteach** page 155.
ON LEVEL	**IF** ... students need more practice,	**THEN** ... have them complete **Skills Practice 2** page 62.
ABOVE LEVEL	**IF** ... students would enjoy a challenging activity,	**THEN** ... have them sort through a variety of **Pocket Chart Picture Cards** to find objects whose names contain the /ī/ sound.

Pickled Peppers Big Book

✦ Display the **Pickled Peppers Big Book,** and turn to page 42, "Tent." Ask a volunteer to come up to the book and to point to the poet's name. Have a volunteer tell what an author, or poet does.

✦ Ask students to share anything they remember about the rhyme.

✦ Tell students you will read the rhyme aloud and you would like them to listen for the words with the /ī/ sound. Ask students to close their eyes as they listen.

✦ Have students share any /ī/ words they noticed while you read the rhyme aloud.

✦ Reread the rhyme, pointing to each word as you say it. Ask students to stop you each time you point to a word with the letter *Ii* in it. *skin, is, like, It's, I, unzip, outside, in, night, within* When you pause, work with students to evaluate the sound the letter *Ii* makes in each word. When you find a word with the /ī/ sound, have students stand up straight and say /ī/. *like, I, outside, night*

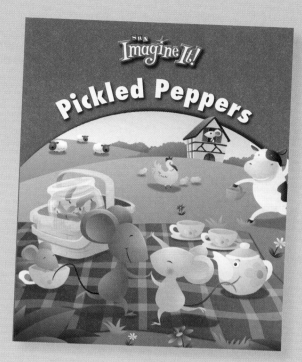

Pickled Peppers Big Book, p. 42

 Teacher Tip

SPELLINGS FOR *Ii* The word *night* in "Tent" displays a spelling for /ī/ besides *i* and *i_e*. If students question the spelling, explain that vowels can say their names in different ways. Tell them they will learn about other ways long *i* is written later.

Technology

Use the **Listening Library CD** to support the **Pickled Peppers** lessons.

 Audio CD

OBJECTIVES

Students will

✦ locate the title and the name of the illustrator.
✦ connect their own life experiences to the information in the poem.
✦ develop an understanding of vocabulary words.
✦ use the comprehension strategy Making Connections.

MATERIALS

✦ *Ready, Set, Grow! Big Book,* pp. 60–61
✦ Routines 5–7

Focus Question Why is it hard to see you are growing?

Something About Me
Anonymous
illustrated by Jeremy Tugeau

There's something about me
That I'm knowing.
There's something about me
That isn't showing.
I'm growing!

60

Ready, Set, Grow! Big Book, pp. 60–61

Poetry

Activate Prior Knowledge ROUTINE 5

✦ Tell students like the plants and butterflies they have been learning about, they are growing also. Ask students *How do you know you're growing? Do people tell you how much you've grown? What signs have you seen for yourselves?* Students might be aware they have grown out of some clothes or they can reach higher than they could before. Encourage students to share any changes they have noticed.

✦ Tell students you will read them a poem about a child growing. As you read the poem, relate what you already know to what you are reading, and encourage students to do the same.

✦ Have students discuss what they are learning about their own growing. A key concept of the poem is that on a day-to-day basis, we are unaware of our physical growth.

Preview the Poem ROUTINE 5

✦ Display the *Ready, Set, Grow! Big Book* opened to pages 60–61. Follow Routine 5, the previewing the selection routine, as you introduce the poem's title and the name of the illustrator. Point out that instead of the poet's name, the word *anonymous* appears. Explain that the word *anonymous* means the poet's name is either unknown or not given.

✦ Prepare to read the poem. Invite students to examine the picture and to share what they see. Ask if their families have charted their growth over the years.

Technology

To promote independent reading, encourage students to use Workshop to listen to the recording of the selection on the *Listening Library CD.* Invite them to follow along and say the words whenever they can.

Audio CD

Vocabulary

ROUTINE**6**

Vocabulary

knowing　　　　growing

✦ Follow Routine 6, the selection vocabulary routine, as you introduce the vocabulary words for this selection.

✦ Explain to students that the word *knowing* means "understanding." Use the following sentence to illustrate: *I would like knowing how plants make their own food.*

✦ Tell students if they are *growing,* they are getting bigger. Remind students of the ways they recognized they are growing.

Read the Poem

ROUTINE **7**

✦ Before reading the poem, read the Focus Question above it. Tell students to keep this question in mind as they listen to the poem.

✦ Follow Routine 7, the reading the selection routine, as you read aloud "Something About Me." Ask students to listen for rhyming words as you read.

✦ Invite students to ask questions or to think aloud about anything in the poem that interests or puzzles them.

Comprehension Strategies

For this poem, model the comprehension strategy Making Connections to help students connect information in the poem with their own experiences.

 Teacher Tip

MAKING CONNECTIONS Remind students to be active readers who make connections as they read. Encourage them to share the connections they make with the class.

 Differentiating Instruction **English Learners**

IF ... students are native speakers of Spanish, Urdu, or some other languages, **THEN ...** they may find the /ng/ sound difficult to pronounce, because it does not occur in their native languages. Demonstrate the position of the tongue and lips, and have students practice producing the sound alone and in simple words such as *song, sing,* and *sang.*

Ready, Set, Grow! Big Book, pp. 60–61

Comprehension Strategies

Teacher Modeling

1 Making Connections *This picture reminds me of the wall in our kitchen on which my parents kept track of how much I was growing. One year I grew three inches. I remember how surprised I was when that happened. But I couldn't tell I was growing. Thinking about my experience helps me understand how the boy in this picture feels.*

Discussing the Poem

✦ Review the Focus Question with students: Why is it hard to see you are growing? *Growing happens so slowly you can't see it happen.*

✦ Invite students to share their thoughts and ideas about the poem. Encourage students to discuss how they know they are growing and how that feels.

Purposes for Reading

✦ Remind students that they were listening to find out what the poem tells them about growing. Ask students what they learned about their own growing process from listening to this poem.

✦ Ask them what they liked best about the poem and why they liked it.

Vocabulary Review

Review with students the selection vocabulary words *knowing* and *growing*. Ask students the following questions:

• *What is the boy knowing in the poem?*
• *What does it mean that he is growing?*

Monitor Progress
Formal Assessment

to Differentiate Instruction

Making Connections Note how easily students can make connections.

APPROACHING LEVEL

IF ... students need help making connections,

THEN ... refer to Unit 8 Lesson 9 of the *Intervention Guide.*

ON LEVEL

IF ... students need to practice making connections,

THEN ... give them pictures of different situations, and ask them to explain to partners each connection they make to their own life experiences.

ABOVE LEVEL

IF ... students understand making connections,

THEN ... ask them to draw pictures or series of pictures that express their own growing and how that has changed their lives.

Language Arts

Students will
✦ revise text by moving, adding, and deleting.
✦ learn about the past tense of action words.
✦ extend story lines through words and illustrations.

✦ *Language Arts Big Book,* p. 9
✦ *Skills Practice 2,* pp. 63–64
✦ *Story Lines Big Book,* pp. 16–23

Writing Process 🕐

Revise: Revising Text

Teach

Display **Language Arts Big Book** page 9, and read the sentence *How Can I Make It Better?* Remind students that revising is an important step in writing something. Review the revising checklist.

Apply

✦ Retrieve the chart paper you have been using to write the class list of instructions.

✦ Focus students' attention on the revised list, and read it to them. Invite volunteers to make other suggestions for revision that might make the list better. Ask students to tell why they think their suggestions will make the writing better.

✦ Encourage students to look for ways to revise the text by moving items, adding ideas, and deleting text.

✦ On a new sheet of chart paper, create a final list of instructions for the class how-to description. Tell students they will continue the writing process in the next lesson.

Grammar, Usage, and Mechanics 🕐

Teach

✦ Remind students words that show action tell us what someone or something is doing. Explain that when someone did something before now, the word that shows action is in the past. Say *Yesterday, we walked to school.* Explain that when someone is doing something now, the word that shows action is in the present. Say *Today we walk to school.*

✦ Make two columns on the board: Past and Present. Write the following in the appropriate column: *I talk. I talked.* Explain that *I talk* is present tense because it is happening now. Explain that *I talked* is past tense because it happened before now.

✦ Point out the different spellings of *talk.* Explain that *-ed* usually shows the past tense, or something that happened before now. Present-tense action words might end in *s,* or they might have a helping word such as *is* or *are.* Repeat with other examples such as *jump, like,* and *play.*

Differentiating Instruction | **English Learners**

IF ... students have difficulty with the pronunciation of the *-ed* endings, **THEN ...** over time, they will assimilate how the pronunciation of the *-ed* ending varies; it may be /ed/ (*painted*), /d/ (*played*), or /t/ (*jumped*).

How can I make it better?

Revising
▶ I can name it.
▶ I can tell what it looks like.
▶ I can tell what it is.
▶ I can tell what it is doing.

doodle rides in a red wagon

The Writing Process · Revising

Language Arts Big Book, p. 9

Grammar, Usage, and Mechanics continued

Guided Practice

✦ Have students open their *Skills Practice 2* to pages 63–64.

✦ Work through the pages with students, and review their answers when you finish.

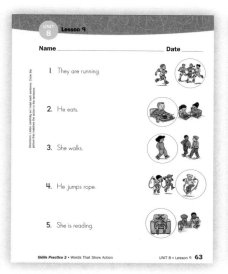 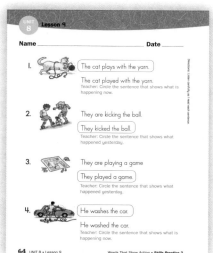

Skills Practice 2, pp. 63–64

Monitor Progress

Formal Assessment ✓

to Differentiate Instruction

Grammar Note how easily students use action words.

APPROACHING LEVEL

IF ... students are having difficulty,

THEN ... with your help, ask them to create a list of simple action words.

ON LEVEL

IF ... students need more practice,

THEN ... have them role-play simple action words.

ABOVE LEVEL

IF ... students are comfortable,

THEN ... have them complete *Challenge Activities* page 117.

Story Crafting

Story Lines

✦ Display the *Big Books Story Lines* interactive book, and open it to page 16, "Plants Move! I Can Prove It."

Story Lines Big Book, p. 16–23

✦ Review the story once again, pointing to each story frame as you read its accompanying text.

✦ When you reach page 21, spend some additional time discussing the extender frames students completed in the previous lesson. Ask students *Would you like to change or add anything to this frame?* Have volunteers tell why they think their suggestions will make the story better.

✦ Then turn to page 22, and tell students today they will complete the story. Guide students by asking questions to spark their creativity.

✦ Fill in the remaining extender frames, and guide the class in crafting story text to accompany the drawings.

✦ When students have completed the story, initiate a class discussion in which students reflect on their experiences with story extensions.

 Teacher Tip

REVISITING A STORY LINE During this activity that revisits "Plants Move! I Can Prove It," try to engage students who did not contribute to the story crafting process last time. Even students who are too shy to volunteer their ideas might enjoy sharing them if they are called upon.

OBJECTIVES

Students will
✦ review the letters of the alphabet.
✦ substitute medial phonemes to make new words.
✦ attach the /ī/ sound to the letter *li*.
✦ review how to write the numerals *2* and *3*.
✦ read and respond to a **Decodable.**

MATERIALS

✦ Routines 2, 4
✦ Supply Icons
✦ **Skills Practice 2,** p. 65
✦ **Decodable** 15

Calendar

Su	M	T	W	Th	F	S
		1	2	3	4	5
6	7	8	9	10	11	12
13	14	15	16	17	18	19
20	21	22	23	24	25	26
27	28	29	30	31		

Point to the box that represents today. Then ask students to identify the next weekend day. Invite a volunteer to point to Saturday. If necessary, review the differences between school days and weekend days.

Warming Up

MORNING MESSAGE

Today is _____.

In class we will _____.

_____, _____, and _____ are things that are tiny.

Kindergarten News

✦ Copy the text above on the board or on chart paper. Make several errors in the message; for example, omit the period at the end of the first sentence, spell *is* with the letter *z* instead of *s*, and begin the last sentence with a lowercase letter when you fill it in.

✦ After volunteers say some things that are small, invite students to proofread your writing. If possible, have students come up to the board to correct the errors.

✦ Reread the sentences. Ask students to tell you the word in the message with the /ī/ sound. *tiny*

Oral Language

Tell students they can make silly sentences with the letter of their choice. Ask a student to say a letter, and have the class work together to brainstorm words that begin with the letter and sound. Make a list on the board, and then have students mix up the words to create silly sentences.

✦ Sit with students in a circle to play the The Ship Is Loaded with _____ game. Choose a focus letter/sound, and say *This ship is loaded with things that begin with /f/. Flowers.* Then roll a ball to a student, and ask him or her to say another word that begins with the /f/ sound.

✦ Continue until students cannot think of any more /f/ words. If time permits, choose another letter, and continue the game.

Phonemic Awareness

Phoneme Manipulation: Medial Sounds

✦ Bring out the **Lion Puppet,** and tell students he wants to play the game in which he changes the sounds in words to make new words.

✦ Say a word, and have students repeat it. Then have the puppet tell students to change the medial phoneme, or vowel sound. Everyone will then say the new word. For example:

Teacher: *The word is* his.

Students: *his*

Puppet: *Now change the /i/ to /a/. How do you say the word now?*

Everyone: *has*

✦ Continue with these words:

got got /e/ get	*met* met /a/ mat
red red /o/ rod	*fan* fan /u/ fun
pit pit /a/ pat	*sock* sock /i/ sick
cut cut /a/ cat	*pink* pink /u/ punk

Teacher Tip

LETTER/SOUND FLUENCY Review the letters of the alphabet with students by writing on the board six to eight different letters, chosen randomly and presented in both small and capital form. Have students identify each letter, say the sound attached to the letter, and then continue with several other letters also out of alphabetical order. When students are presented with the vowels *Aa* and *Ii,* prompt them to give both the short- and long- vowel sounds.

Teacher Tip

BLENDING During these early lessons of blending long vowels, you may need to support students by blending with them. Gradually reduce your voice, and let students take more responsibility for the blending.

Alphabetic Principle

ROUTINE
2

Blending with the Sound of Long Ii

✦ Tell students today they are going to begin blending with the /ī/ sound written *i_e*. Write *i_e* on the board.

✦ To begin blending, first write on the board and blend the word *hid,* using the sound-by-sound blending routine. /h/ /i/ /d/

✦ Then next to *hid* write the letter *h,* and ask students to say the letter's sound. /h/ Write *i_e,* making sure to underscore the blank between the letters *i* and *e.* Ask the class for the sound of *i_e.* /ī/ If necessary, remind students that *i_e* says /ī/. Then blend the sounds with students. /h/ /ī/

✦ Point to the blank between *i* and *e,* and tell students we need to have another sound and letter to make a word. Then write the letter *d* in the blank to make the word *hide.* Have students give the sound /d/, and then have students blend the word. /h/ /ī/ /d/

✦ Ask students to read both words on the board. *hid, hide* Help them blend if necessary.

✦ Reread the words, and ask students to say the vowel sound in *hid* and the vowel sound in *hide.* Then ask volunteers to point to the letter or letters that make the vowel sounds.

✦ Continue this blending procedure using the following word pairs. After blending each pair, have students reread the words naturally as they would speak them.

pin ... pine	*Tim ... time*
bid ... bide	*sit ... site*

✦ When the blending is completed, choose a couple of words, and have students use them in sentences. Encourage students to extend the sentences by asking them to tell where, why, how, or when. Have them answer in complete sentences.

Technology

Have students use the *eGames* activity to practice the vowel sounds they have learned.

Audio CD

Penmanship

✦ Distribute a sheet of writing paper to each student, or use **White Boards** turned to the sides with writing lines.

✦ Place the Supply Icon for *pencil* on the board or in the **Pocket Chart.**

✦ Review with students the procedure for forming the numeral *2* while they make the strokes in the air with their fingers.

✦ Repeat the review for the numeral *3*.

✦ Ask students to write one row of numeral *2*s and one row of numeral *3*s on the writing paper.

Guided Practice

✦ Have students complete **Skills Practice 2** page 65 for additional practice writing the numerals *2* and *3*.

✦ Have students practice writing the numerals *2* and *3* on the lines.

✦ Then ask students to identify the number of apples on each tree and to write the numbers *2* and *3* on the appropriate lines.

✦ After students have finished, be sure to review their work. Help them proofread, using the established procedure.

 Differentiating Instruction **English Learners**

IF . . . students have difficulty writing in rows, **THEN . . .** bear in mind that some languages are written and read vertically or from right to left. Make sure that English Learners are writing from left to right.

Skills Practice 2, p. 65

Monitor Progress to Differentiate Instruction

Formal Assessment ✓

Penmanship Note how easily students write the numerals *2* and *3*.

APPROACHING LEVEL

IF . . . students are having difficulty,　　THEN . . . help them complete **Reteach** page 156.

ON LEVEL

IF . . . students need more practice,　　THEN . . . have them draw pictures of two objects and then write the numeral *2* beneath the picture. Continue with the numeral *3*.

ABOVE LEVEL

IF . . . students would enjoy a challenging activity,　　THEN . . . have them work independently to complete page 118 in **Challenge Activities.**

Mike and
Spike

by Tristan Horrom   illustrated by Kate Flanagan

Decodable 15

Teacher Tips

HIGH-FREQUENCY WORDS Take every opportunity to focus students' attention on the words *they* and *down,* as well as the previously introduced high-frequency words, in the context of their daily **Big Book** reading and in other classroom print. Tell students these are words they will see often in books and other print.

STUDENT PRACTICE Before sending home the takehome versions of the **Decodables,** listen to students read a page or two during Workshop to be sure they are comfortable and confident reading their books.

Technology

Use **eDecodable** *Mike and Spike* to reinforce high-frequency words *down* and *they* and the /ī/ sound.

 Audio CD

Reading a Decodable

ROUTINE ROUTINE

Decodable 15: Mike and Spike

High-Frequency Words: *down, they*

✦ The high-frequency words introduced are *down* and *they.* Write *down* on the board, and read it aloud. Have students repeat it aloud with you. Then have students say the word on their own. Repeat the process with *they.*

✦ Explain to students that the word *down* is used to talk about where something is. Ask all the students to stand, and then say *Look down at the floor.* Point out that *down* is where the floor is. Remind students of the high-frequency word *up.* Discuss how *up* is the opposite of *down.* Have students stand again, and say *Look up at the ceiling.*

✦ Tell students the word *they* is used when talking about a group made of two or more people, not including oneself. Say *The students in Mrs. Martin's class are nice. They are nice.*

✦ Point again to *down* written on the board, and have students read the word independently. Do the same with *they.*

✦ Have students work with partners to say a few sentences using the words *down* and *they.* Review the high-frequency words introduced in previous lessons.

Blending

Before reading **Decodable** 15, review the blending procedure with students. Choose words with the /ī/ sound written *i_e,* such as *time, kite,* and *lime.* After blending, have students make and extend sentences for each word.

Reading Recommendations

✦ Distribute copies of **Decodable** 15. Have students browse the books and look at the pictures, commenting on what they see and making predictions about what they think the story will be about.

✦ Point to the high-frequency words *down* and *they* in the text, and pronounce them. Then have students point to the words and read them aloud.

✦ Hold up your book, and read the title, pointing to each word. Read the names of the author and the illustrator aloud, pointing to each name as you say it. Ask students to explain the jobs of author and illustrator.

✦ Read the **Decodable,** following the established procedure. (See Routine 4 for a detailed description.) After you have read the story, reread the title, and have students repeat after you. Then have students read it chorally with you.

Mike and Spike

by Tristan Horrom   illustrated by Kate Flanagan

Mike did not have a pup.

3

Mike is five! Mike gets Spike!

4

Mike and Spike hike up and down.

5

They like to hike and have fun.

6

They like to ride a bike.

7

Spike is big! Down, Spike, down!

8

Responding

✦ Display the **High-Frequency Flash Cards** for *down* and *they*. Have students find and point to these high-frequency words in the story. Ask students to identify in the story any of the previously introduced high-frequency words.

✦ Ask students to tell about any difficult or interesting words they read in the story. Review each word that students identify.

✦ Have students retell the story event by event using the familiar "and then" format. Remind them to use the words and the pictures to understand story events. Encourage them by asking questions such as *What's happening on this page?* or *What is Spike doing now?* Have students point to the page as they answer.

✦ Have volunteers take turns reading pages of the story aloud. Guide them as necessary.

✦ Make copies of the story for students to take home. A black-and-white version of the story is available in *Pre-Decodable and Decodable Takehomes Blackline Masters.*

Decodable 15, inside back cover

Reading and Responding

Students will

✦ experiment with growing things.
✦ describe their observations orally.
✦ record their observations with drawings.
✦ develop an understanding of vocabulary words.

✦ Assorted plants
✦ Drawing paper
✦ Crayons, markers
✦ Index card

INQUIRY PLANNER

WEEK 1	✦ Begin discussing and sharing ideas. ✦ Think about a question for the **Concept/Question Board.**
WEEK 2	✦ Begin investigating and collecting information. ✦ Generate a question and/or idea for the **Concept/Question Board.**
WEEK 3	✦ Share your findings with others. ✦ Do you have **more questions?**

Inquiry

✦ Talk with students about the selection "Becoming Butterflies." Ask questions such as the following:

- *Why did Miss Dana bring caterpillars to her classroom?*
- *What grew in this selection?*
- *How does the caterpillar change into a butterfly?*
- *Why was it important to watch the caterpillar over a period of time?*
- *How is what the children did in Miss Dana's class like what you are doing in our class?*

✦ Ask students to share what they are learning from their observations. Share some of the students' tables.

✦ Have students start thinking about how they can share this information with other people, such as other kindergartners or their families. They may want to use their tables. They can write their conjectures on other sheets of paper. Over the next few days, they can write how the changes they are seeing support or do not support their conjectures, or they may want to use their observations to write daily logs of what happened. They may want to take photographs of what they are observing and write about how it has changed. They may want to write about how their knowledge grew.

✦ Over the next few days, have students continue to make their observations. During Workshop, have the groups take time to decide on how they want to share their findings and begin working on the product.

Small-Group Time [Small Group]

✦ Have the groups check the results of their plant investigations and discuss any changes they notice in the plants. Remind students to record the results of their findings by making another drawing of their plants.

✦ Tell groups they will share the results of their investigations with the class when they get together as a large group.

Whole-Group Time Whole Group

✦ Invite each group to share what they learned about growing things from their investigations. You may need to prompt students with questions such as the following:

- *Did you learn anything new about plants from your investigation?*
- *What did your investigation tell you about how plants grow and change?*

✦ Discuss with students how sharing knowledge helps us and others learn. Invite them to think about a way to share what they have learned about growing things.

Concept Vocabulary

The word *plant* is the second concept vocabulary word for Unit 8. Write the word on an index card, and post it in your classroom. Explain to students that the word *plant* means "to put in the ground to grow." Tell students people with gardens have to *plant* seeds in the spring to have flowers and vegetables in the summer. Discuss how the word *plant* relates to the concept of growing things. Use the word in a sentence, and have students repeat the word after you. Tell students you will use the word *plant* every day, and encourage them to do the same. If you use the word frequently, students will feel comfortable using it too. Encourage students to bring in pictures and drawings that illustrate the word *plant* to post on the **Concept/Question Board.**

Concept/Question Board

Point out to students that as scientists do research, they discover new questions. Encourage students to share any new questions they have about growing things. Explain that as they think of new ideas, they will discover new questions. Invite students to bring in additional items to post on the Board, such as photographs they have taken and drawings they have made of plants, animals, insects, and people showing growth.

Teacher Tips

QUESTIONS Some seeds take less time to germinate than others, so some groups may not actually see their seeds sprout. Capitalize on this, and take time to raise more questions: *Why is it that not all seeds sprouted at the same time? Why did only one tadpole have the beginning of its frog legs? The plant in the dark did not die. What do you think will happen if we keep it in the dark longer? Why?*

RECREATIONAL READING Because it is important to read daily to your students, choose a book from the Additional Reading listed in the Unit Overview, and find a time during the day to read the book aloud to your students.

Differentiating Instruction   English Learners

IF ... students have difficulty with pronunciation, **THEN ...** give them an opportunity to practice their responses with you before they present them to the class.

Students will
✦ draw pictures to illustrate instructions.
✦ review present-tense and past-tense action words.
✦ review action words through game play.

✦ *Skills Practice 2,* p. 66

Writing Process

Draft: Drawing Pictures to Illustrate Instructions

Teach

✦ Remind students that they can tell a story with pictures, with words, or with both. Tell them they will draw pictures to show the steps of their instructions for how to do something.

✦ Take out the chart paper from the previous lesson, and review the revised text for the how-to instructions.

✦ Tell students you would like them each to draw three pictures to help show the important steps in the instructions.

Apply

✦ Distribute drawing paper to each student, and make art supplies available.

✦ Allow students time to begin drawing their pictures. Invite students to tell you why they are making the pictures look the way they do. Be sure students create their drawings with an awareness of the proper order of the list of instructions.

✦ Ask students to sign their names to their work. Collect students' pictures, and store them until the next lesson.

 Teacher Tip

PLAN AHEAD In preparation for the Writing Process activity, have drawing paper and art supplies on hand.

Grammar, Usage, and Mechanics

Teach

✦ Remind students the present tense of a word that shows action explains something that is happening now.

✦ Remind students the past tense of a word that shows action explains something that happened before now.

✦ Ask students what they are doing right now. Explain that they are listening or learning. Write *You learn* and *You listen* on the board.

✦ Ask students what they did in school yesterday. Explain that they listened and learned. Write *You learned* and *You listened* on the board. Compare verb endings as you point to and read aloud each phrase.

Differentiating Instruction **English Learners**

IF . . . students confuse verb inflections that use *s* with plural endings, **THEN . . .** use example sentences to show how they can use context to determine whether an *s* ending is a plural or a verb inflection. (Confusion is especially likely with words such as *roll* and *brush* that can be both nouns and verbs.) Example: *The brushes are in the drawer. My mom brushes my hair.*

Grammar, Usage, and Mechanics continued

Guided Practice

✦ Have students open their **Skills Practice 2** to page 66.

✦ Work through the page with students, and review their answers when you finish.

Skills Practice 2, p. 66

Monitor Progress

Formal Assessment ✔

to Differentiate Instruction

Grammar Note how quickly students understand the concepts of past and present.

APPROACHING LEVEL

IF ... students are having difficulty,

THEN ... have them complete **Reteach** page 157.

ON LEVEL

IF ... students need more practice,

THEN ... have them look at three sentences that you have written on the board and tell you which show past and present tense.

ABOVE LEVEL

IF ... students are comfortable,

THEN ... have them work with a partner to identify three sentences you have written on the board, and circle the words which show past and present tense.

GAME Day

Action Words Charades

✦ In advance of Game Day, create a list of simple action words to assign to students when it is their turn. Choose a few more action words than you have students. You will need one word to demonstrate how to play, one word for each student to role-play, and a few words in case a tiebreaker is necessary.

✦ On Game Day, group the class into two even-numbered teams. If you have an odd number of students, one team will have a student perform twice to even out the game.

✦ Remind students one student from each team will silently role-play a word that shows action.

✦ Only one team performs at a time, so flip a coin to determine which team goes first. Allow each performer a one-minute time frame to get their team members to guess the word they are role-playing.

✦ Write Yesterday and Today in columns on the board. When the correct answer is said, guide the students in listing both the past and present tenses of the verb.

✦ List each team's correct guesses on the board. The team with the most correct guesses wins.

✦ In the case of a tie, have a final tiebreaker in which you role-play a more difficult action word and the first team that shouts out the correct word wins.

 Teacher Tip

GAME RULES Tell students it is very important to be silent; any students who speak while they role-play a word will, after one warning, lose their turn and, after two warnings, lose a point for their team.

Lesson Planner

Day 1

Day 2

Sounds and Letters

MATERIALS

- ✦ *Pocket Chart Letter Cards*
- ✦ *Alphabet Letter Cards: Aa* and *Ii*
- ✦ Routines 2, 4
- ✦ *Skills Practice 2*, pp. 67, 68, 71–73
- ✦ *Pocket Chart Picture Cards*
- ✦ *Pickled Peppers Big Book*, pp. 13, 16, 40–41
- ✦ *Teacher's Resource Book*, p. 38
- ✦ *Decodable* 16

Day 1

Warming Up, p. T170
Phonemic Awareness
Phoneme Manipulation: Medial Sounds, p. T171
Alphabetic Principle
- Reviewing the Long Sounds of *Aa* and *Ii*, p. T172
- Listening for Medial /ā/ and /ī/, p. T172
- Linking the Sound to the Letter, p. T172
- Penmanship, p. T173

Day 2

Warming Up, pp. T180–T181
Phonemic Awareness
Phoneme Segmentation, p. T181
Alphabetic Principle
- Reviewing the Long Sounds of *Aa* and *Ii*, p. T182
- Blending, p. T182
- *Pickled Peppers Big Book*, p. T183

Reading and Responding

MATERIALS

- ✦ *Science Lap Book*, pp. 28–35
- ✦ Routines 5–7
- ✦ *Story Time Collection:* Zinnia's Flower Garden
- ✦ *Read Aloud Collection:* What's Alive?
- ✦ *Ready, Set, Grow!* Big Book
- ✦ *Home Connection*, pp. 65–66

Day 1

Science Link, p. T174
Vocabulary, p. T175
Read the Selection, p. T175
Comprehension Strategies, p. T176
Print and Book Awareness, p. T177
Vocabulary Review, p. T177

Day 2

Science Link, p. T184
Vocabulary, p. T184
Read the Selection, p. T185
Comprehension Strategies, p. T186
Reading with a Writer's Eye, p. T187
Discussing the Selection, p. T187
Vocabulary Review, p. T187

Language Arts

MATERIALS

- ✦ *Ready, Set, Grow! Big Book,* p. 62
- ✦ *Language Arts Big Book,* p. 10
- ✦ *Skills Practice 2,* pp. 69–70, 74
- ✦ *Willy the Wisher,* p. 83
- ✦ *Transparency* 42
- ✦ *Thinking Crowns*
- ✦ *Teacher's Resource Book,* p. 39

Day 1

Writing Process
Revise: Revising Pictures to Clarify, p. T178
Fine Art
Discussing Fine Art, p. T179

Day 2

Writing Process
Model: Locating Errors in Text, p. T188
Grammar, Usage, and Mechanics, pp. T188–T189
Willy the Wisher, p. T189

Monitor Progress

- ✔ = Formal Assessment
- ⑧ = Benchmark Assessment

Day 1

✔ Numeral Identification, p. T173

Day 2

✔ *Lesson Assessment Annotated Teacher's Edition,* pp. 79A–79B
✔ Blending, p. T182
✔ Past and Future Tenses, p. T189

Day 3

Warming Up, pp. T190–T191
Phonemic Awareness
Phoneme Segmentation, p. T191
Alphabetic Principle
- Reviewing the Long Sounds of *Aa* and *Ii*, p. T192
- Listening for Medial /ā/ and /ī/, p. T192
- Linking the Sounds to the Letter, p. T192
- Penmanship, p. T193

Preview and Prepare, p. T194
Vocabulary, p. T195
Read the Selection, p. T195
Comprehension Strategies, pp. T196, T198, T200, T202
Print and Book Awareness, pp. T197, T199, T201, T203
Discussing the Selection, p. T203
Vocabulary Review, p. T203

1st READ

Writing Process
Revise: Proofreading and Making Changes, p. T204
Story Crafting
Working with the New: Developing Characters and Plots, p. T205

- ✔ *Lesson Assessment Book,* p. 79
- ✔ **Numeral Identification,** p. T193

Day 4

Warming Up, p. T206
Phonemic Awareness
Phoneme Segmentation, p. T207
Alphabetic Principle
- Reviewing the Long Sounds of *Aa* and *Ii*, p. T208
- Blending, p. T208
- *Pickled Peppers Big Book,* p. T209

Preview and Prepare, p. T210
Vocabulary, p. T210
Read the Selection, p. T211
Comprehension Strategy, pp. T212, T214, T216, T218
Comprehension Skills, pp. T213, T215, T217
Reading with a Writer's Eye, pp. T213, T215, T217, T219
Discussing the Selection, p. T219
Vocabulary Review, p. T219

2nd READ

Writing Process
Present: Sharing Drawings, p. T220
Grammar, Mechanics, and Usage, pp. T220–T221
Story Crafting
Working with the New: Developing Characters and Plots, p. T221

- ✔ *Lesson Assessment Book,* pp. 79–80
- ✔ **Blending,** p. T208
- ✔ **Action Words,** p. T220

Day 5

Warming Up, pp. T222–T223
Phonemic Awareness
Phoneme Segmentation, p. T223
Alphabetic Principle
- Reviewing the Long Sounds of *Aa* and *Ii*, p. T224
- Listening for Initial /ā/ and /ī/, p. T224
- Blending, p. T224
- Penmanship, p. T225
Reading a *Decodable*
Decodable 16: *A Nut Pile,* pp. T226–T227

Theme Wrap-Up and Review, p. T228

Writing Process
Present: Sharing Their Drawings, p. T229
Grammar, Usage, and Mechanics, p. T229
Unit Assessment, pp. T230–T231
Unit Celebration
- Celebrate Growth!, p. T232
- Inquiry Wrap-Up, p. T233

- ✔ *Lesson Assessment Book,* pp. 81–83
- Comprehension Observation Log
- ✔ **Numeral Review,** p. T225
- ✔ **Action Words,** p. T229
- Ⓑ *Benchmark Assessment,* Benchmark 5

Student Resources

Story Time Selection

Zinnia's Flower Garden

by Monica Wellington

Audio CD

Big Books

Science Lap Book

Ready, Set, Grow!

Pickled Peppers

Decodable 16: *A Nut Pile*

Teacher Support

Language Arts Big Book

Teacher's Resource Book

Willy the Wisher

Curriculum Connections

- Math Card
- Social Studies Card
- Science Card
- Art Card

Additional Skills Practice

Approaching Level	On Level	English Learner	Above Level
Reteach	**Skills Practice 2**	**English Learner Support Activities**	**Challenge Activities**
• Blending, p. 158	Blending, pp. 68, 72	Lessons 11–15	Blending, p. 119
• Numeral Identification, p. 160	Numeral Identification, pp. 67, 71, 73		Numeral Identification, pp. 120–121
• Past, Present, and Future Tenses, p. 159	Past, Present, and Future Tenses, pp. 69–70, 74		Past, Present, and Future Tenses, p. 122

Lessons **11-15** Overview

Differentiating Instruction
for Workshop

Day 1

Approaching Level	On Level	English Learner	Above Level
Sounds and Letters			
Alphabetic Principle: Refer to Unit 8 Lesson 11 of the **Intervention Guide** for additional support activities.	**Alphabetic Principle:** Have students think of words with the /ī/ sound as you write them on the board or chart paper.	**Alphabetic Principle:** Refer to Unit 8 Lesson 11 of the **English Learner Support Guide.**	**Alphabetic Principle:** Students use the **eGames** activity for this unit to review vowels and their sounds.
Reading and Responding			
Preview: Students browse the illustrations from "All Living Things" in the *Science Lap Book* and point out any words they recognize or illustrations that interest them.	**Preview:** Have students discuss the importance of living things and how animals and plants depend on one another for survival.	**Preview:** Refer to Unit 8 Lesson 11 of the **English Learner Support Guide.**	**Preview:** Students research on the Internet or in the school library about plant growth. Post their findings on the **Concept/Question Board.**
Language Arts			
Writing: With your help, students create one simple sentence.	**Writing:** Show students two sentences you have written with errors.	**Writing:** Students select words from a list to complete simple sentence frames.	**Writing:** Each student writes one sentence with errors.

Day 2

Approaching Level	On Level	English Learner	Above Level

Sounds and Letters

Alphabetic Principle: Work with students to use *eGames* for practice identifying vowels and their sounds.

Alphabetic Principle: Have students use *eSkills* to review the sounds of /ā/ and /ī/.

Alphabetic Principle: Refer to Unit 8 Lesson 12 of the *English Learner Support Guide.*

Alphabetic Principle: Students write down all the words they can think of that begin with /ā/ and /ī/.

Reading and Responding

Comprehension: Say each selection vocabulary word (*carried, sunflower,* and *provide*) and have students repeat the word. If students need further help with definitions, use illustrations and demonstrations to aid in their comprehension.

Comprehension: Invite students to discuss "All Living Things" and what they liked best about the selection.

Comprehension: Preview *Zinnia's Flower Garden* with students, and have them point to any words or illustrations that interest them.

Comprehension: Bring in pictures and information about gardens, and have students discuss things that interest them about the pictures or the selection.

Language Arts

Writing: Rewrite the simple sentence on the board—this time with errors.

Grammar: Refer to Unit 8 Lesson 12 of the *Intervention Guide* for additional support for this Grammar activity.

Writing: Students work as a group to proofread the sentences from Day 11.

Grammar: Students make lists of three action words.

Writing: Show students two sentences you have written with errors.

Grammar: Refer to Unit 8 Lesson 12 of the *English Learner Support Guide.*

Writing: Students challenge partners to proofread and identify the errors in their sentences.

Grammar: Students write simple sentences in present tense.

Differentiating Instruction
for Workshop

Day 3

Approaching Level	On Level	English Learner	Above Level
Sounds and Letters			
Alphabetic Principle: Refer to Unit 8 Lesson 13 of the **Intervention Guide** for activities to help students.	**Alphabetic Principle:** Students make a collage of the letters *Aa* and *Ii* cut out from magazines and catalogs and identify their long- and short-vowel sounds.	**Alphabetic Principle:** Refer to Unit 8 Lesson 13 of the **English Learner Support Guide.**	**Alphabetic Principle:** Students work independently to use the *eSkills* activities for review of the /ā/ and /ī/ sounds.
Reading and Responding			
Preview: Have students browse *Zinnia's Flower Garden* and point out any illustrations that interest them or what they might learn about plants from the story.	**Preview:** Have students discuss connections between Zinnia's garden and what they have learned about how plants grow.	**Preview:** Refer to Unit 8 Lesson 13 of the **English Learner Support Guide.**	**Preview:** Discuss with students connections between *Zinnia's Flower Garden* and gardens the students have seen in their own lives.
Language Arts			
Writing: Students help you proofread and identify the errors you have made.	**Writing:** Students discuss as a group what errors they see in the sentences from Day 11.	**Writing:** Circle the errors in the sentences from Day 12. Help students identify each error from a list you write on the board.	**Writing:** Students challenge partners to correct the errors.

T164   Theme: Ready, Set, Grow!

Approaching Level	On Level	English Learner	Above Level
Sounds and Letters			
Phonemic Awareness: Continue phoneme segmentation with students, having them identify the initial, medial, and final phonemes in words such as *dog, fun,* and *hat.*	**Phonemic Awareness:** Use *eSkills* to review phoneme manipulation.	**Phonemic Awareness:** Refer to Unit 8 Lesson 14 of the *English Learner Support Guide.*	**Phonemic Awareness:** Give students an assortment of decodable *Pocket Chart Word Cards,* and have them segment the phonemes in the words.
Reading and Responding			
Comprehension: Have students retell the story *Zinnia's Flower Garden* in their own words. Encourage them to use words such as *first, then,* and *last.*	**Comprehension:** On chart paper, write down the words *first, then,* and *last.* Ask students to discuss the sequence of events in *Zinnia's Flower Garden.*	**Comprehension:** Refer to Unit 8 Lesson 14 of the *English Learner Support Guide.*	**Comprehension:** Have students browse past units and discuss the sequence of events in each selection.
Language Arts			
Writing: Students help you revise your sentence. **Grammar:** Have students complete *Reteach* page 159.	**Writing:** Students work as a group to revise the sentences. **Grammar:** Students write each action word in past and present tenses.	**Writing:** Help students recall the rules that apply to each error and revise to correct the errors. **Grammar:** Refer to Unit 8 Lesson 14 of the *English Learner Support Guide.*	**Writing:** Students share what they learned with the group. **Grammar:** Students rewrite the sentences in past tense.

Day 5

Approaching Level	On Level	English Learner	Above Level
Sounds and Letters			
Reading a *Decodable*: Reread ***Decodable*** 16 with students, reviewing what is happening in the illustrations and having individual students read pages independently.	**Reading a *Decodable*:** Students reread ***Decodable*** 16 with partners and track print from left to right.	**Reading a *Decodable*:** Review ***Decodable*** 16 with students, pointing to the high-frequency words *some* and *there* as you read aloud to them.	**Reading a *Decodable*:** Have students reread using ***eDecodable*** *A Nut Pile.*
Reading and Responding			
Review: Have students discuss unit selections they liked best and why.	**Review:** Students group into pairs and retell each selection to one another in their own words.	**Review:** Review the selection *Zinnia's Flower Garden,* and have students talk about any questions or wonderings they have about the selection.	**Review:** Students review each selection and how they relate to the unit theme.
Language Arts			
Writing: Discuss with students how easy or difficult they found this activity. **Grammar:** Help students choose one action word and write it in past, present, and future tenses.	**Writing:** Students share their findings with you. **Grammar:** With your help, students write each word in the future tense.	**Writing:** Discuss with students how easy or difficult they found this activity. **Grammar:** Refer to Unit 8 Lesson 15 of the ***English Learner Support Guide.***	**Writing:** Students discuss whether or not they found this activity challenging. **Grammar:** Have students complete ***Challenge Activities*** page 122.

Resources for
Differentiating Instruction

English Learner

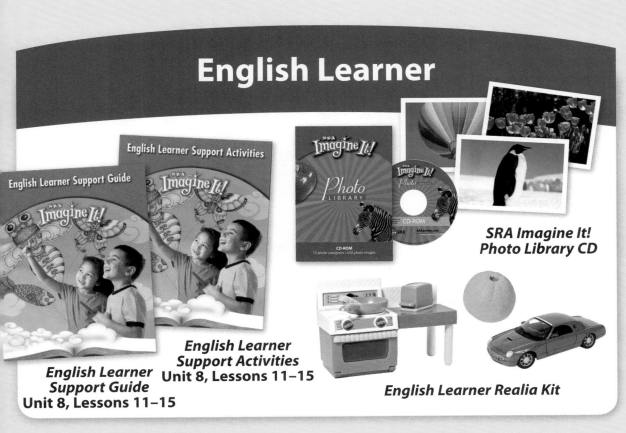

English Learner Support Guide

English Learner Support Activities

SRA Imagine It! Photo Library CD

English Learner Support Activities Unit 8, Lessons 11–15

English Learner Support Guide Unit 8, Lessons 11–15

English Learner Realia Kit

Approaching Level

Intervention

Intervention Guide

Intervention Workbook

Intervention Guide

Workshop Kits

- High Frequency Words
- Letter Recognition
- Phonemic Awareness
- Print and Book Awareness
- Sequencing

Technology

eDecodable A Nut Pile

eSkills & eGames

Listening Library CD

Listening Library Unit 8

Lesson Assessment

Monitor Progress to Differentiate Instruction

Use these summative assessments along with your informal observations to assess student mastery.

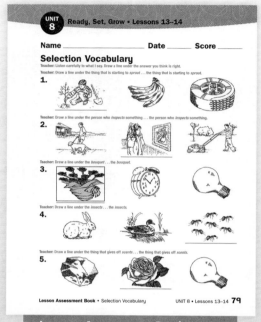

Lesson Assessment Book, p. 79

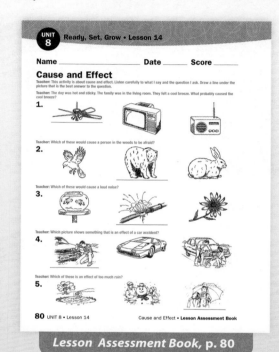

Lesson Assessment Book, p. 80

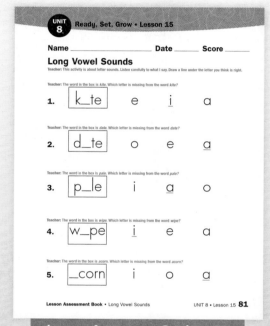

Lesson Assessment Book, p. 81

Lesson Assessment Book, p. 82

UNIT 8 Ready, Set, Grow • Lesson 15

Name _____ Date _____ Score _____

High-Frequency Words
Teacher: This activity is about words you have learned. Look at each group of words and listen to what I say. Draw a line under the word I say.

Teacher: The word is can. Draw a line under can.

1. <u>can</u>   is   was

Teacher: The word is it. Draw a line under it.

2. me   <u>it</u>   way

Teacher: The word is go. Draw a line under go.

3. him   my   <u>go</u>

Teacher: The word is up. Draw a line under up.

4. no   <u>up</u>   her

Teacher: The word is at. Draw a line under at.

5. <u>at</u>   be   so

Lesson Assessment Book • High-Frequency Words   UNIT 8 • Lesson 15 **83**

Lesson Assessment Book, p. 83

Lesson Assessment Book

Comprehension Observation Log

Student _____ Date _____

Unit _____ Lesson _____ Selection Title _____

General Comprehension
Concepts discussed: _____

Behavior Within a Group
Articulates, expresses ideas: _____

Joins discussions: _____

Collaborates (such as works well with other students, works alone): _____

Role in Group
Role (such as leader, summarizer, questioner, critic, observer, non-participant): ___

Flexibility (changes roles when necessary): _____

Use of Reading Strategies
Uses strategies when needed (either those taught or student's choice of strategy)/Describes strategies used:
_____
_____

Changes strategies when appropriate: _____

Changes Since Last Observation

110   Comprehension Observation Log • **Lesson Assessment Book**

Lesson Assessment Annotated Teacher's Edition, p. 110

The Comprehension Observation Log, found in the **Lesson Assessment Annotated Teacher's Edition,** is a vehicle for recording anecdotal information about individual student performance on an ongoing basis. Information such as students' strengths and weaknesses can be recorded at any time the occasion warrants. It is recommended that you maintain a folder for each student where you can store the logs for purposes of comparison and analysis as the school year progresses. You will gradually build up a comprehensive file that reveals which students are progressing smoothly and which students need additional help.

Use **Benchmark Assessment,** Benchmark 5, to target students at risk for reading failure.

Sounds and Letters

OBJECTIVES

Students will

✦ create words that have the /ī/ sound.
✦ substitute medial phonemes to make new words.
✦ review the /ā/ and /ī/ sounds.
✦ practice writing the numeral 4.

MATERIALS

✦ **Pocket Chart Letter Cards** *d, e, f, i, l, m, n*
✦ **Alphabet Letter Cards** *Aa* and *Ii* for each student
✦ Supply Icon
✦ **Skills Practice 2,** p. 67
✦ **Pocket Chart Picture Card** 5

Calendar

Su	M	T	W	Th	F	S
		1	2	3	4	5
6	7	8	9	10	11	12
13	14	15	16	17	18	19
20	21	22	23	24	25	26
27	28	29	30	31		

Point to the box that represents today. Ask a student to identify on the calendar the last day they were in school. Help students count how many days ago that was.

Teacher Tip

ACTIVITY EXTENSION If time allows, extend the Grab Bag of Letters activity, using a word with the long *a* sound. For example, you might use the word part *-ake* along with any of these initial letters: *b, f, l, m, r, s, t, w.*

Warming Up

MORNING MESSAGE

Today is _____.

(Child's name)'s favorite game is _____.

The color of a fire truck is red.

Kindergarten News

✦ Copy the text above on the board or on chart paper. Create a Secret Word by covering the word *red* in the last sentence with a self-sticking note. Tell students there is a Secret Word today. Ask volunteers to use clues to find the answer. When a student gives the correct word, ask how he or she knew. Point out that the rest of the sentence is a clue as to what the Secret Word is.

✦ Discuss the letters and words in the message. You might ask students to identify a word with the long *a* sound or the long *i* sound. *Today, game; fire*

Phoneme Replacement

✦ This version of Grab Bag of Letters is slightly different from earlier versions. Place the selected **Pocket Chart Letter Cards** on a low table so students can choose the correct letter to make the change you call for.

✦ Put the letters *i, n,* and *e* in the **Pocket Chart,** or have three students line up in front of the class, each one holding a card: *i, n, e.* Blend the sounds, and say *ine.* Remind students the *e* signals the vowel and says its name, and *i_e* says /ī/. Place on the table the letters *d, f, l,* and *m.* Ask *How can we make the word* line? Students can put the **Pocket Chart Letter Card** in the **Pocket Chart** or take it and stand in front of the three students holding the *i, n,* and *e* letters.

✦ Ask other students to make *dine, fine,* and *mine.*

Phonemic Awareness 🕐

Phoneme Manipulation: Medial Sounds

✦ Bring out the **Lion Puppet,** and tell students he wants to play the game in which he changes the sounds in words to make new words.

✦ Say a word, and have students repeat it. Then have the puppet tell students to change the medial phoneme, or vowel sound. Everyone will then say the new word. For example:

Teacher:	*The word is* last.
Students:	*last*
Puppet:	*Now change the /a/ to /i/. How do you say the word now?*
Everyone:	*list*

✦ Continue with these words:

duck duck /e/ deck	*sack* sack /i/ sick
hall hall /i/ hill	*want* want /e/ went
miss miss /a/ mass	*suck* suck /a/ sack
best best /u/ bust	*fill* fill /u/ full

Technology

Have students use the *eSkills* activity for this unit for additional practice with phoneme manipulation.

Audio CD

Teacher Tip

BODY MOVEMENTS Work with students to create motions that accompany the *Aa* and *Ii* rhymes. For example, students might point their thumbs at their chests for the first line, put their hands to their ears for the second line, crouch down for the third line, and stand tall with their fingertips touching for the final line.

Alphabetic Principle

Reviewing the Sounds of Long *Aa* and Long *Ii*

✦ Point to **Alphabet Sound Wall Card** Long *Aa*, and have students recite the rhyme for the sounds of *Aa*:

A's my name.

Two sounds I make:

Short a *in* lamb,

Long a *in* cake.

✦ Continue in the same way with **Alphabet Sound Wall Card** Long *Ii*, and have students recite the rhyme:

I's my name.

Two sounds have I:

Short i *in* pig,

Long i *in* pie.

Listening for Medial /ā/ and /ī/

Give each student one **Alphabet Letter Card** *Aa* and one **Alphabet Letter Card** *Ii*. Ask students to raise the *Aa* cards when they hear a word that has the /ā/ sound. They should raise the *Ii* cards when they hear the /ī/ sound. Try the following words:

date	*rice*	*bite*	*tame*
dive	*gave*	*wave*	*paste*
mine	*bake*	*fine*	*bride*

Linking the Sound to the Letter

✦ Write a pair of words on the board, one with the /ī/ sound spelled *i_e* and one with the /ā/ sound spelled *a_e*.

✦ Tell students you will say one of the words and they should give you the thumbs-up signal when you point to it. Try these words:

time . . . tame	*wide . . . wade*
rate . . . rite	*lane . . . line*
pine . . . pane	*rice . . . race*

Penmanship

✦ Distribute a sheet of writing paper to each student, or use **White Boards** turned to the sides with writing lines.

✦ Place the Supply Icon for *pencil* on the board or in the **Pocket Chart.**

✦ Using the established procedure, review with students how to form the numeral *4*. Say *Begin here. Go straight down halfway, and then go right. Now begin here, and go straight down to the bottom, crossing the line in the middle. Four.*

✦ Now invite students to practice writing numeral *4*s across the top row of the paper or **White Boards.** Make sure they are writing from left to right.

✦ Remind students the number *4* means we have four of something, and draw four stars on the board to illustrate.

Guided Practice

✦ Have students complete **Skills Practice 2** page 67 for additional practice with the numeral *4*.

✦ Ask students to trace the *4*s that are outlined across the first penmanship row. Then have students write a row of *4*s across the next line.

✦ Invite volunteers to identify the letters that make up the word *four,* and have the class practice writing the word by tracing the letters. Then have them write the word on the next line.

✦ After students have finished, review their work, and help them proofread.

Teacher Tip

USING PROGRAM MATERIALS Use **Pocket Chart Picture Card** 5 to help you review the shape of the numeral *4*.

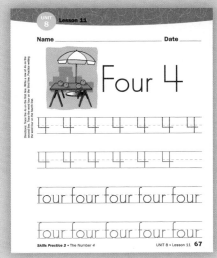

Skills Practice 2, p. 67

Monitor Progress

Formal Assessment ✓

to Differentiate Instruction

Numeral Identification Note how quickly students identify the numeral *4*.

APPROACHING LEVEL	
IF ... students are having difficulty,	THEN ... help them draw four objects on a sheet of paper.
ON LEVEL	
IF ... students need more practice,	THEN ... have them count to four and then write the numeral 4 four times.
ABOVE LEVEL	
IF ... students would enjoy a challenging activity,	THEN ... they can work independently to cut out pictures from old magazines with four objects in them.

Reading and Responding

OBJECTIVES

Students will
✦ connect their own life experiences to the text.
✦ develop an understanding of vocabulary words.
✦ use the comprehension strategies Clarifying and Making Connections.
✦ make connections to the unit theme.

MATERIALS

✦ *Science Lap Book,* pp. 28–35
✦ Routines 5–7

Focus Question How do plants and animals help each

All Living Things

From trees to bugs, all living things need each other.

28

1st READ

Science Lap Book, p. 28

Science Link

Activate Prior Knowledge **ROUTINE 5**

✦ Remind students that readers relate what they already know to what they are reading. Explain that this approach will help them better understand what they read.

✦ Tell students they are going to listen to a selection about living things and how they help each other. To prompt a discussion, ask students the following questions:
  • *Who has a pet at home?*
  • *How do you help your pet stay healthy and happy?*
  • *How does your pet help you?*

✦ Ask if anyone has a fish tank with snails. Then ask the following:
  • *How do the snails help the plants and fish in your fish tank?*
  • *How do the plants help the snails?*

✦ Encourage students to think about the living things in their neighborhoods as they listen to the selection "All Living Things."

Preview the Selection **ROUTINE 5**

✦ Open the *Science Lap Book* to pages 28–29, the opening pages of "All Living Things." Follow Routine 5, the previewing the selection routine, as you introduce the title of the selection.

✦ As you prepare to read the selection, turn through the pages, and focus students' attention on the photographs. Ask them if the photos give them any clues as to what the story might be about.

✦ Encourage students to suggest reasons for reading the selection. Ask them to think what the story might teach them about living things.

✦ Have students discuss what they are learning about living things as you read the selection. Ask students how plants and animals connect with the unit theme Ready, Set, Grow!

Technology

To promote independent reading, encourage students to use Workshop to listen to the recording of the selection on the *Listening Library CD.* Invite them to follow along and say the words whenever they can.

Audio CD

Vocabulary

ROUTINE
6

✦ Follow Routine 6, the selection vocabulary routine, as you introduce the vocabulary words for this selection.

✦ Explain to students that *gardens* are places to grow plants. Ask them if they have gardens at home. Explain that some gardens grow in pots on porches or balconies.

✦ Tell students *seeds* are what plants grow from. Ask them what fruits have seeds inside.

✦ Explain that *insects* are bugs with six legs. Ask students to name several insects. Tell them spiders are not insects because they have eight legs.

Read the Selection

ROUTINE
7

✦ Before beginning the selection, read the Focus Question at the top of the first page. Tell students to keep this question in mind as they listen to the story.

✦ Follow Routine 7, the reading the selection routine, and read the entire selection.

✦ Before, during, and after this first reading, invite students to ask questions or to think aloud about anything in the selection that interests or puzzles them.

Comprehension Strategies

✦ As you read, model the following comprehension strategies:
  • Clarifying
  • Making Connections

✦ Think aloud through each strategy, and encourage students to share their ideas as well.

Vocabulary

gardens   insects

seeds

 Teacher Tip

VOCABULARY Encourage students to use a variety of sources to build their vocabulary, such as making word banks, discussing characters and events from a story, talking with other people, and thinking about their own life experiences.

Differentiating Instruction   **English Learners**

IF ... students need help understanding vocabulary, **THEN ...** use pictures to show meanings.

Comprehension Strategies

Teacher Modeling

1 Clarifying *I'm not sure how living things need each other. Maybe looking at the photo will help us understand. This looks like a rain forest. The plants make a lot of shade for the animals to keep cool, and they probably make homes for them too. Plus, some animals might eat the plants. But how do the plants need the animals? Let's read on to find out.*

2 Making Connections *I know how much rabbits like gardens. They've eaten almost all the lettuce in my grandmother's garden. Thinking about this helps me understand how some animals need plants for food.*

3 Clarifying *I'm confused. How could animals help plants grow in new places? And how could seeds get carried on animals' bodies? Maybe the photo will explain.*

4 Making Connections *I'll bet the bird will drop seeds because it tried to put too many in its mouth. The extra seeds will fall out as it tries to eat. Sometimes I put too much food in my mouth. Then I can't chew it. I have to remove some first. Thinking about how I eat sometimes helps me understand how the bird might drop seeds as it flies away.*

Focus Question How do plants and animals help each other?

All Living Things

From trees to bugs, all living things need each other. **1**

28

Some animals, like rabbits, eat plants for food. They love gardens! **2**

29

Birds eat berries from bushes. They eat seeds and insects too.

30

Animals help plants grow in new places. Sometimes seeds get carried on animals' bodies. **3**

31

Teacher Tip

GLOSSARY The words *gardens*, *seeds*, and *insects* can be found in the Glossary of the *Science Lap Book.*

This bird will drop seeds from this gigantic sunflower as it flies away. ❹

32

New plants will grow from where the seeds are dropped.

33

The new plants will provide more food for people and animals.

34

Can you think of other ways living things need each other?

35

Science Lap Book, pp. 28–35

Science Link

Discuss with students how plants and animals depend on each other for survival. Encourage students to use examples from the selection.

Print and Book Awareness

Picture-Text Relationship

Reread pages 31, 33, and 34, and ask students what the photos tell them that the words do not. If students have difficulty responding, reread the text without showing the photos. Then ask them what questions they have about the story. Next read the text while showing the photos, and ask what additional information the photos provide.

Sentences

Have a volunteer come to the *Lap Book* and move his or her hand under the first sentences on pages 30 and 31. Ask students how they know where each sentence begins and ends. If necessary, point out that capital letters and periods tell us where sentences begin and end.

Vocabulary Review

Review with students the selection vocabulary words *gardens, seeds,* and *insects.* Ask students the following questions:

- *What kinds of things could we find in gardens?*
- *How do we make seeds grow?*
- *What do insects look like?*

OBJECTIVES

Students will
+ revise pictures to clarify information.
+ view, appreciate, and react to fine art.

MATERIALS
+ *Ready, Set, Grow! Big Book,* p. 62

Teacher Tip

PLAN AHEAD In preparation for the following activity, have drawing paper and art supplies on hand.

Traits of Good Writing

Conventions Writers often proofread their writing to clarify what they are trying to say.

Writing Process

Revise: Revising Pictures to Clarify

Teach

+ Ask students to think about when the class worked on the list of instructions last week. Remind them of how they helped you revise the list by moving, adding, and deleting information and ideas.

+ Tell students today they will do the same thing to the pictures they drew in the previous lessons.

Apply

+ Distribute the drawings students made in the previous lesson, and again have available any necessary art supplies. Some students might even want to completely redo one of their drawings; in that case you should have clean sheets of drawing paper available as well.

+ Display the final text for the class list of instructions. Review aloud each item on the list, and have students look at their drawings as you do.

+ Ask students to think about how well their drawings show the instructions. Suggest that as they listen to you read the instructions they should think about something else they could add to, delete from, or move around in each drawing to make it better.

+ Give students time to make the changes to their drawings, offering your help and advice as needed.

+ Ask students to return their drawings to you, and tell them you will resume the writing process in the next lesson.

Fine Art

Discussing Fine Art

✦ Turn to page 62 in the ***Ready, Set, Grow! Big Book.*** Focus students' attention on *Orange Tree in Bloom (Naranjo En Flor)* by Carlos Scaglione.

✦ Encourage students to talk about the painting, using questions such as the following:

- *What is the main thing you see in the painting? What kind of tree is it? How do you know?*
- *What does this painting remind you of? Why?*
- *Which words match the painting the best:* cheerful *and* happy, *or* sad *and* lonely?
- *Do you like the painting? Why or why not?*

✦ Ask students to describe the setting presented in the painting. Identify the building behind the tree and the gate separating the tree from the building.

✦ Next have them discuss the colors that are used in the painting. Draw students' attention to the sky. Ask them if they have ever seen a sky that looked like the one in the painting. Discuss whether the colors look like how it actually looks outside.

✦ Finally ask students how the painting relates to the unit theme. Point out that if students have ever eaten an orange or drunk orange juice, those oranges grew on a tree that looked similar to this one.

Background Information

Carlos Scaglione (1942–) was born near the bustling capital of Argentina, Buenos Aires. However, it is landscapes—not cityscapes—that have dominated as subjects throughout his body of work. Like *Orange Tree in Bloom,* many of Scaglione's paintings present one tree against a sparse natural background, a technique that tends to evoke moods rather than to make statements.

Carlos Scaglione.
Orange Tree in Bloom. 1995.

 **Teacher Tip**

FINE ART You may want to share with students other examples of art that can serve as a comparison or contrast in style or culture.

Sounds and Letters

Students will

✦ identify and produce rhyming words.

✦ identify and count the number of phonemes in words.

✦ review the /ā/ and /ī/ sounds.

✦ *Pickled Peppers Big Book,* p. 16

✦ *Teacher's Resource Book,* p. 38

✦ *Alphabet Letter Cards Aa* and *Ii* for each student

✦ *Skills Practice 2,* p. 68

Point to the box that represents today. Ask students to find the day that happens seven days from today. Have a volunteer count out each day, and point to the correct one.

Warming Up

Kindergarten News

✦ Copy the text above on the board or on chart paper. Make some mistakes in the message today; for example, you might use a small *g* for the word *Good,* or you might end the last sentence with a period instead of a question mark.

✦ Invite students to proofread your writing and correct your errors, where appropriate.

✦ Have students change the first sound in the word *date* to generate rhyming words with the /ā/ sound. *fate, gate, late, mate, Nate, rate*

Make a Rhyme

✦ Open the *Pickled Peppers Big Book* to the Table of Contents. Ask a student to help you find the page number for the poem "One Hungry Monster." *page 16* Turn to the page, then point to and say the title and the names of the author and the illustrator.

✦ Read the poem. As you read, pause to let students say the rhymes:

One hungry monster
underneath my bed,
moaning and groaning
and begging to be ___fed___.

✦ After reading, say these words from the poem, and tell students to raise their hands if they can say a word that rhymes with each:

fed	door	hall	lick
bug	beans	years	plates

Phonemic Awareness

Phoneme Segmentation

✦ Distribute a copy of ***Teacher's Resource Book*** page 38 or a ***White Board*** to each student, along with four counters.

✦ Tell students you will say a word and they should put a counter in a box on the grid for each sound they hear in the word. Demonstrate this process to students, using the word *let*.

✦ Say the word *set,* stretching the sounds: */s-s-s/ /e-e-e/ /t/*. Have students place a counter in the correct box for each sound.

✦ Call on volunteers to tell how many sounds the word has. *three* Then guide the class in blending and saying aloud the word *set*.

✦ Continue the activity with the following words: *it, bun, rap, be, land, in, milk,* and *pen*. Always have students tell how many sounds are in each word; then guide them in identifying each sound and the letters attached to the sounds.

✦ Choose one word, and have students say and write in the boxes on the grid the letter for each sound in the word. Have them use the ***Alphabet Sound Wall Cards*** if they need help.

 Teacher Tip

PRINT TRACKING Remind students to place the counter for the first sound they hear in the box above the arrow. Explain that this is because we read and write from the left side of a page to the right side.

Alphabetic Principle ⏱

Reviewing the Sounds of Long *Aa* and Long *Ii*

Give each student one **Alphabet Letter Card** *Aa* and one **Alphabet Letter Card** *Ii*. Ask students to raise the *Aa* cards and say /ā/ when they hear a word that has the /ā/ sound. They should raise the *Ii* cards and say /ī/ when they hear the /ī/ sound. Try the following words:

vine	line	side	lame
hive	Kate	gate	Mike
make	lake	nine	fake

Blending

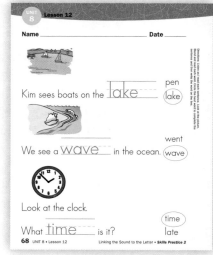

✦ Guide students in completing **Skills Practice 2** page 68.

✦ Explain to students that you will read aloud each sentence. Ask them to look at the picture, to listen to the sentence, and then to blend two words to decide which word best fills the blank. Have them write the word in the blank.

✦ Review each sentence, blending the words aloud. Invite students to proofread their own work.

Skills Practice 2, p. 68

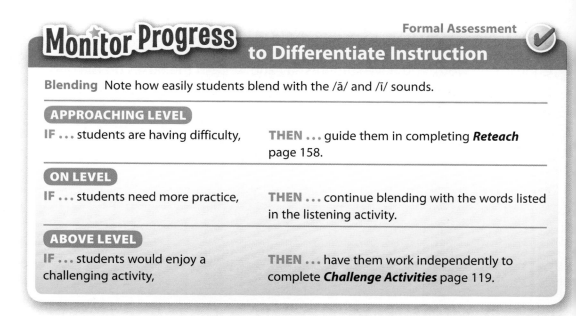

Monitor Progress to Differentiate Instruction

Formal Assessment ✔

Blending Note how easily students blend with the /ā/ and /ī/ sounds.

APPROACHING LEVEL

IF ... students are having difficulty,

THEN ... guide them in completing **Reteach** page 158.

ON LEVEL

IF ... students need more practice,

THEN ... continue blending with the words listed in the listening activity.

ABOVE LEVEL

IF ... students would enjoy a challenging activity,

THEN ... have them work independently to complete **Challenge Activities** page 119.

Pickled Peppers Big Book

✦ Display the **Pickled Peppers Big Book,** and turn to page 8, "One, Two, Buckle My Shoe." Ask a volunteer to come to the book and to point to the title of the rhyme. Have the class help you count the words in the title. *five* Then have the class help you count the spaces in the title. *four*

✦ Tell students you will read aloud the rhyme and you would like them to listen for the words with the /ā/ sound. Ask students to close their eyes as they listen.

✦ Invite students to say any /ā/ words they noticed while you read aloud the rhyme. *lay, eight, straight*

✦ Tell students you will read the rhyme again but this time you want them to listen for words with the /ī/ sound.

✦ Have students share any /ī/ words they remember.

✦ Reread the rhyme once more, and have students stop you when you say a word with the /ā/ or /ī/ sound and repeat the word. *Five, eight, lay, straight, Nine*

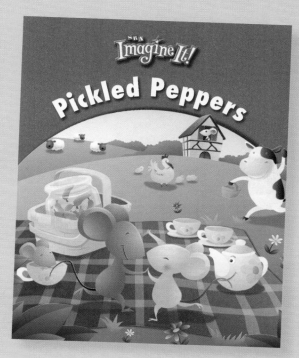

Pickled Peppers Big Book, p. 8

 Teacher Tip

VOWEL SPELLINGS Note that in this activity, students are not asked to visually identify the target words in the rhyme. The words that make the long-vowel sounds use more advanced spellings for the long vowels, with the exception of *Five* and *Nine.* Use this lesson to have students practice their listening identification skills only.

Technology

Use the **Listening Library CD** to support the **Pickled Peppers** lessons.

Audio CD

OBJECTIVES

Students will

✦ develop an understanding of vocabulary words.
✦ review the comprehension strategies Clarifying and Making Connections.
✦ use the comprehension skill Cause and Effect.
✦ discuss the author's purpose in writing the selection.

MATERIALS

✦ *Science Lap Book,* pp. 28–35
✦ Routines 5–7

Focus Question How do plants and animals help each other?

All Living Things

From trees to bugs, all living things need each other.

28

2nd READ

Science Lap Book, p. 28

Vocabulary

carried	provide
sunflower	

Science Link

Preview the Selection ROUTINE 5

✦ Display the *Science Lap Book* opened to the Table of Contents page. Use Routine 5, the previewing the selection routine, to guide students in understanding and using the Table of Contents. Then turn to the selection, and say the title.

✦ As you prepare to reread the selection, have students use the photographs to retell important facts from the selection.

Vocabulary ROUTINE 6

✦ Follow Routine 6, the selection vocabulary routine, as you introduce the vocabulary words for this selection.

✦ Tell students if the wind *carried* something, it held the object in the air. Use the following sentence to illustrate: *The wind carried the feather in the breeze.*

✦ Explain to students that a *sunflower* is a plant with large yellow flowers.

✦ Tell students the word *provide* means "give." Use the following sentence to illustrate: *The teacher will provide paper and pencils for students.*

Read the Selection

ROUTINE
7

Comprehension Strategies

✦ During the first reading of "All Living Things," you modeled the following comprehension strategies:

- Clarifying
- Making Connections

✦ In this second reading of the selection, you will revisit each comprehension strategy model from the first reading.

Reading with a Writer's Eye

✦ In this rereading of "All Living Things," students will learn about the author's purpose in writing the selection.

✦ By discussing the writing strategies an author uses, students will learn how to be better writers themselves.

Concept/Question Board

Tell students readers keep thinking about any questions they think of as they are reading. As they read, tell them to keep in mind the questions on the **Concept/Question Board.** Tell them readers are always thinking about what is important in selections and they try to remember this important information.

Technology

To promote independent reading, encourage students to use Workshop to listen to the recording of the selection on the **Listening Library CD.** Invite them to follow along and say the words whenever they can.

Audio CD

Comprehension Strategies

Teacher Modeling

1 Clarifying *I wasn't sure how living things needed each other, so we looked at the photo for clues. We noticed the plants in the picture were making shade for the animals and keeping them cool. We also knew the animals ate the plants and found homes among them. But we weren't sure how the plants needed the animals. When we read on, we discovered that animals help plant seeds spread to new places.*

2 Making Connections *I understood why rabbits would love gardens when I thought about the rabbits in my grandmother's garden. They've eaten almost all her lettuce! Thinking about this helped us understand how some animals need plants for food.*

3 Clarifying *We didn't understand how animals could help plants grow in new places or how seeds could get carried on animals' bodies. So we looked at the photo for clues. Then we understood. We saw a prickly thistle stuck to an animal's fur. We knew it would drop off at some point and fall to the ground. Then its seeds would grow in a new place.*

4 Making Connections *We understood how a bird could drop seeds from its mouth when we thought about how we eat. Thinking about how we eat helped us understand why birds might drop seeds.*

Focus Question How do plants and animals help each other?

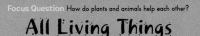

From trees to bugs, all living things need each other. **1**

28

Some animals, like rabbits, eat plants for food. They love gardens! **2**

29

Birds eat berries from bushes. They eat seeds and insects too.

30

Animals help plants grow in new places. Sometimes seeds get carried on animals' bodies. **3**

31

Vocabulary Tip

Review the meaning of the word *carried*. Then have students use the word in a sentence.

This bird will drop seeds from this gigantic sunflower as it flies away. **4**

32

New plants will grow from where the seeds are dropped.

33

The new plants will provide more food for people and animals.

34

Can you think of other ways living things need each other?

35

Science Lap Book, pp. 28–35

Science Link

Discuss with students how the activities of people might affect the abilities of plants and animals to survive. Ask students how the construction of shopping centers and highways might affect plants and animals. Ask how the smoke from factories and car exhaust might affect them.

Reading with a Writer's Eye

Author's Purpose

✦ Ask students why they think the author wrote "All Living Things." Model the following questions: *Did the author write the story to make us laugh? Did the author write it to talk us into believing something? Did the author write to share an experience? Did the author write the story to share information?*

✦ Ask students what they learned from the story. Identify the facts and details that the author shares.

Discussing the Selection

Review the Focus Question with students: How do plants and animals help each other?

Vocabulary Review

Review with students the selection vocabulary words *carried, sunflower,* and *provide.* Ask students the following questions:

• *What kinds of things can be carried with the wind?*

• *What does a sunflower look like?*

• *How do plants provide food for people?*

Vocabulary Tip

Review the meanings of the words *sunflower* and *provide.* Then have students use the words in sentences.

OBJECTIVES

Students will
+ learn how to locate errors in text.
+ learn about the future tense of action words.
+ participate in a Thinking Story experience.

MATERIALS
+ *Language Arts Big Book,* p. 10
+ *Skills Practice 2,* pp. 69–70
+ *Willy the Wisher,* p. 83

Writing Process

Model: Locating Errors in Text

Teach

+ Display **Language Arts Big Book** page 10, and read aloud the sentence *How do I make it right?*

+ Discuss each item on the Checking list one by one, using the sentence on Doodle's poster to illustrate each point.

+ Explain that a piece of writing is not finished until the writer has checked it for errors.

Guided Practice

+ Write a model sentence on the board, and use the think-aloud method to model how one checks his or her writing. For example, use this sentence: *a good writer checks his work for mistakes*

+ Note the following errors aloud: *Missing capital letter to begin the sentence; missing space between the words* his *and* work; *and no mark at the end of the sentence.* You might also identify a word or letter not written in your best handwriting and rewrite it more neatly.

+ Tell students in the next lesson they will help you check the class instructions for errors.

Grammar, Usage, and Mechanics

Teach

+ Remind students words that show action appear in past and present tenses. Explain that a future tense tells what will happen after today.

+ Write the following sentences on the board: *I walked. I walk. I will walk.* Explain that *I walked* tells that the action happened in the past, *I walk* tells that the action happens in the present, and *I will walk* tells that the action will happen in the future.

+ Write *walked* and *will walk* on the board. Circle *ed.* Explain that *ed* at the end of some words shows the past tense. Circle *will.* Explain that *will* in front of a word shows an action that will happen after today.

Language Arts Big Book, p. 10

Differentiating Instruction **English Learners**

IF ... students have difficulty understanding the concept of future tense, **THEN ...** use the calendar to indicate that you are speaking of things that will happen in the future.

Grammar, Usage, and Mechanics continued

Guided Practice

✦ Have students open their **Skills Practice 2** to pages 69–70.

✦ Work through the pages with students, and review their answers when you finish.

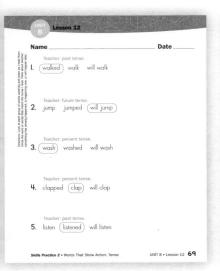
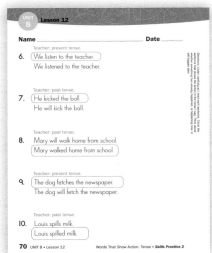

Skills Practice 2, pp. 69–70

Monitor Progress

Formal Assessment ✔

to Differentiate Instruction

Grammar Note how easily students distinguish between past and future tenses.

APPROACHING LEVEL

IF ... students are having difficulty,

THEN ... refer to Unit 8 Lesson 12 of the **Intervention Guide** for additional support of this Grammar activity.

ON LEVEL

IF ... students need more practice,

THEN ... ask them to talk about what they did last night and what they will do tonight.

ABOVE LEVEL

IF ... students are comfortable,

THEN ... have students come to the board and help you make a list of activities that the class has completed and will complete.

Willy the Wisher

✦ Display the book **Willy the Wisher,** and turn to the story "First Things First" on page 83 of the book.

✦ Before reading the story to students, invite them to tell you what they know about Phil. In this story, Phil does not think to ask questions to clarify what he is to do. Phil also has difficulty doing things in the correct order.

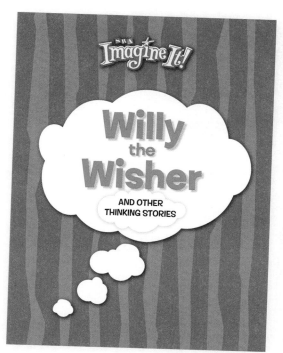

Willy the Wisher, p. 83

✦ After reading the story, discuss Phil's experience in the morning. Talk about how his parents try to tell him just what to do, but they can never seem to offer Phil every detail he needs to successfully complete a task. Discuss how Phil never asks questions to clarify things he does not understand.

✦ Encourage students to think about some advice they would give Phil's parents to help teach Phil a better way to complete tasks.

🍎 Teacher Tip

ORIGINAL STORIES Students might enjoy making up their own stories using the **Willy the Wisher** characters. Collaborate with students to make up a brief story about Phil. For example, students might enjoy writing a story that pretends Phil is a cook in a busy restaurant, but no one is there to tell him how to make the food. Write the story on the board or on chart paper. If time permits, help students create a few story frames with basic line drawings to illustrate their original story.

Sounds and Letters

OBJECTIVES

Students will
+ identify the order of words.
+ identify and count the number of phonemes in words by segmenting.
+ review the /ā/ sound and the /ī/ sound.
+ practice writing the numeral *5*.

MATERIALS

+ **Pickled Peppers Big Book,** p. 13
+ **Teacher's Resource Book,** p. 38
+ **Alphabet Letter Cards** *Aa* and *Ii* for each student
+ Supply Icons
+ **Skills Practice 2,** p. 71
+ **Pocket Chart Picture Card** 6

Calendar

Su	M	T	W	Th	F	S
		1	2	3	4	5
6	7	8	9	10	11	12
13	14	15	16	17	18	19
20	21	22	23	24	25	26
27	28	29	30	31		

Point to the box that represents today. Say the name of a date that occurs within the current week. Invite a volunteer to point to that date on the calendar. Count aloud the number of days until that date.

Warming Up 🕐

MORNING MESSAGE

Today is _____.

Today we will read about _____.

(Child's name)'s favorite game is _____.

Kindergarten News

+ Copy the above text on the board or on chart paper. Change the letter *m* in *game* to a *t*. Also make other mistakes such as writing two words together without any space between them or leaving a period missing at the end of a sentence.

+ Ask students if they can find the wrong letter in a word in the last sentence. If students cannot find it on their own, blend the word *game* with them. Invite a volunteer to come up to the board, cross out the *t*, and write the letter *m*. If the student writes the letter incorrectly, cover his or her attempt with a self-sticking note, and guide him or her on the second attempt.

+ Ask students to find other mistakes you made and to help you correct them.

Word Order

+ Turn to page 13 of the **Pickled Peppers Big Book.** Tell students to close their eyes and listen as you read the nursery rhyme "Humpty Dumpty."

+ Tell students you are going to say the first line of the rhyme again. This time, say the following:

Humpty Dumpty wall on a sat.

+ Ask students to tell what is wrong, and then have them say the line in the correct order. *Humpty Dumpty sat on a wall.*

+ Say the third line as follows:
  All the horses' kings and all the men's kings.

+ Continue, switching words in other lines.

+ Ask students to talk about the word-order changes and what they do to the meaning of the rhyme. Discuss why word order is important to meaning.

Phonemic Awareness

Phoneme Segmentation

+ Continue the phoneme-counting activity from yesterday, but this time focus students' attention more on the positions of each sound.

+ Distribute a copy of **Teacher's Resource Book** page 38 or a **White Board** to each student, along with four counters.

+ Say the word *wet,* stretching the sounds: /w-w-w-w/ /e-e-e-e/ /t/. Give students a moment to place a counter in the correct box for each sound. Then have a volunteer tell how many sounds the word has. *three* Have the class blend and say the word *wet.*

+ Continue the activity with the following words: *wit, win, ten, son, sob, bank.* Have students identify which sound is different in each word change. Say, for example, *Which sound in this word is different from the sounds in the word wet—the first, middle, or last? What is the sound?*

+ Choose one word, and have students say and write in the boxes on the grid the letter for each sound in the word. Remind them to use the **Alphabet Sound Wall Cards** if they need help.

 Teacher Tip

STUDENT RESPONDING Remember to switch unpredictably between asking for whole-class responses and responses from individual students. This will not only encourage students' full attention and participation, but it will also help you identify individual students who are struggling with the skills.

IF ... students are native speakers of Spanish or certain other languages, **THEN ...** they may associate the letter name *a* with the letter *e* because in their native languages, *e* represents a sound similar to English long *a*. These students will need extra practice associating the letter *a* with its English name and with the long *a* sound.

Alphabetic Principle 🕐

Reviewing the Sounds of Long *Aa* and Long *Ii*

✦ Point to **Alphabet Sound Wall Card** *Long Aa*, and have students recite the rhyme for the sounds of *Aa*:

A's my name.

Two sounds I make:

Short a *in* lamb,

Long a *in* cake.

✦ Continue with **Alphabet Sound Wall Card** *Long Ii*, and have students recite the rhyme:

I's my name.

Two sounds have I:

Short i *in* pig,

Long i *in* pie.

Listening for Medial /ā/ and /ī/

Give each student one **Alphabet Letter Card** *Aa* and one **Alphabet Letter Card** *Ii*. Ask students to raise the *Aa* cards and say /ā/ when they hear a word with the /ā/ sound. They should raise the *Ii* cards and say /ī/ when they hear the /ī/ sound. Try the following words:

nice	*face*	*wade*	*same*
cave	*mile*	*wire*	*fine*
tame	*base*	*mine*	*space*

Linking the Sound to the Letter

✦ Write a pair of words on the board, one with the /ī/ sound spelled *i_e*, and one with the /ā/ sound spelled *a_e*.

✦ Tell students you will say one of the words and they should give you the thumbs-up signal when you point to it. Then ask a student to tell you how he or she knows which word you said. Try these words:

lime ... lame	*Dave ... dive*
dime ... dame	*mine ... mane*
make ... Mike	*mite ... mate*

Penmanship

✦ Distribute a sheet of writing paper to each student, or use **White Boards** turned to the sides with writing lines.

✦ Place the Supply Icon for *pencil* on the board or in the **Pocket Chart.**

✦ Using the established procedure, review with students how to form the numeral 5. Say *Begin here. Go straight down halfway, and then curve to the right and up a little. Now go back to the starting point, and go straight across (right). Five.*

✦ Now invite students to practice writing numeral 5s across the top row of the paper or **White Boards.**

✦ Remind students the number *5* means we have five of something, and draw five stars on the board to illustrate.

Guided Practice

✦ Have students complete **Skills Practice 2** page 71 for additional practice with the numeral 5.

✦ Ask students to trace the 5s outlined across the first penmanship row. Then have them practice writing a row of 5s across the next line.

✦ Invite volunteers to identify the letters that make up the word *five,* and have the class practice writing the word by tracing the letters. Then have them write the word on the next line.

✦ After students have finished, review their work. Help them proofread using the established procedure.

 Monitor Progress to Differentiate Instruction

Formal Assessment ✓

Numeral Identification Note how quickly students identify the numeral 5.

APPROACHING LEVEL

IF ... students are having difficulty,

THEN ... look through the **Ready, Set, Grow! Big Book** with them, and have them point to the numeral 5.

ON LEVEL

IF ... students need more practice,

THEN ... have them look through "Becoming Butterflies" with partners to find the numeral 5.

ABOVE LEVEL

IF ... students would enjoy a challenging activity,

THEN ... have them work independently to complete page 120 in **Challenge Activities.**

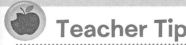 **Teacher Tip**

USING PROGRAM MATERIALS Use *Pocket Chart Picture Card* 6 to help you review the shape of the numeral 5.

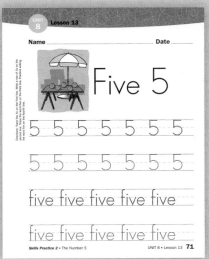

Skills Practice 2, p. 71

Reading and Responding

Students will

✦ locate the title and the name of the author and illustrator.

✦ develop an understanding of vocabulary words.

✦ use the comprehension strategies Asking Questions and Predicting.

✦ identify print and book features.

✦ *Story Time Collection: Zinnia's Flower Garden*

✦ Routines 5–7

✦ *Home Connection,* pp. 65–66

Zinnia's Flower Garden

Preview and Prepare

1st READ

Activate Prior Knowledge ROUTINE 5

✦ *Zinnia's Flower Garden* is fiction about a little girl named Zinnia who plants and carefully tends her flower garden until it blooms into a wide assortment of pretty flowers. As you read aloud the selection, relate what you already know to what you are reading, and encourage students to do the same.

✦ Ask students if they have ever helped plant and/or tend a garden. Some may have only observed a neighbor's or relative's garden or seen gardens on television or in books and magazines. Encourage students to share their gardening experiences and what they know about gardening. Prompt a discussion of gardening with the following questions:

• *What kinds of things can grow in a garden?*

• *What must you do to get a garden ready to plant?*

• *What do plants need to grow?*

✦ Encourage students to discuss what they are learning about the unit theme as they listen to the selection. Key concepts include the following:

• A garden needs lots of attention to grow well.

• Plants need sunshine, rain, and good soil.

• Weeds and bugs hurt garden plants and should be removed.

• You need to be patient when growing things.

Preview the Selection ROUTINE 5

✦ Display the cover of *Zinnia's Flower Garden.* Follow Routine 5, the previewing the selection routine, as you introduce the title and the name of the author and illustrator. Ask students why only one name appears on the cover.

✦ Turn through the pages, and focus students' attention on the illustrations. Invite students to look for clues as to what the story might be about.

✦ Encourage students to think of reasons for reading *Zinnia's Flower Garden.* Invite students to wonder how the story might add to the unit theme.

Technology

To promote independent reading, encourage students to use Workshop to listen to the recording of the selection on the **Listening Library CD.** Invite them to follow along and say the words whenever they can.

Audio CD

Vocabulary

ROUTINE **6**

- Follow Routine 6, the selection vocabulary routine, as you introduce the vocabulary words for this selection.

- Tell students the word *pats* means "to tap lightly." Demonstrate the word *pats*, and have students demonstrate as well.

- Explain that the word *sprinkles* means "to water lightly." Use the following sentence to illustrate: *Grandpa sprinkles his garden with water each evening.*

- Tell students the word *sprout* means "just starting to grow." Use the following sentence to illustrate: *These flower seeds will sprout in about ten days.*

- Explain to students that sprouts will start *poking,* or pushing, through the soil to get sun.

- Explain to students the word *sprouts* means "small plants." Use the following sentence to illustrate: *I water my garden so my sprouts will grow into big plants.*

- Tell students the word *inspects* means "observe or watch carefully." Tell them a good gardener inspects plants for hungry bugs.

Read the Selection

ROUTINE **7**

- Before reading *Zinnia's Flower Garden,* read the Focus Question at the top of the first page. Tell students to keep this question in mind as they listen to the story.

- Follow Routine 7, the reading the selection routine, as you read the entire story. Identify and discuss the border art on the pages of text. Ask students how it adds to each page.

- Before, during, and after the first reading, encourage students to ask questions and to think aloud about anything that interests or puzzles them.

Comprehension Strategies

- You will introduce and model the following comprehension strategies:
  - Asking Questions
  - Predicting

- Think aloud through each comprehension strategy, and encourage students to share their ideas as well.

Vocabulary

pats	poking
sprinkles	sprouts
sprout	inspects

Teacher Tip

ACTIVATING PRIOR KNOWLEDGE Tell students readers relate what they know to a reading. As you are reading, make certain you relate what you already know to what you are reading. As students read the selections, they encounter familiar ideas as well as new ideas. When they read something they already know, encourage them to make a note of the information. When they learn something new, have them be sure to notice that too. This will help students learn as they are reading.

From Your Teacher **Home Connection**

Give each student a copy of **Home Connection** page 65. This same information is also available in Spanish on **Home Connection** page 66. Encourage students to discuss the selection "*Zinnia's Flower Garden*" with their families and complete the activity provided.

Comprehension Strategies

Teacher Modeling

1 **Predicting** *Zinnia is getting her garden ready for planting. I see some of the tools she'll use to plant her garden. I also see a pencil and a little notebook that says "My Garden Journal." I think Zinnia is going to write in the journal. I think she'll write what happens in her garden. Let's read on to see if I'm right.*

2 **Predicting** *I was right! Zinnia wrote in her journal on May 3 when she planted her seeds. I wonder what kinds of flowers Zinnia is planting. I'll look at the pictures to see if they can tell me. Yes, the flower names are printed on the packets of seeds. Zinnia is planting sunflowers, zinnias, marigolds, cosmos, black-eyed Susans, asters, and sweet peas.*

3 **Predicting** *Zinnia's seeds are getting the rain they need. Her journal says it's May 12. Zinnia planted her seeds on May 3, so nine days have passed. I predict Zinnia will soon see little sprouts poke up through the soil just like our sprouts. What do you think? Let's read on to see.*

4 **Predicting** *I was right! The first sprout has appeared! Zinnia's journal says the date is May 20. That's only eight days after I made my prediction.*

Focus Question How does Zinnia make sure her flowers will grow?

Spring has arrived. Zinnia is getting her garden ready for planting. She digs up the soil and turns it over with her shovel. She takes out stones and rakes the dirt smooth. The warm sun feels good as she works. **1**

Zinnia carefully plants many kinds of flower seeds in rows. She covers the seeds with dirt and pats it all down very gently. She sprinkles the ground with water. **2**

Print and Book Awareness

Zinnia's Flower Garden, pp. 4–11

Capital Letters

Invite a volunteer to point to the first word in each sentence on these pages. Ask him or her what kind of letter we use at the beginning of a sentence. *We use a capital letter.*

Word Recognition

Write the word *seeds* on the board, and ask a volunteer to find and point to the word wherever it appears on page 8. Then say the entire sentence in which the word appears.

Comprehension Strategies

Teacher Modeling

5 Asking Questions *Now Zinnia's garden is full of sprouts. Pictures of the sprouts are at the top of the page. But why do the sprouts in each picture look different? Are they sprouts from different flowers? The next page gives me an answer. Each row of sprouts looks different, and each has a different label. The sprouts are from different flowers. Our sprouts look different. I guess flower sprouts don't all look the same.*

6 Predicting *Zinnia has been taking really good care of her plants. She's been watering them, pulling up pesky weeds, and picking off greedy bugs. I predict her garden will be a big success. Let's read on to see.*

7 Asking Questions *Oh, look! The first buds have appeared! How long has it been since Zinnia planted her seeds? She planted her seeds on May 3. Her journal says it's now July 18. Let's see ... That's more than two months! Zinnia's plants have been growing for two months and two weeks. What other things are growing on this page?*

Now Zinnia's garden is full of green sprouts growing toward the sun. Little stems grow taller. Little leaves get bigger. Little roots burrow deeper into the earth. **5**

Zinnia takes care of her garden every day. When the sun is hot and the soil is dry, she waters her thirsty plants.

 Teacher Tip

ASKING QUESTIONS Inform students they should keep asking questions and trying to answer them as they read.

Print and Book Awareness

Zinnia's Flower Garden, pp. 12–19

Word Recognition

Write the word *Little* on the board, and ask a volunteer to find and point to the word wherever it appears on page 12. Then say the entire sentences in which the word appears.

Picture-Text Relationships

Reread the text on pages 12 and 14, and have students comment about the pictures that accompany them. For each page of text, ask students *What do the pictures on these pages tell you that the story does not?* Tell students that the pictures and words work together to tell the whole story.

Sentences: Periods

Display page 16 of *Zinnia's Flower Garden*, and have volunteers point to the first and last words of each sentence. *She, plants; She, bugs; She, growing; Every, bigger* Have them point to the periods at the ends of sentences and say *This is a period.*

Comprehension Strategies

Teacher Modeling

8 **Predicting** *Zinnia's garden is a big success! Colorful flowers are growing everywhere! These pictures confirm the prediction I made earlier. And the story tells how much Zinnia enjoys her flowers.*

9 **Predicting** *Zinnia has so many flowers! I wonder what she'll do with all of them. Look at the pretty bouquets she's made! I predict Zinnia will find a way to share her pretty flowers. What are some clues that can help us predict? Let's read on to see if our prediction is confirmed.*

10 **Predicting** *We were right! Zinnia sets up a stand to sell lemonade, and she invites people to pick their own flowers. Zinnia did find a way to share her pretty flowers.*

Teacher Tip

CONFIRMING PREDICTIONS Remind students that readers continuously make predictions as they read. They also confirm and update their predictions as they go along.

Zinnia's Flower Garden, pp. 20–27

Print and Book Awareness

Exclamation Points

Have a volunteer find and point to the exclamation points on page 20. Tell them to look at the words on the page as well as in Zinnia's journal. Then ask students what an exclamation point means. If necessary, remind students an exclamation point shows that a character is very excited. Then read what the character says in a normal voice and an excited voice, and invite students to do the same. Ask students why Zinnia is so excited.

Sentences, Directionality

Display page 22, and have a volunteer show where to start reading each sentence and where to stop. Remind students we read from left to right, a sentence begins with a capital letter, and some sentences end with periods.

Capital Letters

Have a volunteer find and point to the word printed in capital letters on page 26. Ask students why someone might print a word on a sign in capital letters. If necessary, point out that words printed in capital letters are more noticeable than other words. Ask students why Zinnia would want people to notice the word *FLOWERS.*

Comprehension Strategies

Teacher Modeling

⓫ **Asking Questions** *Hmm . . . I wonder how you can tell when a seed is ripe and ready to be collected. Let's look at the pictures for an answer. I see some seeds falling out of a dried flower. But they would be hard to find on the ground. There must be a way to tell when the seeds are ready before they fall or get eaten by birds. But the story doesn't say. We may have to look in another book to find the answer. Asking this question helps us want to find out more.*

⓬ **Asking Questions** *How is Zinnia planning next year's garden? Let's look at the picture for an answer. Look! Zinnia is writing in two notebooks. One is her journal. But what is the other notebook for? It says "Order seeds." I get it. Zinnia is planning her garden by writing what she needs to do before next spring. She also seems to be looking off into space. I bet she's thinking about what she wants to grow next year.*

stigma
maturing ovary
growing seed
stamen
sepal
petal
stem
In the autumn, as it gets colder, Zinnia picks the last flowers from her garden. She finds ripe seeds that have formed. They are ready to be collected. She will save them to plant next year. 11
October 13 Lots of seeds! (I'll leave some for the birds.)
From Flower to Seed
28
29

Zinnia
Sunflower
spring
early summer
midsummer
The winter days are short. The sun is dim, and the ground is covered with snow. But Zinnia is already planning next year's garden. When spring comes, she will be ready to grow her very own flowers again. 12
winter
autumn
late summer
30
31

Zinnia's Flower Garden, pp. 28–31

Differentiating Instruction English Learners

IF . . . students need additional help with Asking Questions, **THEN . . .** refer to Unit 8 Lesson 13 of the ***English Learner Support Guide.***

Concept/Question Board

Tell students readers keep thinking about any questions they think of as they are reading. As they read, tell them to keep in mind the questions on the **Concept/Question Board.** Tell them readers are always thinking about what is important in selections and they try to remember this important information.

Print and Book Awareness

Tracking Sentences

Have a volunteer run his or her hand under the words as you read the text on pages 28 and 30. Point out to students that the sentence does not end after the first line; it ends at the period.

Capital Letters

Ask volunteers to find and point to the capital letters on pages 28 and 30. Then say the word that each letter begins, and ask students why the word is capitalized.

Discussing the Selection

Review the Focus Question with students: How does Zinnia make sure her flowers will grow? Continue the discussion with questions such as the following: *Does anyone know what Zinnia's name means? Does anyone remember another story we have read in which the main character was also named after a flower?*

Vocabulary Review

Review with students the selection vocabulary words *pats, sprinkles, sprout, poking, sprouts,* and *inspects.* Ask students the following questions:

- *What happens when Zinnia pats the soil?*
- *Why do the flowers begin to grow when Zinnia sprinkles them with water?*
- *How long will it take the flower to sprout?*
- *What are the plants doing when they are poking out of the ground?*
- *How does Zinnia make sure her sprouts will turn into flowers?*
- *What is Zinnia doing when she inspects her flowers?*

Language Arts

Students will
✦ proofread text and make appropriate changes.
✦ retell a story plot through drawings.
✦ consider how changing story details can change the plot.

✦ *Language Arts Big Book,* p. 10
✦ *Transparency* 42
✦ *Thinking Crowns*

Teacher Tip

STUDENT PRESENTATIONS In the next lesson, one half of the class will present their drawings that illustrate the how-to instructions. Today help students write the instructions on their drawings or on sheets of paper they can attach to their drawings. Or, because all students are using the same text, you might simply write the list in large letters on the board to accompany the presentations.

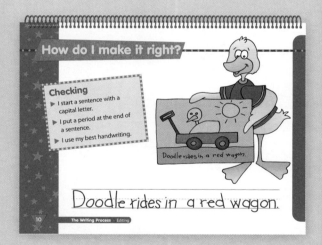

How do I make it right?

Checking
▶ I start a sentence with a capital letter.
▶ I put a period at the end of a sentence.
▶ I use my best handwriting.

Doodle rides in a red wagon.

10
The Writing Process · Editing

Doodle rides in a red wagon.

Language Arts Big Book, p. 10

Writing Process

Revise: Proofreading and Making Changes

Teach

✦ Display **Language Arts Big Book** page 10, and read aloud the sentence *How do I make it right?*

✦ Review with students each item on the Checking list. Remind them of the example you gave them in the previous lesson: *A good writer checks his work for mistakes.*

✦ Tell students today they will help you look for errors in the list of instructions the class wrote.

Guided Practice

✦ Display the chart paper with the class' final list of instructions, or rewrite the list on the board. Also write on the board a checklist: *capital letters, end marks, spelling, best handwriting.*

✦ Read the first item on the list of instructions. Then, point to the first item on the checklist: *capital letters.* Guide the class in checking that the correct letters are capitalized.

✦ Continue with the rest of the items on the list.

✦ Congratulate students on completing this writing assignment. Tell them they will begin sharing their drawings with their classmates in the next lesson.

Story Crafting ⏱

Working with the New: Developing Characters and Plots

✦ Before the activity, make a class set of *Transparency* 42, "Zinnia's Flower Garden."

✦ Display *Transparency* 42, and distribute a copy to each student. Using the line drawings, have students retell the story frame by frame.

✦ After you are certain all students are familiar with the story of *Zinnia's Flower Garden,* ask students to put on their *Thinking Crowns.* Tell them you want them to think about how "*Zinnia's Flower Garden*" might be different if something in the story were changed.

✦ Discuss each of the following scenarios independently. Ask students *How might* "Zinnia's Flower Garden" *be different if*

• *Zinnia lived in a big city such as New York City?*

• *Zinnia had a big pet dog?*

• *Zinnia's best friend helped with the flower garden?*

✦ Add any scenarios to which you think students would enjoy responding.

✦ Close the activity by discussing how different a story can become by changing one simple thing. Point out authors must plan their stories very carefully to create a story they want to share.

Transparency 42

🍎 Teacher Tip

LOOKING AHEAD As students think about different versions of *Zinnia's Flower Garden,* keep a list of the scenarios the class discusses today. During the next lesson, students will choose one scenario to develop.

Differentiating Instruction **English Learners**

IF ... students have difficulty contributing to the discussion, **THEN ...** ask them how the story would be different if Zinnia lived in their native countries or home cultures. If necessary, ask questions that can be answered *yes* or *no* or with a word; for example, you might ask *What name might Zinnia have?*

Day 14 — Sounds and Letters

OBJECTIVES

Students will

✦ blend initial phonemes to make words.

✦ identify and count the number of phonemes in words.

✦ review the /ā/ sound and the /ī/ sound.

MATERIALS

✦ **Pocket Chart Picture Cards** 92, 147

✦ **Alphabet Letter Cards** Aa and Ii for each studer

✦ **Skills Practice 2,** p. 72

✦ **Pickled Peppers Big Book,** pp. 40–41

Point to the box that represents today. Ask students to count with you to find out how many days come before and after today in the month. Point to each day as you count aloud.

Differentiating Instruction

English Learners

IF . . . students need to practice counting in English, **THEN . . .** use this activity to informally assess their proficiency and as an opportunity to provide extra practice.

Warming Up

Kindergarten News

✦ Copy the above text on the board or on chart paper. Choose a student whose birthday is approaching. Use the calendar to count how many days it is until the student's birthday. Have a student fill in the blank with the number of days.

✦ Use the following prompts to discuss the letters and words in the message: *How many y's can you find in the message?* four *Come up, and circle and count them. Which word has the most letters?* birthday *Come up, and point to it. How many letters does it have?* eight *What are they?* b, i, r, t, h, d, a, y

Phoneme Blending: Initial Sounds

Tell students the **Lion Puppet** wants to play a blending game again. Tell them you will say the beginning sound of a word and the puppet will say the rest. When the puppet asks what the word is, students should put together the parts and say the word. Use the following words:

/g/ /g/ . . . *obble* gobble	/k/ /k/ . . . *orner* corner	/s/ /s/ . . . *upper* supper
/t/ /t/ . . . *ender* tender	/j/ /j/ . . . *acket* jacket	/d/ /d/ . . . *aughter* daughter
/m/ /m/ . . . *iddle* middle	/r/ /r/ . . . *eady* ready	/f/ /f/ . . . *orward* forward

Phonemic Awareness

Phoneme Segmentation

✦ Tape **Pocket Chart Picture Card** 92—jam onto the board. Beneath the picture, draw three connected boxes. Have ready several self-sticking notes.

✦ Point to each box, from students' left to right, and tell them each box stands for a sound in the word.

✦ Continue, using the following procedure:

Teacher:	*What is the name of the picture?*
Students:	*jam*
Teacher:	*What is the first sound you hear in the word* jam?
Students:	*/j/*
Teacher:	(placing a blank self-sticking note in the first box) *Yes. What is the middle sound you hear in* jam?
Students:	*/a/*
Teacher:	(note in middle box) *That's right. What is the last sound you hear in* jam?
Students:	*/m/*
Teacher:	(note in third box) *Now let's say the whole word again.*
Everyone:	*jam*
Teacher:	*How many sounds are in the word* jam?
Students:	*three*

✦ Point to each box in turn, and say the sound once more. Ask students what letter represents that sound, and write that letter on the note.

✦ Remove the notes from the boxes, and display **Picture Card** 147—rug. Call on volunteers, and give them self-sticking notes. Ask them to identify the first, middle, and last sounds in the word and to place the notes in the appropriate boxes. Have students blend and say the words.

✦ Repeat with several other three-phoneme words and **Picture Cards.**

Teacher Tips

LISTENING SKILLS Remember that you can play a brief game of Simon says with students to focus them on their listening skills. Ask a volunteer to be the leader, giving directions for others to follow. Play several rounds, and then move into a listening activity such as the one in this lesson.

ACTIVITY SUGGESTION You can use a red self-sticking note for the vowel sounds to help students associate the middle sound with the vowel in the word. Ask students to tell you when to use the red note during the activity.

Teacher Tip

SKILL REVIEW If students still cannot discriminate the /ā/ sound and /ī/ sound, note that they will have one more review activity in Lesson 15. However, you might want to work with these students individually in Workshop before they move on to learning the sounds of other long vowels in Unit 9.

 Monitor Progress ✓

to Differentiate Instruction
Formal Assessment

Blending Note how easily students blend with the /ā/ and /ī/ sounds.

APPROACHING LEVEL

IF ... students are still having difficulty,	**THEN** ... refer to Unit 8 Lesson 14 of the *Intervention Guide* for additional activities.

ON LEVEL

IF ... students need more practice,	**THEN** ... continue blending with the words listed in the listening activity.

ABOVE LEVEL

IF ... students would enjoy a challenging activity,	**THEN** ... have them read *Decodables* 14, 15, or 16 to partners.

Alphabetic Principle 🕐

Reviewing the Sounds of Long *Aa* and Long *Ii*

Give each student one **Alphabet Letter Card** *Aa* and one **Alphabet Letter Card** *Ii*. Ask students to raise the *Aa* cards when they hear a word with the /ā/ sound. They should raise the *Ii* cards when they hear the /ī/ sound. Try the following words:

wade	dice	dive	slide
grace	knife	shame	whine
slime	brake	trade	crate

Blending

✦ Guide students in completing **Skills Practice 2** page 72.

✦ Tell students you will read aloud each sentence. Ask them to look at the picture, to listen to the sentence, and then to blend the two words to decide which word best fills the blank. Have them write the word in the blank.

✦ Review each sentence, blending the words aloud. Invite students to proofread their own work.

Skills Practice 2, p. 72

Pickled Peppers Big Book

✦ Display the **Pickled Peppers Big Book,** and turn to pages 40–41, "Rhyme." Point to the title, and read it aloud. Have students share anything they remember about the rhyme.

✦ Tell students you will play the rhyme on the **Listening Library CD** and you would like them to listen for the words with the /ā/ sound. Ask students to close their eyes as they listen.

✦ Ask students to say any /ā/ words they noticed while you played the rhyme. *shake*

✦ Tell students you will play the rhyme again but this time you want them to listen for words with the /ī/ sound. Have students share any /ī/ words they remember. *I, like*

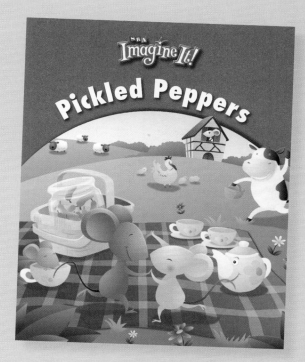

Pickled Peppers Big Book, pp. 40–41

Teacher Tip

VOWEL SPELLINGS Note that some of the words with the letters *a* and *i* do not make the /ā/ sound or the /ī/ sound using the spellings students have so far learned. If students ask about the letters making different sounds and/or having different spellings, tell them they will learn about these other spellings later.

Technology

Use the **Listening Library CD** to support the **Pickled Peppers** lessons.

Audio CD

Reading and Responding

OBJECTIVES

Students will
+ develop an understanding of vocabulary words.
+ review the comprehension strategies Asking Questions and Predicting.
+ use the comprehension skill Cause and Effect.
+ analyze the author's development of the setting.

MATERIALS

+ **Story Time Collection:** *Zinnia's Flower Garden*
+ Routines 5–7

Preview and Prepare

Preview the Selection ROUTINE **5**

+ Show students the front cover of *Zinnia's Flower Garden*. Use Routine 5, the previewing the selection routine, as you say the title and the name of the author and illustrator.

+ As you prepare to reread the story, have students use the illustrations to retell the main events in the story and describe characters and setting.

Vocabulary ROUTINE **6**

+ Follow Routine 6, the selection vocabulary routine, as you introduce the vocabulary words for this selection.

+ Explain to students that if someone *measures* something, he or she uses a tool to find the size of the object. Ask students if someone measures how much they have grown each year.

+ Tell students *buds* are unopened flowers. Use the following sentence to illustrate: *The buds will open into flowers in a few days.*

+ Tell students the word *flutter* means "to flap wings quickly." Demonstrate how a butterfly or bird might flutter its wings, and have students demonstrate as well.

+ Explain to students that *bouquets* are bunches of flowers. Ask them if they have ever picked bouquets of flowers from a garden or a field.

+ Tell students *scents* are the ways things smell. Ask students if the scents in a bakery ever make them feel hungry.

+ Explain to students that *dim* means "not bright." Use the following sentence to illustrate: *The clouds in the sky made the sun very dim.*

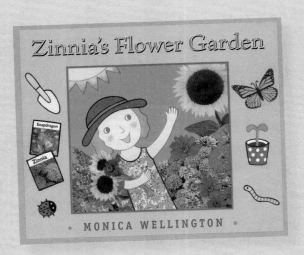

Zinnia's Flower Garden

Vocabulary

measures	bouquets
buds	scents
flutter	dim

Read the Selection

ROUTINE **7**

Comprehension Strategies

✦ During the first reading of *Zinnia's Flower Garden,* you modeled the following comprehension strategies:

- Asking Questions
- Predicting

✦ In this second reading of the selection, you will revisit each comprehension strategy model from the first reading.

Comprehension Skills

In this lesson for *Zinnia's Flower Garden,* students will use the comprehension skill Cause and Effect.

Reading with a Writer's Eye

✦ In this rereading of *Zinnia's Flower Garden,* you will discuss how the author develops the setting.

✦ By discussing the writing strategies the author uses, students become more aware of how they can be better writers.

 Teacher Tip

COMPREHENSION STRATEGIES Readers are also listeners. Reading aloud to students provides an opportunity to teach the reader responses and problem-solving strategies readers employ. In addition to reading aloud with expression and enthusiasm, model your own comprehension strategies while reading aloud to students. This makes the use of strategies "real" for students and encourages them to begin to respond to text similarly.

Technology

To promote independent reading, encourage students to use Workshop to listen to the recording of the selection on the *Listening Library CD.* Invite them to follow along and say the words whenever they can.

 Audio CD

Comprehension Strategies

Teacher Modeling

1 Predicting *Zinnia is busy getting her garden ready for planting. When we looked at the pictures, we saw a pencil and a notebook that says "My Garden Journal." These clues helped us predict Zinnia was going to write what happens in her garden.*

2 Asking Questions *Our prediction was confirmed. Zinnia had written in her journal on May 3 when she planted her seeds. Then we wondered what kinds of flowers Zinnia was planting. The pictures told us she was planting sunflowers, zinnias, marigolds, cosmos, black-eyed Susans, asters, and sweet peas.*

3 Predicting *Here we noticed Zinnia's journal said May 12. We knew she had planted her seeds on May 3, so we figured out nine days had passed. We also knew the seeds had been getting plenty of rain and sunshine. So we predicted Zinnia would soon see little sprouts poke up through the soil.*

4 Predicting *The first sprout appeared! This confirmed our prediction. The sprout appeared only eight days later.*

Focus Question How does Zinnia make sure her flowers will grow?

Spring has arrived. Zinnia is getting her garden ready for planting. She digs up the soil and turns it over with her shovel. She takes out stones and rakes the dirt smooth. The warm sun feels good as she works. **1**

Zinnia carefully plants many kinds of flower seeds in rows. She covers the seeds with dirt and pats it all down very gently. She sprinkles the ground with water. **2**

Zinnia waits for the seeds to sprout. The seeds need the sun to shine, the rain to fall, and many days to pass. It is hard to wait so long for her seeds to grow. ③

Every day Zinnia checks her garden to see if anything has happened. Look! The first seedling is poking its way up through the dirt. ④

Zinnia's Flower Garden, pp. 4–11

Comprehension Skills

Cause and Effect

✦ Review *cause and effect* with students by explaining that certain things make other things happen. When one thing makes something else happen, the first thing is called the *cause,* and the second thing is called the *effect.*

✦ Help students use the selection to find the answers to these cause-and-effect questions:

- *What* causes *Zinnia to dig up the soil in her garden?* *She wants to get her garden ready for planting.*

- *What* causes *Zinnia to check her garden every day?* *She wants to see if any sprouts have appeared.*

- *What will be the* effect *of labeling the rows of seeds?* *Zinnia will know what kind of flowers she has planted in each row.*

- *What is the* effect *of the sun and rain on the seeds?* *The seeds sprout into young plants.*

Reading with a Writer's Eye

Setting

✦ Point out the author/illustrator of *Zinnia's Flower Garden* uses words and pictures to develop the setting. Ask students to identify the setting of *Zinnia's Flower Garden. a flower garden in Zinnia's front yard*

✦ Ask students what the pictures on these pages show about the location and appearance of Zinnia's garden.

Differentiating Instruction **English Learners**

IF . . . students have difficulty identifying or expressing cause and effect, **THEN . . .** introduce the linguistic patterns _____ because _____; _____ caused _____.

Comprehension Strategies

Teacher Modeling

5 Asking Questions *Here we wondered why the sprouts in each picture look different. The next page answered our question. Each row of seeds has a different label. This told us the sprouts look different because they are from different flowers.*

6 Predicting *This page tells the steps Zinnia takes in caring for her plants. So we predicted her garden would be a big success.*

7 Asking Questions *When we saw the first buds had appeared, we wondered how long it had taken. We knew Zinnia had planted her seeds on May 3 and it was now July 18. We counted the months and then the extra days. We decided Zinnia's plants had been growing for two months and two weeks.*

Zinnia's Flower Garden, pp. 12–19

Comprehension Skills

Cause and Effect

Help students use the selection to find the answers to these cause-and-effect questions:

- *What* causes *Zinnia to water her garden?* *She sees the soil is dry.*
- *What* causes *Zinnia to pull up pesky weeds?* *She doesn't want the weeds to crowd out her plants.*
- *What is the* effect *of Zinnia measuring her plants?* *She sees how much they have grown.*
- *What is the effect of Zinnia checking her garden early one morning?* *She sees little buds on some of her plants.*

Reading with a Writer's Eye

Setting

✦ Ask students what new information they learn about the setting of the story on these pages. Ask *Does the garden look any different?*

✦ Ask students if Zinnia's flower garden is a place they would enjoy. Ask them how the author/illustrator makes the garden, or setting, so pleasant.

Vocabulary Tip

Review the meanings of the words *measures* and *buds*. Then have students use the words in sentences.

Teacher Tip

CAUSE AND EFFECT If students seem to have trouble understanding the concept of cause and effect, try demonstrating some simple cause-effect relationships. For example, roll a ball, and knock down some blocks. Have students tell the cause and the effect. *You rolled a ball; the blocks fell down.*

Comprehension Strategies

Teacher Modeling

8 Predicting *When we saw all the colorful flowers, we knew Zinnia's garden had been a big success—just as we had predicted. And the story tells how much Zinnia enjoys relaxing among her flowers.*

9 Predicting *Zinnia's garden has so many flowers! We wondered what she would do with all of them. When we saw the pretty bouquets Zinnia had made, we predicted she would find a way to share her flowers with others.*

10 Predicting *Our prediction was confirmed. Zinnia did find a way to share her flowers. She set up a stand to sell lemonade and invited people to pick their own flowers.*

Vocabulary Tip

Review the meaning of the word *flutter*. Then have students use the word in a sentence.

Teacher Tip

COMPREHENSION Readers should interact with the text as they read—by emoting, reacting, responding, and problem solving—in their efforts to construct and maintain meaning.

Comprehension Skills

Cause and Effect

Help students use the selection to find the answers to these cause-and-effect questions:

- *What* causes *Zinnia to spend so much time in her garden?* *All the flowers make it a lovely place to be.*

- *What* causes *people to come to Zinnia's garden?* *They see her sign and want to pick some flowers.*

- *What is an* effect *of having so many flowers?* *Fragrant scents are everywhere. Zinnia can make lots of bouquets. Zinnia has plenty of flowers to share with others.*

Zinnia's Flower Garden, pp. 20–27

Reading with a Writer's Eye

Setting

✦ Browse pages 20–27. Ask students what new information they learn about the setting of the story on these pages. Ask *Does the flower garden look any different?*

✦ Ask students how the garden setting makes them feel. Point out that the bright, colorful pictures make the garden setting seem like a cheerful, friendly place.

Vocabulary Tip

Review the meanings of the words *bouquets, scents* and *dim.* Then have students use the words in sentences.

Comprehension Strategies

Teacher Modeling

11 Asking Questions *Here we wondered how to tell when a seed is ripe and ready to be collected. We couldn't find an answer in the pictures or the story. I decided we might need to look for the answer in another book. Sometimes we have to look other places to find answers to our questions.*

12 Asking Questions *We wondered how Zinnia was planning next year's garden. When we looked at the picture, we noticed she was writing in two notebooks—her journal and another one that says "Order seeds." This told us she was writing down what she needs to do before next spring. She also seemed to be thinking about something. We decided she could be thinking about what to grow next year.*

Zinnia's Flower Garden, pp. 28–31

 ## Teacher Tip

DISCUSSING THE SELECTION Tell students after reading, they should always ask *What did I find interesting? What is important here?* Later remind students again whenever they conclude a reading, they should ask themselves questions about what was in the text.

Reading with a Writer's Eye

Setting

✦ Ask students *How have the colors changed on page 28?* *The bright colors have changed to orange, brown, and gold.* **What do the colors tell you about the time of year and the changes in the setting?** *It is now autumn, and the leaves have changed to these colors. The flowers have also turned brown.*

✦ Ask *Does the flower garden look any different on pages 28–31?* *In autumn, only a few last flowers remain in the garden. Autumn leaves fall to the ground. When winter comes, the garden is covered with snow. It is no longer the sunny, cheerful place it once was.*

Discussing the Selection

Help students review the stages of a flower's growth.

Purposes for Reading

Ask students what they liked best about *Zinnia's Flower Garden* and what they learned about growing things from this selection.

Vocabulary Review

Review with students the selection vocabulary words *measures, buds, flutter, bouquets, scents,* and *dim.* Ask students the following questions:

- *What is Zinnia doing when she measures her plants?*
- *Why is Zinnia happy to see buds on her plants?*
- *How do butterflies flutter their wings?*
- *Why does Zinnia make bouquets with her flowers?*
- *What kinds of scents do you smell in the summer?*
- *Why are winter days dim?*

OBJECTIVES

Students will

+ share and describe drawings of how-to instructions.
+ review the present, past, and future tenses of action words.
+ rework the plot of a story by changing story details.

MATERIALS

+ *Transparency* 42
+ *Teacher's Resource Book,* p. 39

Writing Process

Present: Sharing Drawings

Teach

+ In preparation for class, group the students into two lists: The students on one list will present their drawings on the first day, and those on the other list will present theirs on the second day.

+ Tell students today is the day they will begin sharing their drawings with their classmates. Explain that half the class will present their drawings today and that the other half will share theirs in the next lesson.

Apply

+ Distribute the drawings for students who are presenting today. Have them review their drawings and think about what they want to say about them.

+ Model how you would like the students to begin their presentations. Use the high-frequency words *they* and *said* that students learned earlier in the unit. As students share their drawings, encourage them to say a few words to describe their drawings.

+ Ask the other students to notice how their classmates' drawings are different from their own.

+ After the last student has presented his or her drawings, tell the remaining students they will have their opportunity to present in the next lesson.

Grammar, Usage, and Mechanics

Teach

+ Remind students that the present tense of a word shows action happening now, the past tense of a word shows action that happened before now, and the future tense of a word shows action that will happen in the future.

+ List the following on the board in Past, Present, and Future columns: *ate, ran, wrote, slept, listened; eat, run, write, sleep, listen; will eat, will run, will write, will sleep, will listen.* Discuss how each tense looks. Explain that some words do not use *ed* in the past tense, such as *eat, run, write,* and *sleep.* Remind students that the correct tense tells us when action happened.

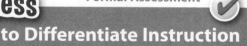

Monitor Progress
to Differentiate Instruction

Formal Assessment ✓

Grammar Note how easily students understand action words.

APPROACHING LEVEL

IF ... students are having difficulty,

THEN ... have them complete **Reteach** page 159.

ON LEVEL

IF ... students need more practice,

THEN ... have them discuss what they did last night and identify action words in the sentences they say.

ABOVE LEVEL

IF ... students are comfortable,

THEN ... have them draw pictures of other children doing some sort of action.

Grammar, Usage, and Mechanics continued

Guided Practice

✦ Review the illustrations and text of the story "Becoming Butterflies," and guide students in identifying the three tenses in the story.

✦ Turn to page 34, and read aloud the text for students. Then guide students in identifying examples of present- and past-tense verbs on the page. For example, you might identify the words *lay, hatch,* and *eat* as present tense and the word *helped* as past tense. (Other past-tense verbs are irregular verbs.) Continue with other pages.

✦ Have students identify the future tense by locating the word *will* on page 56.

Teacher Tip

ACTIVITY PREPARATION Return to each student a copy of *Transparency* 42. It might benefit students to reference this visual representation of the story during this activity.

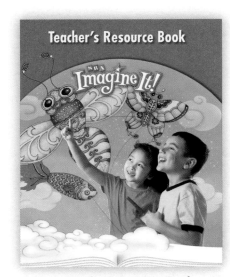

Teacher's Resource Book, p. 39

Story Crafting

Working with the New: Developing Characters and Plots

✦ Display *Transparency* 42, and lead students in a brief retelling of the story.

✦ Write on the board and review each of the scenarios the class discussed in the previous lesson. Have students vote for their favorite one.

✦ Display *Teacher's Resource Book* page 39. Tell students you would like them to help you retell *"Zinnia's Flower Garden,"* using one of the changes they considered in the previous lesson.

✦ Guide students in using line drawings to retell the story, reflecting the change in character or plot. You might take responsibility for the majority of the drawing, but invite students to come up and draw certain details in the frames.

✦ Again, close the activity by discussing how changing one detail in a story can make the story very different.

Transparency 42

Calendar

Su	M	T	W	Th	F	S
		1	2	3	4	5
6	7	8	9	10	11	12
13	14	15	16	17	18	19
20	21	22	23	24	25	26
27	28	29	30	31		

Point to the box that represents today. Ask students to count aloud with you how many days are in this month. Begin with the first day of the month, and point to each day as you count aloud.

Warming Up 🕐

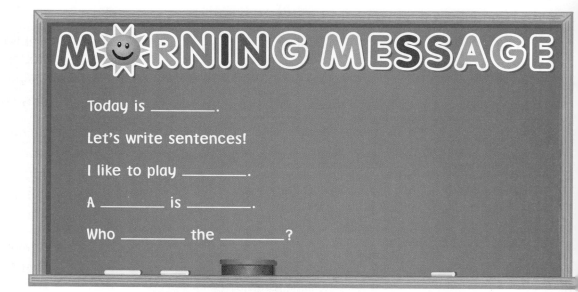

Today is _____.

Let's write sentences!

I like to play _____.

A _____ is _____.

Who _____ the _____?

Kindergarten News

✦ Copy the text above on the board or on chart paper.

✦ Ask students if they can read any words in the message today. Have students point to and say any words they can read.

✦ Invite volunteers to say words to complete the sentences. Have them come up to the board and write the words in the blanks. You might write the words first in dotted lines and have students trace them. Or you could help them write the words hand over hand.

✦ Discuss the letters and words in the message. For example, ask students to underline the letters that say long *i* in *write* or *like,* or have them identify the exclamation point or question mark.

Phoneme Replacement

✦ Tell students they are going to play the rhyme game. Remind them that in the game they use what they are learning about sounds and letters to make rhymes. Say you are going to give them a riddle and the answer is a word that begins with the sound you say.

✦ Try these riddles:

What rhymes with hug *but starts with /b/?* bug

What rhymes with sag *but starts with /n/?* nag

What rhymes with dream *but starts with /k/?* cream

What rhymes with moose *but starts with /g/?* goose

What rhymes with test *but starts with /r/?* rest

Phonemic Awareness

Phoneme Segmentation

✦ Have students sit around a table. Place the following **Pocket Chart Picture Cards** facedown in the center of the table: 19—bat, 31—box, 36—cat, 49—dog, 77—hen, 92—jam, 127—pig, 140—red, and 7—six.

✦ Call on a student to choose a card, and tell him or her not to show it to anyone. Tell the student to think about the name of the picture and then to say the first sound in that name. When the student says the sound, have the other students repeat it.

✦ Continue with the second and third sounds.

✦ When all the sounds in the word have been said, call on a volunteer to say them again and to identify the picture.

✦ Have the first student show the picture to confirm the answer.

✦ Continue with other students and other **Picture Cards.**

 Teacher Tip

ACTIVITY SUPPORT To offer students more support, have them also identify the letters that make each sound in the words. Then write the letters on the board. Students can refer to the letters when they are putting together the sounds to identify the words. Near the end of the activity, have students try to identify the words without the visual support.

Differentiating Instruction | **English Learners**

IF ... students have difficulty with the phonemic awareness activity, **THEN ...** refer to Unit 8 Lesson 15 of the *English Learner Support Guide.*

Teacher Tip

SKILL REVIEW This is the final review of the /ā/ sound and the /ī/ sound before students move on to learning new long-vowel sounds in Unit 9. Take this opportunity to identify students who are still struggling with differentiating sounds or linking the sounds to the proper letters. Work with these students individually, and guide them in redoing a few of the *Skills Practice 2* or *Reteach* pages they completed in this unit.

Alphabetic Principle

Reviewing the Sounds of Long *Aa* and Long *Ii*

✦ Point to **Alphabet Sound Wall Card** Long *Aa*, and have students recite the rhyme for the sounds of *Aa*:

A's my name.

Two sounds I make:

Short a *in* lamb,

Long a *in* cake.

✦ Do the same with **Alphabet Sound Wall Card** Long *Ii*, and have students recite the rhyme:

I's my name.

Two sounds have I:

Short i *in* pig,

Long i *in* pie.

Listening for Initial /ā/ and /ī/

✦ Give each student one **Alphabet Letter Card** *Aa* and one **Alphabet Letter Card** *Ii*. Ask students to raise the *Aa* cards and say the /ā/ sound when you say a word that begins with the /ā/ sound. They should raise the *Ii* cards and say the /ī/ sound when they hear a word that begins with the /ī/ sound.

✦ Tell students to listen closely because not all of the words will begin with the /ā/ sound or the /ī/ sound. Try the following words:

able	**iron**	**April**	ocean
eat	**ate**	**idea**	**island**
ape	**ice**	unit	**apron**
offer	eve	obey	umpire

Blending

✦ Review long-vowel blending with students using the sound-by-sound blending routine. Begin by blending words with the /ā/ sound using the following words:

name　　　*gave*　　　*made*

✦ Continue the activity, blending words with the /ī/ sound:

pine　　　*nine*　　　*bite*

✦ After blending each word, have students reread the words naturally as they would speak them.

Penmanship

✦ Distribute a sheet of writing paper to each student, or use **White Boards** turned to the sides with writing lines.

✦ Place the Supply Icon for *pencil* on the board or in the **Pocket Chart.**

✦ Review with students the procedure for forming the numeral *4* while they make the strokes in the air with their fingers.

✦ Repeat the review for the numeral *5.*

✦ Ask students to write one row of numeral *4*s and one row of numeral *5*s on the writing paper or board. Make sure students write from top to bottom and left to right.

Guided Practice

✦ Have students complete **Skills Practice 2** page 73 for additional practice writing the numerals *4* and *5.*

✦ Have students practice writing the numerals *4* and *5* on the lines.

✦ Then ask students to identify the number of apples on each tree and to write the numbers *4* and *5* on the appropriate lines.

✦ After students have finished, be sure to review their work. Then have them proofread using the established procedure.

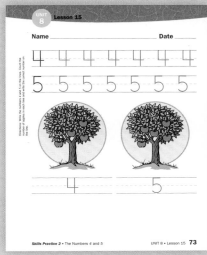

Skills Practice 2, p. 73

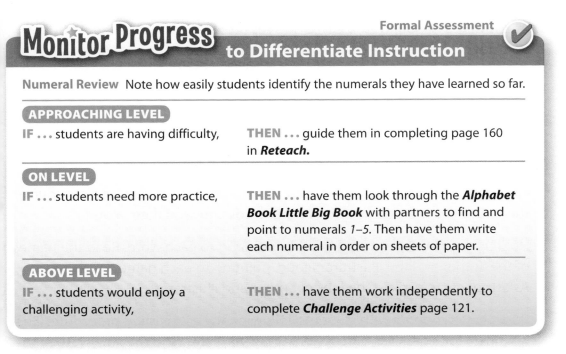

Monitor Progress

Formal Assessment ✓

to Differentiate Instruction

Numeral Review Note how easily students identify the numerals they have learned so far.

APPROACHING LEVEL

IF ... students are having difficulty,

THEN ... guide them in completing page 160 in **Reteach.**

ON LEVEL

IF ... students need more practice,

THEN ... have them look through the **Alphabet Book Little Big Book** with partners to find and point to numerals *1–5*. Then have them write each numeral in order on sheets of paper.

ABOVE LEVEL

IF ... students would enjoy a challenging activity,

THEN ... have them work independently to complete **Challenge Activities** page 121.

A Nut Pile

by Sean Sanders   illustrated by Eileen Hine

Decodable 16

Teacher Tip

SEGMENTATION FLUENCY Take this opportunity to help students practice segmentation of words with the long *i* vowel sound. Give students the word *Pile* from the title, and have them identify all the sounds in the word. Continue with other story words such as *side, five,* and *wide.*

Technology

Use *eDecodable* A Nut Pile to reinforce high-frequency words *some* and *there* and the /ī/ sound.

Audio CD

Reading a Decodable

Decodable 16: A Nut Pile

High-Frequency Words: *some, there*

✦ The high-frequency words introduced are *some* and *there.* Write *some* on the board, and read it aloud. Have students repeat it aloud with you. Then have students say the word on their own. Repeat the process with *there.*

✦ Offer students a few examples of sentences that use *some* and *there.* You might say *Some books are funny* or *There are three pretty flowers.*

✦ Point again to *some* written on the board, and have students read the word independently. Do the same with *there.*

✦ Have volunteers use the words *some* and *there* in sentences. You might provide frames such as the following: *There is a_____. I have some _____.* Ask them to find and point to the words *some* and *there* on any classroom posters, bulletin boards, or the covers of any books.

✦ Review the high-frequency words introduced in previous lessons.

Blending

Before reading **Decodable** 16, review the blending procedure with students. Choose words with the /ā/ sound written *a_e,* such as *game, lake,* and *fade,* and words with the /ī/ sound written *i_e,* such as *ride, like,* and *mile.* After blending, have students make and extend sentences for each word.

Reading Recommendations

✦ Distribute copies of **Decodable** 16. Have students browse the books and look at the pictures, commenting on what they see and making predictions about what they think the story will be about.

✦ Point to the high-frequency words *some* and *there* in the text, and pronounce them. Then have students point to the words and read them aloud.

✦ Hold up your book, and read the title, pointing to each word. Read the names of the author and the illustrator aloud, pointing to each name as you say it. Ask students to explain the jobs of author and illustrator.

✦ Read the **Decodable** with students, following the established procedure. (See Routine 4 for a detailed description.) After you have read the story, reread the title, and have students repeat after you. Then have students read it chorally with you.

A Nut Pile

by Sean Sanders   illustrated by Eileen Hine

Some nuts drop on the side.

3

Five nuts land there in a pile.

4

Can nuts make big plants?

5

Look there! Some plant buds pop up!

6

Look at the plants get big and wide.

7

Five nuts made five big plants!

8

Decodable 16
A Nut Pile

**High-Frequency Words
Introduced in Decodable 16**
some
there

**Previously Introduced
High-Frequency Words**
a
all
am
and
as
at
but
can
did
down
for
girl
go
had
has
have
he
her
him
his
I
in
is
it
look

of
on
said
see
that
the
they
to
up
was
we
were
what
with
you

**Sound-Spelling Correspondences in
Decodables**
1. /s/, /m/, /d/, /p/, /a/
2. /h/, /t/
3. /n/, /l/
4. /i/
5. /b/, /k/ spelled c
6. /o/, /r/
7. /g/
8. /j/, /f/
9. /u/, /ks/ spelled x
10. /z/
11. /w/, /k/ spelled k
12. /e/, /kw/ spelled qu
13. /y/, /v/
14. Long a spelled a_e
15. Long i spelled i_e
16. Review long a, long i

Responding

✦ Display the **High-Frequency Flash Cards** for *some* and *there*. Have students find and point to these high-frequency words in the story. Ask students to identify in the story any of the previously introduced high-frequency words.

✦ Have students connect the story to their prior knowledge. Ask them to share anything they know about how things grow. They might also enjoy sharing stories about something they once planted or watched grow.

✦ Have students work to answer the following questions and point to the answer on the page: *On what page do the plant buds pop up? On what page is the word* and*?*

✦ Have students look at the end marks in the story. Ask a volunteer to say the page number on which a period appears. Ask other students to say the page numbers on which a question mark and an exclamation point appear.

✦ Make copies of the story for the students to take home. A black-and-white version of the story is available in **Pre-Decodable and Decodable Takehomes Blackline Masters.**

***Decodable** 16, inside back cover*

Students will

✦ share and describe drawings of how-to instructions.

✦ review the present, past, and future tenses of action words.

✦ participate in a celebration of the unit theme.

✦ *Skills Practice 2,* p. 74
✦ *Read Aloud Collection: What's Alive?*
✦ *Ready, Set, Grow! Big Book*
✦ *Story Time Collection: Zinnia's Flower Garden*

Theme Wrap-Up and Review 🕐

✦ Show students the covers of *What's Alive?*, "A Tree Is a Plant," "Becoming Butterflies," and *Zinnia's Flower Garden*. Assist students in retelling each story. Invite them to share any comments, and then ask the following questions:

• *What did you learn about living things in* What's Alive?

• *What did you learn about how the parts of a tree help it grow in "A Tree Is a Plant"?*

• *What do the caterpillars need to turn into butterflies in "Becoming Butterflies"?*

• *How did Zinnia help her flowers grow in* Zinnia's Flower Garden?

• *How did Zinnia keep track of the changes in her garden? How is this the same as or different from what we did when we observed?*

✦ Invite students to ask other questions they have, and discuss them as a group. Encourage students to share their thoughts and feelings about the unit theme Ready, Set, Grow! Begin a discussion by asking the following questions:

• *What do plants and animals need to grow?*

• *What do you need to grow?*

• *How does a seed sprout?*

• *How did our knowledge about how things grow increase from the beginning to the end of the unit?*

• *How did our investigations help increase our understanding about how things grow?*

🍎 Teacher Tip

PLANT INVESTIGATIONS If students are doing investigations that require them to observe plants under different growing conditions, you may want to give them this additional week to record the findings of their investigations. Begin the unit celebration after students have recorded their latest findings.

Read Aloud Collection:
What's Alive

Ready, Set, Grow! Big Book

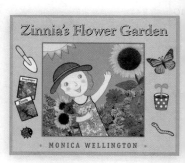

Story Time Collection:
Zinnia's Flower Garden

Writing Process

Present: Sharing Their Drawings

Teach

Tell students today they will finish sharing their drawings with their classmates.

Apply

Distribute the drawings for students who have not yet presented their work. They should review their drawings and think about what they want to say about them.

Ask students to listen attentively to each speaker and to notice how their classmates' drawings are different from their own.

Remind each presenter to say a few words to describe their pictures.

After the last student has presented his or her drawings, have a whole-class discussion about the writing process.

Monitor Progress to Differentiate Instruction

Formal Assessment

Grammar Note how quickly students are able to identify action words.

APPROACHING LEVEL

IF ... students are having difficulty,

THEN ... have students form pairs and talk about an action they will be completing today in class.

ON LEVEL

IF ... students need more practice,

THEN ... ask them to discuss as a group the things they do to get ready for bed and the action words in those sentences.

ABOVE LEVEL

IF ... students are comfortable,

THEN ... have them complete **Challenge Activities** page 122.

Grammar, Usage, and Mechanics

Teach

Draw a web on chart paper. Write *Yesterday after School* in the center circle. Ask students to tell you some things they did yesterday after school. Write each phrase on a line of the web, underlining the word that shows action in the past tense. Continue in this way with the phrases *Next Saturday* and *Class Today*.

Guided Practice

Have students open their **Skills Practice 2** to page 74. Work through the page with students, and review their answers when you finish.

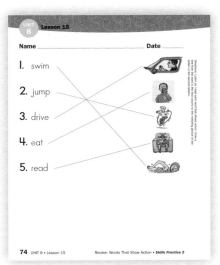

Skills Practice 2, p. 74

Teacher Tip

HIGH-FREQUENCY WORDS Ask students to point out the high frequency word *some* in the story "A Tree Is a Plant."

Monitor Progress ✓
Formal Assessment Options

You will need the following materials, along with your informal observations and Lesson Assessment results, to monitor student progress throughout the year.

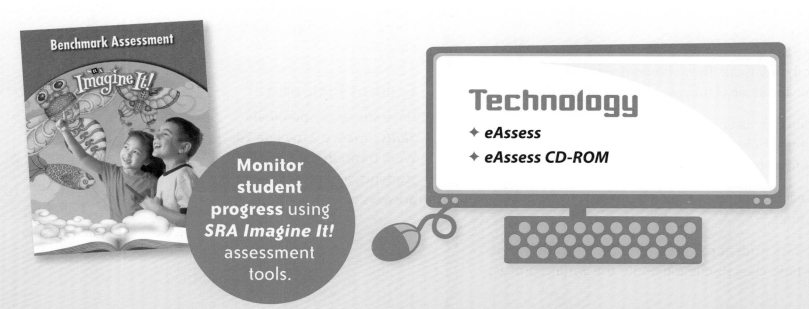

Benchmark Assessment

Monitor student **progress** using *SRA Imagine It!* assessment tools.

Technology
- ✦ *eAssess*
- ✦ *eAssess CD-ROM*

Benchmark Assessment for Unit 8 addresses the following skills:

- Phonemic Awareness
- Letter Recognition
- Phonics/Word Reading
- Comprehension
- Grammar, Usage, and Mechanics

Results on **Benchmark Assessment** will serve as a performance indicator that shows how well students are prepared to take an end-of-the-year standardized test. **Benchmark Assessment** results also will allow you to intervene with students who are at risk for failure.

Monitor Progress with Benchmark Assessment

Below are two sets of **Benchmark Assessment** cutoffs that can be used for predicting student performance—one for Benchmark Skills Assessments and the other for Oral Fluency Assessments. Each cutoff begins with a baseline score under Benchmark 1, which is given at the beginning of the year and ends with Benchmark 6, which is given at the end of the year. The cutoffs are determined by finding the amount of growth a student must make over the course of the year to ensure he or she will not be at risk for reading failure.

Benchmark Skills Assessment

The Benchmark Skills Assessment is a 100-point test, consisting of questions covering phonemic awareness; letter recognition; phonics/word reading; comprehension; and grammar, usage, and mechanics. The table below shows how many points out of 100 kindergarten students should score on a particular Benchmark Skills Assessment over the course of the year. The highlighted score indicates where your students should be at this time.

Benchmark 1	Benchmark 2	Benchmark 3	Benchmark 4	Benchmark 5	Benchmark 6
7	23	38	54	70	85

Oral Fluency Assessment: Letter Sounds

The Oral Fluency Assessment is an individually administered assessment, consisting of letter sounds, phonetically regular words, and high-frequency words that students read aloud to the teacher to assess fluency. The table below shows how many letter sounds and words kindergarten students should read on a particular Oral Fluency Assessment over the course of the year. The highlighted score indicates where your students should be at this time.

Benchmark 1	Benchmark 2	Benchmark 3	Benchmark 4	Benchmark 5	Benchmark 6
0	6	12	18	24	30

Independent Tools to Monitor Progress

DIBELS and TPRI

Based on your DIBELS or TPRI scores, use manipulatives from the **Workshop Kit** to practice letter sounds and letter recognition.

What makes living things grow?

Write the Big Idea question on the board or on chart paper. Ask students what they have learned about things that grow. Ask which selections added something new to their understanding about growth.

Celebrate Growth! 🕐

✦ In advance of the activity, prepare the materials students will need to share the final product of their inquiry. The necessary materials will depend on the method students chose for sharing.

✦ Congratulate students on all their hard work in this unit as they learned about how things grow. Remind them the unit celebration is a reward for all their hard work.

✦ Support students through each step of their preparation for the celebration. For example, if students have decided to demonstrate how something grows, provide the materials and information they need to make their experiments successes.

✦ To ensure all students are taking part, guide students as they plan individual roles in the celebration.

✦ Help students create a forum for sharing the final product of their inquiry. Encourage them to think of new ideas for sharing their inquiry with people outside the classroom. If students need help sparking their creativity, make suggestions for how students might share their celebration with others.

Inquiry Wrap-Up

✦ As students share their inquiry findings, be sure they begin by telling what their conjecture was, what they observed, and if their observations supported their conjectures. Encourage students to ask questions after the presentation.

✦ In the previous unit, students talked about evaluating their inquiry. Take a few minutes to do this.

- *What did you learn from our inquiry activities? How did your knowledge "grow?"*
- *Why was it important to keep track of our observations?*
- *What problems did you have? How can we solve those problems?*

Concept/Question Board

Encourage students to discuss what they have learned about growing things. Invite them to share how their ideas about growing things have changed since the unit began. Focus students' attention on the **Concept/Question Board** postings, and peel back the layers of self-sticking notes to see how their knowledge has changed. Read aloud each question, and determine if it has been answered and can be moved to the Concept side of the Board. Invite volunteers to add ideas to the questions that still need answers.

 Teacher Tip

RECREATIONAL READING Because it is important to read daily to your students, choose a book from the Additional Reading listed in the Table of Contents, and find a time during the day to read the book aloud to your students.

B

bark
The **bark** on the tree is rough.

blossoms
The cherry **blossoms** are pink and white.

branches
Birds live in the tree **branches**.

E

enormous
We like to sit under the **enormous** umbrella.

64

65

H

hatch
Chickens **hatch** from eggs.

P

peeled
Grandma **peeled** the potatoes.

R

roots
Roots carry water to the tree.

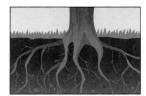

S

shell
The turtle has a **shell** on its back.

66

67

soil
We planted seeds in the soil.

striped
The **striped** caterpillar crawls on the stick.

T

trunk
We hid behind the tree **trunk**.

U

underneath
The ball is **underneath** the bed.

68

69

The Program Appendix includes a step-by-step explanation of procedures for research-based, effective practices in reading instruction that are repeatedly used throughout **SRA Imagine It!** These practices may also be used in other instructional materials.

Table of Contents

Phonological and Phonemic Awareness

The key to learning to read is the ability to identify different sounds and to connect those sounds to the letters of the alphabet. The basic purpose of providing structured practice in phonemic awareness is to help students hear and understand the sounds from which words are made. Before students can be expected to understand the sound/symbol correspondence that forms the base of written English, they need to have a strong working knowledge of the sound relationships that make up the spoken language. This understanding of spoken language lays the foundation for the transition to written language.

Phonological awareness is an umbrella term. It incorporates a range of oral language skills that involve the ability to notice, think about, and manipulate individual sounds in words. Phonological awareness involves working with sentences, words, rhyme, syllables, and sounds. The objective is for students to be able to manipulate words, word parts, and sounds without regard to meaning.

Phonological and phonemic awareness activities initially provide students with the opportunity to think about sentences and to break them into words and then to play with words and to break them into parts. It involves easy and fun activities that engage students in playing with and exploring the parts and sounds of language. The goal of these gamelike activities is to help students understand that speech is made of distinct, identifiable sounds. The playful nature of the activities makes them appealing and engaging, while giving students practice and support for learning about language. When students begin reading and writing, this experience with manipulating sounds will help them use what they know about sounds and letters to sound out and spell unfamiliar words when they read and write.

Developing phonological awareness engages students in activities that move from working with words and syllables — the larger units of language — to individual sounds (phonemes). Students progress by

- Identifying sentences
- Identifying words
- Working with rhymes
- Exploring compound words
- Listening for syllables

- Blending syllables
- Oral blending
- Deleting and substituting sounds
- Segmenting phonemes

As students progress through various phonemic awareness activities, they will become proficient at listening for and reproducing the sounds they hear. It is essential for their progression to phonics and reading that they are able to hear the sounds and the patterns used to make up recognizable words. The phonemic awareness activities support the phonics instruction. Initially students are not expected to read the words they are exploring and manipulating, so any consonant and vowel sounds may be used, even if students have not been formally taught the sounds and their spellings.

> *As students progress through various phonemic awareness activities, they will become proficient at listening for and reproducing the sounds they hear.*

After students have an awareness of phonemes, they can begin to connect sounds to letters and to engage in a variety of activities in which sounds and letters are substituted to make new words. Students begin to understand that if a sound changes, a letter must change, and a new word is created. As students move into phonics, research suggests that connecting sounds to spellings actually heightens their awareness of language. Phonological and phonemic awareness is both a prerequisite for and a consequence of learning to read.

Research suggests that the majority of instructional time should be focused on two critical phonemic awareness formats: phoneme or oral blending and phoneme

segmentation. These are supported by discrimination and elision activities (deleting and substituting sounds) and general wordplay. Oral blending encourages students to combine sounds to make words and lays the foundation for decoding and reading. Segmentation, conversely, requires students to break words into discrete sounds and lays the foundation for spelling. Other activities support discrimination, or recognition, of particular sounds. Sometimes simple songs, rhymes, or games engage students in wordplay. In these, students manipulate words in a variety of ways. From these playful activities, students develop serious knowledge about their language.

Oral Blending
Purpose

In oral blending, students are led through a progression of activities designed to help them hear how sounds are put together to make words.

Until students develop an awareness of the component parts of words, they have no tools with which to decode words or to put letters together to form words. Oral blending helps students understand these component parts of words, from syllables down to single sounds, or phonemes. Oral blending is not to be confused with the formal blending of specific sounds whose spellings students will be taught through phonics instruction. Oral blending does not depend on the recognition of written words; it focuses instead on hearing the sounds.

Oral blending focuses on hearing sounds through a sequence that introduces the most easily distinguished word parts and then systematically moves to oral blending of individual sounds that contains all the challenges of phonic decoding (except letter recognition). This sequence provides support for the least-prepared student—one who comes to school with no concept of words or sounds within words. At the same time, the lively pace and playful nature of oral blending activities hold the interest of students who already have some familiarity with words and letters.

Oral blending prepares students for phonics instruction by developing an awareness of the separate sounds that make up speech. Oral blending activities then continue in concert with phonics instruction to reinforce and extend new learning. And because these activities involve simply listening to and reproducing sounds, oral blending need not be restricted to the sounds students have been or will be taught in phonics.

The tone of the activities should be playful and informal and should move quickly. Although these activities will provide information about student progress, they are not diagnostic tools. Do not expect mastery. Those students who have not caught on will be helped more by varied experiences than by more drilling on the same activity.

Procedure

The following is a description of the progression of oral blending activities.

Word-Part Blending

Syllables are easier to distinguish than individual sounds (phonemes), so students can quickly experience success in forming meaningful words. Tell students that you are going to say some words in two parts. Tell them to listen carefully so they can discover what the words are. Read each word, pronouncing each part distinctly with a definite pause between syllables. The lists of words that follow are arranged in sequence from easy to harder. They cover different types of cues. Whenever they fit into the sequence, include multisyllabic names of students in the class.

Model

Teacher: dino . . . saur. What's the word?
Students: dinosaur

Example Words

✦ First part of the word cues the whole word:
vita . . . min
vaca . . . tion
hippopot . . . amus
ambu . . . lance

✦ Two distinct words easily combined:
butter . . . fly
straw . . . berry
surf . . . board
basket . . . ball

✦ Two distinct words, but first word could cue the wrong ending:
tooth . . . ache
tooth . . . paste
water . . . fall
water . . . melon

✦ First part, consonant + vowel, not enough to guess whole word:
re . . . member
re . . . frigerator
bi . . . cycle
bi . . . ology

✦ Identifying cues in second part:
light . . . ning
sub . . . ject
in . . . sect

✦ Last part, consonant + vowel sound, carries essential information:
yester . . . day
rain . . . bow
noi . . . sy
pota . . . to

✦ Changing the final part changes the word:
start . . . ing
start . . . er
start . . . ed

Initial Consonant Sounds

Initial consonant blending prepares students for consonant replacement activities that will come later. Tell students that you will ask them to put some sounds together to make words. Pronounce each word part distinctly, and make a definite pause at the breaks indicated. When a letter is surrounded by slash marks, pronounce the letter's sound, not its name. When you see /s/, for example, you will say "ssss," not "ess." The words that follow are arranged from easy to harder. Whenever they fit into the sequence, include names of students in the class.

Model

Teacher: /t/ . . . iger. What's the word?
Students: tiger

Example Words

✦ Separated consonant blend, with rest of word giving strong cue to word identity:
/b/ . . . roccoli   */k/ . . . racker*
/f/ . . . lashlight   */k/ . . . reature*

✦ Held consonant that is easy for students to hear, with rest of word giving strong cue:
/s/ . . . innamon   */l/ . . . adybug*
/s/ . . . eventeen   */n/ . . . ewspaper*

✦ Stop consonant that is harder for students to hear preceding vowel, with rest of word giving strong cue:
/t/ . . . adpole   */p/ . . . iggybank*
/d/ . . . ragonfly   */b/ . . . arbecue*

✦ Single-syllable words and words in which the second part gives a weaker cue:
/s/ . . . ing   */l/ . . . augh*   */v/ . . . ase*

Final Consonant Sounds

In this phase of oral blending, the last sound in the word is separated.

Model

Teacher: cabba . . . /j/. What's the word?
Students: cabbage

Example Words

✦ Words that are easily recognized even before the final consonant is pronounced:
bubblegu . . . /m/   *Columbu . . . /s/*
crocodi . . . /l/   *submari . . . /n/*

✦ Multisyllabic words that need the final consonant for recognition:
colle . . . /j/ (college)   *come . . . /t/ (comet)*

✦ Single-syllable words:
sa . . . /d/   *gra . . . /s/ (grass)*   *snai . . . /l/*

Initial Consonant Sound Replacement

This level of oral blending further develops awareness of initial consonant sounds. The activity begins with a common word then quickly changes its initial consonant sound. Most of the words produced are nonsense words, which helps keep the focus on the sounds in the word. Note that the words are written on the board, but students are not expected to read them. The writing is to help students see that when the sounds change, the letters change, and vice versa.

Model

Teacher: [Writes word on board.] This word is *magazine*. What is it?
Students: magazine
Teacher: Now I'm going to change it. [Erases initial consonant.] Now it doesn't start with /m/; it's going to start with /b/. What's the new word?
Students: bagazine
Teacher: That's right . . . [Writes *b* where *m* had been.] It's *bagazine*. Now I'm going to change it again. . . .

Repeat with different consonant sounds. Then do the same with other words such as *remember, Saturday, tomorrow, lotion,* and *million.* Continue with single-syllable words such as *take, big, boot, cot, seat, look, tap, ride,* and *late.* There are two stages in using written letters:

✦ The replacement letter is not written until *after* the new "word" has been identified.

✦ Later, the replacement letter is written at *the same time* the change in the initial phoneme is announced. For example, erase *d* and write *m* while you say, "Now it doesn't start with /d/; it starts with /m/."

When the consonants used have already been introduced in phonics, you may wish to alter the procedure by writing the replacement letter and having students sound out the new word. Feel free to switch between the two procedures within a single exercise. If students are not responding orally to written spellings that have been introduced in phonics, do not force it. Proceed by saying the word before writing the letter, and wait until another time to move on to writing before pronouncing.

One-Syllable Words

Students now begin blending individual phonemes to form words. This important step can be continued well into the year. Continued repetitions of this activity will help students realize how they can use the sound/spellings they are learning to read and write real words.

At first, the blended words are presented in a story context that helps students identify the words. They soon recognize that they are actually decoding meaningful words. However, the context must not be so strong that students can guess the word without listening to the phonemic cues. Any vowel sounds and irregularly spelled words may be used because there is no writing involved.

Model

Teacher: When I looked out the window, I saw a /l/ /ī/ /t/. What did I see?
Students: A light.
Teacher: Yes, I saw a light. At first I thought it was the /m/ /o͞o/ /n/. What did I think it was?
Students: The moon.
Teacher: But it didn't really look like the moon. Suddenly I thought, maybe it's a space /sh/ /i/ /p/. What did I think it might be?
Students: A spaceship!

When students are familiar with this phase of oral blending, they can move to blending one-syllable words without the story context.

Example Words

✦ CVC (consonant/vowel/consonant) words beginning with easily blended consonant sounds (/sh/, /h/, /r/, /v/, /s/,

/n/, /z/, /f/, /l/, /m/):
nip   nap
✦ CVC words beginning with any consonant:
ten   bug   lip
✦ Add CCVC words:
flap   step
✦ Add CVCC words:
most   band   went
✦ Add CCVCC words:
stamp   grand   scuffs

Final Consonant Sound Replacement

Final consonant sounds are typically more difficult for students to use than initial consonants.

✦ Begin with multisyllabic words, and move to one-syllable words.
✦ As with initial consonants, first write the changed consonant after students have pronounced the new word.
✦ Then write the consonant as they pronounce it.
✦ For sound/spellings introduced in phonics instruction, write the new consonant spelling, and have students identify and pronounce it.

Model

Teacher: [Writes word on board.] This word is *teapot*. What is it?
Students: teapot
Teacher: Now I'm going to change it. [Erases final consonant.] Now it doesn't end with /t/; it ends with /p/. What's the word now?
Students: teapop
Teacher: That's right . . . [Writes *p* where *t* had been.] It's *teapop*. Now I'm going to change it again. . . .

Example Words

✦ Words that are easily recognized even before the final consonant is pronounced:
picnic   picnit   picnis   picnil   picnid
airplane   airplate   airplabe   airplafe
✦ Multisyllabic words that need the final consonant for recognition:
muffin   muffil   muffim   muffip   muffit
amaze   amate   amake   amale   amade
✦ Single-syllable words:
neat   nean   neap   neam   neaj   nead   neaf
broom   broot   brood   broof   broop   broon

Initial Vowel Replacement

Up to now, oral blending has concentrated on consonant sounds because they are easier to hear than vowels. As you move to vowel play, remember that the focus is still on the sounds, not the spellings. Use any vowel sounds.

Model

Teacher: [Writes word on board.] This word is *elephant*. What is it?
Students: elephant
Teacher: Now I'm going to change it. [Erases initial vowel.] Now it doesn't start with /e/; it starts with /a/. What's the word now?
Students: alephant
Teacher: That's right . . . [Writes *a* where *e* had been.] It's *alephant*. Now I'm going to change it again. . . .

Example Words

✦ Multisyllabic words:
angry   ingry   oongry   ungry   engry
ivy   avy   oovy   evy   ovy   oivy
✦ One-syllable words:
ink   ank   oonk   unk   onk   oink
add   odd   idd   oudd   edd   udd

Segmentation

Purpose

Segmentation and oral blending complement each other: Oral blending puts sounds together to make words, while segmentation separates words into sounds. Oral blending will provide valuable support for decoding when students begin reading independently.

Procedure

Syllables

The earliest segmentation activities focus on syllables, which are easier to distinguish than individual sounds, or phonemes. Start with students' names, and then use other words. As with the oral blending activities, remember to move quickly through these activities. Do not hold the class back waiting for all students to catch on. Individual progress will vary, but drilling on one activity is less helpful than going on to others. Return to the same activity often. Frequent repetition is very beneficial and allows students additional opportunities to catch on.

- Say, for example, "Let's clap out Amanda's name. A-man-da."
- Have students clap and say the syllables along with you. Count the claps.
- Tell students that these word parts are called syllables. Don't try to explain; the idea will develop with practice. After you have provided the term, simply say, "How many syllables?" after students clap and count.
- Mix one-syllable and multisyllabic words: *fantastic   tambourine   good   imaginary   stand   afraid*

> *Oral blending will provide valuable support for decoding when students begin reading independently.*

Comparative Lengths of Words

Unlike most phonemic awareness activities, this one involves writing on the board or on an overhead transparency. Remember, though, that students are not expected to read what is written. They are merely noticing that words that take longer to say generally look longer when written.

- Start with students' names. Choose two names, one short and one long, with the same first letter (for example, *Joe* and *Jonathan*).
- Write the two names on the board, one above the other, so that the difference is obvious.
- Tell students that one name is *Jonathan* and that one is *Joe*. Have them pronounce and clap each name. Then have them tell which written word they think says *Joe*.
- Move your finger under each name as students clap and say it syllable by syllable.
- Repeat with other pairs of names and words such as *tea/telephone, cat/caterpillar, and butterfly/bug*. Be sure not to give false clues. For example, sometimes write the longer word on top, sometimes the shorter one; sometimes ask for the shorter word, sometimes the

longer; sometimes ask for the top word, sometimes the bottom; and sometimes point to a word and ask students to name it, and sometimes name the word and ask students to point to it.

Listen for Individual Sounds

Activities using a puppet help students listen for individual sounds in words. Use any puppet you have on hand. When you introduce the puppet, tell students that it likes to play word games. Each new activity begins with the teacher speaking to and for the puppet until students determine the pattern. Next, students either speak for the puppet or correct the puppet. To make sure all students are participating, alternate randomly between having the whole group or individuals respond. The activities focus on particular parts of words, according to the following sequence:

I. Repeating last part of word. Use words beginning with easy-to-hear consonants such as *f, l, m, n, r, s,* and *z*. The puppet repeats only the rime, the part of the syllable after the initial consonant.

Model
Teacher: farm
Puppet: arm
After the pattern is established, students
respond for the puppet.
Teacher: rope
Students: ope

Example Words
Use words such as the following:
mine . . . ine   soup . . . oup   feet . . . eet

2. Restoring initial phonemes. Now students correct the puppet. Be sure to acknowledge the correction.

Model
Teacher: lake
Puppet: ake
Teacher: No, Illlake. You forgot the /l/.
Teacher: real
Puppet: eal
Teacher: What did the puppet leave off?
Students: /r/. It's supposed to be *real*.
Teacher: That's right. The word is *real*.

Example Words
Use words such as the following:
*look . . . ook   mouse . . . ouse
sand . . . and*

3. Segmenting initial consonants. The puppet pronounces only the initial consonant.

Model
Teacher: pay
Puppet: /p/

Example Words
Use words such as the following:
moon . . . /m/   nose . . . /n/   bell . . . /b/

4. Restoring final consonants. Students correct the puppet. Prompt if necessary: "What's the word? What did the puppet leave off?"

Model
Teacher: run
Puppet: ru
Students: It's run! You left off the /n/.
Teacher: That's right. The word is *run*.

Example Words
Use words such as the following:
meet . . . mee   cool . . . coo   boot . . . boo

5. Isolating final consonants. The puppet pronounces only the final consonant.

Model
Teacher: green
Puppet: /n/

Example Words
Use words such as the following:
glass . . . /s/   boom . . . /m/   mice . . . /s/

6. Segmenting initial consonant blends. The sounds in blends are emphasized.

Model
Teacher: clap
Puppet: lap
Next have students correct the puppet.
Teacher: stain
Puppet: tain
Students: It's stain! You left off the /s/.
Teacher: That's right. The word is *stain*.

Example Words
Use words such as the following:
*blaze . . . laze   draw . . . raw
proud . . . roud*

Discrimination

Purpose

Discrimination activities help students focus on particular sounds in words.

Listening for long-vowel sounds is the earliest discrimination activity. Vowel sounds are necessary for decoding, but young students do not hear them easily. This is evident in students' invented spellings, where vowels are often omitted. Early in the year, students listen for long-vowel sounds, which are more easily distinguished than short-vowel sounds:

✦ Explain to students that vowels are special because sometimes they say their names in words.

✦ Tell students which vowel sound to listen for.

✦ Have them repeat the sound when they hear it in a word. For example, if the target-vowel sound is long *e*, students will say long *e* when you say *leaf*, but they should not respond when you say *loaf*.

✦ Initially students should listen for one long vowel sound at a time. Later they can listen for two vowel sounds. All Example Words, however, should contain one of the target vowels.

Procedure

Listening for short-vowel sounds

These discrimination activities should be done after the short vowels /a/ and /i/ have been introduced. Short vowels are very useful in reading. They are generally more regular in spelling than long vowels, and they appear in many short, simple words. However, their sounds are less easily distinguished than those of long vowels. Thus, the activities focus only on /a/ and /i/. All the words provided have one or the other of these sounds. Either have students repeat the sound of a specified vowel, or vary the activity as follows: Write an *a* on one side of the board and an *i* on the other. Ask students to point to the *a* when they hear a word with the /a/ sound and to point to the *i* when they hear a word with the /i/ sound. Use words such as the following:

> bat   mat   sat   sit   spit
> pit   pat   pan   pin   spin

Consonant sounds in multisyllabic words

Discriminating these sounds helps students attend to consonant sounds in the middle of words.

✦ Say the word *rib,* and have students repeat it. Ask where they hear the /b/ in *rib.*

✦ Then say *ribbon,* and ask students where they hear the /b/ in *ribbon.*

✦ Tell students that you will say some words and that they will repeat each word.

✦ After they repeat each word, ask what consonant sound they hear in the middle of that word. Use words such as the following:
> famous   message   picky
> jogger   flavor   zipper

Phonemic Play

Purpose

Wordplay activities help students focus on and manipulate sounds, thus supporting the idea that words are made of specific sounds that can be taken apart, put together, or changed to make new words. Through wordplay, students gain important knowledge about language.

Procedure

Producing rhymes

Many phonemic play activities focus on producing rhymes. A familiar or easily learned rhyme or song is introduced, and students are encouraged to substitute words or sounds. An example is "Willaby Wallaby Woo," in which students change the rhyming words in the couplet "Willaby Wallaby Woo/ An elephant sat on you" so that the second line ends with a student's name and that the first line ends with a rhyme beginning with *W*; for example, "Willaby Wallaby Wissy/An elephant sat on Missy."

Generate alliterative words

Students can also say as many words as they can think of that begin with a given consonant sound. This is a valuable complement to discrimination activities in which the teacher produces the words and students identify them.

The Alphabetic Principle: How the Alphabet Works

The Alphabetic Principle

Purpose

A major emphasis in the kindergarten program is on letter recognition and attending to sounds. Students need to learn the alphabetic principle: that letters work together in a systematic way to connect spoken language to written words. This understanding is the foundation for reading. Students are not expected to master letter/sound correspondence at the beginning of kindergarten, nor are they expected to blend sounds into words themselves. They are expected to become an "expert" only on their Special Letters as they learn how the alphabet works. Through this introduction to the alphabetic principle, students will have the basic understanding required to work through the alphabet letter by letter, attaching sounds to each.

Key concepts of the alphabetic principle include the following:

◆ A limited number of letters combine in different ways to make many different words.

◆ Words are composed of sounds, and letters represent those sounds.

◆ Anything that can be pronounced can be spelled.

◆ Letters and sounds can be used to identify words.

◆ Meaning can be obtained by using letters and sounds to determine words.

Procedures for Kindergarten

The following steps can be used for introducing letters and sounds in kindergarten. These steps may be adapted for students at other grades if they do not understand the alphabetic principle. The tone of these activities should be informal, fun, and fast-paced. The purpose of these activities is to familiarize students with how the alphabet works by having them participate in group play with letters and sounds.

I Can Spell Anything

◆ Reinforce the idea that anything that can be pronounced can be spelled with the letters of the alphabet.

◆ Tell students that you can spell any word. Have them give you words to spell.

◆ Write the words on the board, naming each letter as you write it. This shows students that the words contain the letters displayed on the **Alphabet Sound Wall Cards.**

◆ Have students help you spell the words again by pointing to letters as you say them.

◆ Encourage students to spell each word letter by letter.

> *The alphabetic principle is the understanding that speech sounds can be mapped onto print.*

Letter Expert Groups

◆ Have **Alphabet Letter Cards** (Levels K and 1) available for the following set of letters: *b, d, f, h, l, m, n, p, s, t.* You will need two or three cards for each letter. (You will not need the **Alphabet Sound Cards** until later.)

◆ You will be the letter expert for the vowels.

◆ Organize the class into groups of two or three, and assign each group a letter. Give each student the appropriate **Alphabet Letter Card.**

◆ Tell students that they are now in their Letter Expert groups and that they are going to become experts on their Special Letter's name, shape, and sound.

Making Words

◆ Begin each lesson with a rehearsal of each group's letter name.

◆ Demonstrate how letters work by writing a word in large letters on the board.

◆ Tell students the experts for each letter in the word should hold up their **Alphabet Letter Cards** and name the letter. One member of the group should stand in front of their letter on the board.

◆ Continue until all letters in the word are accounted for. Remember that you are responsible for the vowels.

◆ Demonstrate that you can make different words by changing a letter or by changing the letter order.

Identifying Sounds in Words

◆ Use the **Alphabet Sound Cards** to demonstrate that every letter has at least one sound.

◆ Give each student the **Alphabet Sound Card** for his or her Special Letter.

◆ Point out the pictures on the cards. Explain that each card has a picture of something that makes the letter's sound. The picture will help them remember the sound.

◆ Tell each group the sound for its letter. (Remember, you are the expert for the vowels.)

◆ Quickly have each group rehearse its letter's name and sound.

◆ Write a word on the board in large letters. First say the word sound by sound, and then blend the word.

◆ For each letter/sound in the word, have one student from each Letter Expert group come forward, stand in front of the appropriate letter, and hold his or her card. Although only one member of the group may come forward with the **Alphabet Letter Card** or **Alphabet Sound Card,** all students in a Special Letter group should say the name or sound of their letter when it occurs in words.

◆ Say the word again, pointing to the **Alphabet Sound Cards.**

◆ Ask students who are not already standing to help you hold the vowel cards.

◆ Vary the activity by changing one letter sound and having an expert for that letter come forward.

End the activity for each word by saying the sounds in the words one by one and then saying the entire word. Encourage students to participate.

Tips

- Remind students to use the picture on the *Alphabet Sound Card* for their Special Letter to help them remember the letter's sound. Students are expected to "master" only their own Special Letter and to share the information with their classmates. At this point in the year, they are not expected to blend and read the words by themselves. These are group activities in which you work with students to help them gain insight into the alphabet.

- Be sure to connect what students learn about the letters and words to the words they work with in *Big Book* selections.

- Occasionally, have students find their special letters in a *Big Book* selection. Play some of the letter replacement and rearrangement games with words encountered in the *Big Books.*

Developing the Alphabetic Principle

Purpose

The alphabetic principle is the understanding that speech sounds can be mapped onto print. It is the association of sounds with letters and the understanding that speech can be turned into print and that print can be turned into speech sounds. Activities associated with the alphabetic principle help kindergarten students develop a more thorough understanding of how sounds "work" in words. In this group of activities, students are introduced to specific letter/sound correspondences, consonants, and short vowels. While students have previously been introduced to vowels and their special characteristics, students' understanding is extended by introducing students to the convention that a vowel has a short sound in addition to its long sound. With this information and a carefully structured set of activities, students can begin to explore and understand the alphabetic principle in a straightforward and thorough manner. Students not only listen for sounds in specified positions in words, they also link sounds to their corresponding letters. The

activities in this group of lessons lay the groundwork for students to work their way through the entire alphabet as they learn letter-sound associations and to understand the purpose and the value of this learning.

Move students quickly through these activities. Do not wait for all students to master each letter/sound correspondence before going on. They will have more opportunities to achieve mastery. The goal of these activities is for students to obtain a basic understanding of the alphabetic principle.

> *Students need to learn the alphabetic principle: that letters work together in a systematic way to connect spoken language to written words. This understanding is the foundation for reading.*

Procedures

Introducing Consonant Letters and Sounds

- Point to the *Alphabet Sound Wall Card* and ask students what they know about the card (the letter name, the capital and lowercase letter, and so on).

- Turn the card, and point to the picture. Name the picture, and point to and name the letter. Tell students the sound of the letter and how the picture helps them remember the sound. Repeat the sound several times.

- Tell students you will read them the short story or an alliterative sentence to help them remember the sound of the letter. Read the story several times, emphasizing the words with the target sound. Have students join in and say the sound.

- After introducing and reviewing a letter/sound correspondence, summarize the information on the *Alphabet Sound Wall Card:* the name of the card, the sound, and the letter.

Generating Words with the Target Sound

Brainstorm to create a list of words that begin with the target sound. Write the words on the board or on a chart. Include any of the students' names that begin with the target sound.

Listening for Initial Sounds

- Give each student an *Alphabet Letter Card* for the target sound.

- Point to the picture on the *Alphabet Sound Wall Card,* and have students give the sound.

- Tell students to listen for the first sound in each word you say. If it is the target sound, they should hold up their cards. Establish a signal so that students know when to respond.

- Read the list of words, some beginning with the target sound and some beginning with other sounds.

Listening for Final Sounds

The procedure for listening for the final sound of a word is the same as that for listening for the initial sound. Students may need to be reminded throughout the activity to pay attention to the final sound.

Read a list of words, some ending with the target sound and some ending with other sounds. Avoid words that begin with the target sound.

Linking the Sound to the Letter

- **Word Pairs (initial sounds).** Write pairs of words on the board. One of each pair should begin with the target sound. Say the word beginning with the target sound, and ask students to identify it. Remind them to listen for the target sound at the beginning of the word, to think about which letter makes that sound, and to find the word that begins with that letter. For example,
Target sound: /s/
Word pair: *fit sit*
Which word is *sit?*

- **Word Pairs (final sounds).** Follow the same procedure used for initial sounds, and direct students to think about the sound that they hear at the end of the word. Because it is often more difficult

Explicit, Systematic Phonics

The purpose of phonics instruction is to teach students the association between the sounds of the language and the written symbols—spellings—that have been chosen to represent those sounds.

As with all alphabetic languages, English has a limited number of symbols—twenty-six—that are combined and recombined to make the written language. These written symbols are a visual representation of the speech sounds we use to communicate. This is simply a code. The faster students learn the code and how it works, the faster the whole world of reading opens up to them.

Beginning at the kindergarten level, students are introduced to sounds and letters. Students learn that sounds can be mapped onto letters and that those sounds and letters can be blended to read words.

In Grade 1, students make the shift from mapping sounds onto letters to mapping sounds onto spellings. The introduction of both sounds and letters in kindergarten and the sounds and spellings in Grade 1 is done in a very systematic, sequential manner. This allows students to continually build on what they learned the day before. As each sound/symbol relationship is introduced, students learn about and practice with words containing the target sound and letter in kindergarten and sound/spelling in Grade1. This new knowledge is then reinforced through the use of engaging text specifically written for this purpose.

It can be very difficult for students to hear the individual sounds, or phonemes, that make up words. When phonics instruction is explicit—students are told the sounds associated with the different written symbols—there is no guesswork involved. They know that the sound /b/ is spelled *b*. Therefore, students in an **SRA Imagine It!** classroom spend time learning to discriminate individual speech sounds, and then they learn the spellings of those sounds. This systematic, explicit approach affords students the very best chance for early and continuing success.

Sound/Spelling Wall Cards

(Grade 1 on) See The Alphabetic Principle for information on the introduction of sounds and letters in pre-kindergarten and kindergarten.

Purpose

The purpose of the **Sound/Spelling Wall Cards** (Levels 1–3) is to remind students of the sounds in English and their spellings. The name of the picture on each card contains the target sound at the beginning of the name for consonants and in the middle for the short vowels. Long vowels are represented by elongated pictures of the vowel. The variant vowels such as /aw/ and /oi/ contain the vowel sound in the name as well. In addition, the picture associates a sound with an action. This association is introduced through an interactive story in which the pictured object or character "makes" the sound. This "action" cue is particularly helpful for students whose primary language is not English. In some cases, the name of the card and the initial sound may be similar to words in other languages. For example, the word for *lion* in Spanish is *león,* which begins with the same sound as the English word. This is not true for other languages. In Russian the word for *lion* is лев and in Japanese it is *raion.* The word for *zipper* in Spanish is *cremallera,* in Russian it is застежка-молния and in Japanese it is *jippa.* But all students can remember the actions and sounds and use them as a resource for both reading and writing.

> *The faster students learn the code and how it works, the faster the whole world of reading opens up to them.*

Procedure

Posting the Cards

In Grade 1, initially post the first twenty-six cards with the picture to the wall so that only the alphabet letters on the backs show. As you introduce each card, you will turn it to show the picture and the spellings on the front of the card. Some Grade 1 teachers who have students who are familiar with the cards from kindergarten choose to place the first twenty-six cards (the alphabet) with the pictures facing the class. Because students are familiar with the cards and how to use them, this provides support for writing. Even these first-grade teachers, however, cover the spellings not introduced in kindergarten. In second- or third-grade classrooms in which students are reviewing what they learned the year before, place all the cards with the pictures and the spellings facing forward so students can use these as a resource from the beginning of the school year. Make sure that the cards are positioned so that you can touch them with your hand or with a pointer when you refer to them and so that all students can see them easily. The cards should be placed where students can readily see and reference them throughout the day.

Special Devices

- ✦ Vowel spellings are printed in red to draw attention to them. It is the vowels and their different spellings that challenge us all. Consonants are printed in black. The blank line in a spelling indicates that a letter will take the place of the blank in a word. For example, the replacement of the blank with *t* in the spelling *a_e* makes the word *ate.* The blank lines may also indicate the position of a spelling in a word or a syllable. The blank in *h_,* for example, means that the sound /h/ spelled *h_* occurs at the beginning of a word or a syllable.

- ✦ The blanks in *_ie_* indicate that the *ie* spelling will not come at the beginning or the end of a word or a syllable as in *babies,* while the blank in *_oy* shows that the *oy* spelling comes at the end of a word or a syllable as in *toy.* Uses of blanks in specific spellings are discussed in the lessons. Please note now, however, that when you write a spelling of a sound on the board or an overhead transparency, you should include the blanks.

✦ The color of the background behind the spellings also has a meaning. Consonants have a white background. The colors behind vowel spellings are pronunciation clues. Short-vowel spellings have a green background, which corresponds to the green box that appears before some consonant spellings. Thus, before *ck, tch,* or *x,* you will see a green box, which indicates that a short vowel always precedes that spelling. Long-vowel spellings have a yellow background; other vowel spellings such as *r*-controlled vowels, diphthongs, and variant vowels have a blue background. The color code reinforces the idea that vowels are special and have different pronunciations.

Introducing the Sound/ Spelling Wall Cards

In first grade, each sound and spelling is introduced by using a see/hear/say/write sequence. In Grades 2 and 3 the same sequence is used in the review of the cards.

1. *See:* Students see the spelling or spellings on the **Sound/Spelling Wall Card** and the board or an overhead transparency.

2. *Hear:* Students hear the sound used in words and in isolation in the story. The sound is, of course, related to the picture (and the action) shown on the **Sound/ Spelling Wall Card.**

3. *Say:* Students say the sound.

4. *Write:* Students write the spelling(s) for the sound.

There are a number of important points to remember about this routine.

✦ Take down the **Sound/Spelling Wall Card,** tell the class the name of the card, the sound, and the spelling.

✦ Read the alliterative story so students hear the sound used in words as well as in isolation, and say the sound.

✦ After you present the sound and spelling, have several students go to the board to write the spelling. Have them say the sound as they write the spelling. After they have written the spelling of the sound, give them an opportunity to proofread their own work. Then give

the other students the opportunity to help with proofreading by noting what is good about the spelling and then suggesting how to make it better.

✦ Difficulty in blending may be the result of not knowing the sounds or not being able to pronounce the sounds. Teach the sounds thoroughly during the introduction of the **Sound/Spelling Wall Card** and during initial sounding and blending. To help ensure success for all students, make certain that every student is able to see the board or screen.

Introducing the Sound /s/ spelled *s*

✦ Point to the back of **Sound/Spelling Wall Card** 19—Sausages, and have students tell you what they know about the card: it is a consonant and there is an upper and lowercase *s* on the card. Turn the card, and tell the class the name of the card: Sausages. Point to the sausages in the picture, and say the word *sausages,* emphasizing the initial consonant sound—*sssssausages.* Note: teachers usually place a sticky note over the other spellings of /s/—the *ce, ci_,* and *cy*—in order to help students focus on the single spelling being introduced in the lesson.

✦ Point to the spelling *s.* Tell students that /s/ is spelled *s.*

✦ Read the alliterative story. In Grades 2 and 3, the stories for the card are printed in the Level Appendix of the **Teacher's Edition.** If your students in Grades 2 and 3 are familiar with the cards, have them tell you the name of the card, the sound, and the spelling and tell the story.

✦ If students had **SRA Imagine It!** before, you can ask them if they learned an action to help them remember the sound. If your students do not already have an action they associate with the sound, make some up with your students. They will have fun, and it will be another way for them to remember the sound/spelling relationships.

✦ Write *s* on the board or on an overhead transparency, and say the sound. Write the spelling again and ask students to say the sound with you as they write the spelling on slates, on paper, or with their index fingers in the air or in the palm of their hands. Repeat this activity several times.

✦ Have several students come to the board and write the upper- and lowercase spelling while the others continue to write them on slates or with their fingers. Be sure to encourage students to say the sound as they make the spelling. For students writing at the board, take time to have them proofread their work.

✦ Have students listen for words beginning with /s/, indicating by some signal, such as thumbs-up or thumbs-down, whether they hear the /s/ sound and saying /s/ when they hear it in a word. Repeat with the sound in various positions in words. Encourage students to tell you and the class words with /s/ at the beginning, as well as at the ends of words.

✦ Check students' learning by pointing to the card. Have students identify the sound, name the spelling, and discuss how the card can help them remember the sound.

Remember that saying the sound, listening to the alliterative story, and listening for the sound (discriminating it from other sounds) in different positions in words are all phonemic awareness activities that have been integrated into phonics.

Individual Sound/Spelling Cards

Use the individual **Sound/Spelling Cards** for review and for small-group reteaching and practice sessions. Students can use them alone or with partners. Here are some suggestions for activities using the individual **Sound/Spelling Cards:**

1. **Saying sounds from pictures.** The leader flashes pictures as the others say the sound each picture represents.

2. **Saying sounds.** The leader flashes the spellings on the cards as the others say the sound that the spellings represent.

3. **Naming spellings from pictures.** The leader flashes pictures. The others name the card, say the sound, and then name as many spellings as they can.

4. **Writing spellings from the pictures.** Working alone, a student looks at a picture and then writes as many spellings for that **Sound/Spelling Card** as he or she can remember.

5. **Saying words from pictures.** The leader presents a series of individual cards, for example, Sausages, Lamb, Timer. The others tell the word by blending the sounds represented—*sat.*

Word Structure

Purpose

As students move into the upper grades, there is a shift from Phonics to Word Structure. Phonology is the study of the sounds that make up words. In the early grades, students learn to map sounds with spellings to read words. However, as students move into the upper grades and encounter more complex and longer words, the understanding of morphology and the morphological units that make up words is important for fluent reading, vocabulary development, and comprehension.

Morphology is the study of Word Structure. Word Structure activities support the development of fluency as students learn to identify and read meaningful chunks of words rather than individual spellings. Word Structure also supports the development of vocabulary as students learn how inflectional endings change a word's tense, number, and so on and how affixes can be added to a base word to create or derive a new but related meaning.

Morphemes are the smallest units that have semantic meaning. Morphemes may be free or bound. A free morpheme can stand alone, such as the words *dog, man,* or *woman.* A bound morpheme, on the other hand, is a unit of meaning that must be combined with another morpheme to make a meaningful word. For example, in *rewrite* the prefix *re-* means "to do again", and in *dogs* the *-s* changes the meaning to plural. Both re- and -s are bound morphemes because they must combine with other words to create new words.

Learning about word structure helps the reader on several levels. Being able to identify key-word parts not only helps with the pronunciation of longer, unfamiliar words but it also helps with meaning. In Word Structure, students learn how to deconstruct words—to identify the root of the word as well as the affixes. When affixes occur at the beginning of a word, they are called prefixes, and when they occur at the end of a word they are called suffixes. The prefix, root word, and suffix are all morphemes.

In the word *restatement,* there are three morphemes: the prefix *re-,* the root *state* and the suffix *-ment.*

prefix	root	suffix
re-	state	-ment

Suffixes, in particular, can impact the root word in different ways. Suffixes such as -s and -ed can change the tense of a verb; suffixes such as -s can change the number of a noun to make it a plural. Derviational morphemes, in contrast, can be added to words to create or derive another word, for example the addition of -ness to *sad* creates the new word *sadness,* or the addition of -ly changes *sad* to an adverb, *sadly.*

Word structure includes the study of the following:

✦ **Compound words** are made of two words that combine to form a new word. Compounds can be open or closed.

✦ **Root words** focus on learning about the basic element of words. Root words are the foundations upon which the meaning of a word is formed. A root may be a real word as in *audio,* meaning "sound," but it can also used with a suffix to become *audible,* changing the noun to an adjective. Although *audible* can have other elements, it does not need other elements to be complete. Most roots, however, do need other elements. Roots such as *duct, anthrop,* and *cred* require affixes to form the words *deduct, anthropology,* and *incredible,* respectively. Knowledge of root words and affixes provides students with critical tools for understanding derived words.

✦ **Prefixes** include any morpheme that is attached to the beginning of a root or word and changes the meaning of that word. Prefixes do not change the form of the word, only the meaning. Common prefixes include: *con-, com-, ad-, de-, di-, dis-, per-, re-, sub-, hyper-, un-,* and so on as well as numbers *(bi-, tri-, uni-, mono-, octo-,* and so on.)

✦ **Suffixes** include any morpheme that is attached to the end of a word or root and that changes the meaning of that word. Suffixes often change the function of the word and often require a spelling change in the root as well. For example, the addition of -ial to *colony* changes a noun to an adjective.

Common Latin Roots

Aud: auditory, auditorium, inaudible, audible, audition

Dict: dictate, predict, contradict, prediction

Ject: reject, inject, project, object, projection, objection

Port: transport, import, export, portable, support, report

Rupt: rupture, erupt, eruption, disrupt, interruption

Scrib/script: scribe, describe, manuscript, inscription, transcript, description, prescription

Spect: spectator, inspect, inspector, respect, spectacle, spectacular

Struct: structure, construct, instruct, destruction, reconstruction

Tract: tractor, traction, attract, subtraction, extract, retract, attractive

Vis: vision, visual, visit, supervisor, invisible, vista, visualize, visionary

Common Greek Roots

Auto: automatic, autograph, autobiography, automobile

Bio: biology, biography

Graph: graphite, geography, graphic, photograph, phonograph

Hydr: hydrogen, hydrant

Meter: speedometer, odometer, thermometer, metronome

Ology: geology, zoology, phonology

Photo: photography, photocopy, photosynthesis, photogenic

Scope: telescope, stethoscope, microscope, microscopic, periscope

Tele: telephone, television, telegraph

Therm: thermos, thermostat

Other examples of suffixes that change the word form include the following:

- Noun suffixes: *-age, -al, -ance, -ant, -ate, -ee, -ence, -ent, -er, -or, -ar, -ese, -ess, -hood, -ice, -isn, -ist, -ment, -ness, -sion, -tain, -tion, -ure*
- Suffixes that form adjectives: *-able, -al, -er, -est, -ette, -let, -ful, -fully, -ible, -ic, -ical, -ish, -ive, -less, -ous, -some, -worthy*
- Suffixes that form adverbs: *-ly, -wards, -ways, -wide, -wise*
- Suffixes that create verb forms: *-ate, -ed, -en, -ing, -ise, -ize, -yze*
- Inflectional endings are a special set of suffixes that change the number (singular to plural), case, or gender when added to nouns and change tense when added to verbs.

Teaching Word Structure

- ✦ *Have students read the words in a line.
- ✦ Tell students that words can be made of several individual parts.
- ✦ Examine the words in each line for meaningful parts, roots, and affixes.
- ✦ Identify the root or base word, and discuss the meaning.
- ✦ Underline and discuss the meaning of the prefix or suffix or both. If there is a prefix and a suffix, begin with the prefix. Tell students a prefix is a group of letters that is attached to the beginning of a base or root word. These letters have a specific meaning. For example, *un-* means "not" or "the opposite of," *non-* means "not," and *re-* means "again." A suffix is a group of letters that comes at the end of the base or root word and changes the meaning of the word. For example, *-er* changes a verb to a noun or the person doing the action as in *sing* and *singer,* or *-al* or *-ial* change nouns to adjectives as in *colony* and *colonial.*
- ✦ Reassemble the word, thinking about the meaning of the word parts.
- ✦ Say the word.
- ✦ Use the word in a sentence.

---

*Sometimes students are intimidated by longer words. Understanding syllable breaks helps when reading these longer words. The following chart includes information on syllable "generalizations." These may help your students when reading longer words during Word Structure activities and in the reading.

Word	Break into Syllables	Syllable Generalizations
Puppet	Pup-pet	Closed. If a word has two consonants in the middle, divide the word between the two consonants. The first syllable is closed, and the vowel pronunciation is short.
Music	Mu-sic	Open. If a word has a VCV pattern, break the syllables before the consonant, which makes the first syllable an open syllable and the first vowel long.
Closet	Clos-et	Some VCV patterns have the break after the consonant, which makes the first syllable a closed syllable and the vowel pronunciation short.
Hundred	Hun-dred	When there is a VCCCV pattern, the break is usually between the consonants. The first syllable is closed, and the vowel pronunciation is short.
Coward	Cow-ard	When there are two diphthongs, the syllable break comes between them.
Chaos	Cha-os	When there is a VV pattern, the syllable break comes between the vowels, and the first vowel is usually long.
Handle	Han-dle	Consonant plus *-le.* If a word has an *-le* (or *-el*) at the end, it usually forms a separate syllable and is pronounced with the consonant and /ə/ /l/.
Excitement Reform	Ex-cite-ment Re-form	Prefixes and suffixes are separate syllables.
Entertain Hurdle	En-ter-tain Hur-dle	*R*-controlled vowels. In most syllables where the vowel is followed by an *r*, the vowel sound is *r*-controlled.
Complete	Com-plete	Final *e.* When there is a vowel, consonant, and then an *e* at the end, the vowel before the consonant is pronounced long, and the *e* is silent.

Developing Vocabulary

For students to develop a deeper understanding of words, they should have multiple experiences with them. There are any number of activities that students can do to help them use words and internalize their meanings. The following activities can be used with the whole class or in small groups during Workshop.

- ✦ Give a word, and ask the student to find it in the line and to give a definition.
- ✦ Give a word, and ask the student to add a prefix or a suffix and to tell the meaning of the new word and the new part of speech.

- ✦ If the word is a multiple-meaning word, have the student point to the word, and then have the student give one meaning and use it in a sentence. Then have a second student give another meaning and use it in a sentence. (Be sure that the words that are used are truly multiple-meaning words and not words that can be used as different parts of speech, for example, a verb and a noun that have the same basic meaning.)
- ✦ Give two words, and have the student point to them. Ask what is the difference between these two words. For example, *hot* and *cold* are antonyms. The same could be done for synonyms, homonyms,

and homophones. This gets students to use the vocabulary and do the thinking. Point to two words, and have students tell how they are alike and different. For example, *history, historical,* and *historian* all have the same roots. All three words have a common root, but *history* and *historian* are nouns, and *historical* is an adjective.

✦ Give students a word, and have them point to the word. If it is a singular noun, have them change it to a plural or vice versa. If it is a verb, have students change the tense, or if it is an adjective, change it into an adverb if appropriate. In all cases, be sure that students spell the new word.

✦ Give students a word, have them point to and read the word, and then give the part of speech.

✦ Give a student a word, and have him or her use the word in a sentence. Have the class decide if the sentence truly shows the meaning of the word. For example, if the word is *camouflage,* and the student says, "Animals use camouflage," have the class add to the sentence to show the meaning: "Animals use camouflage to protect themselves from predators."

✦ Give students a word with a base word, and ask them to point to the word and read it and then to tell the root of the word.

✦ Give students a word with a Greek or Latin root. Have them point to and read the word, and then have them identify the root. Challenge students to think of other words that have the same root.

✦ Give students a word with a prefix or suffix. Have a student point to and read the word and then identify the prefix or suffix and tell the meaning of the affix. Then, if appropriate, have the student or a different student replace the affix with a different one and tell the meaning of the new word.

✦ When appropriate, give students a word, and have them give a synonym or antonym. When appropriate, work on gradations of words. For example, if the word is *hot* then the opposite is *cold.* Gradations would be *hot, warm, tepid, cool, cold.* These kinds of activities expand vocabulary.

✦ Give two words that are connected in some way, for example, *colony* and *colonial.* Have students come to the board, point to the words, and read them. Then have them tell why or how the words are connected.

✦ Have students find other words that follow comparable patterns to those taught in the lesson. If *colony, colonial, colonist* is a line in Word Structure, many students could find related nouns and use them with affixes, *(history, historical, historian).* Challenge students to think more about words.

Tips

✦ Be sure students understand the limits of structural analysis. The *un-* in *unhappy* is a prefix, but the *un* in *under* and *uncle* is not.

✦ Help students realize that many words are related and that using their knowledge of a word can help them understand related words.

✦ Encourage students to use their knowledge of word structure during all reading to clarify unfamiliar words.

Fluency

Fluency is the ability to read or access words effortlessly with seemingly little attention to decoding. Fluent readers decode words not only automatically but accurately. In addition, fluent readers group words into meaningful units, utilize punctuation to guide their voices, and use expression appropriately to help them comprehend what they are reading. Fluent readers also adjust their reading rate as necessary.

To become proficient readers who fully understand what they read, the whole process of decoding must become automatic. Readers need to be so familiar with the sound/spellings, with common meaningful units like prefixes and suffixes and with the most common nondecodable sight words that they automatically process the spellings and word chunks. This enables them to read the word effortlessly and expend most of their energy on comprehending the meaning of the text. Automaticity is a key component of fluency.

The concept of fluency is introduced in the early grades, even before students are reading. When reading aloud, teachers are modeling fluency and using expression and intonation to support meaning. In pre-kindergarten and kindergarten, emergent readers learn about concepts of print that support fluency: learning about spaces and ending punctuation, reading from left to right, and automatically recognizing high-frequency sight words. Students apply this knowledge to reading *Pre-Decodables.* These skills are then applied to reading *Decodables.* While fluency begins in first grade, many students will continue to need practice in building fluency in second and third grades. Initially students can use the *SRA Imagine It! Decodable Stories* in Grades 2 and 3, but fluency practice should include using materials from a variety of different sources, including selections from the *Student Readers, Leveled Readers,* and the *Leveled Science* and *Social Studies Readers.* At all grade levels using *Pre-Decodables, Decodables, Readers,* or any other materials, students need to appreciate that fluency is about meaning. Take time to ask questions after students have read, talk about new and interesting words, and discuss any problems students encountered.

Building Fluency: Reading Pre-Decodables (K–1)

Purpose

Pre-Decodables play an important role in students' early literacy development by providing them with meaningful "reading" experiences before they are actually reading on their own and by expanding their awareness of the forms and uses of print. By following along as you read aloud a *Pre-Decodable,* students learn about the left-to-right and top-to-bottom progression of print on a page, the clues that indicate the beginnings and endings of sentences, the connections between pictures and words, and important book conventions such as front and back covers, authors' and illustrators' names, title pages, and page numbers.

The *Pre-Decodables* provide students with opportunities to apply their growing knowledge of letter names, shapes, and sounds and to become familiar with individual words. In addition, students practice reading high-frequency sight words. The automatic recognition of these words, the identification of ending punctuation, and reading with expression support the development of foundational fluency skills.

Through retelling the story in a *Pre-Decodable,* predicting or wondering about what will happen, and asking and responding to questions about the book, students not only learn about the relationship between spoken and written language, they learn to think about what they have read.

About the Pre-Decodables

Each *Pre-Decodable* contains a story that engages students' interest as it provides them with opportunities to practice what they are learning in their lessons. These "pre-decodable" stories each contain several high-frequency words that most students already have in their spoken vocabularies and that are a basic part of all meaningful stories. Learning to identify high-frequency words quickly, accurately, and effortlessly is a critical part of students' development as fluent, independent readers. The inside back cover of each *Pre-Decodable* contains a list of high-frequency words.

How to Use the Pre-Decodables

✦ Before reading a *Pre-Decodable,* take time to familiarize students with any new high-frequency words in the book and to review previously introduced words. To reinforce the idea that it is important to know these words because they are used so often in print, always point out the words in context. For example, focus students' attention on the words in *Big Book* selections or on signs and posters around the classroom.

✦ Give each student a copy of the book. Tell students that you will read the book together. Hold up your book. Read the title. If the title has a rebus picture, point to it, and tell students what it is. Then point to the word beneath it, and explain that the picture represents that word. Point to and read the names of the author and illustrator, reminding students that an author writes a book, and an illustrator draws the pictures. Page through the book, pointing to and naming the rebus pictures. Have students say the name of each rebus. To avoid confusion, always tell them the exact word that a rebus represents. Do not encourage them to guess at its meaning.

✦ Allow students time to browse through the book on their own, commenting on what they see in the illustrations and making predictions about what they think the book will be about. Encourage them to comment on anything special they notice about the story, the illustrations, or the words in the book.

✦ Help students find page 3. Read the book aloud without stopping. As you read, move your hand beneath the words to show the progression of print. Pause at each rebus as you say the word it represents, pointing first to the rebus then to the word beneath it.

✦ Reread the book. This time, ask students to point to and read the high-frequency words.

✦ Tell students to follow along in their books as you read the story again. Read the title aloud, and then have students read it with you. Reread page 3. Point to each rebus picture, and ask a volunteer to "read" it. Point to the word beneath the picture, and remind students that the picture shows what the word is. Continue through each page of the book, calling on volunteers to "read" and stopping as necessary to clarify and help students with words.

✦ After reading, answer any questions students might have about the book. Encourage them to discuss the illustrations and to explain what is happening in each one.

Building Fluency: Reading Decodables (K–3)

Purpose

The most urgent task of early reading instruction is to make written thoughts intelligible to students. This requires a balanced approach that includes systematic instruction in phonics as well as experiences with authentic literature. Thus, from the very beginning, **SRA Imagine It!** includes the reading of literature. At the beginning of first grade, when students are learning phonics and blending as a tool to access words, the teacher reads aloud. During this time students are working on using comprehension strategies and skills and discussing stories. As students learn to code and blend words, recognize critical sight words, and develop some level of fluency, they take more responsibility for the actual reading of the text.

This program has a systematic instruction in phonics that allows students to begin reading independently. This instruction is supported by **SRA Imagine It! Decodables.**

About the Decodables

The **SRA Imagine It! Decodables** are designed to help students apply, review, and reinforce their expanding knowledge of sound/spelling correspondences. Each story supports instruction in new phonic elements and incorporates elements and words that have been learned earlier. There are eight-page and sixteen-page **Decodables.** Grade K has eight-page **Decodables.** In Grade 1, the eight-page books focus on the new element introduced in the lesson, while the sixteen-page books review and reinforce the elements that have been taught since the last sixteen-page book. They review sounds

from several lessons and provide additional reading practice. Grades 2–3 have eight-page **Decodable Stories** in Getting Started, and eight- and sixteen-page stories in Units 1–3 in Grade 3 and Units 1–6 in Grade 2. The primary purpose is to provide practice reading the words. It is important that students also attach meaning to what they are reading. Questions are often included in the **Teacher's Edition** to check both understanding and attention to words.

How to use Decodables

Preparing to Read

✦ Introduce and write on the board or cards any nondecodable high-frequency or story words introduced or reviewed in the story. Tell students how to pronounce any newly introduced high-frequency words. Then point to each new word, and have students spell and say it. Have them read any previously introduced sight words in the Word Bank list. All the **SRA Imagine It! Decodables** contain high-frequency words that may not be decodable. For example, the word *said* is a common high-frequency word that is not decodable. Including words such as *said* makes the language of the story flow smoothly and naturally. Students need to be able to recognize and read these words quickly and smoothly.

✦ Read the title. At the beginning of the year, you may need to read the title of the book to students, but as the year goes on, you should have a student read it whenever possible. In Grade 1, selected sixteen-page **SRA Imagine It! Decodables** contain two related chapters, each using the same sounds and spellings. In such cases, read the title of the **Decodable,** and then point out the two individual chapter titles. Have volunteers read the title of the chapter you are about to read.

✦ Browse the story. Have students look through the story, commenting on whatever they notice in the text or illustrations and telling what they think the story will tell them.

Reading the Story

After this browsing, students will read the story a page at a time. Again, these stories are designed to support the learning of sounds and spellings. The focus should not

be on comprehension. Students should understand what they are reading, and they should feel free to discuss anything in the story that interests them. Any areas of confusion are discussed and clarified as they arise, as described below.

✦ Have students read a page to themselves. Then call on one student or groups of students to read the page aloud, or have the entire group read it aloud.

✦ If a student has difficulty with a word that can be blended, help her or him blend the word. Remind the student to check the **Sound/Spelling Cards** for help. If a word cannot be blended using the sound/spellings learned so far, pronounce the word for the student.

✦ If a student has trouble with a word or sentence, have the reader call on a classmate for help and then continue reading after the word or sentence has been clarified. After something on a page has been clarified or discussed, have a different student reread that page before moving on to the next page.

✦ Repeat this procedure for each page.

✦ Reread the story twice more, calling on various students to read or reading it in unison. These readings should go more quickly, with fewer stops for clarification.

Responding to the Story

After the story has been read aloud a couple of times, have students respond as follows:

✦ Ask students which difficult words they found in the story and how they figured them out. They may mention high-frequency words they did not recognize, words they had to blend, and words whose meanings they did not know.

✦ Have students tell about the story, retelling it in their own words, describing what they liked about it, or citing what they found interesting or surprising. Specific suggestions to use are listed in the **Teacher's Edition.**

✦ Questions are often provided in the **Teacher's Edition.** They are designed to focus students' attention on the words and not just the pictures. Ask students the questions, and have all students point to the answer in the story rather than having one student respond orally. Having students point to the answers is important. First, it ensures that all students are engaged in finding the answer, not just one. Second, by pointing to the answer, you know that students know the answer from reading and not just from having heard it read. Third, locating information in a text is an important skill. Finally, by pointing to the answer, you can quickly monitor who is understanding the story and who may still need more support during Workshop.

✦ Have students reread the story with partners. Circulate among the pairs, listening to individual students read. This allows you to monitor students' reading and to identify any students who may need additional help during Workshop.

Building Fluency beyond Decodables (middle of grade 1 on)

For some students, fluency develops naturally, seemingly without instruction. Other students, however, can benefit from more explicit instruction. There are students who can decode and read words but lack the critical phrasing, intonation, and expression that support meaning. Teach the text characteristics that support fluency, model them for students, and then provide students regular opportunities to practice fluency. Instruction can focus on any or all of the following areas:

✦ Discuss and model ending punctuation and what this means in terms of expression and intonation. This should be modeled and then discussed with students. Begin with ending punctuation, and then move to internal punctuation such as commas and semicolons. During modeling,

  • pause longer at a period or other ending punctuation.

  • raise your voice at a question mark.

  • use expression when you come to an exclamation point.

  • pause at commas or other internal punctuation such as semicolons.

  • when you come to quotation marks, think of the character and how he or she might say his or her words.

  • pause at an ellipsis.

  • pause at dashes.

✦ Discuss and model words written in a

special way—typographical signals such as underlined words, boldfaced words, or those in all caps—need to be read with expression and changed in intonation for emphasis.

✦ Talk about reading rate. Oral reading should be done at a normal speaking rate. Students should not be reading so fast that someone listening could not hear the individual words and make sense of what is being read.

✦ Discuss and model intonation. Let students hear how voices change with different ending punctuation, how voices change when reading dialogue, and how intonation changes with cues from the author. In dialogue, think of the difference between "screamed Jennifer" versus "pleaded Jessie."

✦ Work on phrase cue boundaries. A good way to teach this is by using an overhead of what students are reading. Mark natural phrase boundaries—for example, clauses, prepositional phrases, subject phrases, verb phrases, and so on, with slashes. For example, *In the summertime,/Josh likes to play baseball/ at the park/down the street from his house.* Have students listen to you read the text, noticing how you paused at the markers. Then have students read the sentences naturally, using the markers as guides. Scaffold the instruction. In the beginning, mark the boundaries, and have students practice reading using the already marked passages. As students become comfortable, have them mark what they are reading with boundary markers. Gradually fade out the markers or slashes.

Fluency develops over time, and students should be given repeated opportunities to practice fluency with a variety of different texts. After students have read a text, take time to go back and discuss any new vocabulary or interesting words that students encountered while reading. Fluency is not an isolated activity; it is about supporting comprehension.

There are a number of techniques for practicing fluency: repeated readings, partner reading, tape-assisted reading, and Reader's Theater. All of these techniques can be done with a variety of different reading materials, including selections from the *Student Readers,* the *Leveled Readers,* and the *Science* and *Social Studies Leveled Readers.*

✦ Repeated readings increase reading rate, accuracy, and comprehension by providing students with multiple exposures to words and spelling patterns. In addition, it helps students improve their ability to break sentences into meaningful phrases and to use intonation. It is effective with both older and younger students. Repeated readings involve the students reading segments of text between 50 to 200 words, depending upon students' ability. Students should practice repeated readings with a variety of different text types. While repeated readings can be done with materials from *SRA Imagine It!* using segments from science and social studies texts helps students in the upper grades apply their reading knowledge across the curriculum. The goal is to have students read the text fluently and automatically at a per-minute rate commensurate with grade-level norms.

✦ CD-assisted readings help build confidence and are excellent support for second-language learners. Tape-assisted reading allows students to hear good models of reading and to develop their awareness of phrasing and prosody, or expressive reading. Tapes should provide students with experiences from a variety of text types. Tape selections should be read at approximately 80–100 words per minute by fluent readers with natural intonation, phrasing, and expression. Students read along with the text, aloud or subvocalizing. When the student is comfortable with the text, the student should practice reading the text independently and then read a portion of it to the teacher. The CDs in *SRA Imagine It!* can help students develop fluency with selections in the *Student Readers.*

✦ Reader's Theater legitimizes practicing fluency because it involves reading a script. While students do not memorize the script the way actors do in a play, they must be able to read the script fluently so the audience—the rest of the class—can enjoy the play. Several students can work together on a single play or playlet. They will need to practice reading the script several times before presenting it to the class. Reader's Theater also provides students with a writing opportunity. They can use a selection from their *Student Readers,* write a playlet, and then practice it for Reader's Theater.

✦ Radio Reading, like Reader's Theater, connects reading aloud to real-life situations. Students, with copies of the text, read aloud in front of the class as if they were news broadcasters. Expository text works particularly well for this. Students can practice, and then once a week, several students can be the radio announcers. Students can also write weekly news reports and read them.

✦ Partner Reading involves students reading with a partner. They can take turns reading pages or the entire selection. While one student reads, the listening-partner should note misread words and then discuss them with the partner after the reading. If the pairs are reading for one-minute-fluency checks, the nonreading partner can be responsible for timing the reading. Selections should be read multiple times with the goal being that students achieve a higher fluency rate on successive readings.

Assessing Fluency

Fluency should be assessed periodically to determine students' growth and to monitor progess. Listening to students read regularly is key. Fluency assessment should include not just reading rate but decoding accuracy, prosody (phrasing and intonation), and expression. In addition, checks should be done using various text types.

Generally accepted procedures for assessment include the following:

✦ Use a passage of approximately 250 words at student's reading level. In the first half of first grade, use the appropriate **Decodable** in the Practice set. Have two copies—one for the student and one for you to mark.

✦ Have the student read the passage for one minute. Use a timer, if possible, so you do not have to keep watching a stopwatch or the minute hand on a clock. You can also tape-record the reading. The goal is to have students read the text aloud in a natural way, the

way they would speak the words. This is not a race! Use the following scoring conventions. Mark any errors made by the reader.

✦ Draw a line through any misread word, and count it as an error.

✦ Circle any words the student omits or refuses to read, and count them as errors.

✦ Indicate with a caret any extra words the student inserts.

✦ Draw an arrow between words that student reverses, and count as one error.

✦ Put two check marks above a word that a student repeats, but do not count it as an error.

✦ Draw a box around the last word student reads in the one-minute time frame.

To calculate the student's accuracy rate, count the total number of words read in one minute. Subtract the number of errors from the total number of words read, and use that number to find the number of correct words read per minute.

For example, to calculate the rate:
Total words read – errors = words correct per minute
75 words read – 10 errors = 65 words per minute

For example, to calculate the accuracy:
Number of words ÷ the total number of words = percent of accuracy
145 (words correct) ÷ 156 (total number of words) = 93%

Descriptive Statistics for Oral Reading Fluency by Season for Grades 1–6 (Medians)

		Fall	Winter	Spring
Grade	Percentile	WCPM[2]	WCPM	WCPM
1	75		46.75	82
	50		23	53
	25		6	15
2	75	79	100	117
	50	51	72	89
	25	25	42	61
3	75	99	120	137
	50	71	92	107
	25	44	62	78
4	75	119	139	152
	50	94	112	123
	25	68	87	98
5	75	139	156	168
	50	110.25	127	139
	25	85	99	109
6	75	153	167	177
	50	127	140	150
	25	98	111	122

[2]WCPM = words correct per minute

SOURCE
From "Curriculum-Based Oral Reading Fluency Norms for Students in Grades 1 Through 6" (2005) by Jan E. Hasbrouck and Gerald Tindal. *Behavioral Research and Teaching.*

In addition, watch for and note the following:

+ Expression
+ Ability of the reader to read words in natural syntactic clusters

Assessing accuracy, pace or rate, and expression provide information for instruction.

In addition to the qualitative information, some teachers like to use rubrics in their evaluation of fluency.

+ **Level 1:** Reads basically word by word with limited phrasing, little expression. Reading is labored with difficulty in reading words automatically and fluently.

+ **Level 2:** Reads in limited phrases of two words, but grouping of words is not natural. There is little or no appropriate expression or intonation.

+ **Level 3:** Reads in phrases with most having appropriate breaks. Most of the reading has appropriate expression and intonation. There is limited comprehension.

+ **Level 4:** Reads with appropriate phrasing, intonation, and expression and demonstrates understanding of the piece.

Interpreting Fluency Data

First compare the student's number of correct words per minute with accepted fluency norms.

Then examine the student's accuracy percentage. Reading accuracy should remain constant or gradually increase within and between grades until it stabilizes at 90 percent or higher. Compare the student's accuracy percentage after each assessment to ensure that his or her accuracy percentage is holding constant or improving.

Next examine the types of errors the student made, and consider what they mean for instruction.

+ Inserting extra words suggest that the student understands what is being read but is reading perhaps impulsively or carelessly.

+ Refusing to attempt to read words suggests that the student may be uncertain of his or her abilities, unwilling to take risks, or needs additional work with decoding at the sound/spelling or morpheme level. Look at the words the student does not read. Are they one-syllable words or multisyllabic words?

+ Misreading routine CVC and CVCe words suggest that the student may need more work with the sounds and spellings. In some cases, a student may be able to read words with common sounds and spellings but needs more work with long vowels, diphthongs, and diagraphs.

+ Looking for patterns in errors is key.

+ Using or not using intonation, expression, and phrasing but reading quickly and accurately suggests that students need to think about how words combine to make meaning and how our expression can support understanding.

Tips

+ Use Workshop time for building fluency. Introduce different ways to practice fluency one at a time.

+ Set up a listening area for Workshop that students can use for tape-assisted instruction.

+ Make sure **Pre-Decodables, Decodables,** and **Leveled Readers** are available to students.

+ Have simple timers available for students to check their fluency rate.

+ Encourage students to chart their fluency growth. If students are doing repeated reading, have them chart the number of words read each day for several days so they can see their fluency improving.

+ When students have developed some degree of fluency with a **Pre-Decodable, Decodable,** or **Leveled Reader,** send the materials home for additional practice.

+ Use a range of materials to practice building fluency throughout the day. Remember, fluency practice can be as short as one minute several times a day.

Reading Aloud

Purpose

Adults read aloud a variety of materials to students. In this program there are **Big Books,** picture books, novels, and excerpts for reading aloud. Research has shown that students who are read to are more likely to develop the skills they need to read successfully on their own.

In kindergarten and Grade 1, there are **Big Books.** In every grade level of **SRA Imagine It!** there are opportunities for teachers to read aloud to students. At the beginning of each unit is a Read Aloud selection tied to the unit theme. This Read Aloud selection allows students the opportunity to think about the unit theme before reading selections on their own.

Reading aloud at any age serves multiple purposes. Reading aloud

+ provokes students' curiosity about text.
+ conveys an awareness that text has meaning.
+ demonstrates the various reasons for reading text (to find out about the world, to learn useful new information and new skills, or simply for pleasure).
+ exposes students to the "language of literature," which is more complex than the language they ordinarily use and hear.
+ provides an opportunity to teach the problem-solving strategies that good readers employ. As students observe you interacting with the text, expressing your own enthusiasm, and modeling your thinking aloud, they perceive these as valid responses and begin to respond to text in similar ways.

Procedures

The following set of general procedures for reading aloud is designed to help you maximize the effectiveness of any Read Aloud session.

+ **Read-Aloud sessions.** Set aside time each day to read aloud.
+ **Introduce the story.** Tell students that you are going to read a story aloud to them. Tell its title, and briefly comment on the topic. To allow students to anticipate what will happen in the story, be careful not to summarize.

+ **Activate prior knowledge.** Ask whether anyone has already heard the story. If so, ask them to see if this version is the same as the one they have heard. If not, activate prior knowledge by saying, "First, let's talk a little about _____." If the story is being read in two (or more) parts, before reading the second part, ask students to recall the first part.
+ **Before reading.** Invite students to interrupt your reading if there are any words they do not understand or ideas they find puzzling or to ask questions. Throughout the reading, encourage them to do this.
+ **Read the story expressively.** Occasionally react verbally to the story by showing surprise, asking questions, giving an opinion, expressing pleasure, or predicting events. Expressive reading not only supports comprehension but serves as a model for fluency. Think-aloud suggestions are outlined below.
+ **Use Comprehension Strategies.** While reading aloud to students, model the use of comprehension strategies in a natural, authentic way. Remember to try to present a variety of ways to respond to text. These include visualizing, asking questions, predicting, making connections, clarifying, and summarizing.
+ **Retell.** When you have finished reading the story, call on volunteers to retell it.
+ **Discuss.** After reading, discuss with students their own reactions: how the story reminded them of things that have happened to them, what they thought of the story, and what they liked best about the story.
+ **Reread.** You may wish to reread the selection on subsequent occasions, focusing the discussion on the unit theme.

Think-Aloud Responses

The following options for modeling thinking aloud will be useful for reading any story aloud. Choose responses that are most appropriate for the selection you are reading.

+ React emotionally by showing joy, sadness, amusement, or surprise.

+ Ask questions about ideas in the text. This should be done when there are points or ideas that you really do wonder about.
+ Identify with characters by comparing them to yourself.
+ Show empathy with or sympathy for characters.
+ Relate the text to something you already know or something that has happened to you.
+ Show interest in the text ideas.
+ Question the meaning or clarity of the author's words and ideas.

Questions to Help Students Respond

At reasonable stopping points in reading, ask students general questions to get them to express their own ideas and to focus their attention on the text. These types of generic questions will help students discuss their reactions to the reading and demonstrate their comprehension.

+ What do you already know about this?
+ What seems really important here? Why do you think so?
+ Was there anything that you did not understand? What?
+ What did you like best about this?
+ What did you not like about this?
+ What new ideas did you learn from this?
+ What does this make you wonder about?
+ What surprised you in the story?

Vocabulary

Purpose

Strong vocabulary skills are correlated to achievement throughout school. The purpose of vocabulary instruction is to introduce students to new words (and ideas) and to teach students a range of strategies for learning, remembering, and incorporating unknown vocabulary words into their existing reading, writing, speaking, and listening vocabularies.

Words chosen for inclusion in **SRA Imagine It!** are based upon the vocabulary research of Andrew Biemiller, who has developed a comprehensive database of words students with large vocabularies know by the end of sixth grade. Biemiller's work identifies words that all students need to know and provides evidence that students from various backgrounds acquire these word meanings in roughly the same order. It appears that for students with small vocabularies, improving vocabulary mainly means moving them through the sequence faster. Because vocabulary knowledge is so critical to comprehension, vocabulary instruction is integrated throughout **SRA Imagine It!**

Vocabulary is taught throughout every part of the lesson.

Part 1: Preparing to Read

✦ In Grades 2–6, Word Structure develops vocabulary and the understanding that words can be deconstructed and related through known elements to determine meaning. In addition, students are learning about Greek and Latin roots, antonyms, synonyms, and multiple-meaning words. The emphasis on root words and affixes, in particular, serves to expand students' knowledge of words and their vocabulary.

✦ In Grades K–1, students are using words they blend in sentences to develop vocabulary and oral language. Learning about inflectional endings also helps children see the relationship between root words and various forms of the root. Reviews of blending lines focus on using words based on teacher clues as well as finding synonyms and antonyms.

Part 2: Reading and Responding

✦ The selection vocabulary instruction in this part of the lesson focuses on teaching specific vocabulary necessary for understanding the literature selection more completely.

✦ In kindergarten and the first half of Grade 1, the teacher introduces the selection vocabulary orally before reading the selection. Suggestions are made throughout the reading to discuss new and interesting words as the class reads the **Big Books.** Work from Biemiller suggests that clarifying words in the context of reading is an effective technique for expanding student vocabulary. Suggestions for which words to stop and clarify are suggested throughout the lessons. Vocabulary review activities are found throughout the lesson.

✦ From the middle of Grade 1 on, critical word meanings needed to understand the story are pre-taught as students read the Vocabulary Warm-Up in the **Student Reader.** This provides an initial exposure to the selection vocabulary. This is followed by guided vocabulary practice in which students discuss the definitions of critical words; learn to apply critical skills such as context, structure and apposition; use the vocabulary words in a variety of activities, and then return to the Vocabulary Warm-Up to reread the sentences containing the vocabulary words and to discuss the words. The clarification of additional vocabulary words is highlighted throughout the reading of each selection. Vocabulary review activities are found throughout the lesson.

✦ Students write the words and their definitions in their Writer's Notebooks.

✦ Vocabulary words, along with any other words students find interesting, are posted on charts to remind students to use these words in discussion of their reading as well as in their writing.

Part 3: Language Arts

During writing, students are encouraged to use their new vocabulary.

General Strategies

There is no question that having students read and reading to students are effective vocabulary instructional strategies. Most word learning occurs through exposure to words in listening and reading. Multiple exposures to words, particularly when students hear, see, say, and write words, is also effective. Wordplay, including meaning and dictionary games, helps develop a word consciousness as well.

Vocabulary Strategies for Unknown Words

Different strategies have been shown to be particularly effective for learning completely new words. These strategies are included in the Vocabulary Warm-Up lessons and **Skills Practice** activities.

Key Word This strategy involves providing or having students create a mnemonic clue for unknown vocabulary. For example, the word *mole* is defined in chemistry as a "gram molecule." By relating *mole* to *molecule,* students have a key to the meaning of the word.

Definitions Copying a definition from a dictionary is somewhat effective in learning new vocabulary. Combining this with using the word in writing and speaking adds to the effectiveness of this strategy. Requiring students to explain a word or to use it in a novel sentence helps ensure that the meaning is understood. It is not uncommon when students use words in sentences that the meaning of the vocabulary word is not clear. For example, a typical sentence a student might give for the word *camouflage* is "The octopus uses camouflage." The word *camouflage* is correctly used, but there is no real indication that the student knows the meaning of the word. Having students extend the sentence to explain why or how in the sentence helps: "The octopus uses camouflage to protect itself from predators." Or "The camouflage an octopus uses when it is in danger is to change its shape and color."

Context Clues Some words can be inferred from context and can be learned with repeated exposure to words in reading and listening. While using context can be useful, it is not the most effective way to learn new words. Also, as students move into content area reading, context becomes a less effective tool for determining the meaning of unfamiliar words.

✦ **Syntax** How a word is used in a sentence may provide some clue as to its meaning. This is particularly effective with homographs. "The lead pipe is a hazard to the community." Here lead is an adjective and is pronounced with a short e. In the sentence "He will lead the troops into battle," *lead* has a very different meaning, is a verb, and is pronounced with a long e.

✦ **Apposition** Sometimes the word is actually defined within the text. In an appositive, the definition of a word is often set off by commas for the reader.

Word Structure Examining the affixes and roots of a word often provides clues to its meaning. Knowing the meaning of at least part of the word can provide a clue as to its meaning. For example, *unenforceable* can be broken down into meaningful word parts. This is a particularly important tool in content area reading.

Developing Vocabulary

Purpose

Vocabulary is closely connected to comprehension. Considerable vocabulary growth occurs incidentally during reading. A clear connection exists between vocabulary development and the amount of reading a person does, and there are strong indications that vocabulary instruction is important and that understanding the meanings of key words helps with comprehension.

In **SRA Imagine It!** vocabulary is addressed before, during, and after reading. Before reading, the teacher presents vocabulary words from the selection. Students use skills such as context clues, apposition, and structural analysis to determine the meanings of the words. These selection vocabulary words are not only important to understanding the text but are also high-utility words that can be used in discussing and writing about the unit theme.

During reading, students monitor their understanding of words and text. When they do not understand something, they stop and clarify what they have read. Students will use these same skills—context clues, apposition, structural elements, and so on—to clarify the meanings of additional words encountered while reading. Determining the meanings of words while reading prepares students for the demands of independent reading both in and out of school.

After reading, students review the vocabulary words that they learned before reading the selection. They also review any interesting words that they identified and discussed during reading. Students record in their Writer's Notebooks both the selection vocabulary words and the interesting words they identified during their reading and are encouraged to use both sets of words in discussion and in writing.

Procedure

Before students read the selection, they read the Vocabulary Warm-Up in the **Student Reader.** As they read, students use context clues, word structure, or apposition to figure out the highlighted selection vocabulary. If students cannot determine the meaning of a word using one of the skills, they can consult the glossary or dictionary. After reading the Vocabulary Warm-Up, the teacher displays an overhead transparency to review the selection vocabulary.

Below are suggestions for modeling the use of context clues, apposition, or word structure to determine the meaning of a word.

Modeling Using Context Clues

Write the following sentences on the board or on a transparency. Explain to students that

they will use context clues, or other words in the sentence, to determine the meaning of the underlined word.

1. Mrs. Frisby must undertake a <u>treacherous</u> journey to take her son some medicine.

2. We took a <u>treacherous</u> walk near a swamp filled with crocodiles.

Have students look for clues in the sentences that might help them understand the meaning of the underlined word. Point out that a good clue in the second sentence is "near a swamp filled with crocodiles." This clue should help them understand that *treacherous* probably has something to do with danger. Guide students until they can give a reasonable definition of *treacherous*. To consolidate understanding of the word, ask another student to use the definition in a sentence.

Modeling Using Apposition

Write the following sentences on the board or on a transparency. Explain to students that they will use apposition to determine the meaning of the underlined word. In apposition, the word is followed by the definition, which is set off by commas.

1. The conductor thought he was an <u>abolitionist,</u> a person who wanted to end slavery.

2. John Brown was a famous <u>abolitionist</u>, a person who wanted to end slavery.

It should be clear to students using apposition that the definition of the word *abolitionist* is "a person who wanted to end slavery."

Modeling Using Word Structure

Write the following sentences on the board or on a transparency. Explain to students that they will use word structure, or parts of the word, to determine the meaning of the underlined word.

1. The strong wind blew Ivan's ship away into <u>uncharted</u> seas.

2. The explorers Lewis and Clark went into <u>uncharted</u> territory.

Have students look at the word *uncharted* and break it into parts: the prefix *un-*, *chart*, and the suffix *-ed*. Students should know that the suffix *un-* means "not" and that the suffix *-ed* usually indicates the past tense of a verb. However, you may need to remind students about the meanings of these affixes. Ask students for the meaning of the word *chart*. Students should know that a chart could be a map or a table. Guide them as they put together the definitions of the word parts: *un-* (not), *charted* (mapped or tabled). They should be able to come up with the definition "not mapped" or "unmapped" or even "unknown." Have them substitute their definition in the sentences to see if the definition makes sense. For instance, the first sentence would read, "The strong wind blew Ivan's ship away into unmapped (or unknown) seas." Confirm with students that the new sentence makes sense, and then repeat the same process for the second sentence.

Everything students learn about phonemic awareness, phonics, word

structure and decoding has one primary goal—to help them understand what they are reading. Without comprehension, there is no reading.

Take time to review words and their meanings. Help students connect new words to familiar words. Each unit in **SRA Imagine It!** revolves around a theme, and there are key words. In every lesson, there is a concept.

Semantic Mapping Having students create a semantic map of an unknown word after learning its definition helps them learn it. Have students write the new word and then list in a map or web all words they can think of that are related to it.

Semantic Feature Analysis A semantic feature analysis helps students compare and contrast similar types of words within a category to help secure unknown words. Have students chart, for example, the similarities and differences between various types of sports, including new vocabulary such as *lacrosse* and *cricket*.

Reading Comprehension

Purpose

The primary aim of reading is comprehension. Without comprehension, neither intellectual nor emotional responses to reading are possible—other than the response of frustration. Reading is about problem solving. Expert readers bring their critical faculties to bear on everything they read. They generally understand most of what they read, but just as importantly, they recognize when they do not understand, and they have at their command an assortment of strategies for monitoring and furthering their understanding.

The goal of comprehension strategy instruction is to turn responsibility for using strategies over to students as soon as possible. Research has shown that students' comprehension and learning problems are not a matter of mental capacity but rather their inability to use strategies to help them learn. Expert readers use a variety of strategies to help them make sense of the text and to get the most out of what they read. Trained to use a variety of comprehension strategies, students dramatically improve their learning performance. To do this, the teacher models strategy use and gradually incorporates various kinds of prompts and possible student think-alouds as examples of the types of thinking students might do as they read to comprehend what they are reading.

Setting Reading Goals

Even before they begin reading and using comprehension strategies, good readers set reading goals and expectations. Readers who have set their own goals and have definite expectations about the text they are about to read are more engaged in their reading and notice more in what they read. Having determined a purpose for reading, they are better able to evaluate a text and to determine whether it meets their needs. Even when the reading is assigned, the reader's engagement is enhanced when he or she has determined ahead of time what information might be gathered from the selection or how the selection might interest him or her.

Comprehension Strategies

Descriptions of strategies expert readers use to comprehend the text follow.

> *Good readers continually monitor their speed and ability to understand throughout reading.*

Summarizing

Periodically it is important to summarize and check our understanding as we read. Sometimes readers reread to fill in gaps in their understanding. They use the strategy of summarizing to keep track of what they are reading and to focus their minds on important information. The process of putting the information in one's own words not only helps good readers remember what they have read but also prompts them to evaluate how well they understand the information. Sometimes the summary reveals that one's understanding is incomplete, in which case it might be appropriate to reread the previous section to fill in the gaps. The strategy of summarizing is particularly helpful when readers are reading long or complicated text. When to stop and summarize depends on the difficulty of the text as well as the type of text. Often in content area reading, it makes sense to stop and summarize the key ideas after each section. In narratives, the reader often stops to summarize after an episode has been read. Many of us will automatically summarize what has happened if we have put down a book and are about to continue reading it again. Students should think to themselves the following:

✦ Does this make sense? What is this selection about?

✦ What are the big ideas the writer is trying to get at?

✦ What can I delete from my summary? What is not important?

✦ Have I said the same thing more than once in my summary?

✦ How can I put what I just read into my own words?

✦ What is unclear? What is the meaning of the word or sentence? How can I determine this?

Clarifying

Monitoring understanding is key to reading. It allows readers to make sure they understand what they read. They note the characteristics of the text, such as whether it is difficult to read or whether some sections are more challenging or more important than others are. In addition, when readers become aware that they do not understand, they stop and take appropriate action, such as rereading, to understand the text better. As they read, good readers stay alert for problem signs such as loss of concentration, unfamiliar vocabulary, or lack of sufficient background knowledge to comprehend the text. This ability to self-monitor and identify aspects of the text that hinder comprehension is crucial to becoming a proficient reader. Clarifying may occur at the word, the sentence, the paragraph, or at the whole-text level. Students should think to themselves the following:

✦ What does not make sense? If it is a word, how can I figure it out? Do I use context, structure, or apposition, or do I need to ask someone or look it up in the dictionary or glossary?

✦ What does not make sense? The paragraph is long and full of details. What can I do? I can take some notes, I can reread it more slowly; I can discuss it with someone.

✦ These sentences are endless. How can I deal with long, complicated sentences?

✦ What is the main idea of what I just read?

✦ Can I summarize what I just read?

Asking Questions

Asking questions allows the reader to constantly check his or her understanding and to follow the writer's train of thought. Good readers ask questions that may prepare them for what they will learn. If their questions are not answered in the text, they may try to find answers elsewhere and thus add even more to their store of knowledge. Certain kinds of questions occur naturally to a reader, such as to clear up confusion or to wonder why something in the text is as it is. Intentional readers take this somewhat informal questioning one step further by formulating questions with the specific intent of checking their understanding. They literally test themselves by thinking of questions a teacher might ask and then by determining answers to those questions. Students should think to themselves the following:

✦ Why is this the way it is? What else is there to know about this?

✦ What question can I ask to check if I have understood what I just read?

✦ How does this connect to the unit theme? What new information will I learn?

✦ What questions do I think the author will answer as I read this selection?

✦ Do I understand the author? What is not making sense?

✦ What is interfering with my understanding?

Predicting

Predicting what will happen in the story allows the reader to summarize what has been read so far, to identify clues and events in the text, and to use prior knowledge and personal experience to make inferences about what will happen next. When reading fiction, readers make predictions about what they are reading and then confirm or revise those predictions as they go. Predictions are not wild guesses. They are made based on information provided by the author as well as the reader's background knowledge. Students should think to themselves the following: What do I already know that will help me predict? What are the clues in the text that will help me predict?

✦ Why was my prediction confirmed?

✦ Why was my prediction not confirmed?

✦ What clues did I miss that would have helped me make a better prediction?

> *The responsibility for using strategies by students should begin as soon as they understand that reading is about problem solving and making sense of text and that these strategies will help them do both.*

Making Connections

Making connections between the text and what is known from personal experience or previous reading deepens our understanding of text and expands our understanding. Comprehension is enhanced when we relate what is read to what is known. Students should think to themselves the following:

✦ What does this remind me of? What else have I read like this?

✦ What does this remind me of in my own life? In my own experiences?

✦ How does this connect with other selections I have read?

✦ How does this connect with what is going on in the world today?

Visualizing

Creating a mental image about the text involves not just the literal interpretation of the author's word but going beyond the literal to incorporating prior knowledge and experiences that deepen understanding. Readers form mental images as they read. They picture the setting, the characters, and the action in a story. Visualizing can also be helpful when reading expository text. Visualizing helps readers understand descriptions of complex activities or processes. When a complex process or an event is being described, the reader can follow the process or the event better by visualizing each step or episode. Sometimes an author or an editor helps the reader by providing illustrations, diagrams, or maps. If no visual aids have been provided, it may help the reader to create one. Creating mental images helps the reader create pictures that can be stored efficiently in his

or her long-term memory. Students should think to themselves the following:

✦ What picture does the words create in my mind? How do the words suggest feelings, actions, and settings?

✦ Would a drawing help me understand the process?

✦ How does my mental picture extend beyond the words in the text?

✦ How did this picture help me understand what I am reading?

Adjusting Reading Speed

Some texts are easy to read; others are more challenging. How difficult a text is to read depends on both author and reader variables. Good readers understand that not all text is equal. Because of this, they continuously monitor what they are reading and adjust their reading speed accordingly. Efficient readers skim parts of the text that are not important or relevant to their reading goals, and they purposely slow down when they encounter difficulty in understanding the text. Students should think to themselves the following:

✦ When I reread does this make sense?

✦ This is a long and involved sentence. Rereading may help.

Procedures

Modeling and Thinking Aloud

One of the most effective ways to help students understand and use critical comprehension is to make strategic thinking public. Modeling these behaviors and encouraging students to think aloud as they attempt to address comprehension problems and to understand text can demonstrate for everyone in a class how these behaviors are put into practice. Suggestions for think-alouds are provided throughout the ***Teacher's Edition.***

The most effective models you can offer will be those that come from your own reading experiences. What kinds of questions did you ask yourself? What kinds of things surprised you the first time you read a story? What kinds of new information did you learn? What kinds of things were confusing until you reread or read further? Drawing on these questions and on your students' questions and comments as they read will make the strategic reading process more meaningful to students. Below are suggestions for modeling each of the comprehension strategies.

Before Reading

✦ **Modeling Setting Reading Goals.** To model setting reading goals, engage students in the following:

- **Activate prior knowledge.** As you approach a new text, consider aloud what you already know about the subject or what your experiences have been in reading similar material.

- **Browse the text.** To get an idea of what to expect from a text, look at the title and the illustrations. When students are reading fiction, they will browse the text to look for Clues, Problems and Wonderings. Possible clues will support comprehension— for example, genre, content, author, setting, and so on—potential problems might include things such as difficult words or dense paragraphs as well as unfamiliar concepts; and wonderings are the things students are curious to find out about from their reading— questions about the selection. Wonderings are students' purposes for reading. When students read nonfiction, they will use a KWL chart— this is what I know (K), this is what I want to find out (W), and this is what I have learned (L). Both these activities— Clues, Problems, and Wonderings and KWL—engage students in thinking before reading the selection by having them activate their own background knowledge, identify potential problems, and set purposes for reading. Have students glance quickly at the selection, looking briefly at the illustrations and the print. Have them tell what they think they might be learning about as they read the selection. Early in the year, model the thinking involved with these activities and then begin to turn the responsibility for completing them over to students.

During Reading

Modeling— or thinking aloud— about how to use strategies to solve problems is a powerful tool for teaching comprehension. While think-aloud models are included in all lessons, relate your own thinking and experiences to the lesson and the think-alouds. Early in the process you will need to model thinking about how, when, and why to use the strategies. Encourage students to stop and use them as well; engage them in thinking!

✦ **Modeling Summarizing.** Just as the strategy of summarizing the plot and then predicting what will happen next can enhance a student's reading of fiction, so too can the same procedure be used to the student's advantage in reading nonfiction. In expository text, it is particularly logical to stop and summarize at the end of a chapter or section before going on to the next. One way to model the valuable exercise of making predictions and at the same time to expand knowledge is to summarize information learned from a piece of expository writing and then to predict what the next step or category will be. Appropriate times to stop and summarize include the following:

- When a narrative text has covered a long period of time or a number of events
- When many facts have been presented
- When an especially critical scene has occurred
- When a complex process has been described
- Any time there is the potential for confusion about what has happened or what has been presented in the text
- When returning to a selection

✦ **Modeling Clarifying.** A reader may need clarification at any point in the reading. Model this strategy by stopping at points that confuse you or that may confuse your students. Indicate that you are experiencing some confusion and need to stop and make sure you understand what is being read. Difficulty may arise from a challenging or unknown word or phrase. It may also stem from the manner in which the information is presented. Perhaps the author did not supply needed information. As you model this strategy, vary the reasons for stopping to clarify so that students understand that good readers do not simply skip over difficult or confusing material—they stop and determine what they do not comprehend.

✦ **Modeling Asking Questions.** Learning to ask productive questions is not an easy task. Students' earliest experiences with this strategy take the form of answering teacher-generated questions. However, students should be able to move fairly quickly to asking questions like those a teacher might ask. Questions that can be answered with a simple *yes* or *no* are not typically very useful for helping them remember and understand what they have read. Many students find it helpful to ask questions beginning with *Who? What? When? Where? How?* and *Why?* As students become more accustomed to asking and answering questions, they will naturally become more adept at phrasing their questions. As their question asking becomes more sophisticated, they progress from simple questions that can be answered with explicit information in the text to questions that require making inferences based on the text.

✦ **Modeling Predicting.** Predicting can be appropriate at the beginning of a selection—on the basis of the titles and the illustrations—or at any point while reading a selection. At first, your modeling will take the form of speculation about what might happen next, but tell students from the start what clues in the text or illustrations helped you predict to make it clear that predicting is not just guessing. When a student makes a prediction—especially a far-fetched one—ask on what in the selection or in his or her own experience the prediction is based. If the student can back up the prediction, let the prediction stand; otherwise, suggest that the student make another prediction on the basis of what he or she already knows. Often it is appropriate to summarize before making a prediction. This will help students consider what has come before as they make their predictions about what will happen next. When reading aloud, stop whenever a student's prediction has been confirmed or contradicted. Have students tell whether the prediction was correct. If students seem comfortable with the idea of making predictions but rarely do so on their own, encourage them to discuss how to find clues in the text that will help them.

✦ **Modeling Making Connections.** To model making connections, share with students any thoughts or memories that come to mind as you read the selection. Perhaps a character in a story reminds you of a childhood friend, allowing you to better identify with interactions between characters. Perhaps information in an article on Native American life in the Old West reminds you of an article that you have read on the importance of the bison to Native Americans. Sharing your connections will help students become aware of the dynamic nature of reading and show them another way of being intentional, active learners.

✦ **Modeling Visualizing.** Model visualizing by describing the mental images that occur to you as you read. A well-described scene is relatively easy to visualize, and if no one does so voluntarily, you may want to prompt students to express their own visualizations. If the author has not provided a description of a scene, but a picture of the scene would make the story more interesting or comprehensible, you might want to model visualizing as follows: "Let's see. The author says that the street was busy, and we know that this story is set during the colonial period. From what I already know about those times, there were no cars, and the roads were different from the roads of today. The street may have been paved with cobblestones. Horses would have been pulling carriages or wagons. I can almost hear the horses' hoofs going clip-clop over the stones." Remind students that different readers may picture the same scene quite differently, which is fine. Every reader responds to a story in her or his own way.

✦ **Modeling Adjusting Reading Speed.** Just as readers need to monitor for problems, they need to be aware that various texts can be approached in various ways. For example, if reading a story or novel for enjoyment, the reader will typically read at a relaxed speed that is neither so fast as to miss information nor as slow as they might read a textbook. If on the other hand, the reader is reading a textbook, he or she will probably decrease speed to assure understanding and make sure that all important information is read and understood. When modeling this strategy, be sure you indicate why you,

as the reader, have chosen to slow down or speed up. Good readers continually monitor their speed and ability to understand throughout reading.

If your students have not previously engaged in the sort of strategic thinking aloud that is promoted throughout **SRA Imagine It!,** you will have to do all or most of the modeling at first, but encourage students to participate as soon as possible. Remember, however, the goal is for students to use these strategies independently as they read both in and out of school. In addition to the think-alouds for the teachers, there are also prompts to encourage students to do the thinking. The responsibility for using strategies by students should begin as soon as they understand that reading is about problem solving and making sense of text and that these strategies will help them do both.

Reading Aloud

At the beginning of the year, students should be encouraged to read selections aloud. This practice will help you and them understand some of the challenges posed by the text and how individual students approach these challenges.

Reading aloud helps students build fluency, which in turn will aid their comprehension. Students in Grades K–3 can use **Decodables** to build fluency, while students in Grades 4–6 can use the literature from the **Student Readers. Leveled Readers** are also available for Grades 1–6. Fluent second graders read between 79 and 117 words per minute with accuracy and understanding, depending on the time of the year (fall/spring). Fluent third graders can be expected to read between 99 and 137 words per minute; fourth (119/152); fifth (139/168); sixth (123/177).

Make sure that you set aside time to hear each student read during the first few days of class—the days devoted to Getting Started are perfect for this—so that you can determine students' abilities and needs. Workshop is also a good time to listen to any students who do not get to read aloud while the class is reading the selection together.

As the year progresses, students should continue reading aloud often, especially with particularly challenging text. Model your own use of strategies, not only to help students better understand how to use strategies but also to help them understand that actively using strategies is something that good, mature readers do constantly.

Most students are unaccustomed to thinking aloud. They will typically stand mute as they try to determine an unfamiliar word or to deal with a confusing passage. When this happens, students should be encouraged to identify specifically with what they are having difficulty. A student might identify a particular word, or he or she may note that the individual words are familiar but that the meaning of the passage is unclear.

Active Response

Not only are good readers active in their reading when they encounter problems, but they respond constantly to whatever they read. In this way they make the text their own. As students read they should be encouraged to

✦ make as many connections as they can between what they are reading and what they already know.

✦ visualize passages to help clarify their meanings or simply to picture appealing descriptions.

✦ ask questions about what they are reading. The questions that go through their minds during reading will help them examine, and thus better understand, the text. Doing so may also interest them in pursuing their own investigations. The questions may also provide a direction for students' research or exploration.

✦ summarize and make predictions as a check on how well they understand what they are reading.

Tips

✦ Remember that the goal of all reading is comprehension. If a story or article does not make sense, the reader needs to choose whatever strategies will help make sense of it. If one strategy does not work, the reader should try another.

✦ Always treat problems encountered in text as interesting learning opportunities rather than something to be avoided or dreaded.

✦ Encourage students to think aloud about text challenges.

✦ Encourage students to help each other build meaning from text. Rather than telling each other what a word is or what a passage means, students should tell each other how they figured out the meanings of challenging words and passages.

✦ Assure students that these are not the only strategies that can be used while reading. Any strategy that they find helpful in understanding text is a good, useful strategy.

✦ Encourage students to freely share strategies they have devised on their own. You might want to write these on a large sheet of paper and tape them onto the board.

✦ An absence of questions does not necessarily indicate that students understand what they are reading. Be especially alert to students who never seem to ask questions. Be sure to spend tutorial time with these students occasionally, and encourage them to discuss specific selections in the context of difficulties they might have encountered and how they solved them as well as their thoughts about unit concepts.

✦ Observing students' responses to text will enable you to ascertain not only how well they understand a particular selection but also their facility in choosing and applying appropriate strategies. Use the strategy rubrics to evaluate students' understanding of and ability to use the different reading strategies. Take note of the following:

- Whether the strategies a student uses are effective in the particular situation.
- Whether the student chooses from a variety of appropriate strategies or uses the same few over and over.
- Whether the student can explain to classmates which strategies to use in a particular situation and why.
- Whether the student can identify alternative resources to pursue when the strategies she or he has tried are not effective.
- Whether students' application of a given strategy is becoming more effective over a period of time.

✦ Encourage students to use the reading strategies throughout the day in all their reading activities.

Becoming familiar and comfortable with these self-monitoring techniques gives readers the confidence to tackle material that is progressively more difficult. A good,

mature reader knows when understanding what he or she is reading is becoming a problem and can take steps to correct the situation. He or she has internalized the strategies, values them, and uses strategies automatically.

Comprehension Skills

Purpose

An important purpose of writing is to communicate thoughts from one person to another. The goal of instruction in reading comprehension skills is to make students aware of the logic behind the structure of a written piece. If the reader can discern the logic of the structure, he or she will be more able to understand the author's logic and to gain knowledge both of the facts and the intent of the selection. By keeping the organization of a piece in mind and considering the author's purpose for writing, the reader can go beyond the actual words on the page and make inferences or draw conclusions based on what was read. Strong, mature readers utilize these "between the lines" skills to get a complete picture of not only what the writer is saying but what the writer is trying to say.

Effective comprehension skills include the following:

Author's Point of View

Point of view involves identifying who is telling the story. If a character in the story is telling the story, that one character describes the action and tells what the other characters are like. This is first-person point of view. In such a story, one character will do the talking and use the pronouns *I, my,* and *me*. All other characters' thoughts, feelings, and emotions will be reported through this one character.

If the story is told in third-person point of view, someone outside the story who is aware of all of the characters' thoughts, feelings, and actions is relating them to the reader. All of the characters are referred to by their names or the pronouns *he/she, him/her,* and *it*.

If students stay aware of who is telling a story, they will know whether they are getting the full picture or the picture of events as seen through the eyes of only one character.

Sequence

The reader cannot make any decisions about relationships or events if he or she has no idea in which order the events take place. The reader needs to pay attention to how the writer is conveying the sequence. Is it simply stated that first this happened and then that happened? Does the writer present the end of the story first and then go back and let the reader know the sequence of events? Knowing what the sequence is and how it is presented helps the reader follow the writer's line of thought.

Fact and Opinion

Learning to distinguish fact from opinion is essential to critical reading and thinking. Students learn what factors need to be present for a statement to be provable. They also learn that an opinion, while not provable itself, should be based on fact. Readers use this knowledge to determine for themselves the validity of the ideas presented in their reading.

Main Idea and Details

An author always has something specific to say to his or her reader. The author may state this main idea in different ways, but the reader should always be able to tell what the writing is about.

To strengthen the main point or main idea of a piece, the author provides details to help the reader understand. For example, the author may use comparison and contrast to make a point, to provide examples, to provide facts, to give opinions, to give descriptions, to give reasons or causes, or to give definitions. The reader needs to know what kinds of details he or she is dealing with before making a judgment about the main idea.

Compare and Contrast

Using comparison and contrast is one of the most common and easiest ways a writer gets his or her reader to understand a subject. Comparing and contrasting unfamiliar thoughts, ideas, or things with familiar thoughts, ideas, and things gives the reader something within his or her own experience base to use in understanding.

Cause and Effect

What made this happen? Why did this character act the way he or she did? Knowing the causes of events helps the reader see the whole story. Using this information to identify the probable outcomes (effects) of events or actions will help the reader anticipate the story or article.

Classify and Categorize

The relationships of actions, events, characters, outcomes, and such in a selection should be clear enough for the reader to see the relationships. Putting like things or ideas together can help the reader understand the relationships set up by the writer.

Author's Purpose

Everything is written for a purpose. That purpose may be to entertain, to persuade, or to inform. Knowing why a piece is written— what purpose the author had for writing the piece—gives the reader an idea of what to expect and perhaps some prior idea of what the author is going to say.

If a writer is writing to entertain, then the reader can generally just relax and let the writer carry him or her away. If, on the other hand, the purpose is to persuade, it will help the reader understand and keep perspective if he or she knows that the purpose is to persuade. The reader can be prepared for whatever argument the writer delivers.

Drawing Conclusions

Often, writers do not directly state everything—they take for granted their audience's ability to "read between the lines." Readers draw conclusions when they take from the text small pieces of information about a character or event and use this information to make a statement about that character or event.

Reality and Fantasy

Students learn to distinguish reality from fantasy as they read different genres, including expository text, realistic fiction, fables, fairy tales, and so on. As students read, they note that a fantasy contains people, animals, and objects that do things that could not happen in the real world. Reality contains people, animals, and objects that can exist and do things in the real world.

Making Inferences

Readers make inferences about characters and events to understand the total picture in a story. When making inferences, readers use information from the text, along with personal experience or knowledge, to gain a deeper understanding of a story event and its implications.

Procedures

Read the Selection

First, have students read the selection using whatever skills they need to help them make sense of the selection. Then discuss the selection to assure that students did, indeed, understand what they read. Talk about any confusion they may have, and make any necessary clarifications.

Reread

Revisiting or rereading a selection allows the reader to note specific techniques that authors use to organize and present information in narratives and expository genres. When students have a basic understanding of the piece, have them reread the selection in whole or in part, concentrating on selected skills. Students learn to appreciate that writers use different structures, for example, cause and effect or compare/contrast, to organize their work and that recognizing these structures can help readers understand what they have read. It is these same structures that students will use in their own writing.

Limit this concentration on specific comprehension/writing skills to one or two that can be clearly identified in the piece. Trying to concentrate on too many things will just confuse students and make it harder for them to identify any of the organizational devices used by the writer. If a piece has many good examples of several different aspects, then go back to the piece several times over a span of days.

Write

Solidify the connection between how an author writes and how readers make sense of a selection by encouraging students to incorporate these organizational devices into their own writing. As they attempt to use these devices, they will get a clearer understanding of how to identify them when they are reading.

Remind students often that the purpose of any skill exercise is to give them tools to use when they are reading and writing. Unless students learn to apply the skills to their own reading—in every area of reading and study—then they are not gaining a full understanding of the purpose of the exercise.

Writing is a complicated process. A writer uses handwriting, spelling, vocabulary, grammar, usage, genre structures, and mechanics skills with ideas to create readable text. In addition, a writer must know how to generate content, or ideas, and understand genre structures to effectively present ideas in writing. Many students never progress beyond producing a written text that duplicates their everyday speech patterns. Mature writers, however, take composition beyond conversation. They understand the importance of audience and purpose for writing. They organize their thoughts, eliminating those that do not advance their main ideas, applying what they have learned in reading, and elaborating on those that do so that their readers can follow a logical progression of ideas in an essay or story. Mature writers also know and can use the conventions of grammar, usage, spelling, and mechanics. They proofread and edit for these conventions, so their readers are not distracted by errors.

Reading Big Books

Purpose

Many students come from homes where they are read to often, but a significant number of other students have not had this valuable experience. **Big Books** (Levels K and 1) offer all students crucial opportunities to confirm and expand their knowledge about print and reading, to develop vocabulary, and to enjoy literacy experiences. They are especially useful for shared reading experiences in the early grades.

The benefits of reading **Big Books** include engaging even nonreaders in

✦ unlocking the books' messages.

✦ developing print awareness.

✦ participating in good reading behaviors.

✦ observing what a good reader does: remarking on the illustrations and the title, asking questions about the content and what might happen, making predictions, and clarifying words and ideas.

✦ promoting the insights about print, for example, that a given word is spelled the same way every time it occurs as high-frequency words are identified.

✦ reinforcing the correspondence between spoken and written words and spelling patterns.

✦ enjoying the illustrations and connecting them to the text to help students learn to explore books for enjoyment and information.

✦ learning about different genre and the language of print.

✦ developing vocabulary and academic language.

✦ interpreting and responding to literature and expository text before they can read themselves.

Procedure for Reading Big Books

During the first reading of the **Big Books,** you will model reading behaviors and comprehension strategies similar to those that will later apply to their own reading. This focus on strategies encourages students to think about the ideas in the stories, to ask questions, and to learn new vocabulary. During the second reading, you will address print awareness and teach comprehension skills such as classifying and categorizing or sequencing, which help the reader organize information and focus on the specifics in the selection. In addition, you will teach skills such as making inferences and drawing conclusions, which help the reader focus on the deeper meaning of the text. At first, teachers should expect to do all of the reading but should not prevent students from trying to read on their own or from reading words they already know.

✦ **Activate Prior Knowledge.** Read the title of the selection and the author's and illustrator's names. At the beginning of each **Big Book,** read the title of the book and discuss what the whole book is about before going on to reading the first selection. Initiate a brief discussion of any prior knowledge students have that might help them understand the selection.

> **Big Books** *offer all students opportunities to confirm and expand their knowledge about print and reading.*

✦ **Browse the Selection.** Explain to the class that browsing means to look through the pages of the story to get a general idea of what the story is about, to see what interests them, and to ask questions. Ask students to tell what they think the story might be about just from looking at the illustrations. This conversation should be brief so that students can move on to a prereading discussion of print awareness.

✦ **Develop Print Awareness.** The focus of browsing the **Big Books** is to develop awareness of print. Urge students to tell what words or letters they recognize rather than what they expect the selection to be about.

To develop print awareness, have students look through the selection page by page and to comment on whatever they notice in the text. Some students may know some of the words, while others may recognize only specific letters or sounds. The key is to get students to look at the print separately from the illustrations even before they have heard the actual text content. This process isolates print awareness so that it is not influenced by content. It also gives you a clearer idea of what your students do or do not know about print.

✦ **Read Aloud.** Read the selection aloud expressively, using intonation and pauses at punctuation. Not only does this enable students to hear and enjoy the text as it is read through once, it serves as an early model for fluency. Good fluency and expression support comprehension. As you read, you will stop periodically to model behaviors and comprehension strategies that all students will need to develop to become successful readers—for example, asking questions; clarifying unfamiliar words, first by using the pictures and later by using context; or predicting what might happen next.

✦ **Reread.** Read the selection expressively again. During the second reading of the stories, you will focus on teaching comprehension skills. Also, to develop print awareness, point to each word as it is read, thus demonstrating that text proceeds from left to right and from top to bottom and helping advance the idea that words are individual spoken and written units. Invite students to identify the rhyming words in a poem or to chime in on repetitive parts of text as you point to the words. Or students can read with you on this second reading, depending on the text. As students' knowledge of words and phonics grows, they can participate in decoding words and reading high-frequency sight words.

✦ **Discuss Print.** Return to print awareness by encouraging discussion of anything students noticed about the words. Young students should begin to realize that you are reading separate words that are separated by spaces. Later, students will begin to see that each word is made of a group of letters. Students should be encouraged to discuss anything related to the print. For example, you might ask students to point to a word or to count the number of words on a line. Or you might connect the words to the illustrations by pointing to a word and saying it and then asking students to find a picture of that word.

✦ **Responding.** Responding to a selection is a way of insuring comprehension. Invite students to tell about the story by asking them what they like about the poem or story or calling on a student to explain in his or her own words what the poem or story tells about. Call on others to add to the telling as needed. For nonfiction selections, this discussion might include asking students what they learned about the topic and what they thought was most interesting.

Tips for Using Big Books

✦ Make sure the entire group is able to see the book clearly while you are reading.

✦ If some students are able to read words, encourage them to do so during the rereading.

✦ Encourage students to use their knowledge of print.

✦ Encourage students' use of academic language as they talk about reading. Students should be comfortable using strategic reading words such as *predict* and *clarify* and book and print words such as *author* and *illustrator*.

✦ Allow students to look at the *Big Books* whenever they wish.

✦ Provide small versions of the *Big Books* for students to browse through and to try to read at their leisure.

✦ The reader of the *Big Book* should try to be part of the collaborative group of learners rather than the leader.

Strategic Reading

Purpose

Reading is a complex process that requires students not only to decode automatically and correctly what they read but also to understand and respond to it. The purpose of this section is to help you identify various reading behaviors used by good readers and to encourage those behaviors in your students.

Reading Behaviors and Comprehension Strategies

There are four basic behaviors that good readers engage in during reading: Setting Reading Goals and Expectations, Responding to Text, Checking Understanding, and Monitoring and Clarifying Unfamiliar Words and Passages. Engaging in these behaviors involves the application of certain comprehension strategies. These strategies are initially modeled while reading the **Big Books** (Level K and the first half of Level 1) and **Student Readers** (Levels 1–6). The goal of strategy instruction, however, is to ultimately turn over responsibility for using strategies to students so they set their own goals for reading, respond to text, and check their own understanding and solve problems while reading. Students need to take responsibility for doing the thinking and making sense of text.

Setting Reading Goals and Expectations

Good readers set reading goals and expectations before they begin reading. This behavior involves a variety of strategies that will help students prepare to read the text.

✦ **Activate prior knowledge.** When good readers approach a new text, they consider what they already know about the subject or what their experiences have been in reading similar material.

✦ **Browse the text.** To get an idea of what to expect from a text, good readers look at the title and the illustrations. They may look for potential problems, such as difficult words. When browsing a unit, have students glance quickly at each selection, looking briefly at the illustrations and the print. Have them tell what they think they might be learning about as they read the unit.

✦ **Decide what they expect from the text.** When reading for pleasure, good readers anticipate enjoying the story or the language. When reading to learn something, they ask themselves what they expect to find out.

Responding to Text

Good readers are active readers. They interact with text by using the following strategies:

✦ **Making connections.** Good readers make connections between what they read and what they already know. They pay attention to elements in the text that remind them of their own experiences. Readers make connections to personal experiences, to other stories they have read, and to world knowledge.

✦ **Visualizing, or picturing.** Good readers visualize what is happening in the text. They not only form mental images as they read but make inferences based on their own experiences. Visualizing goes beyond the words in text. They imagine the setting and the emotions it suggests, they picture the characters and their feelings, and they visualize the action in a story. When reading expository text, good readers picture the objects, processes, or events described. Visualizing helps readers understand descriptions of complex activities or processes.

✦ **Asking questions.** Good readers ask questions that may prepare them for what they will learn. If their questions are not answered in the text, they may try to find answers elsewhere and thus add even more to their store of knowledge.

✦ **Predicting.** Good readers predict what will happen next. When reading fiction, they make predictions about what they are reading and then confirm or revise those predictions as they go.

✦ **Thinking about how the text makes you feel.** Well-written fiction touches readers' emotions; it sparks ideas.

Checking Understanding

One of the most important behaviors good readers exhibit is the refusal to continue reading when something fails to make sense. Good readers continually assess their understanding of the text with strategies such as the following:

✦ **Interpreting.** As they read, good readers make inferences that help them understand and appreciate what they are reading.

✦ **Summarizing.** Good readers summarize to check their understanding as they read. Sometimes they reread to fill in gaps in their understanding.

✦ **Adjusting reading speed.** Good readers monitor their understanding of what they read. They slow down as they come to difficult words and passages. They speed up as they read easier passages.

Monitoring and Clarifying Unfamiliar Words and Passages

Monitoring understanding involves knowing when meaning is breaking down. The reader needs to stop and identify what the problem or source of confusion is. It might be an unfamiliar word, complex and hard-to-understand sentences or unfamiliar concepts that need clarifying. At the word level, the reader might

✦ apply decoding skills to sound out unknown words.

✦ apply context clues in text and illustrations to figure out the meanings of words.

✦ use structural elements to figure out the meaning of the word.

✦ ask someone the meaning of the word.

✦ reread the passage to make sure the passage makes sense.

✦ check a dictionary or the glossary to understand the meanings of words not clarified by clues or rereading.

Complex sentences may require the reader to look for the main idea in the sentence, to pull out clauses that may interfere with the main idea, or to ask for help. When faced with unfamiliar concepts, readers often ask for clarification from someone.

These cognitive activities engage the reader in thinking about text before, during, and after reading. Readers think about text before they read by activating background knowledge, anticipating content, setting purposes, and wondering about the text and what they will learn. During reading, the reader is constantly checking understanding—asking whether what is being read makes sense and constructing conclusions or summary statements. When the text is not making sense, the reader uses strategies to clarify words, ideas, and larger units of text or may reread more slowly for clarification. After reading, the reader reflects on what was read, connecting new information to prior knowledge, evaluating purposes, and connecting the relevance of the new information to the purpose.

Procedures

Modeling and Thinking Aloud

Modeling and encouraging students to think aloud as they attempt to understand text can demonstrate for everyone how reading behaviors are put into practice. Modeling and thinking aloud helps students learn how to process information and learn important content. It is more than asking students questions; it is letting students in on the thinking that helps readers make sense of text, solve problems while reading, and use strategies differentially and intentionally. The most effective models will be those that come from your own reading. As you model the different strategies, let students know what strategy you are using and why you are using it.

Model comprehension strategies in a natural way, and choose questions and comments that fit the text you are reading. Present a variety of ways to respond to text.

✦ Pose questions that you really do wonder about.

✦ Identify with characters by comparing them with yourself.

✦ React emotionally by showing joy, sadness, amusement, or surprise.

✦ Show empathy with or sympathy for characters.

✦ Relate the text to something that has happened to you or to something you already know.

✦ Show interest in the text ideas.

✦ Question the meaning or clarity of the author's words and ideas.

Encourage Students' Responses and Use of Strategies

Most students will typically remain silent as they try to figure out an unfamiliar word or a confusing passage. Encourage students to identify specifically with what they are having difficulty. When the problem has been identified, ask students to suggest a strategy for dealing with the problem. Remind students to

✦ treat problems encountered in text as interesting learning opportunities.

✦ think aloud about text challenges.

✦ help each other build meaning. Rather than tell what a word is, students should tell how they figured out the meanings of challenging words and passages.

✦ consider reading a selection again with a partner after reading it once alone. Partner reading provides valuable practice in reading for fluency.

✦ make as many connections as they can between what they are reading and what they already know.

✦ visualize to clarify meanings or enjoy descriptions.

✦ ask questions about what they are reading.

✦ notice how the text makes them feel.

In addition, using open-ended questions such as the following, as well as your students' questions and comments, will make both the text and the strategic reading process more meaningful to students.

✦ What kinds of things did you wonder about?

✦ What kinds of things surprised you?

✦ What new information did you learn?

✦ What was confusing until you reread or read further?

Discussion

The more students are able to discuss what they are learning, to voice their confusions, and to compare perceptions of what they are learning, the deeper and more meaningful their learning becomes.

Purpose

Through discussions, students are exposed to points of view different from their own and learn how to express their thoughts and opinions coherently. Through discussion, students add to their own knowledge that of their classmates and learn to explain themselves coherently. They also begin to ask insightful questions that help them better understand what they have read and all that they are learning through their inquiry/research and explorations. The purpose of classroom discussion is to provide a framework for learning.

Procedure

Reflecting on the Selection

After students have finished reading a selection, provide an opportunity for them to engage in discussion about the selection. Students should

✦ check to see whether the questions they asked before reading as part of Clues, Problems, and Wonderings and KWL (What I Know, What I Want to Know and What I Have Learned) have been answered. Encourage them to discuss whether any unanswered questions should still be answered. If unanswered questions are related to the theme, add those questions to the **Concept/ Question Board.**

✦ discuss any new questions that have arisen because of the reading. Encourage students to decide which of these questions should go on the **Concept/ Question Board.**

✦ share what they expected to learn from reading the selection and tell whether expectations were met.

✦ talk about whatever has come to mind while reading the selection. This discussion should be an informal sharing

of impressions of, or opinions about, the selection; it should never take on the aspects of a question-and-answer session about the selection.

✦ give students ample opportunity to ask questions and to share their thoughts about the selection. Participate as an active member of the group, making your own observations about information in a selection or modeling your own appreciation of a story. Be especially aware of unusual and interesting insights suggested by students so that these insights can be recognized and discussed. To help students learn to keep the discussion student-centered, have each student choose the next speaker instead of handing the discussion back to you.

> *The purpose of classroom discussion is to provide a framework for learning.*

Recording Ideas

As students finish discussions about their reactions to a selection, they should be encouraged to record their thoughts, feelings, reactions, and ideas about the selection or the subject of the selection in their Writer's Notebooks. This will not only help keep the selections fresh in students' minds; it will strengthen their writing abilities and help them learn how to write about their thoughts and feelings.

Students may find that the selection gave them ideas for their own writing, or it could have reminded them of some person or incident in their own lives. Perhaps the selection answered a question that has been on their minds or raised a question they had never thought before. Good, mature writers—especially professional writers—learn the value of recording such thoughts and impressions quickly before they fade. Students should be encouraged to do this also.

Handing Off

Handing off (Levels 1–6) is a method of turning over to students the primary responsibility for controlling discussion. Often, students who are taking responsibility for controlling a discussion tend to have all "turns" go through the teacher. The teacher is the one to whom attention is transferred when a speaker finishes, and the teacher is the one who is expected to call on the next speaker—the result being that the teacher remains the pivotal figure in the discussion.

Having students "hand off" the discussion to other students instead of the teacher encourages them to retain complete control of the discussion and to become more actively involved in the learning process. When a student finishes his or her comments, that student should choose (hand off the discussion to) the next speaker. In this way, students maintain a discussion without relying on the teacher to decide who speaks.

When handing off is in place, the teacher's main roles are to occasionally remind students to hand off, to help students when they get stuck, to encourage them to persevere on a specific point, and to get them back to a discussion, and to monitor the discussion to ensure that everyone gets a chance to contribute. The teacher may say, for example, "Remember, not just boys (or girls)." or "Try to choose someone who has not had a chance to talk yet." It is not unusual early in the process for students to roam from the topic and selection. To bring the discussion back to the topic and selection, be a participant, raise your hand, and ask a question or make a statement that refocuses students' thinking and discussion.

For handing off to work effectively, a seating arrangement that allows students to see one another is essential. It is hard to hold a discussion when students have their backs to each other. A circle or a semicircle is effective. In addition, all students need to have copies of the materials being discussed.

Actively encourage this handing-off process by letting students know that they, not you, are in control of the discussion.

If students want to remember thoughts about, or reactions to, a selection, suggest that they record these in the Response Journal section of their Writer's Notebooks.

Encourage students to record the thoughts, feelings, or reactions that are elicited by any reading they do.

Exploring Concepts within the Selection

To provide an opportunity for collaborative learning and to focus on the concepts, you may want to have students form small groups and spend time discussing what they have learned about the concepts from this selection. Topics may include new information that they have acquired, new ideas that they have had, or new questions that the selection raised.

Students should always base their discussions on postings from the **Concept/ Question Board** as well as on previous discussions of the concept. The small-group discussions should be ongoing throughout the unit; during this time, students should continue to compare and contrast any new information with their previous ideas, opinions, and impressions about the concepts. How does this selection help confirm their ideas? How does it contradict their thinking? How has it changed their outlook?

As students discuss the concepts in small groups, circulate around the room to make sure that each group stays focused upon the selection and the concepts. After students have had some time to discuss the information and the ideas in the selection, encourage each group to formulate some statements about the concept that apply to the selection.

Sharing Ideas about Concepts

Have a representative from each group report and explain the group's ideas to the rest of the class. Then have the class formulate one or more general statements related to the unit concepts and write these statements on the **Concept/Question Board.** As students progress through the unit, they will gain more and more confidence in suggesting additions to the **Concept/Question Board.**

✦ **Visual Aids** During this part of the discussion, you may find it helpful to use visual aids to help students as they build the connections to the unit concepts. Not all units or concepts will lend themselves to this type of treatment; however, aids such as time lines, charts, graphs, and pictographs may help students see how each new selection adds to their growing knowledge of the concepts.

Encourage students to ask questions about the concepts that the selection may have raised. Have students list on the **Concept/Question Board** those questions that cannot be answered immediately and that they want to explore further.

> *Through discussions, students are exposed to points of view different from their own and learn how to express their thoughts and opinions coherently.*

Exploring Concepts across Selections

As each new selection is read, encourage students to discuss its connection with the other selections and with the unit concepts. Also encourage students to think about selections that they have read from other units and how they relate to the concepts for this unit.

Ultimately, this ability to make connections between past knowledge and new knowledge allows any learner to gain insights into what is being studied. The goal of the work with concepts and the discussions is to help students to start thinking in terms of connections—how is this like what I have learned before? Does this information confirm, contradict, or add

a completely different layer to that which I already know about this concept? How can the others in the class have such different ideas than I do when we just read the same selection? Why is so much written about this subject?

Learning to make connections and to delve deeper through self-generated questions and substantive discussions give students the tools they need to become effective, efficient, lifelong learners.

Tips

✦ Create an environment that facilitates discussion. Have students sit in circles or some other configuration so everyone can see each other.

✦ When students are discussing the selection, they should have their books with them, and students should feel free to refer to them throughout the discussion.

✦ Discussions offer a prime opportunity for you to introduce, or seed, new ideas about the concepts. New ideas can come from a variety of sources: Students may draw on their own experiences or on the books or videos they are studying; you may introduce new ideas into the discussion; or you may at times invite experts to speak to the class.

✦ If students do not mention an important idea that is necessary to the understanding of some larger issue, you may "drop" that idea into the conversation and, indeed, repeat it several times to make sure that it does get picked up. This seeding may be subtle ("I think that might be important here") or quite direct ("This is a big idea, one that we will definitely need to understand and one that we will return to regularly").

✦ To facilitate this process for each unit, you must be aware of the unit concepts and be able to recognize and reinforce them when they arise spontaneously in discussions. If central unit concepts do not arise naturally, then, and only then, will you seed these ideas by direct modeling. The more you turn over discussions to students, the more involved they will become, and the more responsibility they will take for their own learning. Make it your goal to become a participant in, rather than the leader of, class discussions.

✦ Help students see that they are responsible for carrying on the discussion. After a question is asked, always wait instead of jumping in with a comment or an explanation. Although this wait time may be uncomfortable at first, students will come to understand that the discussion is their responsibility and that you will not jump in every time there is a hesitation.

✦ As the year progresses, students will become more and more adept at conducting and participating in meaningful discussions about what they have read. These discussions will greatly enhance students' understanding of the concepts that they are exploring.

Discussion Starters and Questions

The following examples of discussion starters can be modeled initially, but then the responsibility for using them should be turned over to students. The starters provide the opportunity for open-ended discussions by students.

✦ I didn't know that . . . .

✦ Does anyone know . . . .

✦ I figured out that . . . .

✦ I liked the part where . . . .

✦ I'm still confused about . . . .

✦ This made me think . . . .

✦ I agree with _____ because . . . .

✦ I disagree with _____ because . . . .

✦ The reason I think _____ is . . .

✦ I found _____ interesting because . . . .

✦ I learned . . .

✦ What I learned in this selection reminds me of what we read in _____ because . . .

✦ This author's writing reminds me of . . .

✦ I had problems understanding _____ because . . .

✦ I wonder why the author chose to . . .

✦ I still do not understand . . .

✦ I was surprised to find out . . .

✦ I like the way the author developed the character by . . .

✦ The author made the story really come alive by . . .

In addition to these open-ended discussion starters, students should be encouraged to ask open-ended questions. When students ask questions, other students should respond to the question before moving on to another idea or topic. One student asking a question often helps to clarify something for the whole class and places a value on asking questions as a critical part of learning.

✦ Why did the author . . . ?

✦ What did the author mean when he or she wrote . . . ?

✦ Who can help me clarify . . . ?

✦ Who can help me figure out . . . ?

✦ How does this piece connect to the unit theme?

✦ What does this section mean?

Writing

Purpose

The writing program in **SRA Imagine It!** teaches students how to write skillfully. This is essential, as writing is a powerful tool that fosters learning, communication, creativity, and self-discovery. **SRA Imagine It!** writing teaches students how to use writing effectively for these purposes.

Writing is a complex process. It involves deftly juggling a variety of skills, strategies, and knowledge. Writers must make plans, consider the reader, draw ideas from memory, develop new ideas, organize thoughts, consider the conventions of the genre, translate ideas into words, craft sentences, evaluate decisions, make needed revisions, transcribe words into correctly spelled print, and monitor the writing process, among other things.

SRA Imagine It! writing is designed to ensure that students acquire the skills, knowledge, strategies, and dispositions they need to become skilled writers. This includes the following:

✦ Knowledge about the qualities of good writing, characteristics of different genres, intended audience, and writing topics. Skilled writers know how to obtain information about their topics, are familiar with basic features of different genres, and possess basic schemas or frameworks for accomplishing common writing tasks.

✦ The writing strategies involved in basic composing processes such as prewriting, drafting, monitoring, evaluating, revising, editing/proofreading, and publishing. Skilled writers flexibly employ these strategies to create text.

✦ Command of basic writing skills such as handwriting, spelling, sentence construction, grammar, and usage. Skilled writers execute these basic writing skills with little conscious effort.

✦ Interest and motivation to write as well as perceptions of competence as a writer. Skilled writers possess an "I can do" attitude.

Procedures

With **SRA Imagine It!** writing, evidence-based practices are used to teach students to write skillfully. These evidence-based practices are drawn from research on the effectiveness of specific writing interventions that show that the quality of students' writing can be improved by

✦ explicitly teaching strategies for prewriting, drafting, revising, editing/proofreading, and publishing.

✦ modeling effective use of writing strategies.

> *Children start school wanting to learn how to write and enjoying writing. The goal of **SRA Imagine It!** writing is for children to become lifelong writers— people who enjoy writing and use writing effectively at work as well as in their personal lives.*

✦ having students work together to prewrite, draft, revise, edit/proofread, and publish their compositions.

✦ using prewriting tools such as graphic organizers to gather information.

✦ involving students in inquiry activities designed to help them further develop their ideas for writing.

✦ making the goals for writing assignments clear and specific.

✦ teaching students how to construct more sophisticated sentences.

✦ providing students with the opportunity to read, evaluate, and emulate models of good writing.

✦ teaching students how to use word processing as a tool for composing.

The evidence-based practices in **SRA Imagine It!** are also based on the study of expert teachers who

✦ make sure their students are engaged, spending most of their writing time doing something that involves thoughtfulness, such as crafting a story or learning how to construct a complex sentence.

✦ teach basic writing skills, strategies, and knowledge balanced by ample opportunity to apply what is learned.

✦ involve students in writing for a variety of different purposes.

✦ create a writing classroom environment that is supportive, pleasant, and motivating.

✦ encourage students to accomplish as much as possible on their own (to act in a self-regulated fashion), but who are ready to offer support and instruction as needed.

✦ use reading to support writing development and vice versa.

✦ monitor students' growth in writing and encourage students to monitor their own growth.

✦ provide extra assistance to students who experience difficulty.

✦ are passionate about writing.

Knowledge about Writing

Purpose

Writing can be used to communicate, entertain, inform, reflect, persuade, and learn. To take full advantage of this flexible tool, students must acquire knowledge about the qualities of good writing and the various purposes and forms of writing. They must also carefully consider their audience and be knowledgeable about the topics they write about.

Procedures

Qualities of Good Writing

One way students learn about the qualities of good writing is by directly teaching them that good writing is characterized by the following seven traits:

✦ Clearly presented and fully developed ideas

✦ Writing that is easy to follow and logically organized

✦ Effective and precise word choice

✦ Varied use of sentence structure to promote fluency, rhythm, and natural speech patterns

✦ Writing that captures appropriate tone or mood to make the desired impact on the reader

✦ Correct spelling, usage, and grammar

✦ A written product that is legible, attractive, and accessible

For each writing assignment, teachers concentrate on one or more of these traits, teaching students strategies for enhancing the trait(s) in their writing. For example, students are taught to circle words that are vague in their writing and to replace them with more precise ones.

Another way that students learn about the qualities of good writing is through reading. The reading material in **SRA Imagine It!** provides concrete models that illustrate the characteristics of good writing, such as how authors

✦ present, develop, and organize ideas.

✦ use words to evoke specific images and feelings.

✦ manipulate sentences to speed up or slow down the flow of text.

✦ set and change the mood to match the action of the characters.

✦ use illustrations to reinforce and sharpen readers' understanding.

This knowledge is fostered in **SRA Imagine It!** through Reading with a Writer's Eye. Teachers and students discuss what the author of a reading selection did to achieve certain purposes. For example, after reading a mystery, the class discusses how the author planted a false lead to make the story more interesting and complex. Students are then encouraged to use the same technique in a mystery they write.

Different Purposes and Forms of Writing

Students learn the purposes and forms of a wide range of genres they need to master for success both in and out of school. This includes using writing to do the following:

✦ Communicate with others (personal letters, business letters, notes, cards, and e-mail)

✦ Create personal narratives (journal writing, autobiography, writing about a personal event, and so on)

✦ Entertain (stories, plays, poems, and so on)

✦ Learn (learning logs, reports, journal entries, summarizing, and biographies)

✦ Inform (writing lists, explaining how to do something, describing objects or places, describing events, news reports, reports, and biographies)

✦ Respond to literature (book evaluations, book reports, and book reviews)

✦ Persuade (advertisements, opinions about controversial topics)

✦ Demonstrate knowledge (for example, traditional classroom tests, high-stakes tests involving writing, high-stakes tests involving multiple-choice answers)

In **SRA Imagine It!** writing, students learn to write stories, poetry, plays, journal entries, summaries, book reviews, informative reports, descriptions, explanations, letters, critiques, and e-mail. They also use these various forms of writing to gather, think about, and report what they have learned when doing extended Inquiry projects.

One way they learn about the purposes and forms of these various genres is through the use of models of each type of writing. As students begin working on a new genre, the class analyzes an exemplary model of this type of writing to determine its characteristics and functions. They are encouraged to incorporate these features in their writing. In addition, what they write is frequently tied to what they read, so their reading material provides a model and source of information on the purpose and form of their writing.

Students are also asked to carefully consider the purpose for each of their compositions and include this determination as part of the planning process. As they plan, the form and purpose of their compositions is further emphasized through the use of graphic organizers, in which students typically generate and organize ideas for each of the basic elements included in the type of composition they are composing.

Knowledge of Writing Topics

To write well, students must have something to write about. Good writers typically know a lot about their topics or have strategies for acquiring such information. With **SRA Imagine It!** writing, students are taught effective strategies for gathering information to write about. This includes how to

✦ locate information in written and electronic sources.

✦ obtain information through interviews or surveys.

✦ summarize information in notes.

✦ reference informational sources.

Developing a Sense of Audience

While writing is often viewed as a solitary activity, it is typically meant to be read by others. Children and adults most often use writing to communicate, persuade, or inform others. Because the writer is usually not present when the composition is read, he or she must carefully consider the needs of the readers. **SRA Imagine It!** writing helps students develop a sense of audience by asking them to identify their audience when they write collaboratively or independently. Students are also encouraged to share what they write with their peers and others. The following are procedures for presenting and sharing:

✦ Before presenting, have the writer
  • decide what will be shared.
  • practice what will be shared.

✦ During presenting,
  • have the writer tell what is to be shared and why.

- have the writer read aloud his or her work or idea.
  - remind students to listen carefully.
- After presenting,
  - have students tell what they like.
  - have students offer the writer helpful suggestions.
  - take notes of students' comments to share with the writer.

Tips

- Have students keep a log of new information they have learned about the attributes of good writing.
- Develop wall charts that specify the purpose and attributes of specific writing genres.
- Ask students to evaluate their writing and the writing of others based on seven traits of good writing.
- Before students begin work on a writing assignment, hold a class discussion on the topic to share information, clarify misperceptions, and identify information students still need to locate.

Mastering the Writing Process

Purpose

To write skillfully, young writers must master the basic processes involved in writing. These processes include the strategic "know-how" involved in writing and include the following:

- **Prewriting:** Writers spend time thinking about and planning their topics. They consider their purposes, audience, and the focus of their topics. Writers make plans to guide the composing process, establishing goals for what to do and say. They gather possible ideas for their writing, drawing on memory and external sources such as books, interviews, articles, and the Internet. Writers make decisions about which information to include and how to organize it.
- **Drafting:** Writers draft or put their ideas into words, using the initial plans they developed as a guide. These plans are expanded, modified, and even reworked as writers create a first draft of their composition, often in a rough form.

- **Revising:** While some revising may occur during prewriting and drafting, writers revisit and revise their first drafts. They reread them to see whether the drafts say what the writers intended. Writers check to be sure the drafts make sense and that the meaning is clear for the audience. They consider whether their writing will have the desired impact on the audience. As they make changes in their text, they discover new things to say and new ways to present their ideas.

> *Writers need feedback throughout the writing process. Feedback is one of our most powerful tools for helping developing writers.*

- **Editing/Proofreading:** Writers edit/proofread their work. They recognize that spelling, grammar, and usage errors make it harder for others to understand and enjoy their published work. Writers know that readers are more likely to value their message when they correct these mistakes.
- **Publishing:** Writers share their writing by reading their entire work, or part of their work, to others. They publish their work in books, newspapers, magazines, anthologies, and so on.

Skilled writers move back and forth through these processes—from prewriting to drafting to revising and back—to create their final pieces.

Procedures

Much of what happens during writing is not visible. It occurs inside the writer's head. **SRA Imagine It!** writing makes the processes involved in writing concrete and visible in the following four ways:

- Establishing a predictable writing routine during which students are expected to prewrite, draft, revise, edit/proofread, and publish.

- Using graphic organizers and revising, editing/proofreading, and publishing checklists that help developing writers carry out basic writing processes.
- Teaching strategies for prewriting, drafting, revising, editing/proofreading, and publishing.
- Providing feedback throughout the writing process through writing conferences and students' presentation of their works in progress and completed compositions.

Establishing a Predictable Writing Routine

One way to make the basic writing processes more concrete is to create a predictable classroom writing routine, during which students plan, draft, revise, edit, proofread, and publish their work. This establishes that these processes are important and ensures that time is provided for each process. It also allows students to work with minimum teacher direction and at their own pace.

Tips

- Guide students through the steps of the writing routine. Model each step of prewriting, drafting, revising, editing/proofreading, and publishing.
- Make sure students learn that the processes of writing do not always occur in the same order but are recursive. For example, revising may occur at any stage of the composing process. You should not only model this by showing how this is done, but the predictable routine should vary at times to reflect this flexibility.

Using Graphic Organizers and Revising, Editing/Proofreading, and Publishing Checklists

Graphic organizers and revising, editing/proofreading, and publishing checklists provide students with assistance in carrying out the thinking activities involved in a writing assignment. They provide structure and information for how to carry out the process. The graphic organizer typically includes a series of prompts that ask the student to think about the purpose for writing a particular piece and the intended audience. It also provides prompts designed to help the student generate and organize possible writing ideas. This frequently involves generating possible content for each part of the target composition. The revising, editing/proofreading, and publishing checklists direct students' attention to specific features or aspects of text that would be useful to consider while writing.

Tips

It is important to be sure that students understand how to use graphic organizers and revising, editing/proofreading, and publishing checklists. Be sure to

✦ explain the purpose of the graphic organizer or revising, editing/proofreading, and publishing checklist.

✦ describe how students are to use the graphic organizer or revising, editing/proofreading, and publishing checklist.

✦ model aloud how to carry out the basic activities on the graphic organizer or revising, editing/proofreading, and publishing checklist.

✦ make sure students understand each part of the graphic organizer or revising, editing/proofreading, and publishing checklist.

Teaching Strategies for Carrying Out Basic Writing Processes

A strategy involves a series of actions a writer undertakes to achieve a desired goal. In **SRA Imagine It!** students are taught strategies to help them carry out each of the basic writing processes—prewriting, drafting, revising, editing/proofreading, and publishing. Each strategy is also designed to enhance one or more of the seven traits of good writing. These include clearly presented and fully developed ideas; writing that is easy to follow and logically organized; effective and precise word choice; varied use of sentences to promote fluency, rhythm, and natural speech patterns; writing that captures appropriate tone or mood to make maximum impact on readers; correct spelling, usage, and grammar; and a written product that is legible, attractive, and accessible.

The goal is for students to be able to use the strategy independently and to make it part of their writing tool kit. The steps for teaching writing strategies are to

✦ describe the strategy.

✦ tell why the strategy is important.

✦ tell students when they should use the strategy.

✦ model how to use the strategy when writing, making your thoughts visible by saying aloud each thing you are doing and thinking.

✦ make sure students understand why the strategy is important, when to apply it, and how to use it.

✦ provide students with assistance in applying the strategy until they can do it on their own.

✦ remind students to use the strategy when they write.

Tips

✦ Ask students to evaluate their progress and how the strategy improved their writing.

✦ Be enthusiastic about learning the strategy.

✦ Establish the importance of effort in learning and using the strategy.

✦ Provide opportunities for students to see how the strategy improves their writing.

✦ Praise and reinforce students' use of the strategy.

✦ Foster students' ownership of the strategy.

Providing Feedback through Conferencing and Presentation

Writers need feedback throughout the writing process. They need reactions to ideas, drafts, and revisions. Feedback is one of our most powerful tools for helping developing writers. Writers want to know how their works-in-progress sound to someone else, whether their compositions make sense, whether they contain any incorrect or misleading information, and where and how to make changes.

Regular feedback encourages developing writers to solve problems and make meaningful changes throughout the writing process.

One way of providing feedback is through conferences. Teachers may initiate conferences, but students should also be encouraged to call conferences on an as-needed basis. Because conferences can be held at various times throughout the writing process, the focus will vary. Conferences held during the early stages of the writing process help students identify and refine a topic or identify research references. During the revision process, conferences help students

learn to elaborate and reorganize their writing. During the final stages, students learn to edit and proofread stories before they are published. Conferences offer an excellent opportunity for the teacher and student to evaluate jointly the student's progress and set goals for future growth.

The basic procedures for writing conferences are as follows:

✦ Have the student read aloud his or her work.

✦ Review any feedback the student has received so far.

✦ Identify positive elements of the work.

✦ Use one or more of these strategies to help the student improve his or her work.

• Have the student explain how he or she got his or her ideas.

• Have the student think aloud about how he or she will address the feedback he or she has received.

• Ask the student to help you understand any confusion you may have about his or her writing.

• Have the student add, delete, or rearrange something in the work, and ask how it affects the entire piece.

• Think aloud while you do a part of what the student was asked to do. Then ask the student to compare what you did to what he or she did.

• Have the student prescribe as if to a younger student how to revise the work.

✦ Ask two or three questions to guide the student through revising (see below).

✦ Conclude the conference by having the student state his or her plan for continuing work on the piece of writing.

Tips

✦ Set aside a special area of the classroom for you to work with students or for students to work with each other.

✦ You don't have to meet with every student every day.

✦ Conferences should be brief; don't overwhelm students with too many comments or suggestions. Several short conferences are often more effective than one long one.

✦ If appropriate, suggest that students take notes to help them remember where changes are to be made.

- Don't take ownership of the students' work. Encourage students to identify what is good and what needs to be changed, and let the students make the changes.
- Focus on what is good about the students' work; discuss how to solve problems rather than telling students what to do.
- Peer conferencing should be encouraged during Workshop.
- As students engage in peer conferencing, note which students are participating, the types of questions they ask, and the comments they make. Use this information to help students become more effective in peer conferencing.
- You may need to structure peer conferences by asking students to first explain what they liked about the composition, and then teaching them how to give constructive feedback.

Having students present or share their work provides another opportunity for them to receive feedback about their writing. Student presentations can involve

- presenting an initial idea or plan for a writing assignment.
- sharing a first draft of a paper.
- presenting orally part or all of a final piece of writing.

Tips

- Everyone must listen carefully and provide constructive feedback. Focus on what is good about a piece and ways to make it better.
- The student author has ownership and can decide which suggestions to use. The author does not have to incorporate all suggestions from the audience.
- Have a chair designated as the "Author's Chair" from which the student author can read his or her work or share ideas. This lends importance to the activity.
- The student author should be encouraged to give a bit of background, including where he or she is in the process, why he or she chose a particular part, or what problem he or she is having. This helps orient the audience.

- Short pieces of writing can be read in their entirety. As students become more proficient and write longer papers, they should be encouraged to read just a part of their writing; for example, a part they need help with, a part that has been revised, or a part they particularly like.
- Take notes during the presentations, and encourage older students to do the same.
- Be sensitive to the attention span of the class and the feedback being given. Students have a tendency to repeat the same comments to each author.

Word Processing and Other Aspects of Electronic Composing

Using a word processor to compose a piece of writing makes many aspects of the writing process easier. Text can easily be changed, deleted, or moved during drafting or revising. Software such as spell-checkers or word prediction provides assistance with basic writing skills. Information for writing can be obtained on-line or through other electronic sources, such as encyclopedias. Students can use publishing software to develop a more polished and attractive final product by adding pictures to their composition, developing a cover, changing fonts, and so on. *SRA Imagine It!* supports the use of these technologies.

Teaching Basic Writing Skills

Purpose

Young writers need to learn many basic writing skills to the point that the skills can be executed with minimal effort so they do not interfere with other writing processes. Correct handwriting, spelling, and grammar should be mastered to the point that they require little attention on the part of the writer. While sentences cannot and should not be constructed without conscious attention and effort, developing writers need to become familiar with different sentence types, and they need to become proficient at building them.

Procedures

Sentence Construction

SRA Imagine It! teaches sentence construction skills through the use of sentence frames, sentence expansion, and sentence combining.

- **Sentence Frames** With sentence frames, students are given part of a sentence and asked to generate the rest of it. For example, students can be taught to write a simple sentence, with a single subject and predicate, by giving them a frame containing the subject (The dog _____ _____.) and asking them to complete the sentence by telling what happened (The dog ran.).
- **Sentence Expansion** With sentence expansion, students are given a kernel sentence and asked to expand it by adding additional words. For example, students can be taught to make sentences more colorful by adding descriptive words to a kernel sentence: *Rewrite **The cat and dog like the toy** so the sentence tells more about the cat and dog and the toy — The big dog and gray cat like the fuzzy little toy.*
- **Sentence combining** With sentence combining, students learn how to combine two or more kernel sentences into a more complex single sentence. For example, you can lead students to produce sentences with relative clauses by combining the following two sentences:

  John will win the race.

  John is very fast. (who)

  John, who is very fast, will win the race.

When teaching sentence construction skills, the following three steps should be followed:

- Describe the skill, establish why it is important, and model how to use it.
- Provide students with assistance until they can apply the skill correctly and independently.
- Ask students to apply the skill when they write.

Tips

✦ Use more than one method to teach a sentence construction skill.

✦ Ask students to monitor how often they use the sentence construction skill.

✦ Encourage students to set goals to use sentence construction skills in their writing.

Handwriting

Students need to develop both legible and fluent handwriting. An important aspect of meeting this goal is to teach them an efficient pattern for forming individual letters (both lowercase and uppercase letters). Effective teaching procedures include

✦ modeling how to form the letter.

✦ describing how the letter is similar to and different from other letters.

✦ using visual cues, such as numbered arrows, as a guide to letter formation.

✦ providing practice tracing, copying, and writing the letter from memory.

✦ keeping instructional sessions short, with frequent review and practice.

✦ asking students to identify or circle their best formed letter or letters.

✦ encouraging students to correct or rewrite poorly formed letters.

✦ monitoring students' practice to ensure that letters are formed correctly.

✦ reinforcing students' successful efforts and providing corrective feedback as needed.

In addition to learning how to write the letters of the alphabet correctly, students must be able to produce them quickly. Fluency generally develops as a consequence of writing frequently, but it can also be fostered by having students copy short passages several times, and trying to write them a little faster each time.

Tips

✦ Make sure that each student develops a comfortable and efficient pencil grip.

✦ Encourage students to sit in an upright position, leaning slightly forward, as they write.

✦ Show students how to place or position their papers when writing.

✦ Implement appropriate procedures for left-handed writers, such as how to properly place or position their papers when writing.

✦ Monitor students' handwriting, paying special attention to their instructional needs in letter formation, spacing, slant, alignment, size, and line quality.

✦ Encourage students to make all final drafts of their papers neat and legible.

Spelling

Purpose

To become good spellers, students must learn to spell correctly and easily the words they are most likely to use when writing. They need to be able to generate and check plausible spellings for words whose spellings are uncertain. They also need to learn to use external sources such as spell-checkers to ensure correct spelling during writing. In *SRA Imagine It!* students are taught how to spell words they frequently use when writing as well as spelling patterns that help them spell untaught words.

Tips

✦ Teach students an effective strategy for studying spelling words.

✦ Reinforce the correct spelling of taught words in students' writing.

✦ Have students build words from letters or letters and phonograms, for example, c - at.

✦ Teach strategies for determining and checking the spelling of unknown words.

✦ Model the use of correct spelling and how to correct spelling errors when you write in front of the class.

✦ Encourage students to correct misspelled words in all final drafts of their writing.

✦ Provide instruction and practice in proofreading.

✦ Encourage students to use spell-checkers, dictionaries, and so on to determine the correct spelling of unknown words.

Grammar and Usage

Traditional methods of teaching grammar and usage skills are not effective. With such instruction, students are initially provided with an abstract definition, such as an adjective is a word that describes a noun or pronoun. This is often followed by asking students to practice applying the skill correctly without actually generating any textual material longer than a word or a phrase. For example, students might be asked to complete the following sentence: The _____ wagon rolled through the _____ town. It is not surprising that many students do not understand the rules they are taught or how to use them in their writing, because such instruction is abstract and decontextualized.

To make grammar instruction effective, *SRA Imagine It!* applies the following five principles. To make these principles concrete, the program illustrates each as it would apply to the rule for capitalizing the first letter in a person's name.

✦ Grammar and usage skills need to be defined in a functional and concrete manner. The rule of capitalizing the first letter in a person's name can be introduced by writing a sentence with two or three familiar names on the board. With the students' help, identify each name in the sentence, and ask them what they notice about the first letter in each name—They are capital letters. Repeat this process with a second sentence, and then establish the "capitalization rule" with students' help.

✦ As soon as the skill is functionally described or defined, establish why it is important—Capitalizing the first letter in a person's name makes the name stand out and shows respect for the person named. This is an important rule for writing.

✦ Show students how to use the skill when writing. Generate a sentence using the names of students in the class, or have your students help you generate such a sentence. Write it on the board, capitalizing the first letter while simultaneously telling the class what you are doing.

◆ Provide students with guided practice in applying the skill when writing. Generate with the class another sentence that includes three of your students' names. Tell the class you will write the sentence on the board, but they will need to tell you when to capitalize a word. Next, have students work together in pairs to generate two sentences using names of their friends, capitalizing the first letter in each name. Provide support as needed. Finally, have each student generate one sentence of his or her own containing two names. Monitor to ensure that students capitalize the first letter in each name. Have them share their sentences with a peer.

◆ Ask students to apply the skill in their compositions. Have students look at one of the papers in their writing portfolio and correct any capitalization mistakes involving people's names. Remind students to capitalize people's names when writing and revising subsequent writing assignments.

Tips

◆ Ask students to correct other students' papers, focusing on specific grammar and usage rules and mistakes.

◆ Encourage students to read their papers aloud when revising. This will help them spot grammar and usage mistakes.

Fostering Motivation

Purpose

Children start school wanting to learn how to write and enjoying writing. Too quickly, however, many begin to view writing as a chore or something to be avoided. The goal of *SRA Imagine It!* writing is for children to become lifelong writers—people who enjoy writing and use writing effectively at work as well as in their personal lives.

Procedures

One way to foster an interest in writing is to have students write for real purposes and audiences. This includes having students identify why they are writing and what they hope to accomplish. Likewise, students need to share their writing with others. They are more likely to do their best writing when there is an audience. Students can share their plans, an initial draft, a portion of their composition, or the completed paper with you, their peers, or other children or adults.

Students are also likely to give their best effort when the writing environment is supportive and pleasant. This can be accomplished by the following:

◆ Establishing clear rules for student behavior during the writing period. Keep the rules simple and reasonable in number and consistently reinforce them. Students are not likely to enjoy writing, or learn well, if the classroom environment is chaotic.

◆ Creating a low-risk environment in which students feel comfortable taking risks with their writing. This means being accepting and encouraging of students' efforts and encouraging them to act in the same manner. For example, make it a rule in your class that when someone shares his or her writing, the first thing that you or other students do is say what you liked most about it.

◆ Supporting students as they begin to apply the knowledge, skills, or strategies you teach them. This can include reteaching, providing hints and reminders, giving useful feedback, and initially helping students apply what was taught.

◆ Having students help each other as they plan, draft, revise, edit/proofread, and publish their work. This is most effective when the process of working together is structured. For instance, students are more likely to give good advice for revising if they are asked to focus on specific aspects of the composition, such as identifying places where the writing is unclear or more detail is needed.

◆ Celebrating student success by displaying their work. This can be done by prominently displaying student work in the classroom or in other places in the school. Students can also be asked to publish their work in a class or school newspaper or to read their compositions aloud to younger children, in other classes, or at a special event.

◆ Fostering an "I can do" attitude among your students. Consistently emphasize that the key to good writing is effort and the use of what they have learned.

◆ Setting a positive mood during writing time. Be enthusiastic about writing and what your students write.

Tips

◆ Allow students to make their own decisions and to accomplish as much on their own as possible.

◆ Increase students' ownership of a writing topic by allowing them to develop unique interpretations of the topic.

◆ Encourage students to take ownership of their writing. This includes allowing them to arrange a suitable writing environment, construct a personal plan for accomplishing the writing task, to work at their own pace when possible, and to decide what feedback from you and their peers is most pertinent for revising their writing.

◆ Look for opportunities to give students positive feedback about their work. Let them know when they have done something well in their writing.

◆ Encourage students to monitor their progress. For example, have students select their best writing to keep in a writing portfolio, identifying why they selected each piece.

◆ Show your students that you are a writer too. Share your writing with them. Talk about the various ways you use writing each day.

◆ Connect writing to students' lives and the world in general. Have them document the types of writing they do outside school. Develop a wall chart on which the class can identify how they use writing away from school.

◆ Provide incentives for writing at home. For example, have parents document that their child writes for twenty minutes at home a set number of nights for a month. Provide a special party for these children, allowing each one to select a book to keep from an array of books donated by parents or a sponsoring business partner.

Spelling Strategies

Spelling

Many people find English difficult, because English sound/spelling patterns seem to have hundreds of exceptions. The key to becoming a good speller, however, is not just memorization. The key is recognizing and internalizing English spelling patterns. Some people do this naturally as they read and develop large vocabularies. They intuitively recognize spelling patterns and apply them appropriately. Others need explicit and direct teaching of vocabulary and spelling strategies and spelling patterns before they develop spelling consciousness.

Purpose

Spelling is a fundamental skill in written communication. Although a writer may have wonderful ideas, he or she may find it difficult to communicate those ideas without spelling skills. Learning to spell requires much exposure to text and writing. For many it requires a methodical presentation of English spelling patterns.

English Spelling Patterns

A basic understanding of English spelling patterns will help provide efficient and effective spelling instruction. Just as the goal of phonics instruction is to enable students to read fluently, the goal of spelling instruction is to enable students to write fluently so they can concentrate on ideas rather than spelling.

Sound Patterns Many words are spelled the way they sound. Most consonants and short vowels are very regular. When a student learns the sound/spelling relationships, he or she has the key to spelling many words.

Structural Patterns Structural patterns are employed when adding endings to words. Examples of structural patterns include doubling the final consonant, adding -s or -es to form plurals, and dropping the final e before adding -ing, -ed, -er, or -est. Often these structural patterns are very regular in their application. Many students have little trouble learning these patterns.

Meaning Patterns Many spelling patterns in English are morphological; in other words, the meaning relationship is maintained regardless of how a sound may change. Prefixes, suffixes, and root words that retain their spellings regardless of how they are pronounced are further examples of meaning patterns.

Foreign Language Patterns Many English words are derived from foreign words and retain those language patterns. For example, kindergarten (German), boulevard (French), and ballet (French from Italian) are foreign-language patterns at work in English.

Developmental Stages of Spelling

The most important finding in spelling research in the past thirty years is that students learn to spell in a predictable developmental sequence, much as they learn to read. It appears to take the average student three to six years to progress through the developmental stages and emerge as a fairly competent, mature speller.

Prephonemic The first stage is the prephonemic stage, characterized by random letters arranged either in continuous lines or in wordlike clusters. Only the writer can "read" it, and it may be "read" differently on different days.

Semiphonemic As emergent readers learn that letters stand for sounds, they use particular letters specifically to represent the initial consonant sound and sometimes a few other very salient sounds. This marks the discovery of phonemic awareness that letters represent speech sounds in writing.

Phonemic When students can represent most of the sounds they hear in words, they have entered the phonemic stage of spelling. They spell what they hear, using everything they know about letter sounds, letter names, and familiar words. Many remedial spellers never develop beyond this stage and spell a word the way it sounds whenever they encounter a word they cannot spell.

Transitional or Within-Word Pattern As they are exposed to more difficult words, students discover that not all words are spelled as they sound. They learn that they must include silent letters, spell past tenses with -ed, include a vowel even in unstressed syllables, and remember how words look. The transitional stage represents the transition from primarily phonemic strategies to rule-bound spelling.

Derivational The derivational stage occurs as transitional spellers accumulate a large spelling vocabulary and gain control over affixes, contractions, homophones, and other meaning patterns. They discover that related or derived forms of words share spelling features even if they do not sound the same. As spellers gain control over these subtle word features and spell most words correctly, they become conventional spellers.

Procedures

The spelling lessons are organized around different spelling patterns, beginning with phonetic spelling patterns and progressing to other types of spelling patterns in a logical sequence. Word lists including words from the literature selection focus on the particular patterns in each lesson. In general, the sound patterns occur in the first units at each grade, followed by structural patterns, meaning patterns, and foreign-language patterns in the upper grade levels.

- ✦ As you begin each new spelling lesson, have students identify the spelling pattern and how it is like and different from other patterns.

- ✦ Give the pretest to help students focus on the lesson pattern.

- ✦ Have students proofread their own pretests immediately after the test, crossing out any misspellings and writing the correct spelling.

- ✦ Have them diagnose whether the errors they made were in the lesson pattern or in another part of the word. Help students determine where they made errors and what type of pattern they should work on to correct them.

- ✦ As students work through the spelling pages from *Skills Practice,* encourage them to practice the different spelling strategies in the exercises.

Sound Pattern Strategies

Pronunciation Strategy As students encounter an unknown word, have them say the word carefully to hear each sound. Encourage them to check the *Sound/ Spelling Cards.* Then have them spell each sound. (/s/ + /i/ + /t/: sit). This strategy builds directly on the Dication and Spelling introduced in kindergarten and taught in Levels 1–3.

Consonant Substitution Have students switch consonants. The vowel spelling usually remains the same. (bat, hat, rat, flat, splat) This is a natural extension of Phonemic Awareness activities begun in prekindergarten and kindergarten.

Vowel Substitution Have students switch vowels. The consonant spellings usually remain the same. (CVC: hit, hat, hut, hot; CVCV: mane, mine; CVVC: boat, beat, bait, beet) This is a natural extension of Phonemic Awareness activities begun in prekindergarten and kindergarten.

Rhyming Word Strategy   Have students think of rhyming words and the rhymes that spell a particular sound. Often the sound will be spelled the same way in another word. (cub, tub, rub) This is a natural extension of Phonemic Awareness activities begun in prekindergarten and kindergarten.

Structural Pattern Strategies

Conventions Strategy   Have students learn the rules and exceptions for adding endings to words (dropping *y*, dropping *e*, doubling the final consonant, and so on).

Proofreading Strategy   Many spelling errors occur because of simple mistakes. Have students check their writing carefully and specifically for spelling.

Visualization Strategy   Have students think about how a word looks. Sometimes words "look" wrong because a wrong spelling pattern has been written. Have them double-check the spelling of any word that looks wrong.

Meaning Pattern Strategies

Family Strategy   When students are not sure of a spelling, have them think of how words from the same base word family are spelled. (critic, criticize, critical; sign, signal, signature; nation, national, nationality)

Meaning Strategy   Have students determine a homophone's meaning to make sure they are using the right word. Knowing prefixes, suffixes, and base words will also help.

Compound Word Strategy   Tell students to break apart a compound and to spell each word. Compounds may not follow convention rules for adding endings. (homework, nonetheless)

Foreign-Language Strategy   Have students think of foreign-language spellings that are different from English spelling patterns. (ballet, boulevard, sauerkraut)

Dictionary Strategy   Ask students to look up the word in a dictionary to make sure their spelling is correct. If they do not know how to spell a word, have them try a few different spellings and look them up to see which one is correct. (fotograph, photograph) Have students use the ***Sound/Spelling Cards*** to help them look up words. This develops a spelling consciousness.

Use the post test to determine understanding of the lesson spelling pattern and to identify any other spelling pattern problems. Encourage student understanding of spelling patterns and use of spelling strategies in all their writing to help transfer spelling skills to writing.

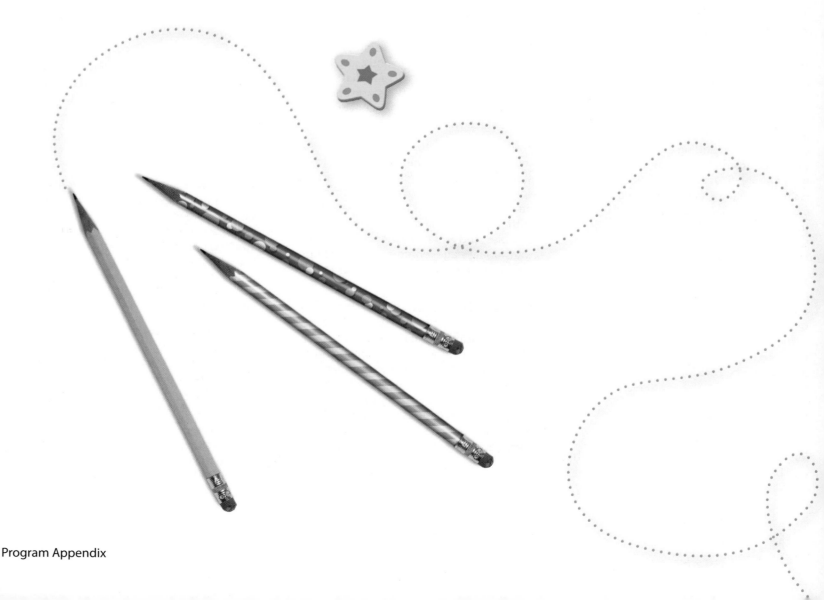

Grammar, Usage, and Mechanics

Purpose

The Study of English Conventions

Over the years the study of grammar, usage, and mechanics has gone in and out of favor. In the past century much research has been done to demonstrate the effectiveness of traditional types of instruction in the conventions of English. Experience and research have shown that learning grammatical terms and completing grammar exercises have little effect on the student's practical application of these skills in the context of speaking or writing. These skills, in and of themselves, do not play a significant role in the way students use language to generate and express their ideas—for example, during the prewriting and drafting phases of the writing process. In fact, emphasis on correct conventions has been shown to have a damaging effect when it is the sole focus of writing instruction. If students are evaluated only on the proper use of spelling, grammar, and punctuation, they tend to write fewer and less complex sentences.

Knowledge of English conventions is, however, vitally important in the editing and proofreading phases of the writing process. A paper riddled with mistakes in grammar, usage, or mechanics is quickly discounted. Many immature writers never revise or edit. They finish the last sentence and turn their papers in to the teacher. Mature writers employ their knowledge of English language conventions in the editing phase to refine and polish their ideas.

The study of grammar, usage, and mechanics is important for two reasons.

1. Educated people need to know and understand the structure of their language, which in large part defines their culture.

2. Knowledge of grammar gives teachers and students a common vocabulary for talking about language and makes discussions of writing tasks more efficient and clearer.

Procedure

The key issue in learning grammar, usage, and mechanics is how to do it. On the one hand, teaching these skills in isolation from writing has been shown to be ineffective and even detrimental if too much emphasis is placed on them. On the other hand, not teaching these skills and having students write without concern for conventions is equally ineffective. The answer is to teach the skills in a context that allows students to directly apply them to a reading or writing activity. Students should be taught proper use of punctuation or subject/verb agreement at the same time they are taught to proofread for those conventions. As they learn to apply their knowledge of conventions during the final stages of the writing process, they will begin to see that correcting errors is an editorial rather than a composition skill.

> *A paper riddled with mistakes in grammar, usage, or mechanics is quickly discounted.*

History of English

A basic understanding of the history and structure of the English language helps students understand the rich but complex resource they have for writing.

Old English

The English language began about A.D. 450 when the Angles, Jutes, and Saxons––three tribes that lived in northern Europe–– invaded the British Isles. Much of their language included words that had to do with farming (*sheep, dirt, tree, earth*). Many of their words are the most frequently used words in the English language today. Because of Latin influences, English became the first of the European languages to be written.

Middle English

In 1066 William the Conqueror invaded England and brought Norman French with him. Slowly Old English and Norman French came together, and Middle English began to appear. Today forty percent of Modern English comes from French. With the introduction of the printing press, English became more widespread.

Modern English

With the Renaissance and its rediscovery of classical Greek and Latin, many new words were created from Greek and Latin word elements. This continued intensively during the Early Modern English period. This rich language was used in the writings of Shakespeare and his contemporaries and profoundly influenced the nature and vocabulary of English. With dictionaries and spelling books, the English language became more standardized, although it continues to be influenced by other languages and new words and trends. These influences continue to make English a living, dynamic language.

Punctuation

Early writing had no punctuation or even spaces between words. English punctuation had its beginning in ancient Greece and Rome. Early punctuation reflected speaking rather than reading. By the end of the eighteenth century, after the invention of printing, most of the rules for punctuation were established, although they were not the same in all languages.

The Structure of English

Grammar is the sound, structure, and meaning system of language. People who speak the same language are able to communicate because they intuitively know the grammar system of that language, the rules to make meaning. All languages have grammar, and yet each language has its own grammar.

Traditional grammar study usually involves two areas:

✦ **Parts of speech** (nouns, verbs, adjectives, adverbs, pronouns, prepositions, conjunctions) are typically considered the content of grammar. The parts of speech involve the form of English words.

✦ **Sentence structure** (subjects, predicates, objects, clauses, phrases) is also included in grammar study. Sentence structure involves the function of English.

Mechanics involves the conventions of punctuation and capitalization. Punctuation helps readers understand writers' messages. Proper punctuation involves marking off sentences according to grammatical structure. In speech students can produce sentences as easily and unconsciously as they can walk, but in writing they must think about what is and what is not a sentence.

In English there are about fourteen punctuation marks (period, comma, quotation mark, question mark, exclamation point, colon, semicolon, apostrophe, hyphen, ellipsis, parenthesis, bracket, dash, and underscore). Most immature writers use only three: period, comma, and question mark. The experienced writer or poet with the command of punctuation adds both flexibility and meaning to his or her sentences through his or her use of punctuation.

Usage is the way in which we speak in a given community. Language varies over time, across national and geographical boundaries, by gender, across age groups, and by socioeconomic status. When the variation occurs within a given language, the different versions of the same language are called dialects. Every language has a prestige dialect associated with education and financial success. In the United States,

this dialect is known as Standard English and is the language of school and business.

Usage involves the word choices people make when speaking certain dialects. Word choices that are perfectly acceptable in conversation among friends may be unacceptable in writing. Usage is often the most obvious indicator of the difference between conversation and composition. Errors in word usage can make a writer seem ignorant and thus jeopardize his or her credibility, no matter how valid or important his or her overall message might be. Usage depends on a student's cultural and linguistic heritage. If the dialect students have learned is not the formal language of school settings or if it is not English, students must master another dialect or language in order to write Standard English.

The Grammar, Usage, and Mechanics lessons in *SRA Imagine It!* are structured to focus on skills presented in a logical sequence. A skill is introduced with appropriate models and then practiced in reading and writing on subsequent days to ensure that skills are not taught in isolation. Encourage students to use the focused English language convention presented in each lesson as they complete each Writing Process Strategies activity. Also encourage them to reread their writing, checking for proper use of the conventions taught. With practice, students should be able to apply their knowledge of conventions to any writing they do.

Tips

✦ Some of the errors students make in writing are the result simply of not carefully reading their final drafts. Many errors occur because the writer's train of thought was interrupted and a sentence is not complete or a word is skipped. These may look like huge errors that a simple rereading can remedy. Most

often the writer can correct these types of errors on his or her own. A major emphasis of any English composition program should be to teach the editing and proofreading phases of the writing process so students can eliminate these types of errors themselves. This involves a shift in perception—from thinking of grammar as a set of discrete skills that involve mastery of individual rules to understanding grammar as it applies to the act of communicating in writing.

✦ As students learn English language conventions, they should be expected to incorporate them into their written work.

✦ Sometimes, students write sentences that raise grammatically complex problems that require a deep understanding of English grammar. Use the Sentence Lifting strategies outlined in the Proofreading part of the Appendix to identify and discuss these more sophisticated types of errors that can include the following:

✦ **Faulty Parallelism.** Parts of a sentence parallel in meaning are not parallel in structure.

✦ **Nonsequiturs.** A statement does not follow logically from something said previously.

✦ **Dangling Modifiers.** A phrase or clause does not logically modify the word next to it.

✦ **Awkwardness.** Sentences are not written simply.

✦ **Wordiness.** Thoughts are not written in as few words as possible. Precise words are not used.

Listening/Speaking/Viewing

Some people are naturally good listeners, and others have no trouble speaking in front of groups. Many people, however, need explicit instruction on how to tune in for important details and how to organize and make an oral presentation. While some people naturally critique what they read, hear, and see, many others need specific guidance to develop skills for analyzing what they encounter in images and the media. The abilities to listen appropriately and to speak in conversations and in groups, as well as to critically evaluate the information with which they are presented, are fundamental skills that will serve students throughout their lives.

Purpose

In addition to reading and writing, listening, speaking, and viewing complete the language arts picture. Through the development of these language arts skills, students gain flexibility in communicating orally, visually, and in writing. When speaking and listening skills are neglected, many students have difficulty speaking in front of groups, organizing a speech, or distinguishing important information they hear. A top anxiety for many adults is speaking in front of groups. Much of this anxiety would not exist if listening, speaking, and viewing skills were taught from the early years.

The Listening/Speaking/Viewing instruction focuses on the literature selection or the Writing Process Strategies to provide context, to reinforce other elements of the lesson, and to integrate the other language arts. Many of the listening, speaking, and viewing skills are very similar to reading or writing skills. For example, listening for details is the same type of skill as reading for details. Preparing an oral report employs many of the same skills as preparing a written report. Learning to use these skills effectively gives students flexibility in how they approach a task. Furthermore, listening and speaking are naturally integrated into all aspects of learning as students listen and respond to each other during discussions, writing, and Inquiry.

Procedure

Listening, speaking, and viewing skills are presented with increasing sophistication throughout every grade level of **SRA Imagine It!** in the Language Arts part of each lesson. Every unit includes at least one lesson on each of the following skills so that students encounter the skills again and again throughout a grade level:

- **Listening.** Listening skills include comprehending what one hears and listening for different purposes, such as to identify sequence or details, to summarize or draw conclusions, or to follow directions.
- **Speaking.** Speaking skills include speaking formally and conversationally, using appropriate volume, giving oral presentations, and using effective grammar. Speaking skills also include using descriptive words, figurative language, and formal and informal language.
- **Viewing.** Viewing skills include comprehending main ideas and messages in images, mass media, and other multimedia.
- **Interaction.** Interaction instruction focuses on a combination of listening and speaking skills. These include asking and responding to questions; nonverbal cues such as eye contact, facial expression, and posture; and contributing to and interacting in group settings.
- **Presenting Information.** The last Listening/Speaking/Viewing lesson in every unit usually focuses on presentation skills. These include sharing ideas, relating experiences or stories, organizing information, and preparing for speeches. These lessons often parallel the Writing Process Strategies instruction so that students can prepare their information in written or oral form. These skills are an integral part of the Inquiry process as students share their ideas, questions, conjectures, and findings.

Tips

- Identify the parallels among the language arts skills: providing written and oral directions, telling or writing a narrative, and so on. Encourage students to see that they have choices for communicating. Discuss the similarities and differences between different forms of communication, and determine whether one is preferable in a given situation.
- Ensure that all students have opportunities to speak in small groups and whole-class situations.
- Provide and teach students to allow appropriate wait time before someone answers a question.
- Encourage students (when they are able) to take notes to help them remember what they heard so they can better respond.
- Remind students to use visuals when appropriate in their presentations to support their presentations and to help keep the listeners' attention.
- Set up simple class rules to show respect for the listener and speaker. These rules should be used during Inquiry or handing off or any time of the day and should foster respect for the speaker and listeners.
  - Students should speak in a voice loud and clear enough for everyone in the class to hear.
  - Students should raise their hands and not interrupt.
  - If someone asks a question, then the person who responds should address the question before going on to another idea or topic.
  - The speaker should look at the audience, and the audience should look at the speaker.

Inquiry

Even in elementary school, students can produce works of genuine research—research that seeks answers to real questions or solutions to real problems.

Inquiry—research, investigation, and exploration—forms the heart of the **SRA Imagine It!** program. To encourage students to understand how reading and writing are tools for learning that can enhance their lives and help them become mature, educated adults, they are asked in each unit to use the content they are learning in the unit as the basis for further inquiry, exploration, and research. The unit information is simply the base for their investigations.

There are two types of units in the **SRA Imagine It!** program—units based on universal topics of interest such as friendship, heritage, and courage and content units that provide students a very solid base of information upon which they can begin their own inquiry and research. Units delving into science-related areas such as camouflage, energy, and ecology or into social studies units that address American history, geography, or money invite students to become true researchers by exploring personal areas of interest driven by problems or questions raised by students. Based upon common areas of interest, students conduct Inquiry in small collaborative groups and then present their findings to their classmates. In this way, students recognize the importance of sharing knowledge and gain much more knowledge of the unit theme than they would have simply by reading the selections in the unit.

The selections in the units are organized so that each selection will add more information or a different perspective to students' growing bodies of knowledge.

Inquiry through Reflective Activities

Purpose

The units in **SRA Imagine It!** that deal with universal topics tend to be explored through reflective activities. These units—such as Courage, Friendship, and Risks and Consequences—are organized to help students expand—perhaps even change—their perspectives of familiar concepts. As they explore and discuss the concepts that emerge from reading selections related to each unit topic, students are involved in activities that extend their experiences and offer opportunities for reflection. Such activities include writing, drama, art, interviews, debates, and panel discussions. Students will choose the activities and presentation format best suited to explore or investigate their research questions. Throughout each unit, students may be involved in a single ongoing investigative activity, or they may participate in a number of different activities. They may choose to produce a final written project or a multimedia presentation. They will share with the rest of the class the new knowledge that they have gained from their investigations. Workshop provides an ideal time for students to work individually or in collaborative groups on their investigation and/or projects.

The Inquiry activities will be those of students' own choosing, thereby allowing them to explore the unit concepts more fully. They are free, of course, to make other choices or to devise activities of their own.

Procedure

Choosing an Area to Investigate

Students may work on activities alone, in pairs, or in small groups. They have the option of writing about or using other methods for presenting their findings to the entire group. Students should decide what concept-related question or problem they wish to explore. Generally, it is better for students to generate wonderings, questions, or problems after they have engaged in some discussion at the beginning of each unit. This should be done, however, before they have had a chance to consult source materials. The goal is to have students ask questions that will drive their inquiry. This approach is more likely to bring forth ideas that students actually wonder about or wish to understand. Students may also look at the questions posted on the **Concept/Question Board** or introduce fresh ideas inspired by material they have just finished reading.

Inquiry pairs or groups are developed based upon common areas of interest or common questions that appear on the **Concept/Question Board.** Students who share a common interest for inquiry should work together to develop a common question to explore. Some of students may need your assistance in deciding upon, or narrowing down, a question or a problem so that it can be explored more easily. A good way to model this process for students is to make webs for a few of your own ideas on the board and to narrow down these ideas to a workable question or problem.

Organizing the Group

After a question or a problem has been chosen, students may choose an activity that will help them investigate that problem or question. For example, if students in Grade 3 are exploring the question "What are the common characteristics that define friendship?" they may want to develop and conduct a survey of classmates, friends, and so on. To develop the survey, group participants may want to do some additional reading about friendship, explore resources on the Internet, and so on to have a sense of the kinds of questions to include in the survey. Students' next responsibility is to decide who is going to investigate which facet of the question or the problem (when they are conducting a literature search, for example) or who is going to perform which activity related to the particular reflective activity (when they are writing and performing an original playlet or puppet show, for example). Lastly, students need to decide how, or if, they want to present their findings. For instance, after conducting a literature search, some students may want to read and discuss passages from a book with a plot or theme that relates to a unit concept. Other students may prefer performing and discussing scenes from the book.

Deciding How to Investigate

The following suggestions may help you and your students choose ways in which to pursue their investigations. For units on universal topics that are more literary in nature, students may want to do one of the following activities to pursue answers to their questions.

✦ Conduct a literature search to pursue a question or a problem. Discussion or writing may follow.

- Write and produce an original playlet or puppet show based on situations related to the concepts.
- Play a role-playing game to work out a problem related to the concepts.
- Stage a panel discussion with audience participation on a question or problem.
- Hold a debate on an issue related to the concept.
- Write an advice column dealing with problems related to the concepts.
- Write a personal-experience story related to the concepts.
- Invite experts to class. Formulate questions to ask.
- Conduct an interview with someone on a subject related to the concepts.
- Produce and carry out a survey on an issue or a question related to the concept.
- Produce a picture or photo-essay about the concept.

You may want to post this list in the classroom so that groups have access to it as they decide what they want to investigate and how they want to proceed. Encourage students to explore other possibilities as well and to add these ideas to the list.

EXAMPLE: In the Heritage unit in Grade 5 of **SRA Imagine It!,** students read "In Two Worlds: A Yup'ik Eskimo Family." This selection is about how three generations of Eskimos living in Alaska near the Arctic strive to adopt the best of modern ways without abandoning their traditional values. During the class discussion, some students may note that Alice and Billy Rivers want their students to learn both the new and the old ways of living. As the discussion continues, many students may conclude from the story that the older generations hope that future generations will continue to value their roots and their cultural traditions. Students then relate this story to their own heritage. Some students may share information about their customs or traditions.

Students choose some reflective activities that will help them learn more about family heritage and that will answer some of their questions about the unit concepts. These questions may relate to the value of maintaining traditional customs and values versus. adopting contemporary ones. Other students may ask exploring questions related to how to maintain traditional

values in the face of contemporary changes. Some students may be interested in interviewing family members or close family friends about their cultural traditions and heritages or interviewing students in their class about their cultural heritage and then looking for commonalities and differences. These students review what they know about interviewing. They should proceed by performing the following:

- Researching examples of interviews to see what they might look like and how to build in space to write answers
- Preparing a list of questions to ask
- Preparing a list of subjects to interview, deciding how to record the interview (by audiotape, videotape, or taking notes)
- Contacting in advance the person(s) they want to interview
- Deciding whether to photograph the person and, if so, getting permission to do so in advance—collecting the equipment necessary for conducting the interview
- After they conduct the interviews, students decide how they wish to present the information that they have collected.

EXAMPLE: Another group of students in the same fifth-grade class may be more interested in planning a photo-essay about one family or about a neighborhood with many families belonging to a particular culture. These students may decide to reexamine "In Two Worlds" in terms of how the text and the photographs complement each other and what information is conveyed in each photograph. They may also decide to examine some photo-essays listed in the unit bibliography. These students will need to make some advance preparations as well. They should proceed by performing the following:

- Determining which neighborhood and which family or families to photograph
- Contacting in advance the persons to be interviewed and photographed
- Touring the neighborhood in advance of the photo shoot
- Making a list of questions to ask the family or families about their heritage or about their neighborhood
- Thinking about what information to include in their essay so that they can

determine what photographs to take
- Collecting the equipment necessary for conducting interviews and photographing subjects

After students collect the information and take photographs, they may write and organize the photo-essay and present it to the class. The teacher should remind students of the phases of the writing process and encourage them to plan, draft, revise, and edit/proofread their work until they are completely satisfied with it.

Not all questions on the **Concept/ Question Board** will be explored in depth. Throughout the unit, students can continue discussing family heritage and raising and posting new questions. The teacher should remind them that as they read further, they may think of additional ways to explore the unit concepts. Students should sign or initial their questions or ideas so that they can identify classmates with similar interests and exchange ideas with them. The teacher should encourage students to feel free to write an answer or a note on someone else's question or to consult the Board for ideas for their own explorations. From time to time, the teacher should post his or her own questions on the **Concept/Question Board.**

Tips

- The **Leveled Readers** contain books related to the unit concepts. Remind students that these are good sources of information and that they should consult them regularly—especially when they are investigating concept-related ideas and questions.
- Some students work better within a specified time frame. Whenever they are beginning a new activity, discuss with students a reasonable period of time within which they will be expected to complete their investigations. Post the completion date somewhere in the classroom so that students can refer to it and pace themselves accordingly. At first, you may have to help them determine a suitable deadline, but eventually they should be able to make this judgment on their own.
- Some teachers like to do the Inquiry for the first unit with a common question decided upon by the whole class. Then students break into small groups and work on different ways to explore the question. One group may do a literature search while another might conduct a survey. The end results in students sharing new knowledge that addresses

the common research question.

Inquiry through Research

Purpose

Students come to school with a wealth of fascinating questions. Educators need to capitalize on this excitement for learning and natural curiosity. A classroom in which the teacher is the only person who asks the questions and defines the assignments, only correct answers are accepted, and students are not allowed to make errors and consider alternative possibilities to questions can quickly deaden this natural curiosity and enthusiasm. The purpose of the inquiry and research aspect of this program is to capitalize on students' questions and natural curiosity by using a framework or structure based upon the scientific method. This structure helps students ask questions and preserve the open-ended character of real research, which can lead to unexpected findings and to questions that were not originally considered.

The conventional approach to school research papers can be found, with minor variations, in countless textbooks and instructional resources. This approach consists of a series of steps such as the following: Select a topic or choose a topic from a list suggested by the teacher, narrow the topic to something of interest, collect materials, take notes, outline, and write. By following these steps, a student may produce a presentable paper, but the procedure does not constitute research in a meaningful sense. Indeed, this restrictive approach gives students a distorted notion of what research is about. We see students in universities and even in graduate schools still following this procedure when they do library research papers or literature reviews; we see their dismay when their professors regard such work as mere cutting and pasting and ask them where their original contribution is.

Elementary school students can produce works of genuine research—research that seeks answers to real questions or solutions to real problems—when they are provided the opportunity, taught how to ask good questions and develop conjectures, and work collaboratively to find information or data that will support or refute their conjecture. Being able to collect, analyze, and evaluate information are critical twenty-first century skills. In the adult world, as knowledgeable consumers, productive members of a sophisticated workforce, and lifelong learners, students will be expected to constantly identify problems, raise questions, analyze new information, and make informed decisions on the basis of this information. Preparing students for the analytic demands of adult life and teaching them how to find answers to their questions are goals of education.

Procedure

To make the research productive, the following important principles are embodied in this approach:

1. Research is focused on problems, not topics.

2. Questions and wonderings are the foundation for inquiry and research.

3. Conjectures—opinions based on less than complete evidence or proof—are derived from questions and guide the research; the research does not simply produce conjectures.

4. New information and data are gathered to test and revise conjectures.

5. Discussion, ongoing feedback, and constructive criticism are important in all phases of the research but especially in the revising of problems and conjectures.

6. The cycle of true research is essentially endless, although presentations of findings are made from time to time; new findings give rise to new problems and conjectures and thus to new cycles of research.

Following a Process

While working with the science and social studies units, students are encouraged to use this framework to keep their research activities focused and on track. Within this framework, there is flexibility. Students may begin with a question, develop a conjecture, and begin collecting information only to find that they need to redefine their conjecture. Like the writing process, there is a recursive nature to this framework. Students may go through these steps many times before they come to the end of their research. Certainly for adult researchers, this cycle of question, conjecture, research, and reevaluation can go on for years and, in some cases, lifetimes.

This cycle uses the following process:

1. Decide on a problem or question to research. Students should identify a question or problem that they truly wonder about or wish to understand and then form research groups with other students who have the same interests.
   - My problem or question is _____.

2. Formulate an idea or conjecture about the research problem. Students should think about and discuss with classmates possible answers to their research problems or questions and meet with their research groups to discuss and record their ideas or conjectures.
   - My idea/conjecture/theory about this question or problem is _____.

3. Identify needs and make plans. Students should identify knowledge needs related to their conjectures and meet with their research groups to determine which resources to consult and to make individual job assignments. Students should also meet periodically with the teacher, other classmates, and research groups to present preliminary findings and to make revisions to their problems and conjectures on the basis of these findings.
   - I need to find out _____.
   - To do this, I will need these resources: _____
   - My role in the group is _____.
   - This is what I have learned so far: _____
   - This is what happened when we presented our findings _____

4. Reevaluate the problem or question based on what we have learned so far and the feedback we have received.
   - My revised problem or question is _____.

5. Revise the idea or conjecture.
   - My new conjecture about this problem is _____.

6. Identify new needs and make new plans.
   - Based on what I found out, I still need to know _____.
   - To do this, I will need these resources: _____
   - This is what I have learned: _____
   - This is what happened when we presented our new findings: _____

Procedure for Choosing a Problem to Research

1. Discuss with students the nature of the unit. Explain to students that the

unit they are reading is a research unit and that they will produce and publish in some way the results of their explorations. They are free to decide what problems or questions they wish to explore, with whom they want to work, and how they want to present their finished products. They may publish a piece of writing, produce a poster, write and perform a play, or use any other means to present the results of their investigations and research. They may work individually, with partners, or in small groups.

2. Discuss with students the schedule you have planned for their investigations: how long the project is expected to take, how much time will be available for research, when the first presentation will be due. This schedule will partly determine the nature of the problems that students should be encouraged to work on and the depth of the inquiry students will be encouraged to pursue.

3. Have students talk about things they wonder about that are related to the unit subject. For example, in the Grade 3 unit Money, students might wonder where money in the money machine comes from or how prices are determined. Conduct a free-floating discussion of questions about the unit subject.

4. Brainstorm possible questions for students to think about. It is essential that students' own ideas and questions be the starting point of all inquiry. Helpful hint: For the first research unit, you might wish to generate a list of your own ideas, having students add to this list and having them choose from it.

5. Using their wonderings, model for students the difference between a research topic and a research problem or question by providing several examples. For example, have them consider the difference between the topic *California* and the problem *Why do so many people move to California?* Explain to them that if they choose to research the topic *California,* everything they look up under the subject heading or index entry *California* will be related in some way to their topic. Therefore, it will be quite difficult to choose which information to record. This excess of information also creates problems in organizing their research. Clearly, then, this topic is too broad and general. Choosing a specific question or problem, one that particularly interests them, helps them

narrow their exploration and advance their understanding. Some possible ideas for questions can be found in the unit introduction. Ideas can also be generated as you and your students create a web of their questions or problems related to the unit concept. For example, questions related to the topic *California* might include the following: Why do so many people move to California? How have the different groups of people living in California affected the state?

6. A good research problem or question not only requires students to consult a variety of sources but is engaging and adds to the groups' knowledge of the concepts. Furthermore, good problems generate more questions. Help students understand that the question *Why do so many people move to California?* is an easy one to research. Many sources will contribute to an answer to the question, and all information located can be easily evaluated in terms of usefulness in answering the question. Helpful hint: Students' initial responses may indeed be topics instead of problems or questions. If so, the following questions might be helpful: What aspect of the topic really interests you? Can you turn that idea into a question?

7. Remember that this initial problem or question serves only as a guide for research. As students begin collecting information and collaborating with classmates, their ideas will change, and they can revise their research problem or question. Frequently, students do not sufficiently revise their problems until after they have had time to consider their conjectures and to collect information.

8. As students begin formulating their research problems, have them elaborate on their reasons for wanting to research their stated problems. They should go beyond simple expressions of interest or liking and indicate what is puzzling, important, or potentially informative, and so forth about the problems they have chosen.

9. At this stage, students' ideas will be of a very vague and limited sort. The important thing is to start them thinking about what really interests them and what value it has to them and the class.

10. Have students present their proposed problems or questions, along with reasons for their choices, and have

an open discussion of how promising proposed problems are. As students present their proposed problems, ask them what new things they think they will be learning from their investigations and how that will add to the group's growing knowledge of the concepts. This constant emphasis on group knowledge building will help set a clear purpose for students' research.

11. Form research groups. To make it easier for students to form groups, they may record their problems on the board or on self-sticking notes. Final groups should be constituted in the way you find best for your class—by self-selection, by assignment on the basis of common interests, or by some combination of methods. Students can then meet during Workshop to agree on a precise statement of their research problem, the nature of their expected research contributions, and lists of related questions that may help later in assigning individual roles. They should also record any scheduling information that can be added to the planning calendar.

Using Technology

Students and teachers can access the Web site **www.SRAonline.com** to find information about the themes in their grade level.

What does Inquiry look like in the classroom?

Inquiry is a new concept for many students and is performed over an extended period of time. The following series of vignettes are an example of what Inquiry might look like in a third-grade classroom that is studying the third-grade unit Money.

Lesson 1

Developing questions

For the unit on money, Ms. Hernandes introduced the theme through "A New Coat for Anna" and now is focusing on having her students generate some questions. To maximize the number of resources available to her students to do their inquiry, she talked with the librarian at her local library as well as local high school teachers who are knowledgeable in the area. Both were able to provide resources for the class. Ms. Hernandes began with a discussion of money. She had prepared some basic questions to get the class started.

- Why do you think it is important to have a system of money like ours?
- What is money?
- Why do you think we have both paper money and coins?
- How have you learned about money?
- How would your life change if suddenly there were no money in the world?
- When people are using credit cards to pay for something, are they paying with real money?
- When someone writes a check, are they paying with real money?
- What is the difference between credit cards and checks and cash, or actual money?
- Why do you think people use credit cards and checks instead of cash?

The teacher felt that using open-ended questions like these would help get her students talking about what they know about money as well as give her an opportunity to informally assess students' background knowledge.

Students were able to provide some basic information such as the following:

- Money is used to buy things.
- There was not always money in the world.
- Some people used things such as animals instead of money.
- Sometimes people traded things to get something they wanted.
- Coins are made of metal.
- Some things cost more than other things.
- Sometimes you need to determine ways to get things when you do not have money.

But there were some basic misunderstandings that arose during the conversation, such as the following:

- All countries use dollars and cents.
- Everything costs the same no matter where you live.

- Money is made of paper.
- You can use credit cards whenever you want.

By discussing money in such general terms, students were able to share basic information.

To move students to the next level—asking questions—Ms. Hernandes began by thinking aloud about things related to the unit that interested her.

"I really am curious about how money is made. And another thing I've wondered about is how the government knows how much money to print." Ms. Hernandes encouraged her students to share some of their wonderings or things they are curious about. Some student wonderings included the following:

- What kind of money do people in other countries use?
- Does everyone make the same amount of money?
- What would happen if there were only credit cards and no money?
- How much money do people make?
- Does ripped money get thrown away?
- How come we cannot make our own money?

Lesson 2

Forming groups based on shared interest

Developing good research questions

Ms. Hernandes and her class have been reading about money for the past week. Many students read different trade books during Workshop to learn more about money. Every day at the end of Workshop, they shared some of their new questions. Some students even started bringing in articles from newspapers and magazines and posting them on the **Concept/Question Board.**

By now there are a number of questions on the **Concept/Question Board** and Ms. Hernandes wants to work with the class to generate more questions that will help students connect what they are learning in school to the real world. She began by modeling or thinking aloud and sharing some of her own thoughts: "I know that at the checkout stand in stores, you can buy plastic cards that have a dollar amount printed on them. I wonder how might this change our whole idea about money. Maybe instead of getting cash from the automatic

money machines, we'll get a coded card."

The focus is on asking questions. She recognized that students' questions needed to be refined to lead to functional conjectures. The class discussed what makes a good question.

- Questions or wonderings should be things that students are truly curious about.
- Questions should be generated without consulting an encyclopedia or a reference source.
- Good questions cannot be answered with a simple *yes* or *no*.
- Questions should help students deepen their understanding of the unit theme rather than focus on a character or incident in a specific story.
- A good research question often begins with *how*.

Ms. Hernandes and the class talked about their questions and how to refine them. For example, one question the class raised earlier was "Does money change?" The class decided to change the question to "How does money change over time?"

- What possible changes might we see in the future?
- Given the changes in technology today, how might our use of money change over time?

Based on the selections the class has read, students generated the following questions to add to their existing ones on the **Concept/Question Board:**

- I wonder when and how the government decided to change coins and bills.
- I wonder if the government can ever run out of money.
- What happens when people make fake money?
- How do people choose the metals they use to make coins?
- How can money be made so people cannot copy it or make counterfeits?
- What do other countries use for money?
- Where do you save money?

To help move students toward developing some good questions for inquiry, the class reviewed all the questions and grouped them together. They discussed these groups of questions and decided to think of a good representative question. The class worked over the next couple of days to think of a question they were all interested in.

Lesson 3

Forming Conjectures

Identifying Needs and Making Plans

A goal of Inquiry is to have students move from asking questions to forming conjectures. Ms. Hernandes explained to the class that they were now going to take their question and develop a conjecture. Developing a conjecture simply means thinking of what they think the best answer is, given what they know now and have read so far.

Ms. Hernandes modeled this by using one of the questions students raised in the earlier lesson. The question was "How do people choose the metals to make coins?" Ms. Hernandes thought aloud about possible answers to this question: "I think that people choose a strong metal that will last a long time but that is not too heavy for people to carry."

Then Ms. Hernandes wrote the question the class thought of last week. They discussed the question and talked about what possible answers they might find. The question the class decided to focus on was "How is money made so that people cannot copy it?"

The class conjecture was "Special paper and really detailed pictures are used so no one can copy it." However, Ms. Hernandes realized that there could be other conjectures for the same question. She arranged the class into small groups and had them think about other possible conjectures. Some additional conjectures included the following:

- Every dollar has a different number that is recorded in a computer.
- Special ink is used so colors cannot be duplicated.
- When you hold up a bill to the light, you can see a special band in it that maybe only a special government machine can make.

At the end of the lesson, Ms. Hernandes created a chart with the question and all the conjectures students developed.

During the week, Ms. Hernandes continued working with the class on Inquiry. To help the group get started on identifying needs and materials related to their conjecture, Ms. Hernandes asked the following questions:

- What information will we need to help us decide if our conjecture is accurate?
- Where can we find this information?
- Who can help us find information related to our conjecture?
- What people in our school might be able to help us?
- What family members might know something about this?
- What words could we plug in on the Internet to help us get more information?

During the rest of this week, students started collecting different resources and reading various books during Workshop. Students were encouraged to take notes and to share with their groups each day.

Lesson 4

Revising Plans as Necessary

Collecting Data and Information

Now that students have started collecting material, they need to identify individual job assignments so they are not duplicating efforts. At the beginning of this week, Ms. Hernandes took time to have students meet in their groups. During this time she met with the small groups to track their progress, discuss any problems, and help them focus their research efforts.

The group working with the conjecture "Every dollar has a different number that is recorded in a computer" was having trouble finding information to support or refute their conjecture. They had looked in books but did not really find anything. As they talked with the teacher, someone mentioned the term *mint*. As they discussed what happened in the mint, someone suggested that they write the mint with their question to see if they could get some help. This simple activity led students to the Internet to find out the address of the mint. They then spent the rest of that period composing a letter.

At the end of Inquiry that day, Ms. Hernandes made time for each group to present a summary of what it had done. If the group had any unsolved problems, it shared them with the class to get possible suggestions on how to solve the problems. When the group who wrote to the mint shared its problem and solution, several other groups realized that the Internet would be a good resource for them to use as well.

Lesson 5

Continuing Working and Planning Final Presentation

At this point students are beginning to conclude their investigations. Several of the groups realized as they collected information that they really needed to change or revise their conjectures. Ms. Hernandes asked in what ways their ideas have changed—what do they know now that they did not know before? For example, the group that had the conjecture that special ink was used so colors cannot be duplicated revised its conjecture by broadening it. After doing some research, their new conjecture was that there are many different things that the government does in addition to using special ink to protect money from being copied.

As groups presented their conjectures and progress, Ms. Hernandes modeled constructive comments such as the following: "Your points are clearly made." "Your charts and graphs help us understand each of your points." "Each one of you presented different pieces of information that all connect to your conjecture." "How was your conjecture supported?" After the lesson, Ms. Hernandes took time to reflect and realized that it was very hard for her students to give constructive feedback. She knew that this is an area they would need to work on. She would have to continue modeling but also thought about having groups exchange conjectures and provide feedback in writing to each other. This might reduce anxiety as well as give students time to reflect on the questions and conjectures and to develop some thoughtful feedback.

During this week, Ms. Hernandes took time to discuss possible ways that students could present their findings. The class brainstormed other ideas including the following:

- Writing a series of articles on their information for a magazine
- Creating a poster with diagrams of a process
- A panel discussion
- A computer presentation

Students returned to their groups to decide how they wanted to present their findings.

Final Presentation

Students have been busy working on completing their investigations and developing their presentations. While the class decided on a single research question at the beginning of the unit, different groups developed their own conjectures. Because their conjectures guided their research, each group will be presenting different information. Ms. Hernandes has created a simple web with the class's research question in the center and circles around the question. After groups present their work, the class will discuss what information was found to address the research question. As presentations are made, students will also be encouraged to make connections not only to the question but to each other's findings.

Throughout the unit, Ms. Hernandes recognized that students need more work on asking questions of each other and providing constructive feedback. She plans on modeling questions and comments as groups complete their presentations. Some examples include the following:

- How does what you presented support or refute your conjecture?
- Would you clarify . . .
- It would be helpful if . . .
- Have you thought about . . .
- Your visuals really helped me better understand your ideas.
- That was a great idea. Where can we find more information on it so we can learn more about it?
- What other questions did you think of as you were researching your conjecture?

Overall, Ms. Hernandes felt that this first attempt at Inquiry with the entire class focusing on a single question but generating multiple conjectures made Inquiry manageable for students and herself. Ms. Hernandes is now thinking about how to plan the next Inquiry unit so there are multiple questions as well as multiple conjectures. From the final presentations, she has really begun to appreciate how Inquiry incorporates all the reading and writing skills she has been teaching and how it takes students to the next level of learning—delving deeper into ideas that personally interest them, taking time and responsibility to learn about something, working collaboratively, and sharing new ideas and information.

Tips

- ✦ Inquiry takes time to develop. You may want to do the first unit as an entire class.
- ✦ Provide time throughout the unit for students to work on Inquiry. Use Workshop as well as computer and library time to support Inquiry.
- ✦ If students are careful about the problems or questions they choose to research, they should have few problems in following through with the research. If the problem is too broad or too narrow, they will have problems.

- ✦ Have students take sufficient time in assessing their needs—both knowledge needs and physical needs in relation to their research. Careful preplanning can help the research progress smoothly with great results.
- ✦ Encourage students to reevaluate their needs often so they are not wasting time finding things they already have or ignoring needs that they have not noticed.
- ✦ Interim presentations of material are every bit as important, if not more so, than final presentations. It is during interim presentations that students have the opportunity to rethink and reevaluate their work and change direction or to decide to carry on with their planned research.
- ✦ Connect Inquiry to learning in the content areas. Have students apply their Inquiry skills to learning science, social studies, and the arts.

Assessment

Assessment can be your most effective teaching tool if it is used with the purpose of informing instruction and highlighting areas that need special attention.

Purpose

The assessment components of **SRA Imagine It!** are designed to help you make informed instructional decisions, make adequate yearly progress, and help ensure you meet the needs of all your students. The variety of assessments is intended to be used continuously and formatively. That is, students should be assessed regularly as a follow-up to instructional activities, and the results of the assessment should be used to inform subsequent instruction.

You can use assessment as a tool to monitor students' progress, to diagnose students' strengths and weaknesses, to prescribe forms of intervention as necessary, and to measure student outcomes. Both formal and informal assessment can be used, though formal assessment will be your main assessment tool. Formal assessment of student learning consists of performance assessment (both reading and writing), objective tests (multiple choice, short answer, and essay), progress assessment (through students' everyday oral and written work), and assessment rubrics (used for writing, inquiry, and comprehension strategies). Informal assessment can be done by observing or listening to students as they work and jotting down notes either in the Comprehension Observation Log or in a notebook.

Procedure

Formal Assessment

Formal assessment is addressed in **SRA Imagine It!** in the form of **Benchmark Assessments** and **Lesson Assessments.** Both will help you use the results to differentiate instruction, especially for students needing some type of intervention to ensure they will not be at risk for reading failure.

Benchmark Assessments

The **Benchmark Assessments** are a form of general outcome measurement that offer an overall framework for assessment and serve as a predictor of how well students will perform at the end of the school year. Each **Benchmark Assessment** has material that students will learn over the course of the school year, and each **Benchmark Assessment** is of equivalent difficulty. Students are not expected to score high on the initial screening benchmark; instead, students are expected to show growth as they move on to each subsequent benchmark. Only at the end of the year are students expected to have mastered the materials on these assessments.

> *Observing students as they go about their regular classwork can be an effective way to learn your students' strengths and areas of need.*

One **Benchmark Assessment** will be administered at the beginning of the year for screening. This can serve as a baseline score against which you can measure students' progress throughout the year. Subsequent benchmarks will also be given at regular intervals—at the end of every other unit in grades K–1, for a total of six assessments, and at the end of each unit for students in grades 2–6, for a total of seven assessments. Since the tests are of equivalent difficulty and contain the same types of items, students' higher scores will reflect their increasing mastery of the curriculum over the course of the year. Use the data from the **Benchmark Assessments** to identify students who are at risk for reading failure, to identify strengths and weaknesses of students, and to gauge student progress toward high-stakes tests.

Depending upon the grade level, tested benchmark skills include the following:

- letter recognition,
- phonemic/phonological awareness,
- phonics,
- high-frequency word recognition,
- vocabulary,
- spelling,
- grammar, usage, and mechanics,
- comprehension,
- oral fluency, and
- maze fluency.

In addition, a writing assessment is given in the initial screening, at midyear, and also again at the end of the year for students in grades 3–6. This assessment is the type of on-demand writing performance students will encounter in high-stakes tests. Each writing assessment is of equal difficulty, and student outcomes should reflect an increased mastery of writing convention and genre expectations.

Lesson Assessments

The **Lesson Assessments** cover the most important skills featured in the lesson of a given unit—skills that are closely related to reading success and are typically in state and national standards. These assessments will help you determine how well students are grasping the skills and concepts as they are taught and will help inform you about any additional instruction they might need.

The **Lesson Assessments** are easily administered and scored. They feature the same language used in the instructional components of **SRA Imagine It!** and correspond to its sequence of instruction. The format of these weekly assessments range from multiple choice questions to short answer to an extended writing response. Depending upon the grade level, skills assessed include the following:

- letter and number recognition
- phonological and phonemic awareness
- phonics
- print and book awareness
- high frequency words

- selection vocabulary
- spelling
- grammar, usage, and mechanics skills
- comprehension skills
- oral fluency
- writing

The *Lesson Assessments* are offered in several formats so that students can demonstrate their knowledge of content in a number of developmentally appropriate ways. Wherever possible, the assessments are designed to be administered to the whole class or small groups of students. In some cases, however, individually administered assessments are included, such as the oral fluency assessments, as well as critical pre-literacy skills such as phoneme blending or segmentation as well as letter and number recognition.

The *Lesson Assessments* will allow you to monitor students' progress as they are assessed on the specific skills taught in a given lesson. The results will provide instructionally relevant information that you can use to differentiate instruction for students who may need additional learning opportunities.

Progress Assessment

Written Practice

Students work on several different skills throughout the day. Each of these assignments can provide you with valuable information about your students' progress. One very helpful resource that students will work in daily is the *Skills Practice Book* (Levels K–6). The *Skills Practice Books* include lessons that act as practice and reinforcement for the skills lessons taught before and during the reading of the lesson as well as in conjunction with the Language Arts lesson. These skills pages give you a clear picture of students' understanding of the skills taught. Use them as a daily assessment of student progress in the particular skills taught through the program.

Also included in the *Skills Practice Books* are lessons that help students with their Inquiry activities. Students can record what they know about the concepts and what they learn, they can keep a record of their research, and they can practice study and research skills that will help them in all of their schooling. You will be able to monitor their growing ability to make connections, find resources, and enhance their knowledge base as they find the answers to the research questions they have posed.

Dictation

In grades 1–3, students use dictation to practice the sound/spelling associations they are learning and/or reviewing. Collect the dictation papers and look through them to see how the students are doing with writing and with proofreading their words. Record notes on the papers and keep them in the student portfolios.

Portfolios

Portfolios are more than just a collection bin or gathering place for student projects and records. They add balance to an assessment program by providing unique benefits to teachers, students, and families.

- Portfolios help build self-confidence and increase self-esteem as students come to appreciate the value of their work. More importantly, portfolios allow students to reflect on what they know and what they need to learn. At the end of the school year, each student will be able to go through their portfolios and write about their progress.

- Portfolios provide the teacher with an authentic record of what students can do. Just as important, portfolios give students a concrete example of their own progress and development. Thus, portfolios become a valuable source of information for making instructional decisions.

- Portfolios allow families to judge student performance directly. Portfolios are an ideal starting point for discussions about a student's achievements and future goals during teacher/family conferences.

You will find that there are many opportunities to add to students' portfolios.

Fluency

- During partner reading, during Workshop, or at other times of the day, invite students, one at a time, to sit with you and read a story from an appropriate *Decodable* (grades 1–3), *Leveled Readers* (grades 1–6), *Leveled Readers for Science* or *Social Studies* (grades 1–6), or the *Student Reader.*

- As each student reads to you, follow along and make note of any recurring problems the student has while reading. Note students' ability to decode unknown words as well as any attempt—successful or not—to use strategies to clarify or otherwise make sense of what they are reading. From time to time,

check students' fluency by timing their reading and noting how well they are able to sustain the oral reading without faltering.

- If a student has trouble reading a particular *Decodable* or *Leveled Reader,* encourage the student to read the story a few times on her or his own before reading it aloud to you. If the *Decodable* has two stories, use the alternate story to reassess the student a day or two later.

- If after practicing with a particular Decodable Book or Leveled Reader and reading it on his or her own a few times, a student is still experiencing difficulty, try the following:
  - Drop back two *Decodables*. (Continue to drop back until the student is able to read a story with no trouble.) If the student can read that book without problems, move up one book. The same is true for *Leveled Readers.*
  - Continue the process until the student is able to read the current *Decodable* or *Leveled Readers.*

Assessment Rubrics

In addition to the formal assessment opportunities available in *Benchmark Assessments, Lesson Assessments,* and progress assessment, *SRA Imagine It!* provides rubrics for you to evaluate students' performance in comprehension, Inquiry, and writing. Rubrics provide criteria for different levels of performance. Rubrics established before an assignment is given are extremely helpful in evaluating the assignment. When students know what the rubrics for a particular assignment are, they can focus their energies on the key issues. Rubrics can be found in the Level Appendix.

Informal Assessment

Observation

Informal assessment is a part of the everyday classroom routine. Observing students as they go about their regular classwork can be an effective way to learn your students' strengths and areas of need. The more students become accustomed to you jotting down informal notes about their work, the more it will become just another part of classroom life that they accept and take little note of. This gives you the opportunity to assess their progress constantly without the interference and possible drawback of formal testing situations.

One tool that will help you make

informal assessment of student progress a part of your everyday classroom routine is the Comprehension Observation Log. You can record information quickly on this observation sheet and even extend your observations over several days, until you have had a chance to observe each student's performance in a particular area.

✦ Enter students' names in the Comprehension Observation Log, found in the *Lesson Assessment Books.*

✦ Before each day's lesson begins, decide which students you will observe.

✦ Keep the Comprehension Observation Log available so that you can easily record your observations.

✦ Decide what aspect of the students' learning you wish to monitor.

✦ During each lesson, observe this aspect in the performances of several students.

✦ When observing students, do not pull them aside; rather, observe students as part of the regular lesson, either with the whole class or in small groups.

✦ Record your observations.

✦ It may take four to five days to make sure you have observed and recorded the performance of each student. If you need more information about performance in a particular area for some of your students, you may want to observe them more than once.

Responding to Assessment Results

The point of assessment is to monitor progress in order to inform instruction, diagnose students' strengths and weaknesses, and differentiate instruction for students who need extra practice in certain skills or an extra challenge. *SRA Imagine It!* offers you opportunities to diagnose areas that may cause problems for students, differentiate instruction according to their abilities, monitor their progress on an ongoing basis, and measure student outcomes through *Lesson Assessments* or *Benchmark Assessments,* in addition to high-stakes state assessments. *SRA Imagine It!* also provides several ways to differentiate instruction based on the results of the various assessments. These include the following:

✦ Reteach lessons are available for students who are approaching level and appear to grasp a given concept but need more instruction and practice to solidify their learning. Many skills taught in the *Skills Practice Books* are available in a *Reteach* format.

✦ Intervention lessons provide options for you to use with students who need more intensive support and who are struggling to understand the on-level material. In addition to the support for the weekly lesson, controlled vocabulary lessons and specific skills lessons can help bring students up to grade level.

✦ *English Learner Support* lessons are available for students who are having difficulty with the concepts because they lack the necessary English language background. These resources will provide English Learners with the vocabulary, phonics, comprehension, grammar, and writing support they need to access the *SRA Imagine It!* lessons.

✦ *Challenge Activities* provide continued stimulation for those students who are doing well and working above grade level. Many skills covered in the *Skills Practice Books* are also available in *Challenge Activities.*

✦ *Workshop Resource Book* activities give students alternative activities to strengthen or extend their skills in areas such as letter recognition, phonics, vocabulary, comprehension, fluency, word structure, and grammar.

✦ *Leveled Readers* provide students at all different levels of instruction— Approaching Level, On Level, Above Level, and English Learners—with additional opportunities to practice fluency, vocabulary, and comprehension skills. Besides the general *Leveled Readers, Leveled Readers for Science* and *Leveled Readers for Social Studies* provide students cross-curricular opportunities.

These materials, along with formal and informal assessments, help ensure that assessment and instruction work together to meet every student's needs.

Workshop

Every teacher and every student needs time during the day to organize, to take stock of work that is done, to make plans for work that needs doing, and to finish up incomplete projects. In addition, teachers need time for differentiating instruction, for holding conferences with students, and for doing fluency checks.

Purpose

Workshop is the period of time each day in which students work independently or collaboratively to practice and review material taught in the lessons.

A variety of activities may occur during this time. Students may work on a specific daily assignment, complete an ongoing project, work on unit inquiry activities, focus on writing, or choose from a wide range of possibilities. With lots of guidance and encouragement, students gradually learn to make decisions about their use of time and materials and to collaborate with their peers.

A goal of Workshop is to get students to work independently and productively. This is essential because Workshop is also the time during which the teacher can work with individuals or groups of students to reinforce learning, to provide extra help for those having difficulties, to extend learning, or to assess the progress of the class or of individuals.

Procedure

Initially for many students you will need to structure Workshop carefully. Eventually students will automatically go to the appropriate areas, take up ongoing projects, and get the materials they will need. Workshop will evolve slowly from a very structured period to a time when students make choices and move freely from one activity to the next.

Setting up Workshop guidelines is key. By the time students have completed the first few weeks of school, they should feel confident during Workshop. If not, continue to structure the time and limit options. For young students, early periods of Workshop may run no more than five to eight minutes. The time can gradually increase to fifteen minutes or longer as students gain independence. Older students may be able to work longer and independently from the very beginning of the school year.

Introducing Workshop

Introduce Workshop to students by telling them that every day there will be a time when they are expected to work on activities on their own or in small groups. For younger students explain that in the beginning there may be just a couple of activities but that gradually new ones will be introduced and that students can choose what they want to do. With older students and for those who have experienced Workshop in early grades, you may want to introduce the concept of Workshop and discuss the range of Workshop options from working on fluency to completing their writing.

> *Workshop is the period of time each day in which students work independently or collaboratively to practice and review material taught in the lessons.*

Establish and discuss rules for Workshop with students. Keep them simple and straightforward. You may want to write the finalized rules on the board or on a poster. You may want to review these rules each day at the beginning of Workshop for the first few lessons or so. You may also wish to revisit and revise the rules from time to time. Suggested rules include the following:

- Share.
- Use a quiet voice.
- Take only the materials you need.
- Return materials.
- Always be working.
- When the teacher is working with a student or small group, do not interrupt.

Early in the process, review rules routinely, and discuss how Workshop is going. Is the class quiet enough for everyone to work on his or her own? Are there any rules that need changing? What problems are students having with materials?

For young students in the beginning you will assign the Workshop activities to help them learn to work on their own. Point out the shelf or area of the classroom where Workshop materials are stored. Tell students that when they finish working with the materials for one activity, they will choose something else from the Workshop shelf. New activity materials will be added to the shelf from time to time. Make sure students know that they may always look at books during Workshop.

Tell older students that they will have an opportunity each day to work on their unit inquiry activities, their writing, and other projects. Students will be working independently and collaboratively during this time.

Guidelines

- ✦ Make sure each student knows what he or she needs to do during Workshop.

- ✦ Demonstrate for the entire group any activity or game assigned for Workshop, for example, teaching students a new game, introducing new materials or projects, or explaining different areas.

- ✦ For young students, it is essential to introduce and demonstrate different activities and games before students do them on their own. With games, you may want to have several students play while the others watch. Make sure that all students know exactly what is expected of them.

- ✦ In the beginning, plan to circulate among students, providing encouragement and help as necessary.

- ✦ When students are engaged in appropriate activities and can work independently, meet with those students who need your particular attention. This may include individual students or small groups.

- ✦ Let students know that they need to ask questions and to clarify assignments during Workshop introduction so that you are free to work with small groups.

- ✦ Be sure that students know what they are to do when they have finished an activity and where to put their finished work.

Setting Up Your Classroom for Workshop

Carefully setting up your classroom to accommodate various Workshop activities will help assure that the Workshop period progresses smoothly and effectively. While setting up your classroom, keep the primary Workshop activities in mind. During Workshop, students will be doing independent and collaborative activities. In kindergarten and first grade, these activities may include letter recognition and phonemic awareness activities and writing or illustrating stories or projects. In addition, they will be working on individual or small-group projects.

Many classrooms have areas that students visit on a regular or rotating basis. Unlike traditional centers, all students do not rotate through all the areas each day.

The following are suggestions for space and materials for use during Workshop:

1. Reading Area supplied with books and magazines. The materials in the Reading Area should be dynamic—changing with students' abilities and reflecting unit themes they are reading. You may wish to add books to your classroom library.

2. Writing Area stocked with various types and sizes of lined and unlined paper, pencils, erasers, markers, crayons, small slates, and chalk. The area should also have various **Letter Cards** and other handwriting models for those students who want to practice letter formation or handwriting. Students should know that this is where they come for writing supplies. In addition to the supplies described above, the Writing Area can also have supplies to encourage students to create and write on their own:

   - Magazines and catalogs to cut up for pictures; stickers, paint, glue, glitter, and so on to decorate books and book covers; precut and stapled blank books for students to write in (Some can be plain and some cut in special shapes.)
   - Cardboard, tag board, construction paper, and so on for making book covers (Provide some samples.)
   - Tape, scissors, yarn, hole punches for binding books
   - Picture dictionaries, dictionaries, thesauruses, word lists, and other materials that may encourage independence

3. Listening Area supplied with tape recorder, CD player, optional headphones, and CDs of stories, poems, and songs for students to listen to and react to. You might also want to provide blank tapes and encourage students to retell and record their favorite stories or to make up and tell stories for their classmates to listen to on tape. You may also want to make available the Listening Library CDs that are available with the program.

4. Phonics Activities supplied with **Alphabet Flash Cards,** individual **Alphabet Sound Card** sets (Kindergarten), individual **Sound/Spelling Cards** and **High-Frequency Flash Cards** (Grades K, 1, 2, and 3), and other materials that enhance what students are learning. Other commonly used classroom materials that enhance reading can be included, for example, plastic letters, puzzles, and games.

5. Fluency Area supplied with **Pre-Decodables and Decodables, Leveled Readers, Leveled Science Readers** and **Leveled Social Studies Readers,** and other resources for practicing fluency. Some teachers have folders for each student with materials to practice during the week. In addition, some Fluency areas have timers and tape recorders as well.

Because students will be working on their inquiry/investigations during Workshop, make sure there are adequate supplies to help them with their research. These might include dictionaries, encyclopedias, magazines, newspapers, and computers—preferably with Internet capability.

Students thrive in an environment that provides structure, repetition, and routine. Within a sound structure, students will gain confidence and independence. This setting allows you to differentiate instruction to provide opportunities for flexibility and individual choice. This will allow students to develop their strengths, abilities, and talents to the fullest.

Suggestions for English Learners

Workshop affords students who are English Learners a wealth of opportunities for gaining proficiency in English. It also encourages them to share their backgrounds with peers. Since you will be working with all students individually and in small groups regardless of their reading ability, students who need special help with language will not feel self-conscious about working with you.

In addition, working in small groups made of students with the same interests rather than the same abilities will provide them with the opportunity to learn about language from their peers during the regular course of Workshop activities.

Some suggestions for meeting the special needs of students with diverse backgrounds are as follows:

✦ Preread a selection with English Learners to help them identify words and ideas they wish to talk about. This will prepare them for discussions with the whole group.

✦ Preteach vocabulary and develop selection concepts that may be a challenge for students.

✦ Negotiate the meaning of selections by asking questions, checking for comprehension, and speaking with English Learners as much as possible.

✦ Draw English Learners into small-group discussions to give them a sense that their ideas are valid and worth attention.

✦ Pair English Learners with native English speakers to share their experiences and to provide new knowledge to other students.

✦ Have English Learners draw or dictate to you or another student a description of a new idea they may have during Workshop activities.

Book Review

Sessions can be small or large. Workshop is a good time for students to share the reading they do on their own. They can discuss a book they have all read, or one person can review a book for the others and answer questions from the group.

During Workshop, students can discuss and review a variety of books:

✦ Full-length versions of **Student Reader** selections

✦ Books that students learn about when discussing authors and illustrators

✦ Books related to the investigations of unit concepts that can be shared with others who might want to read them

✦ Interesting articles from magazines, newspapers, and other sources

When a student reviews a book others have not read, he or she can use some of the sentence starters to tell about the book. These may include "This book is about . . . ," "I chose this book because . . . ," "What I really like/don't like about this book is . . . , " and so on.

✦ When several students read the same book and discuss it during Workshop, they can use discussion starters.

Encouraging Reading

✦ Read aloud to your students regularly. You can read from your classroom library or full-length versions of *Student Reader* selections.

✦ Provide a time each day for students to read silently. This time can be as short as 10–15 minutes but should be strictly observed. You should stop what you are doing and read. Students should be allowed to choose their own reading materials during this time and record their reactions in the response journal section of their Writer's Notebooks.

✦ Establish a classroom library and reading center with books from the school or local library, or ask for donations of books from students, parents, and community members.

✦ Take your students to the school library or to the public library.

Workshop Management Tips

Use the following Workshop management tips to ensure that Workshop runs smoothly.
   Note that these suggestions for a weekly unit/lesson may not exactly correspond to a particular unit/lesson in a given grade level but will give you a sense of how Workshop should progress. All of the time suggestions depend upon the needs of the class and their readiness to work independently.

Kindergarten through Grade 1

Unit 1, Week 1 Introduce Workshop as whole-class workshop. Explain Workshop and its rules. Give the class an activity to do, for example, putting letters in alphabetical order (Grade 1) or copying their names (kindergarten). Tell the class that they will be doing Workshop today. As they do their activity, you will walk around, observing students and noting how well Workshop is going. The class is working quietly and independently. Workshop may last only a few minutes in kindergarten and about ten minutes in first grade.

Unit 1, Weeks 2 and 3 Depending upon your class, you can move to whole-group Workshop with two activities. Give half the class one activity and the other half the other. Explain to the class that for the next few Workshop sessions, there will be two different activities but that the class is supposed to work quietly and independently. Switch activities for the next day, and repeat this format for the next few days or so. Introduce the concept of "debriefing." Take a few minutes at the end, have several students share what they did or learned during Workshop. You may want to have students tell what they like about Workshop and if any changes need to be made.

Unit 2, Week 1 Begin introducing Workshop Areas, explaining the materials and how they can be used. Explain to students that the materials in these areas will be changing regularly so students will be able to practice and use their new reading and writing skills. Workshop activities should change routinely and reflect the changing nature of the curriculum. Often, during the early weeks of Workshop, teachers assign students to different activities and, as students become ready, turn over to students the responsibility for choosing activities.

Unit 3 Add new activities for students. Encourage them to do a couple of Workshop activities each day, perhaps working on their writing in progress and fluency practice (reading a Pre-Decodable or Decodable). Other options might include on-line phonemic awareness and phonics activities, phonics activities such as word sorts, using blended words in written sentences, practicing high-frequency sight words, and so on.

Unit 4 By this time, students should be making choices and working independently. Each Workshop session may be fifteen minutes long with the teacher working with small groups. Take time to review Workshop activities to be sure they are being used and that students are learning from the activities. If activities become stale, vary them, or change them altogether.

Grades 2–6

Unit 1, Lesson 1 Introduce Workshop to students. Make sure they know where materials are located. Post the rules on the board or other prominent place in the classroom. Keep Workshop time short (less than thirty minutes) and very directed during the first few weeks until students can work

independently.

Unit 1, Lesson 2 Discuss using small groups for pre-/reteaching purposes and how you will indicate who will be in the groups. Start by forming one small group randomly and having other students do something specific such as a writing assignment. When you have finished with the small group, send them to do independent work. Call another small group of students to work with you. Continue this each day until students are accustomed to forming groups and working independently.

Unit 1, Lesson 3 Reading Roundtable is a student-formed and student-run book discussion. Encourage students participating in Reading Roundtable to choose a book that they all will read and discuss. Several different Reading Roundtable groups may form on the basis of the books students choose.

Unit 1, Lesson 4 For the first few weeks of the school year, make sure each student has a plan for using Workshop time.

Unit 1, Lesson 5 (Days 1–5) Allow time for presentation and discussion of research activities. Use an entire Workshop day, and have all groups present their findings, or split the presentations over several days, depending on the small-group needs of your class.

Unit 1, Lesson 5 (Days 6–10) Review how students have used Workshop during this unit. Have they used their time well? Do they have the materials they need? Discuss suggestions for improving their use of this time. Take a few minutes at the beginning of each Workshop to make sure students know what they will be doing.

Unit 2, Lesson 1 Form small extra-practice groups with the more advanced students from time to time, as they also need special attention.

Unit 2, Lesson 2 To keep the entire class informed about the independent research being done, every other day or so invite a research group to explain what it is doing, how the research is going, and any problems they are encountering.

Unit 2, Lesson 3 Discuss the use of Workshop time for doing Inquiry and research projects, and share *eInquiry* with different research activities.

Unit 2, Lesson 4 Make sure small extra-practice groups are formed based on your observations of students' work on the different daily lessons. Small groups should be fluid and based on demonstrated need rather than become static and unchanging.

Unit 2, Lesson 5 (Days 1–5) One purpose of Workshop is to help students learn independence and responsibility. Assign students to monitor Workshop materials. They should alert you whenever materials are running low or missing, and they can be responsible for checking on return dates of library books and making sure the books are either returned or renewed.

Unit 2, Lesson 5 (Days 6–10) Students sometimes have difficulty starting discussions in Reading Roundtable. Try some of these discussion starters with students, and print them on a poster for student use.

> *I didn't know that . . .*
> *I liked the part where . . .*
> *Does anyone know . . .*
> *I'm still confused by . . .*
> *I figured out that . . .*
> *This made me think . . .*
> *I agree/disagree with because . . .*

Unit 3, Lesson 1 By this time students should be accustomed to the routines, rules, expectations, and usage of Workshop time and be moving smoothly from small teacher-led groups to independent work. Monitor small groups occasionally to see that they are on task and making progress on their activities.

Unit 3, Lesson 2 Make a practice of reading aloud to students. All students enjoy being read to, no matter their age or grade. Encourage them to discuss the shared reading in groups and to bring books and read them aloud to their classmates.

Unit 3, Lesson 3 Encourage cooperation and collaboration by providing students with opportunities to engage in small groups.

Unit 3, Lesson 4 Spend a few minutes each day circulating around the room and monitoring what students are doing independently or in small groups. Students can then share with you on a timely basis any questions or problems they are having.

Unit 3, Lesson 5 (Days 1–5) Take note of various small groups. Make sure that quieter students are able to participate in the discussions. Often the stronger, more confident students dominate such discussions. Encourage them to give all participants an opportunity to share their ideas.

Unit 3, Lesson 5 (Days 6–10) If students are not productive during Workshop, keep them in the small group you are working with until they can successfully benefit from independent work. Discuss strategies they could use to become more independent.

Unit 4, Lesson 1 Individual students can monitor Workshop materials and alert you when materials or supplies are running low or missing and can check that library books are either returned or renewed.

Unit 4, Lesson 2 From time to time, join a Reading Roundtable group, and take part in their discussion. Make sure students lead the discussion.

Unit 4, Lesson 3 Encourage responsibility and independence by reminding students to show respect for each other and the materials provided.

Unit 4, Lesson 4 Be sure students discuss during Reading Roundtable what they like or dislike about a book, why they wanted to read it, and how the book either lived up to their expectations or disappointed them. Discussions should not be about basic comprehension but should help students think more deeply about the ideas presented in the book.

Unit 4, Lesson 5 (Days 1–5) Make sure students continue to use the activities provided for use with this unit at **SRAonline. com.**

Unit 4, Lesson 5 (Days 6–10) If students are not productive in Workshop, keep them in the small group you are working with until they can successfully benefit from independent work. Discuss strategies they could use to become more independent.

Unit 5, Lesson 1 Students often make great tutors for other students. They are uniquely qualified to understand problems that others might be having. Encourage students to pair up during Workshop to help each other with their daily lessons.

Unit 5, Lesson 2 Form small extra-practice groups with the more advanced students from time to time, as they also need special attention.

Unit 5, Lesson 3 To keep the entire class informed about the independent research being done, every other day or so, invite a research/investigation group to explain what it is doing, how the research is going, and any problems they are encountering.

Unit 5, Lesson 4 Most of the authors of the *Student Reader* selections are well known and have written many, many pieces of fine literature. Encourage students who enjoy the selections to find other books by the same author. Encourage them to think about and discuss what about that particular author's work attracts them.

Unit 5, Lesson 5 (Days 1–5) Share your impressions of books from your classroom library or other readings during Reading Roundtable. Note which students initiate sharing and which are reluctant to share.

Unit 5, Lesson 5 (Days 6–10) Review with students the time they have used in Workshop. Have they used their time well? Do they have the materials they need? Discuss suggestions for improving the use of this time.

Unit 6, Lesson 1 Spend a few minutes each day circulating and monitoring what students are doing independently or in small groups. Students can share with you on a timely basis any questions or problems they are having.

Unit 6, Lesson 2 Students should be accustomed to the routines, rules, expectations, and usage of Workshop time and be moving smoothly from small teacher-led groups to independent work. Make sure to monitor small groups occasionally to see that they are on task and making progress with their activities.

Unit 6, Lesson 3 Make sure students continue to use the activities provided for use with this unit at **SRAonline.com.**

Unit 6, Lesson 4 If the reading selection is an excerpt from a longer piece, encourage students to read the book from which the excerpt is taken and to discuss how the excerpt fits into the larger work.

Unit 6, Lesson 5 (Days 1–5) Students often make great tutors for other students. The fact that they, too, are just learning the materials makes them uniquely qualified to understand problems that others might be having. Encourage students to pair up during Workshop to help each other on their daily lessons.

Unit 6, Lesson 5 (Days 6–10) Allot time for presentation and discussion of research activities. You may want to use a whole Workshop day and have all groups present their findings or split the presentations over several days, depending on the urgency of the small-group instruction your class needs.

Scope and Sequence

Reading

	K	1	2	3	4	5	6
Print/Book Awareness (Recognize and understand the conventions of print and books)							
Capitalization	X	X					
Constancy of Words		X					
Differentiate between Letter and Word	X						
Differentiate between Word and Sentence	X						
End Punctuation	X	X					
Follow Left-to-Right, Top-to-Bottom	X	X					
Letter Recognition and Formation	X	X					
Page Numbering	X	X					
Parts of a Book	X	X					
Picture/Text Relationship	X	X					
Punctuation	X	X					
Quotation Marks	X	X					
Relationship Between Spoken and Printed Language	X	X					
Sentence Recognition	X	X					
Spacing Between Sentences	X	X					
Spacing Between Words	X	X					
Table of Contents	X	X					
Text Features		X					
Text Relationships		X					
Word Length	X	X					
Word Boundaries		X					
Write Left-to-Right, Top-to-Bottom	X	X					
Phonemic Awareness (Recognize Discrete Sounds in Words)							
Oral Blending: Words/Word Parts	X	X					
Oral Blending: Onset and Rime	X	X					
Oral Blending: Syllables	X	X					
Oral (Phoneme) Blending: Initial Sounds	X	X					
Oral (Phoneme) Blending: Final Sounds	X	X					
Oral Blending: Initial Vowels		X					
Oral Blending: Vowel Replacement		X					
Rhyming	X	X					
Phoneme Matching: Initial Sounds	X	X					
Phoneme Matching: Final Sounds	X	X					
Phoneme Matching: Medial Sounds	X	X					
Phoneme Manipulation: Initial Sounds	X	X					
Phoneme Manipulation: Final Sounds	X	X					
Phoneme Manipulation: Medial Sounds	X	X					
Segmentation: Final Consonants	X	X					
Segmentation: Initial Consonants/Blends		X					
Segmentation: Words/Word Parts	X	X					
Segmentation: Syllables	X	X					
Segmentation: Identifying the Number and Order of Sounds in Words	X	X					

Reading (continued)

	K	1	2	3	4	5	6
How the Alphabet Works							
Letter Knowledge (Alphabetic Knowledge)	X	X					
Letter Order (Alphabetic Order)	X	X					
Letter Sounds	X	X					
Sounds in Words	X	X					
Phonics (Associate Sounds and Spellings to Read Words)							
Blending Sounds into Words	X	X	X	X			
Consonant Clusters		X	X	X			
Consonant Digraphs		X	X	X			
Phonograms		X	X	X			
Schwa			X	X			
Silent Consonants			X	X			
Syllables		X	X	X			
Vowel Diphthongs		X	X	X			
Vowels: Long Sounds and Spellings	X	X	X	X			
Vowels: r-controlled		X	X	X			
Vowels: Short Sounds and Spellings	X	X	X	X			
Comprehension Strategies							
Adjusting Reading Speed			X	X	X	X	X
Asking Questions/Answering Questions	X	X	X	X	X	X	X
Clarifying	X	X	X	X	X	X	X
Making Connections	X	X	X	X	X	X	X
Predicting/Confirming Predictions	X	X	X	X	X	X	X
Summarizing		X	X	X	X	X	X
Visualizing	X	X	X	X	X	X	X
Comprehension Skills							
Author's Point of View			X	X	X	X	X
Author's Purpose			X	X	X	X	X
Cause and Effect	X	X	X	X	X	X	X
Classify and Categorize	X	X	X	X	X	X	X
Compare and Contrast	X	X	X	X	X	X	X
Drawing Conclusions	X	X	X	X	X	X	X
Fact and Opinion			X	X	X	X	X
Main Idea and Details	X	X	X	X	X	X	X
Making Inferences		X	X	X	X	X	X
Reality and Fantasy	X	X	X	X			
Sequence	X	X	X	X	X	X	X
Vocabulary							
Apposition		X	X	X	X	X	X
Concept Words		X	X	X	X	X	X
Context Clues		X	X	X	X	X	X
Expanding Vocabulary		X	X	X	X	X	X
High-Frequency Words	X	X	X	X			
Idioms					X	X	X
Multiple-Meaning Words		X	X	X	X	X	X
Selection Vocabulary	X	X	X	X	X	X	X
Time and Order Words (Creating Sequence)	X	X	X	X	X	X	X
Utility Words (Colors, Classroom Objects, etc.)	X	X					

Reading (continued)

Reading with a Writer's Eye	K	1	2	3	4	5	6
Author's Purpose	X		X	X	X	X	
Alliteration			X		X		X
Captions and Headings			X	X		X	X
Characterization	X	X	X	X	X	X	X
Choosing Good Examples				X	X		
Description			X	X	X	X	X
Diagrams							X
Dialect						X	
Dialogue			X	X	X	X	X
Effective Beginnings					X	X	
Effective Endings					X		
Event Sequence	X	X	X	X		X	
Expository Writing Techniques					X	X	
Fable Characteristics					X		
Figurative Language			X	X	X	X	X
Flashback							X
Genre Knowledge	X		X	X	X	X	X
Idiom						X	X
Irony					X		
Language Use	X		X	X	X	X	X
Mood and Tone		X	X	X			X
Onomatopoeia			X	X	X		X
Personification			X	X		X	X
Persuasive Techniques					X	X	
Plot (Problem/Solution)	X	X	X	X	X	X	X
Point of View					X	X	
Punctuation					X	X	
Quoting Sources					X		
Rhyme	X		X			X	X
Sensory Details		X		X		X	
Sentence Variety						X	
Setting	X	X	X	X	X	X	X
Sidebars							X
Similes and Metaphors					X	X	X
Stage Directions					X		
Style							X
Suspense and Surprise					X		X
Text Structure	X		X	X	X	X	X
Theme	X		X	X	X	X	X
Transitions					X		X
Using Comparisons		X	X	X		X	
Voice					X	X	X
Word Choice					X		X

Word Structure	K	1	2	3	4	5	6
Antonyms			X	X	X	X	X
Comparatives/Superlatives			X	X	X	X	
Compound Words	X	X	X	X	X	X	X
Contractions			X	X	X	X	
Connotation and Denotation							X
Content/Concept Words							X

Reading (continued)

	K	1	2	3	4	5	6
Foreign Words and Phrases						X	X
Gerunds							X
Greek and Latin Roots				X	X	X	X
Homographs			X	X	X	X	X
Homonyms/Homophones			X	X	X	X	X
Inflectional Endings			X	X	X	X	X
Irregular Plurals			X	X	X	X	
Multiple-Meaning Words					X	X	X
Multisyllabic Words			X	X	X	X	
Plurals			X	X	X	X	
Position Words	X	X					
Prefixes			X	X	X	X	X
Root or Base Words			X	X	X	X	X
Shades of Meaning/Levels of Specificity						X	X
Suffixes			X	X	X	X	X
Synonyms			X	X	X	X	X
Word Families			X	X	X	X	X
Word Origins					X	X	X

Inquiry and Study Skills

Study Skills	K	1	2	3	4	5	6
Comparing Information across Sources		X		X		X	
Charts, Graphs, and Diagrams/Visual Aids	X	X	X	X	X	X	X
Collaborative Inquiry	X	X	X	X	X	X	X
Communicating Research Progress Results		X	X	X	X	X	X
Compile Notes				X	X	X	X
Conducting an Interview		X	X	X	X	X	X
Finding Needed Information	X	X	X	X	X	X	X
Follow Directions	X		X	X	X		X
Formulate Questions for Inquiry and Research	X	X	X	X	X	X	X
Give Reports	X		X	X	X	X	X
Make Outlines			X	X	X	X	X
Making Conjectures	X	X	X	X	X	X	X
Maps	X	X	X	X	X	X	
Note Taking		X	X	X	X	X	X
Parts of a Book	X	X	X	X	X		
Planning Inquiry		X	X	X	X	X	X
Recognizing Information Needs		X	X	X	X	X	X
Revising Questions and Conjectures	X	X	X	X	X	X	X
Summarize and Organize Information		X	X	X	X	X	X
Time Lines			X	X	X	X	
Use Appropriate Resources (Media Sources, Reference Books, Experts, Internet)		X	X	X	X	X	X
Using a Dictionary/Glossary		X	X	X	X		
Using a Media Center/Library		X	X	X	X		
Using a Thesaurus			X	X	X	X	
Using an Encyclopedia		X	X	X	X		
Using Newspapers and Magazines		X	X		X		X
Using Technology	X	X	X	X	X	X	X

Language Arts

Writing/Composition

	K	1	2	3	4	5	6
Approaches							
Collaborative Writing	X	X	X	X	X	X	X
Individual Writing	X	X	X	X	X	X	X
Writing Process							
Brainstorming/Prewriting	X	X	X	X	X	X	X
Drafting	X	X	X	X	X	X	X
Revising	X	X	X	X	X	X	X
Editing	X	X	X	X	X	X	X
Proofreading	X	X	X	X	X	X	X
Publishing	X	X	X	X	X	X	X
Writing Genres							
Action Tale			X				
Autobiography/Biography	X	X	X	X	X	X	X
Book Review		X	X	X	X	X	
Business Letter			X	X		X	X
Describe a Process		X	X	X	X	X	X
Descriptive Writing	X	X	X	X	X	X	X
Expository/Informational Text	X	X	X	X	X	X	X
Fantasy		X	X	X			
Folklore (Folktales, Fairy Tales, Tall Tales, Legends, Myths)		X	X	X	X	X	
Friendly Letter	X	X	X	X	X	X	X
Historical Fiction					X		X
Invitation		X		X		X	
Journal Writing			X	X	X		
Magazine Article						X	X
Making a List	X	X	X	X	X	X	X
Mystery				X			
Narrative	X	X	X	X	X	X	X
News Story		X	X	X	X		
Personal Writing	X	X	X	X	X	X	X
Persuasive Writing	X	X	X	X	X	X	X
Play/Dramatization			X	X	X	X	X
Poetry	X	X	X	X	X	X	X
Realistic Fiction		X	X	X	X	X	X
Summary		X	X	X	X	X	X
Timed Writing		X	X	X	X	X	X
Writing Traits							
Audience		X	X	X	X	X	X
Conventions	X	X	X	X	X	X	X
Elaboration		X	X	X	X	X	X
Focus		X	X	X	X	X	X
Ideas/Content	X	X	X	X	X	X	X
Organization		X	X	X	X	X	X
Presentation	X	X	X	X	X	X	X
Purpose		X	X	X			
Sentence Fluency	X	X	X	X	X	X	X
Sentence Variety		X			X	X	X
Vocabulary		X	X	X	X	X	X
Voice	X	X	X	X	X	X	X
Word Choice	X	X	X	X	X	X	X

Language Arts
Writing/Composition (continued)

Writing Strategies	K	1	2	3	4	5	6
Action and Describing Words	X	X	X	X			
Adding Details	X	X	X	X	X	X	X
Addressing Audience Needs		X	X	X	X	X	X
Brainstorming	X	X	X	X	X	X	X
Categorizing Ideas						X	
Cause and Effect					X	X	X
Character Sketch					X	X	
Choosing a Topic	X	X	X	X	X	X	X
Compare and Contrast			X			X	X
Conveying a General Mood					X	X	X
Creating Suspense					X		X
Creating Vivid Images		X		X	X	X	
Dialogue	X	X	X	X	X	X	X
Effective Beginnings					X	X	X
Elements of a Letter		X	X	X	X	X	X
Elements of Persuasion			X	X	X	X	
Eliminating Irrelevant Information		X	X	X	X	X	X
Eliminating Wordiness			X	X	X	X	X
Evaluate Personal Growth as a Writer			X	X	X	X	
Explanatory Paragraphs		X					
Figurative Language			X	X	X	X	X
Formality of Language		X	X	X	X	X	
Format		X			X	X	X
Generate Additional Ideas		X	X	X	X		
Highlight a Memorable Event		X			X		
Identifying Best Feature of Something Written			X	X			
Illustrations and Drawings	X	X	X	X			
Information from Multiple Sources					X	X	X
Main Idea and Details					X	X	
Making Connections							X
Organizing a Multi-Paragraph Composition					X	X	X
Planning		X			X	X	X
Plot Structure—Beginning, Middle, Climax, and End		X		X	X	X	X
Point of View						X	X
Presenting Facts and Examples Objectively					X	X	X
Proofreading	X	X	X	X	X	X	X
Purpose		X	X	X	X	X	X
Realism					X	X	X
Referencing a Source					X	X	
Revising	X	X	X	X	X	X	X
Rhythm and Rhyme		X	X			X	
Sensory Details				X	X	X	X
Sentence Combining			X	X	X	X	X
Sequence	X	X	X	X		X	
Setting		X	X	X	X	X	X
Story Elements		X	X	X	X	X	
Style							X
Summary			X	X	X	X	X
Taking Notes		X	X	X	X	X	X

Language Arts

Writing/Composition (continued)

	K	1	2	3	4	5	6
Timed Writing		X	X	X	X	X	X
Time Line			X	X		X	
Transition Words/Devices			X	X	X	X	X
Using a Checklist		X	X	X	X	X	
Using a Graphic Organizer		X	X	X	X	X	X
Using a Model as a Guide to Writing			X	X		X	
Using Outlines to Organize Information				X	X	X	X
Using Multimedia Sources			X	X	X	X	X
Vary Sentence Beginnings			X	X	X	X	
Vary Sentence Length		X	X			X	
Vary Sentence Types	X	X	X	X	X	X	
Voice					X	X	
Voicing an Opinion		X				X	X
Word Choice		X	X	X	X	X	X
Working Collaboratively						X	X
Writing Coherent Paragraphs		X	X	X	X	X	X

Language Arts

Grammar

	K	1	2	3	4	5	6
Parts of Speech							
Adjectives (Describing Words)	X	X	X	X	X	X	X
Adverbs			X	X	X	X	X
Conjunctions			X	X	X	X	X
Nouns	X	X	X	X	X	X	X
Prepositions				X	X	X	X
Pronouns	X	X	X	X	X	X	X
Verbs	X	X	X	X	X	X	X
Sentences							
Complete and Incomplete Sentences		X	X	X	X	X	X
Fragments			X	X	X	X	X
Independent and Dependent Clauses							X
Parts (Subjects and Predicates)			X	X	X	X	X
Run-on Sentences					X		X
Sentence Combining			X	X	X	X	X
Structure (Simple, Compound, Complex, Compound-Complex)			X	X	X	X	X
Subject/Verb Agreement		X	X	X	X	X	X
Types (Declarative, Interrogative, Exclamatory, Imperative)	X	X	X	X	X	X	X
Usage							
Adjectives		X	X	X	X	X	X
Adverbs			X	X	X	X	X
Antonyms		X	X				
Articles			X	X		X	X
Contractions			X	X	X		
Nouns		X	X	X	X	X	X
Pronouns		X	X	X	X	X	X
Regular and Irregular Plurals					X	X	X
Synonyms		X	X				
Verb Tenses		X	X	X	X	X	X
Verbs (Action, Helping, Linking, Regular/Irregular)		X	X	X	X	X	X

Language Arts
Grammar (continued)

	K	1	2	3	4	5	6
Mechanics							
Capitalization (Sentence, Proper Nouns, Titles, Direct Address, Pronoun "I")	X	X	X	X	X	X	X
Punctuation (End Punctuation, Comma Use, Quotation Marks, Apostrophe, Colon, Semicolon, Hyphen, Parentheses)	X	X	X	X	X	X	X
Spelling							
Antonyms					X	X	X
Base or Root Words					X	X	
Comparatives/Superlatives				X	X	X	X
Compound Words				X	X	X	
Connotation and Denotation							X
Content/Concept Words							X
Contractions				X	X		X
Foreign Words and Phrases							X
Gerunds							X
Greek and Latin Roots				X	X	X	X
Homographs				X	X	X	X
Homonyms/Homophones				X	X	X	X
Inflectional Endings		X		X	X	X	X
Irregular Plurals		X		X	X	X	
Irregular Verbs					X		
Long Vowel Patterns		X	X	X	X		
Multiple-Meaning Words					X	X	X
Multisyllabic Words		X	X	X	X		X
Phonograms		X					
Prefixes				X	X	X	X
r-Controlled Vowel Spellings		X	X				
Shades of Meaning					X		X
Short Vowel Spellings		X	X	X	X		
Silent Letters			X	X	X		
Sound/Letter Relationships	X	X	X				
Special Spellings Patterns/Rules		X	X	X	X	X	
Special Vowel Spellings		X	X	X			
Suffixes		X		X	X	X	X
Synonyms					X	X	X
Word Families		X		X		X	X

Listening/Speaking/Viewing

	K	1	2	3	4	5	6
Listening							
Analyze/Evaluate Intent and Content of Speaker's Message		X	X	X		X	X
Ask Questions		X	X	X	X	X	X
Determine Purposes for Listening		X	X	X	X	X	X
Drawing Conclusions and Making Inferences						X	
Follow Directions	X	X		X	X	X	X
Learn about Different Cultures through Discussion					X	X	
Listen for Poetic Language (Rhythm/Rhyme)	X	X				X	X
Listening for Details			X	X	X		
Listening for Information				X	X		
Participate in Group Discussions	X	X	X	X	X	X	X
Recalling What Was Heard				X			
Recognizing Fact and Opinion				X			
Respond to Speaker	X	X	X	X	X	X	X
Use Nonverbal Communication Techniques		X		X	X	X	X
Speaking							
Answer Questions	X	X	X	X	X	X	X
Asking Questions		X		X	X		
Describe Ideas and Feelings	X	X	X				X
Effective Word Choice/Voice			X	X	X	X	
Engaging the Audience					X	X	
Give Directions		X			X	X	X
Learn About Different Cultures through Discussion		X		X			X
Listen and Respond		X		X	X		
Making Announcements and Introductions		X					
Organizing Presentations					X	X	X
Paraphrasing			X	X			
Participate in Group Discussion	X	X	X	X	X	X	X
Present Oral Reports		X	X	X	X	X	X
Purposes of Speech			X				
Read Fluently with Expression, Phrasing, and Intonation		X	X	X	X	X	X
Read Orally	X	X	X	X	X	X	X
Share Information		X	X	X	X	X	X
Small Group Discussion			X	X	X	X	X
Speak Clearly at Appropriate Volume		X	X	X	X	X	X
Speaking Strategies					X	X	
Staying on Topic		X					
Summarize/Retell Stories	X	X	X	X	X	X	X
Understand Formal and Informal Language		X		X	X	X	X
Use Appropriate Language for Audience		X		X	X	X	X
Use Nonverbal Communication Techniques		X	X	X	X	X	X

Listening/Speaking/Viewing (continued)

	K	1	2	3	4	5	6
Viewing							
Analyze Purposes and Techniques of the Media			X	X	X	X	X
Appreciate/Interpret Artist's Techniques		X					
Compare Visual and Written Material on the Same Subject		X					X
Culture in Media		X			X	X	
Describe Pictures			X				
Gather Information from Visual Images		X	X	X	X	X	X
Interpreting Media				X	X		
Language Development							X
Literary Devices				X			X
Relating to Content				X	X		
Understanding Gestures				X	X		
Using Multimedia				X	X	X	
View Critically		X		X	X	X	X
Penmanship							
Cursive Letters			X	X			
Manuscript Letters	X	X					
Numbers	X	X					

Unit Themes

	Level K	Level 1	Level 2
Unit 1	Off to School	Back to School	Kindness
Unit 2	Patterns	Where Animals Live	Let's Explore
Unit 3	Finding Friends	I Am Responsible!	Around the Town
Unit 4	By the Sea	Our Neighborhood at Work	Look Again
Unit 5	Stick to It	What's the Weather?	Courage
Unit 6	My Shadow	North, South, East, West	America's People
Unit 7	Teamwork	I Think I Can	
Unit 8	Ready, Set, Grow!	Away We Grow!	
Unit 9	Red, White, and Blue	Home, Sweet Home	
Unit 10	Windy Days	I Am Brave	

Level **3**	Level **4**	Level **5**	Level **6**
Friendship	Risks and Consequences	Heritage	Taking a Stand
Animals and Their Habitats	Nature's Delicate Balance	Energy at Work	Ancient Civilizations
Money	A Changing America	Making a New Nation	Ecology
Earth, Moon, and Sun	Science Fair	Our Corner of the Universe	Great Expectations
Communities across Time	America on the Move	Going West	Earth in Action
Storytelling	Dollars and Sense	Call of Duty	Art and Impact

Glossary of Reading Terms

This glossary includes linguistic, grammatical, comprehension, and literary terms that may be helpful in understanding reading instruction.

acronym a word formed from the initial letter of words in a phrase, **scuba (self-contained underwater breathing apparatus)**.

acrostic a kind of puzzle in which lines of a poem are arranged so that words or phrases are formed when certain letters from each line are used in a sequence.

adjective a word or group of words that modifies or describes a noun.

adventure story a narrative that features the unknown or unexpected with elements of excitement, danger, and risk.

adverb a word or group of words that modifies a verb, adjective, or other adverb. An adverb answers questions such as **how, when, where,** and **how much.**

affective domain the psychological field of emotional activities such as interests, attitudes, opinions, appreciations, values, and emotional sets

affix a word part, either a prefix or a suffix, that changes the meaning or function of a word root or stem.

affricate a speech sound that starts as a stop but ends as a fricative, the /ch/ in **catch.**

agreement the correspondence of syntactically related words; subjects and predicates are in agreement when both are singular or plural.

alliteration the repetition of the initial sounds in neighboring words or stressed syllables.

alphabet the complete set of letters representing speech sounds used in writing a language. In English there are twenty-six letters.

alphabet book a book for helping young children learn the alphabet by pairing letters with pictures whose sounds they represent.

alphabetic principle the association between sounds and the letters that represent them in alphabetic writing systems.

alveolar a consonant speech sound made when the tongue and the ridge of the upper and lower jaw stop to constrict the air flow, as /t/.

anagram a word or phrase whose letters form other words or phrases when rearranged, for example, **add** and **dad.**

analogy a likeness or similarity.

analytic phonics also deductive phonics, a whole-to-part approach to phonics in which a student is taught a number of sight words and then phonetic generalizations that can be applied to other words.

antonym a word that is opposite in meaning to another word.

appositive a word that restates or modifies a preceding noun, for example, **my daughter, Charlotte.** Appositives are also definitions of words usually set off by commas.

aspirate an unvoiced speech sound produced by a puff of air, as /h/ in **heart.**

aspirated stop a stop consonant sound released with a puff of air, as /k/, /p/, and /t/.

auditory discrimination the ability to hear phonetic likenesses and differences in phonemes and words.

author's purpose the motive or reason for which an author writes; includes to entertain, inform, persuade, and explain how.

automaticity fluent processing of information, requiring little effort or attention.

auxiliary verb a verb that precedes another verb to express time, mood, or voice; includes verbs such as **has, is,** and **will.**

ballad a narrative poem, composed of short verses to be sung or recited, usually containing elements of drama and often tragic in tone.

base word a word to which affixes may be added to create related words.

blank verse unrhymed verse, especially unrhymed iambic pentameter.

blend the joining of the sounds of two or more letters with little change in those sounds, for example, /spr/ in **spring;** also **consonant blend** or **consonant cluster.**

blending combining the sounds represented by letters or spellings to sound out or pronounce a word; contrast with **oral blending.**

breve the symbol placed above a vowel to indicate that it is a short vowel.

browse to skim through or look over in search of something of interest.

canon in literature, the body of major works that a culture considers important at a given time.

case a grammatical category that indicates the syntactic/semantic role of a noun phrase in a sentence.

cause-effect relationship a stated or implied association between an outcome and the conditions that brought it about; also the comprehension skill associated with recognizing this type of relationship as an organizing principle in text.

chapter book a book long enough to be divided into chapters, but not long or complex enough to be considered a novel.

characterization the way in which an author presents a character in a story, including describing words, actions, thoughts, and impressions of that character.

choral reading oral group reading to develop oral fluency by modeling.

cinquain a stanza of five lines, specifically one that has successive lines of two, four, six, eight, and two syllables.

cipher a system for writing in code.

clarifying a comprehension strategy in which the reader rereads text, uses a dictionary, uses decoding skills, or uses context clues to comprehend something that is unclear.

clause a group of words with a subject and a predicate used to form a part of or a whole sentence, a dependent clause modifies an independent clause, which can stand alone as a complete sentence.

collaborative learning learning by working together in small groups.

command a sentence that asks for action and usually ends with a period.

common noun in contrast to **proper noun,** a noun that denotes a class rather than a unique or specific thing such as **girl** versus **Susan.**

comprehension the understanding of what is written or said.

comprehension skill a skill that aids in understanding text, including identifying **author's purpose, author's point of view,** comprehending **cause-and-effect** relationships, **clarifying, comparing and contrasting** items and events, **drawing conclusions,** distinguishing **fact from opinion,** identifying **main ideas, making inferences,** distinguishing **reality from fantasy,** and understanding **sequence.**

comprehension strategy a sequence of steps for monitoring and understanding text, includes adjusting reading speed, asking questions, clarifying, making connections, predicting, summarizing, and visualizing.

conjugation the complete set of all possible inflected forms of a verb.

conjunction a part of speech used to connect words, phrases, clauses, or sentences, including the words **and, but,** and **or.**

consonant a speech sound, and the alphabet letter that represents that sound, made by partial or complete closure of part of the vocal tract, which obstructs air flow and causes audible friction.

context clue information from the immediate and surrounding text that helps identify a word.

contraction a short version of a written or spoken expression in which letters are omitted, for example, **can't.**

convention an accepted practice in spoken or written language, usually referring to spelling, mechanics, or grammar rules.

cooperative learning a classroom organization that allows students to work together to achieve their individual goals. Related term is **collaboration.**

creative writing prose and poetic forms of writing that express the writer's thoughts and feelings imaginatively.

cueing system any of the various sources of information that help identify an unrecognizable word in reading, including phonetic, semantic, and syntactical information.

cumulative tale a story, such as "The Gingerbread Man," in which details are repeated until the climax.

dangling modifier usually a participle that because of its placement in a sentence modifies the wrong object.

decodable text text materials controlled to include a majority of words whose sound/spelling relationships are known by the reader.

decode to analyze spoken or graphic symbols for meaning.

diacritical mark a mark, such as a breve or macron, added to a letter or graphic character to indicate a specific pronunciation.

dialect a regional variety of a particular language with phonological, grammatical, and lexical patterns that distinguishes it from other varieties.

dialogue a piece of writing written as conversation, usually punctuated by quotation marks.

digraph two letters that represent one speech sound, for example, /sh/ or /ch/.

diphthong a vowel sound produced when the tongue glides from one vowel sound toward another in the same syllable, for example, /oi/ or /ou/.

direct object the person or thing that receives the action of a verb in a sentence, for example, the word **cake** in this sentence: **Madeline baked a cake.**

drafting the process of writing ideas in rough form to record them.

drama a story in the form of a play, written to be performed.

edit in the writing process, to revise or correct a manuscript. Often this is part of the final step in the process with a focus on correcting grammar, spelling, and mechanics rather than content, structure, and organization.

emergent literacy the development of the association of meaning and print that continues until a child reaches the stage of conventional reading and writing.

emergent reading a child's early interaction with books and print before the ability to decode text.

encode to change a message into symbols, for example, to change speech into writing.

epic a long narrative poem, usually about a hero.

exclamatory sentence a sentence that shows strong emotion and ends with an exclamation point.

expository writing or **exposition** a composition in writing that explains an event or process.

fable a short tale that teaches a moral.

fantasy a highly imaginative story about characters, places, and events that cannot exist.

fiction imaginative narrative designed to entertain rather than to explain, persuade, or describe.

figure of speech the expressive, nonliteral use of language usually through metaphor, simile, or personification.

fluency freedom from word-identification problems that hinder comprehension in reading. Fluency involves rate, accuracy, and expression.

folktale a narrative form of genre such as an epic, myth, or fable that is well-known through repeated storytellings.

foreshadowing giving clues to upcoming events in a story.

free verse verse with irregular metrical pattern.

freewriting writing that is not limited in form, style, content, or purpose; designed to encourage students to write.

genre a classification of literary works, including tragedy, comedy, novel, essay, short story, mystery, realistic fiction, and poetry.

grammar the study of the classes of words, their inflections, and their functions and relations in sentences; includes phonological, morphological, syntactic, and semantic descriptions of a language.

grapheme a written or printed representation of a phoneme, such as **c** for /k/.

guided reading reading instruction in which the teacher provides the structure and purpose for reading and responding to the material read.

handing off a method of turning over to students the primary responsibility for controlling discussion.

indirect object in a sentence, the person or thing to or for whom an action is done, for example, the word **dog** in this sentence: **Madeline gave the dog a treat.**

inference a conclusion based on facts, data, or evidence.

infinitive the base form of a verb, usually with the infinitive marker, for example, **to go.**

inflectional ending an ending that expresses a plural or possessive form of a noun, the tense of a verb, or the comparative or superlative form of an adjective or adverb.

interrogative word a word that marks a clause or sentence as a question, including **interrogative pronouns who, what, which, where.**

intervention a strategy or program designed to supplement or substitute instruction, especially for those students who fall behind.

invented spelling the result of an attempt to spell a word based on using the sounds in the letter names to determine the sound the letter names. Gradually sounds are connected to letters, which leads to conventional spelling..

irony a figure of speech in which the literal meanings of the words is the opposite of their intended meanings.

journal a written record of daily events or responses.

juvenile book a book written for children or adolescents.

legend a traditional tale handed down from generation to generation.

leitmotif a repeated expression, event, or idea used to unify a work of art such as writing.

letter one of a set of graphic symbols that forms an alphabet and is used alone or in combination to represent a phoneme, also **grapheme.**

linguistics the study of the nature and structure of language and communication.

literary elements the elements of a story such as **setting, plot,** and **characterization** that create the structure of a narrative.

macron a diacritical mark placed above a vowel to indicate a long vowel sound.

main idea the central thought or chief topic of a passage.

making connections a reading strategy used to connect information being read to one's own experiences to other reading materials or to one's knowledge of the world. Making connections fosters engagement, while reading helps the reader make sense of the text and connect information.

mechanics the conventions of capitalization and punctuation.

metacognition awareness and knowledge of one's mental processes or thinking about what one is thinking about.

metaphor a figure of speech in which a comparison is implied but not stated; for example, **She is a jewel.**

miscue a deviation from text during oral reading in an attempt to make sense of the text.

modeling an instructional technique in which the teacher makes public the thinking needed to use critical reading and writing behaviors.

mood the literary element that conveys the emotional atmosphere of a story.

morpheme a meaningful linguistic unit that cannot be divided into smaller units, for example, **word**; **a bound morpheme** is a morpheme that cannot stand alone as an independent word, for example, the prefix **re-**; a **free morpheme** can stand alone, for example, **dog.**

myth a story designed to explain the mysteries of life.

narrative writing or **narration** a composition in writing that tells a story or gives an account of an event.

nonfiction prose designed to explain, argue, or describe rather than to entertain with a factual emphasis; includes biography and autobiography.

noun a part of speech that denotes persons, places, things, qualities, or acts.

novel an extended fictional prose narration.

onomatopoeia the use of a word whose sound suggests its meaning, for example, **purr.**

oral blending the ability to fuse discrete phonemes into recognizable words; oral blending puts sounds together to make a word, **see also segmentation.**

orthography correct or standardized spelling according to established usage in a language.

oxymoron a figure of speech in which contrasting or contradictory words are brought together for emphasis.

paragraph a subdivision of a written composition that consists of one or more sentences, deals with one point, or gives the words of one speaker, usually beginning with an indented line.

participle a verb form used as an adjective, for example, **the skating party.**

personification a figure of speech in which animals, ideas, or things take on human characteristics.

persuasive writing a composition intended to persuade the reader to adopt the writer's point of view.

phoneme the smallest sound unit of speech, for example, the /k/ in **book.**

phonemic awareness the ability to recognize that spoken words are made of discrete sounds and that those sounds can be manipulated.

phonetic spelling the respelling of entry words in a dictionary according to a pronunciation key.

phonetics the study of speech sounds.

phonics a way of teaching reading that addresses sound/symbol relationships, especially in beginning instruction.

phonogram a letter or symbol that represents a phonetic sound.

phonological awareness the ability to attend to the sound structure of language; includes sentence, word, syllable rhyme and phonological awareness.

plot the literary element that provides the structure of the action of a story, which may include rising action, climax, and falling action leading to a resolution or denouement.

plural a grammatical form of a word that refers to more than one in number; an irregular plural is one that does not follow normal patterns for inflectional endings.

poetic license the liberty taken by writers to ignore conventions.

poetry a metrical form of composition in which language is chosen and arranged to create a powerful response through meaning, sound, or rhythm.

possessive showing ownership either through the use of an adjective, an adjectival pronoun, or the possessive form of a noun.

predicate the part of the sentence that expresses something about the subject and includes the verb phrase; a **complete predicate** includes the principal verb in a sentence and all its modifiers or subordinate parts.

predicting a comprehension strategy in which the reader attempts to anticipate what will happen, using clues from the text and prior knowledge, and then confirms predictions as the text is read.

prefix an affix attached before a base word that changes the meaning of the word.

preposition a part of speech in the class of function words such as **of, on,** and **at** that precede noun phrases to create prepositional phrases.

prewriting the planning stage of the writing process in which the writer formulates ideas, gathers information, and considers ways to organize them.

print awareness in emergent literacy, a child's growing recognition of conventions and characteristics of written language, including reading from left to right and from top to bottom in English and that words are separated by spaces.

pronoun a part of speech used as a substitute for a noun or noun phrase.

proofreading the act of reading with the intent to correct, clarify, or improve text.

pseudonym an assumed name used by an author; a pen name or nom de plume.

publishing the process of preparing written material for presentation.

punctuation graphic marks such as commas, periods, quotation marks, and brackets used to clarify meaning and to give speech characteristics to written language.

question an interrogative sentence that asks a question and ends with a question mark.

realistic fiction a story that attempts to portray characters and events as they actually are.

rebus a picture or symbol that suggests a word or syllable.

revise in the writing process, to change or correct a manuscript to make its message more clear.

rhyme identical or very similar recurring final sounds in words, often at the ends of lines of poetry.

rime a vowel and any following consonants of a syllable.

segmentation the ability to break words into individual sounds; **see also oral blending.**

semantic mapping a graphic display of a group of words that are meaningfully related to support vocabulary instruction.

semantics the study of meaning in language, including the meanings of words, phrases, sentences, and texts.

sentence a grammatical unit that expresses a statement, question, or command; a **simple sentence** is a sentence with one subject and one predicate; a **compound sentence** is a sentence with two or more independent clauses usually separated by a comma and conjunction, but no dependent clause; a **complex sentence** is a sentence with one independent and one or more dependent clauses.

sentence combining a teaching technique in which complex sentence chunks and paragraphs are built from basic sentences.

sentence lifting the process of using sentences from children's writing to illustrate what is wrong or right to develop children's editing and proofreading skills.

sequence the order of elements or events.

setting the literary element that includes the time, place, and physical and psychological background in which a story takes place.

sight word a word that is taught to be read as a whole word, usually words that are phonetically irregular.

simile a figure of speech in which a comparison of two things that are unlike is directly stated, usually with the words **like** or **as**; for example, **She is like a jewel.**

spelling the process of representing language by means of a writing system.

statement a sentence that tells something and ends with a period.

study skills a general term for the techniques and strategies that help readers comprehend text with the intent to remember; includes following directions, organizing, locating, and using graphic aids.

style the characteristics of a work that reflect the author's particular way of writing.

subject the main topic of a sentence to which a predicate refers, including the principal noun; a **complete subject** includes the principal noun in a sentence and all its modifiers.

suffix an affix attached at the end of a base word that changes the meaning and the function of the word.

summarizing a comprehension strategy in which the reader constructs a brief statement that contains the essential ideas of a passage.

syllable a minimal unit of sequential speech sounds comprised of a vowel sound or a vowel-sound combination.

symbolism the use of one thing to represent something else to represent an idea in a concrete way.

synonym a word that means the same as another word.

syntax the grammatical pattern or structure of word order in sentences, clauses, and phrases.

tense the way in which verbs indicate past, present, and future time of action.

text structure the various patterns of ideas that are built into the organization of a written work.

theme a major idea or proposition that provides an organizing concept through which, by study, students gain depth of understanding.

topic sentence a sentence intended to express the main idea of a paragraph or passage.

tragedy a literary work, often a play, in which the main character suffers conflicts and which presents a serious theme and has an unfortunate ending.

usage the way in which a native language or dialect is used by the members of the community.

verb a word that expresses an action or state that occurs in a predicate of a sentence; an irregular verb is a verb that does not follow normal patterns of inflectional endings that reflect past, present, or future verb tense.

visualizing a comprehension strategy in which the reader constructs a mental picture of a character, setting, or process.

vowel a voiced speech sound and the alphabet letter that represents that sound, made without stoppage or friction of the air flow as it passes through the vocal tract.

vowel digraph a spelling pattern in which two or more letters represent a single vowel sound.

word calling proficiency in decoding with little or no attention to word meaning.

writing also **composition** the process or result of organizing ideas in writing to form a clear message; includes persuasive, expository, narrative, and descriptive forms.

writing process the many aspects of the complex act of producing a piece of writing, including prewriting, drafting, revising, editing/proofreading, and publishing.

Songs and Games

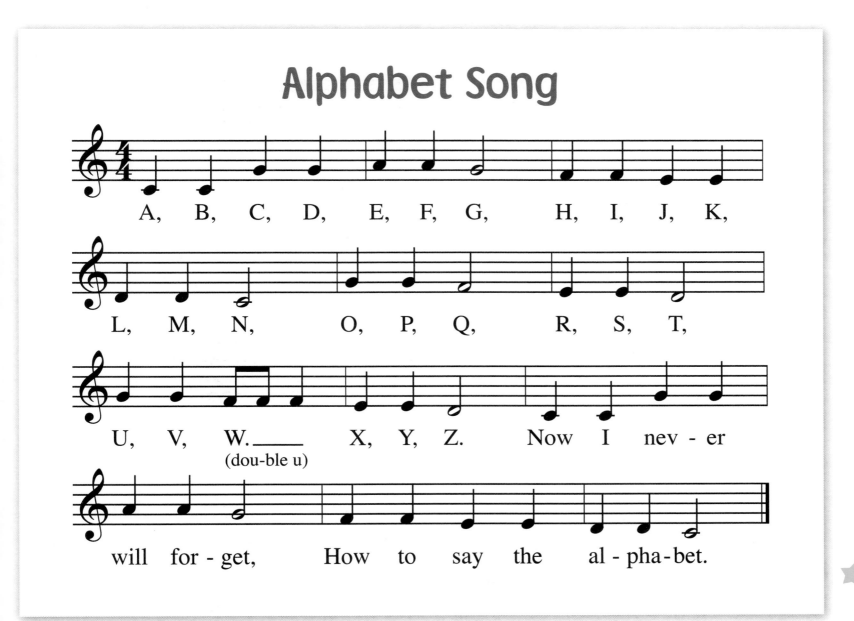

Alphabet Song

A, B, C, D, E, F, G, H, I, J, K,

L, M, N, O, P, Q, R, S, T,

U, V, W.____ X, Y, Z. Now I nev - er
(dou-ble u)

will for - get, How to say the al - pha-bet.

a b c d e f g
h i j k l m n
o p q
r s t
u v w
x y z

Alphabet Rap

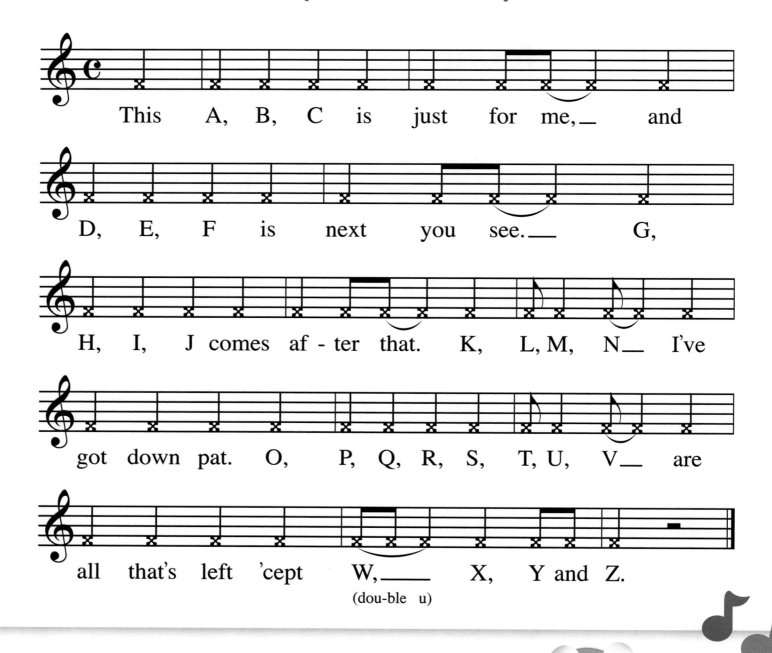

This A, B, C is just for me,___ and

D, E, F is next you see.___ G,

H, I, J comes af-ter that. K, L, M, N___ I've

got down pat. O, P, Q, R, S, T, U, V___ are

all that's left 'cept W,___ X, Y and Z.
(dou-ble u)

Alphabet Cheer

We're So Glad You're Here

We're so glad you're here.
We're so glad you're here.
We're so glad that Jor - dan's here.
We're so glad he's here.

We're so glad you're here
We're so glad you're here
We're so glad that <u>Katie</u>'s here
We're so glad <u>she</u>'s here

We're so glad you're here
We're so glad you're here
We're so glad that _____'s here
We're so glad ___'s here

If You're Happy and You Know It

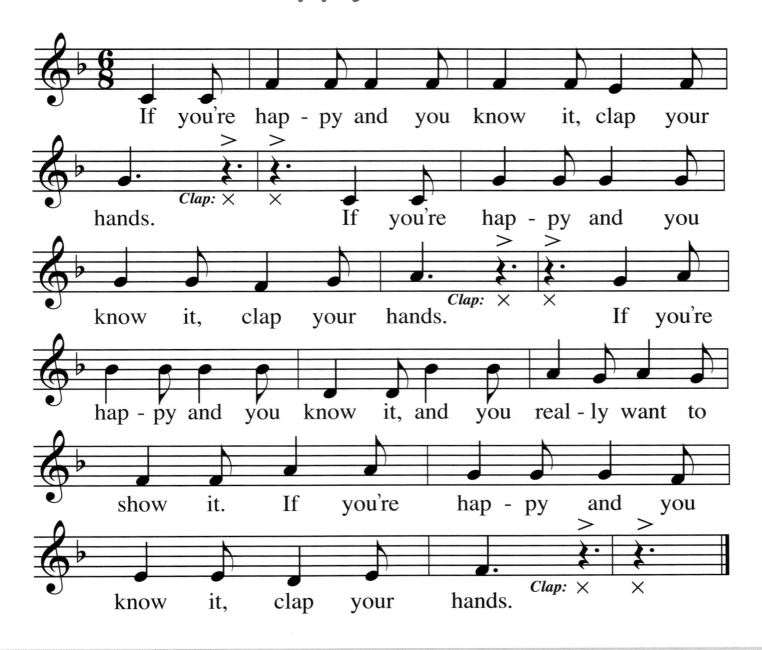

This is the Way We Come to Circle

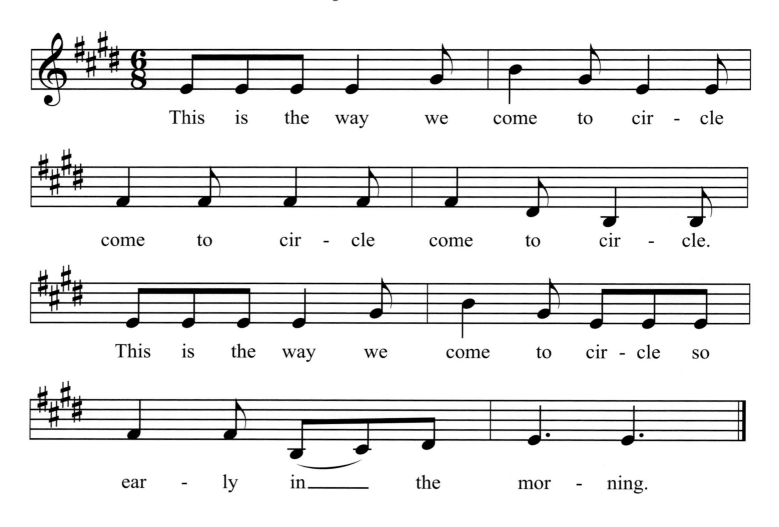

This is the way we sit right down,
Sit right down, sit right down.
This is the way we sit right down,
So early in the morning.

This is the way we fold our hands,
Fold our hands, fold our hands.
This is the way we fold our hands,
So early in the morning.

Hello

Hel - lo   Lu - cy.   Hel - lo   Lu - cy.

Hel - lo   Lu - cy   please   stand   and   take   a   bow.

Hello <u>Jose</u>, hello <u>Jose</u>,
Hello <u>Jose</u>, please stand, and take a bow.

Hello _____, hello _____,
Hello _____, please stand, and take a bow.

I'm a Little Teapot

I'm a lit - tle tea - pot short and stout,

Here is my han - dle, here is my spout.

When I get all steamed up, hear me shout,

Tip me o - ver and pour me out.

Are You Sleeping?

Where   is   Char - lotte?   Where   is   Char - lotte?

Here   I   am!   Here   I   am!

Hel - lo   to   you, Char - lotte.   We   are   glad   to   see   you.

Take   a   bow.   Take   a   bow.

Where is <u>Charlotte</u>? Where is <u>Charlotte</u>?
Here I am! Here I am!
Hello to you <u>Charlotte</u>. We are glad to see you.
Take a bow. Take a bow.

Where is _____? Where is _____?
Here I am! Here I am!
Hello to you _____. We are glad to see you.
Take a bow. Take a bow.

Hokey Pokey

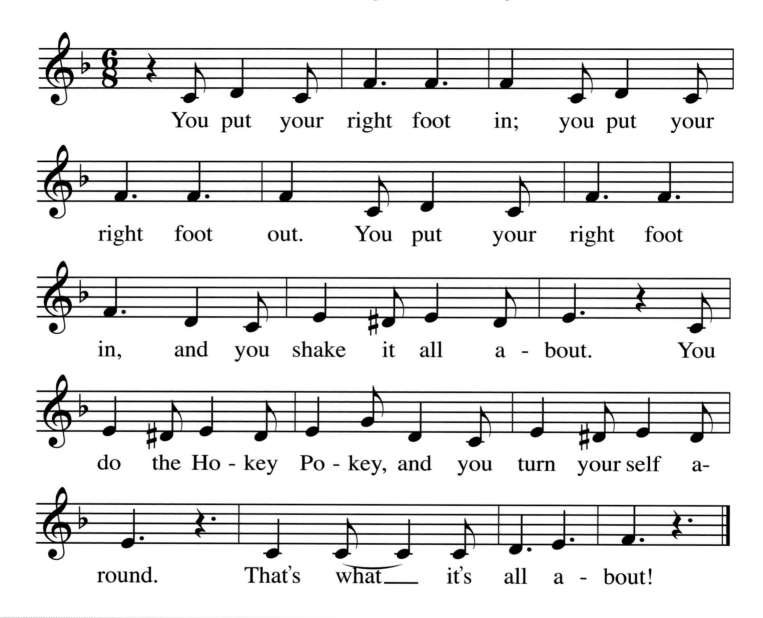

You put your right hand in; you take your right hand out.
You put your right hand in, and you shake it all about.
You do the hokey pokey, and you turn yourself around.
That's what it's all about!

You put your left foot in; you take your left foot out.
You put your left foot in, and you shake it all about.
You do the hokey pokey, and you turn yourself around.
That's what it's all about!

You put your left hand in; you take your left hand out.
You put your left hand in, and you shake it all about.
You do the hokey pokey, and you turn yourself around.
That's what it's all about!

Teddy Bear, Teddy Bear

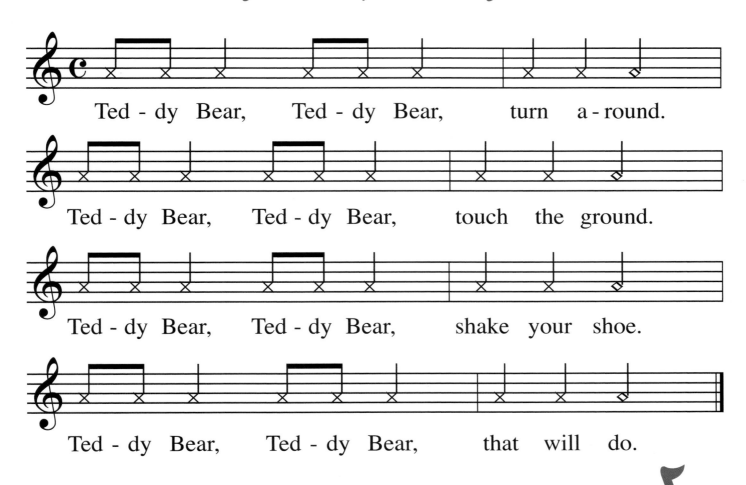

Ted - dy Bear,   Ted - dy Bear,   turn a - round.

Ted - dy Bear,   Ted - dy Bear,   touch   the   ground.

Ted - dy Bear,   Ted - dy Bear,   shake   your   shoe.

Ted - dy Bear,   Ted - dy Bear,   that   will   do.

Down By the Bay

Down by the bay
Where the watermelons grow
Back to my home
I dare not go
For if I do
My mother will say
"Did you ever see a bear
Combing his hair?"
Down by the bay

Down by the bay
Where the watermelons grow
Back to my home
I dare not go
For if I do
My mother will say
"Did you ever see a moose
Kissing a goose?"
Down by the bay

Down by the bay
Where the watermelons grow
Back to my home
I dare not go
For if I do
My mother will say
"Did you ever see a whale
With a polka dot tail?"
Down by the bay

Apples and Bananas

1.) I like to eat, eat, eat,___ ap - ples and ba-
2.) I like to ate, ate, ate,___ ay - ples and bay-

nan - as._____ I like to eat, eat,
nay - nays._____ I like to ate, ate,

eat,_____ ap - ples and ba - nan - as.
ate,_____ ay - ples and bay - nay - nays.

Vowel Song

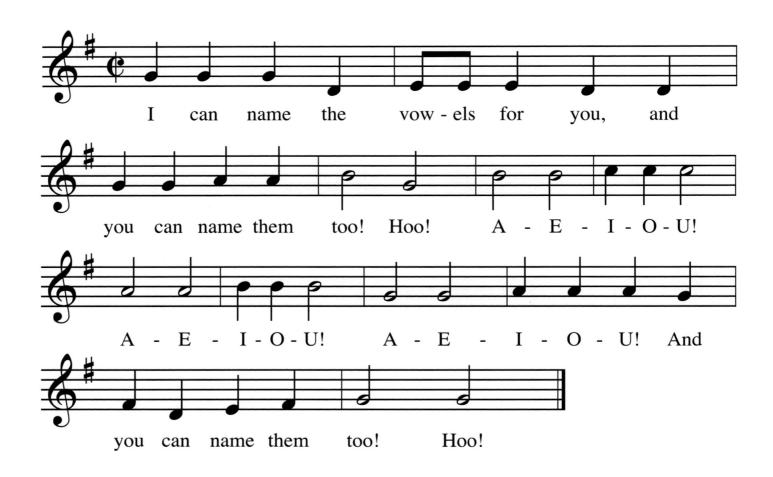

I can name the vow - els for you, and

you can name them too! Hoo! A - E - I - O - U!

A - E - I - O - U! A - E - I - O - U! And

you can name them too! Hoo!

The Ship Is Loaded With _____

Purpose

To provide students with a movement activity that will reinforce rhyming words and initial consonant sounds

Instruction

Have students sit in a circle. Explain that you are loading a ship with items that sound alike. Each student will have a chance to say a rhyming word. Use a ball or anything that can be rolled from student to student. Ask for a volunteer, and have that student say *The ship is loaded with cheese.* The student then rolls the ball to someone else who must repeat the line, substituting a rhyming word for cheese (for example, *peas, bees, keys, breeze, fleas,* or *trees).*

At this point, you might have the student roll the ball back to the first student, who will repeat *The ship is loaded with* cheese. Or have the student roll the ball to someone else for a new rhyming word.

Play the game using the following words:

The ship is loaded with *cats (mats, rats, bats, hats).*

The ship is loaded with *logs (frogs, hogs, dogs, bogs).*

The ship is loaded with *cans (fans, bans, Dans, pans).*

Play The Ship Is Loaded with _____ game, and have students choose words with the same initial sound. For example, if they choose /b/, students can say *The ship is loaded with* basketballs, begonias, baseballs, balls, *and* blankets.

Ordering Letters Game

Give each student a set of **Alphabet Letter Cards** *Aa–Nn.* (You may add letters as the student's knowledge of new letters increases). The cards in each set should be shuffled out of order and should face different ways.

Tell students they should do two things with these cards. First they should turn all the cards so they are showing either all capitals or all small letters. Then students should each show the set to a partner to check.

Next have each student work with a partner and match each capital letter with a small letter.

Simon Says

Purpose

To reinforce word concepts using a game format

Instruction

Tell students you are going to play Simon says. For those unfamiliar with the game, explain that when Simon says to do something, they must follow the instructions. Also, tell them they should not follow any directions that do not start with the words *Simon says*. Give the following instructions:

Simon says pat your head.
(Students pat their heads.)

Simon says rub your tummy.
(Students rub their tummies.)

Simon says hop on one foot.
(Students hop on one foot.)

Simon says hop on your left foot.
(Students hop on their left feet.)

After giving several different instructions, give another one, omitting *Simon says:*

Jump in place.

(Students should stand still.)

Students are "out" when they

- do something Simon does not say to do.
- do something other than what Simon says.
- do not do what Simon says.

When a student is "out," you can have him or her sit down. Continue the game until one student is left standing. Another alternative is to give each student an **Alphabet Letter Card** to identify if they miss an instruction. If the student correctly identifies the letter, he or she can stay in the game.

To reinforce language skills, try different and gradually more challenging instructions, such as the following:

- Students can touch their noses and then turn around.
- Add numbers *(jump three times; clap four times; pat tummy once).*
- Add prepositions and prepositional phrases designating location *(over, under, in front of, behind).*
- Add conjunctions (hop *and* skip).
- Use adjectives (take *big* steps).
- Use adjectival strings (*take three big* steps).
- Use adverbs *(clap softly).*
- Add negatives *(don't clap your hands).*
- Add conditionals *if, when, unless, until, while (rub your tummy while you pat your head).*

Mat Games

Purpose

To help students match sounds to letters

Instruction

Play each of these games on a **Game Mat,** using game markers to move around the squares. Place the mat on a table or on the floor. Have students gather around the mat, and explain to them that as they move around the squares, they will be naming letters and sounds.

Each of the **Game Mats** is generic and can be used for not only the games described here, but also for games you create with students. You and your class might enjoy creating variations of the games described here or creating entirely new games to play on the mats.

Create new rules and difficulty levels as your class needs or wants them. Challenge students to think of new games to play on the mats.

Difficulty Levels

The levels of difficulty described here are simply suggestions. Your students may need to begin with much easier tasks, or they may not be challenged enough by them. Always suit the games to the activities and levels of difficulty where you know your class will be most comfortable. The games should be difficult enough to challenge students yet easy enough for them to experience success and have fun.

Hop Along Game

The object of this game is to move the game marker from the bunny to the carrot at the end of the trail. Use a number cube to determine how many spaces a student may move the marker along the trail. If the student lands on a letter, he or she must do one of the following, depending on the level of difficulty you have chosen:

Name the letter	(Level 1)
Name the sound of the letter	(Level 2)

If the student does not name the correct letter or sound, he or she must do one of the following:

Lose a turn	(Level 1)
Go back a space until he or she is able to name the correct letter or sound	(Level 2)

If the student lands on a happy face, he or she may take an extra turn.

Ball Diamond, School Yard, A Day at the Beach, My Neighborhood, Race Track

Play all these games with the same rules. Each student rolls the number cube and moves the game marker the correct number of spaces. Use the **Alphabet Letter Cards** for Level 1 and the **Alphabet Sound Cards** for the card pack on Levels 2, 3, and 4. Have each student draw a card. Depending on the level, students will do the following:

State the name of the letter   (Level 1)

State the sound the letter makes   (Level 2)

Name a word that begins with   (Level 3)
the sound

Name the letter, the sound,   (Level 4)
and a word that begins with the sound

If students do not guess correctly, they lose the next turn.

Winning the Games

These games can be played quickly, or you can have students extend them. For a quick game, have them play until the first student reaches the goal at the end of the trail. If a student has not reached the goal when the cards run out, the student closest to the goal wins.

To extend the games, tell students to shuffle the cards when the last card has been chosen and to keep playing. The number of times the cards are shuffled will determine the length of the game. Again, the student who reaches the goal or is closest to the goal when the cards run out for the last time wins the game.

Challenges

These games are designed to be played independently by students. This means students must determine whether each given answer is correct. Encourage them to discuss any differences of opinion they may have. If they are not able to decide whether the answer is correct, tell them to raise their hands so you can help them.

Penmanship

SRA Imagine It! develops handwriting skills through Penmanship lessons three days each week. The instruction for these lessons appears in the Sounds and Letters part in this grade level. The purpose of these lessons is to develop important handwriting skills necessary for producing legible, properly spaced documents. In kindergarten, penmanship practice reinforces the sound-letter correspondence in the lesson.

The overhead projector, in addition to the board, can be an effective device for teaching penmanship. Students can move their pencils at the same time you form letters on the transparency. To further help students, you should also recite the descriptions or chants that go with each letter.

Penmanship in Grades K–1

Beginning in kindergarten, the Penmanship lessons expand on the sound/letter instruction by introducing letters students study in Sounds and Letters. Students learn that those letters are made of four basic lines: curved lines, horizontal lines, vertical lines, and slanted lines.

Next students learn letter and number formation. Students practice letter formation by writing the letter being studied and then words that contain the particular letter. This instruction continues in Level 1 and is tied to the letter formation instruction in Language Arts.

Manuscript Penmanship Models

The lessons present ball-and-stick models of manuscript handwriting, while this appendix offers an alternative method with continuous stroke models.

Hand and Paper Positioning

The **hand and paper positioning** models are for your reference and enhance the written instruction of positioning lessons. The diagrams give you a visual aid so you may better understand and demonstrate an effective technique of positioning.

A right-handed student should hold the pencil loosely about one inch above the point, between the thumb and middle finger. A left-handed student should hold the pencil the same way, but up to one half inch farther away from the point. The index fingers of both writers should rest lightly on the top of the pencil. The wrist should be level and slightly raised from the desk.

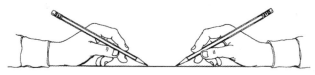

Left-handed writers   Right-handed Writers

For both kinds of writers, the paper should lie straight in front of the student with the edges parallel to the edges of the desk. A left-handed writer may find it easier to slant the paper slightly to the right and parallel to the left forearm. A right-handed writer's writing hand should be kept well below the writing. The left hand should hold down the paper.

Left-handed writers   Right-handed Writers

Ball and Stick Penmanship Models

The **ball-and-stick** models of manuscript handwriting provide you with a systematic method for teaching students to form uppercase and lowercase letters of the alphabet. The dots on the letters indicate starting points for students. The numbered arrows show students in which order and direction the line they are drawing should go to form the particular letter. You may use the chants to describe the letter step by step as students model the formation on the board. Students may also recite the chants in unison as they practice the formation, whether they are writing the letter or tracing it on the board.

Ball-and-Stick Penmanship Models

capital *A*

a   Starting point, around left all
the way
Starting point, straight down,
touching the circle: small *a*

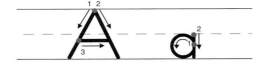

A   Starting point, slanting down left
Starting point, slanting down right
Starting point, across the middle:

B   Starting point, straight down
Starting point, around right and in
at the middle, around right and in at

d   Starting point, around left all
the way
Starting point, straight down,
touching the circle: small *d*

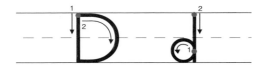

D   Starting point, straight down
Starting point, around right and in
at the bottom: capital *D*

E   Starting point, straight down
Starting point, straight out
Starting point, straight out

g   Starting point, around left all
the way
Starting point, straight down,
touching the circle, around left to
stopping place: small *g*

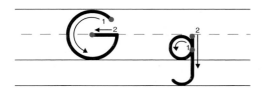

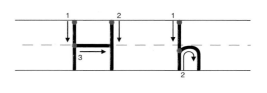

G   Starting point, around left, curving
up and around
Straight in: capital *G*

H   Starting point, straight down
Starting point, straight down
Starting point, across the middle:

Ball-and-Stick Penmanship Models

j   Starting point, straight down,
around left to stopping place
Dot exactly above: small *j*

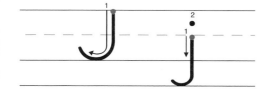

J   Starting point, straight down,
around left to stopping place:
capital *J*

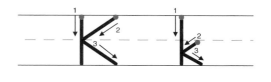

K   Starting point, straight down
Starting point, slanting down left,
touching the line, slanting down

right, straight down: capital *M*

m   Starting point, straight down, back
up, around right, straight down,
back up, around right, straight
down: small *m*

n   Starting point, straight down, back
up, around right, straight down:
small *n*

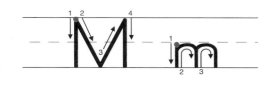

M   Starting point, straight down
Starting point, slanting down right
to the point, slanting back up to the

N   Starting point, straight down
Starting point, slanting down right,
straight back up: capital *N*

p   Starting point, straight down
Starting point, around right all the
way, touching the line: small *p*

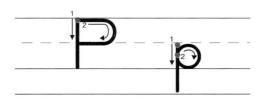

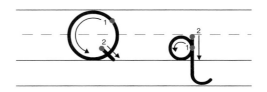

P   Starting point, straight down
Starting point, around right and in
at the middle: capital *P*

Q   Starting point, around left all the
way
Starting point, slanting down right:

Ball-and-Stick Penmanship Models

S   Starting point, around left, curving right and down around right,

curving left and up to stopping place: small s

S   Starting point, around left, curving right and down around right, curving left and up: capital S

T   Starting point, straight across Starting point, straight down: capital T

V   Starting point, slanting down right, slanting up right: small v

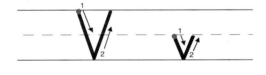

V   Starting point, slanting down right, slanting up right: capital V

Y   Starting point, slanting down right, stop
Starting point, slanting down left, stop
Starting point, straight down: capital Y

y   Starting point, slanting down right
Starting point, slanting down left, connecting the lines: small y

Z   Starting point, straight across, slanting down left, straight across: capital Z

W   Starting point, slanting down right, slanting up right, slanting down right, slanting up right: capital W

z   Starting point, straight across, slanting down left, straight across: small z

Continuous Stroke Penmanship Models

Continuous stroke models of manuscript handwriting provide you with an alternative to the ball-and-stick method. The purpose of these models is geared toward teaching students to write letters without lifting their pencils.

A a B b C c D d E e

F f G g H h I i J j

K k L l M m N n O o

P p Q q R r S s T t

U u V v W w X x

Y y Z z

Numbers

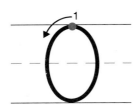

0 Starting point, curving left all the way around to starting point: *0*

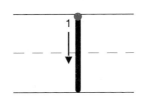

1 Starting point, straight down: *1*

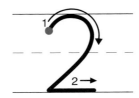

2 Starting point, around right, slanting left and straight across right: *2*

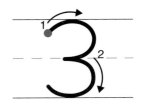

3 Starting point, around right, in at the middle, around right: *3*

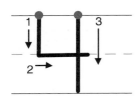

4 Starting point, straight down
Straight across right
Starting point, straight down, crossing line: *4*

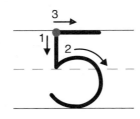

5 Starting point, straight down, curving around right and up
Starting point, straight across right: *5*

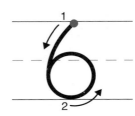

6 Starting point, slanting left, around the bottom curving up, around right and into the curve: *6*

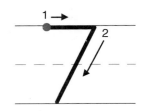

7 Starting point, straight across right, slanting down left: *7*

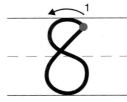

8 Starting point, curving left, curving down and around right, slanting up right to starting point: *8*

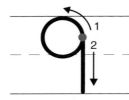

9 Starting point, curving around left all the way, straight down: *9*

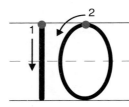

10 Starting point, straight down
Starting point, curving left all the way around to starting point: *10*

Alphabet Activities

Purpose

To provide students with activities for reinforcement of letter shapes

About the Activities

During Workshop of lessons in which you introduce letters, include activities in which students can make letters. Activities like these are included in the lessons already, while some letter-making activities you can establish in your classroom are listed below.

Most students will probably need a visual model to help them get started. Use red, blue, or green markers to print the letters on sturdy cardboard or poster board cards. Students will make yarn letters, glue letters, or other types by tracing the model.

All these activities, in addition to reinforcing letter formation, will help students' visual, perceptual, and fine-motor development.

Yarn Letters

Give each student four 4-inch pieces, four 8-inch pieces, and four 12-inch pieces of heavy yarn (such as rug yarn) to form letters. Each different length of yarn can be a different color (for example, 4-inch—red, 8-inch—blue, and 12-inch—green). When you work with students to form a particular letter, you can help them by using colors. For example, if students are making a capital A, they can use one blue piece and one red. Keep the yarn pieces in small plastic bags for reuse each time you introduce a new letter.

Clay Letters

Have students roll modeling clay into sticks that can be broken into different lengths and curved as necessary to form letters. When they are finished, have students roll their letters back into balls of clay. Keep these in sealed plastic bags for reuse.

Sand Letters

Provide each student with a small Styrofoam grocery tray filled halfway with sand. Have students trace with their fingers the letters they are practicing. In later lessons, have students trace words.

Pipe Cleaner Letters

Cut 12-inch pipe cleaners into 4-inch and 8-inch pieces, leaving some 12-inch pieces. Instruct students to form letters with the different lengths of pipe cleaners.

Glue Letters

Provide each student with large printed models of the letters. Tell students to trace the letters with glue and then sprinkle the glue with glitter, colored sand, confetti, salt, oatmeal, rice, or any other material that is not too bulky to stick to the glue. After the glue has begun to dry, have students shake off any excess material.

Drinking Straw Letters

Cut 8-inch drinking straws in half to make 4-inch pieces. Then cut them in fourths to make 2-inch pieces. Leave some the 8-inch length. Have students form letters using the pieces. Drinking straws are not suitable for letters that have curved lines but work well for those with straight and slanted lines.

Floor Letters

Have students form letters from various classroom materials, such as jump ropes, building blocks, beads, string, and so on.

Finger-Paint Letters

Using finger paints and finger-paint paper, have students trace letters with their fingers.

Board Letters

Encourage students to use the board or chart paper to practice their letters.

The Pocket Chart

Purpose

To provide a device that will allow students to practice word substitutions and to play with words

Developing Concepts Using the *Pocket Chart*

The ***Pocket Chart*** will help students understand written language. They will begin to understand the concept of words, phrases, and sentences. It is easy to substitute and play with words in the ten-line ***Pocket Chart.***

Introducing Print At the beginning of the year, use the ***Pocket Chart*** to introduce print in another way to students. Seeing the words in the ***Pickled Peppers Big Book*** on the board, on chart paper, or in the ***Pocket Chart*** gives students several opportunities to understand print.

Words Take the ***Pocket Chart Word Cards*** out of the ***Pocket Chart,*** and allow students to handle the individual cards. Students will begin to comprehend the concept of words and learn that words vary in length.

Sequence Arrange the ***Pocket Chart Word Cards*** and ***Pocket Chart Picture Cards*** out of sequence and "read" them. Have students help you rearrange the cards in order, reinforcing their understanding of word order in phrases and sentences.

Matching Words to Pictures Show students a ***Pocket Chart Picture Card.*** Have them say the name of the picture, and ask them for the beginning and ending sounds of the picture name. Allow them to choose the matching ***Pocket Chart Word Card*** based on their answers to your questions. After students have had many experiences with written words and the ***Pocket Chart,*** place the ***Word Cards*** in the ***Pocket Chart,*** and have students match the ***Picture Cards*** with the ***Word Cards.***

Matching Words to Words Use ***Pickled Peppers*** selections that repeat words or entire lines several times. Place portions of a selection in the ***Pocket Chart,*** leaving space for students to complete the excerpt by placing the appropriate repeated ***Pocket Chart Word Cards*** in the ***Pocket Chart.***

Rhyme and Substituting Words After students have learned a ***Pickled Peppers*** selection, place a portion of it in the ***Pocket Chart,*** then substitute rhyming ***Pocket Chart Word Cards*** or ***Picture Cards*** for various words. Although the result may be a change in meaning, students will hear a new rhyme. You may want to place ***Alphabet Letter Cards*** over the letters that make the initial sound of key words to create rhyming words with different initial sounds. For example, you may want to place the *Mm* card over the initial consonants in "Peter Piper picked" to make "Meter Miper micked."

Position Words and Prepositional Phrases Place in the ***Pocket Chart*** a phrase such as "under the [picture of a bed]" and substitute the ***Pocket Chart Word Cards*** to make other phrases. Ask students to change the phrase by changing the position word or the ***Pocket Chart Picture Card.*** Position words include *after, against, at, behind, down, here, in, on, out, over, right, underneath,* and *up.*

Framing Sentences Place only the beginning of a sentence in the ***Pocket Chart Pocket Chart,*** such as "I hear a ⎯⎯⎯."

Ask students to finish the sentence by placing a ***Pocket Chart Word Card*** or ***Picture Card*** at the end. You may also choose to set incomplete lines from "Keep a Poem in Your Pocket" in the ***Pocket Chart,*** asking students to complete the line with an appropriate card.

Pocket Chart Card Lists

The following lists are intended to save time in gathering ***Pocket Chart Word Cards*** and ***Picture Cards*** for ***Pickled Peppers*** selections and other activities. ***Picture Cards*** are in **boldfaced type.**

Numbers

0/zero, **1**/one, **2**/two, **3**/three, **4**/four, **5**/five, **6**/six, **7**/seven, **8**/eight, **9**/nine, **10**/ten

Colors

black/black, **blue**/blue/azul, **brown**/brown, **gray, green**/green/verde, **orange**/orange/anaranjada, **pink**/pink, **purple**/purple, **red**/red, **white**/white, **yellow**/yellow/amarilla

Foods

apple, apple juice, berry/berry, **bowls of spaghetti, cherry**/cherry, **corn**/corn, **eggplants, ice, jam, juice, loaf, bread, loaves of bread, meat, noodle,** orange, **peanut butter, peppers**/peppers, **pickled pears, pie, pizza pies, potatoes, pumpkins, rice, roasted turkeys, tomatoes, vegetables, water**/water, **watermelons, yam**

Opposites

big, little; **black**/black, **white**/white; **day, night**/night; for, against; in, out; short, tall; up, down

Pickled Peppers Big Book Selections

I'm a Little Teapot* a, all, and, and, get, handle, hear, here, Here, I, I'm, is, is, little, me, me, me, my, my, out, over, pour, short, shout, spout, stout, **teapot**/teapot, Tip, up, When

One, Two, Buckle My Shoe* **1**/One, **2**/two, **3**/Three, **4**/four, **5**/Five, **6**/six, **7**/Seven, **8**/eight, **9**/Nine, **10**/ten, A, big, Buckle, **door**/door, fat, **hen**/hen, Lay, my, Pick, **shoe**/shoe, Shut, **sticks**/sticks, straight, the, them, up

Little Boy Blue**** after, blow, **boy**/boy, **Boy Blue**/Boy Blue, Come, **corn**/corn, cow's, **horn**/horn, in, in, is, looks, meadow, **sheep**/sheep, sheep's, the, the, the, the, The, The, Where, Who, your

Jack and Jill* a, after, and, And, And, broke, came, **crown**/crown, down, fell, fetch, **hill,** hill, his, **Jack**/Jack, Jack, **Jill**/Jill, Jill, of, **pail**/pail, the, To, tumbling, up, **water**/water, Went

Humpty Dumpty* a, a, again, all, All, and, Couldn't, fall, great, had, **horses**/horses, Humpty, **Humpty Dumpty**/Humpty Dumpty, Humpty Dumpty, King's, King's, **men**/men, on, put, sat, the, the, together, **wall**/wall

Little Bo Peep* alone, and, And, behind, **Bo Peep**/Bo Peep, come, doesn't, find, has, her, know, Leave, Little, lost, **sheep**/sheep, **tails**/tails, them, them, their, them, they'll, to, Wagging, where

Peter Piper** a, A, of, of, **peck**/peck, peck, **peppers**/peppers, peppers, **Peter Piper**/Peter Piper, Peter Piper, picked, picked, pickled, pickled

One Hungry Monster** **1**/One, **2**/two, **3**/Three, **4**/four, **5**/Five, **6**/six, **7**/Seven, **8**/eight, **9**/Nine, **10**/ten, and, **apple juice,** be, **bed**/bed, begging, **bowls of spaghetti, clam, eggplants,** fed, groaning, hungry, **jam, loaves of bread,** moaning, **monster**/monster, **monsters,** my, **orange**/orange, **peanut butter, pickled pears, pizza pies, pumpkins, purple**/purple, **roasted turkeys,** to, underneath, **watermelons**

Rope Rhyme** and, and, and, Bounce, clappedy-slappedy, Get, giggle, **ground**/ground, hits, in, it, jump, kick, Listen, Listen, now, ready, right, **rope**/rope, set, sound, spin, that, the, the, to, to, when

Who Said Red?** A, A, A, **berry**/berry, **cherry**/cherry, Did, **red**/red, red, red, red, red, red, Santa, say, sign, stop, **stop sign,** very, Who, you

Rhyme*** a, A, A, and, **black**/black, blunder, Come, down, dunder, **hills**/hills, I, I, it, like, like, see, see, slow, **storm**/storm, storm, storm, stumbling, the, thunder, to, to

Tent***** A, **bone**/bone, bone, canvas, cut, for, from, I, is, It's, It's, Just, like, me, measure, My, sewn, **skin**/skin, stretched, **tent**/tent, That's, to, to, where, wonder

Little Pine* a, a, against, But, doesn't, even, feet, few, grows, have, I, I, is, it, it, it, It, just, keep, little, measuring, more, My, myself, **pine**/pine, slower, tall, the, the, **tree**/tree, trunk, watch, yet

Houses/Casitas (English)* **1**/one, A, a, a, a, an, **blue**/blue, bouquet, **bouquet of flowers,** down, **flowers**/flowers, **green**/green, **house**/house, house, house, house, is, Just, Like, look, of, **orange**/orange, ours, **street**/street, the, The, **yellow**/yellow

Houses/Casitas (Spanish)*** a, **amarilla**/amarilla, **anaranjada**/anaranjada, Asómate, **azul**/azul, **calle**/calle, **casita**/casita, casita, casita, casita, la, mira, Una, una, una, una, **verde**/verde, y

Keep a Poem in Your Pocket** a, a, and, and, at, **bed**/bed, feel, **head**/head, in, in, in, Keep, lonely, never, night, picture, **pocket**/pocket, poem, when, you'll, your, your, you're

* There are **Pocket Chart Word** or **Picture Cards** for the entire selection.

There are **Pocket Chart Word or **Picture Cards** for the first four lines of the selection.

***There are **Pocket Chart Word** or **Picture Cards** for the first five lines of the selection.

****There are **Pocket Chart Word** or **Picture Cards** for the first six lines of the selection.

*****There are **Pocket Chart Word** or **Picture Cards** for the first eight lines of the selection.

Introduction of Letters and Sounds

Lesson	Letters and Sounds	Pre-Decodables/Decodables	High-Frequency Words
Unit 1			
Lesson 1	A		
Lesson 2	B	*Pre-Decodable* 1: The First Day of Kindergarten	
Lesson 3	C		
Lesson 4	D	*Pre-Decodable* 2: Apple Pie	
Lesson 5	E		
Lesson 6	F		
Lesson 7	A-F	*Pre-Decodable* 3: A Farm	a
Lesson 8	G		
Lesson 9	H	*Pre-Decodable* 4: The Lunch	the
Lesson 10	I		
Lesson 11	J		
Lesson 12	K	*Pre-Decodable* 5: School	and
Lesson 13	L		
Lesson 14	M	*Pre-Decodable* 6: Go Play!	go
Lesson 15	G-M		
Unit 2			
Lesson 1	N		
Lesson 2	O	*Pre-Decodable* 7: The Zoo	had
Lesson 3	P		
Lesson 4	Q	*Pre-Decodable* 8: Colors	he
Lesson 5	R		
Lesson 6	S		
Lesson 7	N-S	*Pre-Decodable* 9: Shapes	I
Lesson 8	T		
Lesson 9	U	*Pre-Decodable* 10: Animal Tracks	see
Lesson 10	V		
Lesson 11	W		
Lesson 12	X	*Pre-Decodable* 11: The Tree	has
Lesson 13	Y		
Lesson 14	Z	*Pre-Decodable* 12: Flowers	you
Lesson 15	T-Z		

Lesson	Letters and Sounds	Pre-Decodables/Decodables	High-Frequency Words
Unit 3			
Lesson 1	initial /s/		
Lesson 2	final /s/		
Lesson 3	initial /m/		
Lesson 4	final /m/		
Lesson 5	review /s/ and /m/	*Pre-Decodable* 13: We Go	we
Lesson 6	initial /d/		
Lesson 7	final /d/		
Lesson 8	initial /p/		
Lesson 9	final /p/		
Lesson 10	review /d/ and /p/	*Pre-Decodable* 14: We Carry	of
Lesson 11	/a/		
Lesson 12	/a/		
Lesson 13	review /s/, /m/, and /a/	*Pre-Decodable* 15: In the Park	in
Lesson 14	blending		
Lesson 15	/s/, /m/, /a/, /d/ and /p/	*Decodable* 1: Sam and Pam	am
Unit 4			
Lesson 1	initial /h/		
Lesson 2	initial /h/		
Lesson 3	initial /t/		
Lesson 4	final /t/		
Lesson 5	review /h/ and /t/	*Decodable* 2: A Hat!	at, to
Lesson 6	initial /n/		
Lesson 7	final /n/		
Lesson 8	initial /l/		
Lesson 9	final /l/		
Lesson 10	review /n/ and /l/	*Decodable* 3: Nan and Lad	as, have
Lesson 11	/i/		
Lesson 12	/i/		
Lesson 13	review /h/, /t/, and /i/		
Lesson 14	review /n/, /l/, and /i/		
Lesson 15	/h/, /t/, /i/, /n/, and /l/	*Decodable* 4: Tim in Sand	is, it

Lesson	Letters and Sounds	Pre-Decodables/Decodables	High-Frequency Words
Unit 5			
Lesson 1	initial /b/		
Lesson 2	final /b/		
Lesson 3	/k/ spelled *Cc*		
Lesson 4	/k/ spelled *Cc*		
Lesson 5	/b/ and /k/	*Decodable* 5: Cal Can Bat	can, his
Lesson 6	/o/		
Lesson 7	/o/		
Lesson 8	initial /r/		
Lesson 9	final /r/		
Lesson 10	initial /g/	*Decodable* 6: Ron Hops	him, on
Lesson 11	final /g/		
Lesson 12	review /r/ and /g/		
Lesson 13	review /b/, /k/, and /o/		
Lesson 14	review /r/, /g/, and /o/		
Lesson 15	/b/, /k/, /o/, /r/, and /g/	*Decodable* 7: Glad Pam	did, girl
Unit 6			
Lesson 1	initial /j/		
Lesson 2	initial /j/		
Lesson 3	initial /f/		
Lesson 4	final /f/		
Lesson 5	review /j/ and /f/	*Decodable* 8: Jam Pot	for
Lesson 6	/u/		
Lesson 7	/u/		
Lesson 8	/ks/ (*Xx*)		
Lesson 9	/ks/ (*Xx*)		
Lesson 10	/z/	*Decodable* 9: Bud and Max	but, up
Lesson 11	/z/ spelled Ss		
Lesson 12	review /ks/ and /z/		
Lesson 13	review /j/, /f/, and /u/		
Lesson 14	review /ks/, /z/, and /u/		
Lesson 15	/j/, /f/, /u/, /ks/, and /z/	*Decodable* 10: Liz and Tad	all

Lesson	Letters and Sounds	Pre-Decodables/Decodables	High-Frequency Words
Unit 7			
Lesson 1	initial /w/		
Lesson 2	final /w/		
Lesson 3	/k/ spelled Kk		
Lesson 4	/k/ spelled Kk		
Lesson 5	review /w/ and /k/	*Decodable* 11: Kim and Sam	look, with
Lesson 6	/e/		
Lesson 7	/e/		
Lesson 8	initial /kw/ (*Qu*)		
Lesson 9	initial /kw/ (*Qu*)		
Lesson 10	initial /y/	*Decodable* 12: Quin and the Jets	her, what
Lesson 11	initial /v/		
Lesson 12	review /y/ and /v/		
Lesson 13	review /w/, /k/, and /e/		
Lesson 14	review /kw/, /y/, /v/, and /e/		
Lesson 15	/w/, /k/, /e/, /kw/, /y/, and /v/	*Decodable* 13: Vic Yelps	was, were
Unit 8			
Lesson 1	initial /ā/		
Lesson 2	initial and medial /ā/		
Lesson 3	medial /ā/		
Lesson 4	medial /ā/ and a_e		
Lesson 5	blending with /ā/	*Decodable* 14: Jake Plants Grapes	said, that
Lesson 6	initial /ī/		
Lesson 7	initial and medial /ī/		
Lesson 8	medial /ī/		
Lesson 9	medial /ī/ and i_e		
Lesson 10	blending with /ī/	*Decodable* 15: Mike and Spike	down, they
Lesson 11	review /ā/ and /ī/		
Lesson 12	review /ā/ and /ī/		
Lesson 13	review /ā/ and /ī/		
Lesson 14	review /ā/ and /ī/		
Lesson 15	blending with /ā/ and /ī/	*Decodable* 16: A Nut Pile	some, there

Lesson	Sound and Letters	Pre-Decodables/Decodables	High-Frequency Words
Unit 9			
Lesson 1	initial /ō/		
Lesson 2	initial and medial /ō/		
Lesson 3	medial /ō/		
Lesson 4	medial /ō/ and o_e		
Lesson 5	blending with /ō/	*Decodable* 17: An Old Flag	boy, out
Lesson 6	initial /ū/		
Lesson 7	initial and medial /ū/		
Lesson 8	medial /ū/		
Lesson 9	medial /ū/ and u_e		
Lesson 10	blending with /ū/	*Decodable* 18: Cute Little Mule	do, little
Lesson 11	review /ō/ and /ū/		
Lesson 12	review /ō/ and /ū/		
Lesson 13	review /ō/ and /ū/		
Lesson 14	review /ō/ and /ū/		
Lesson 15	blending with /ō/ and /ū/	*Decodable* 19: The Cutest Pet	when, then
Unit 10			
Lesson 1	initial /ē/		
Lesson 2	initial and medial /ē/		
Lesson 3	medial /ē/		
Lesson 4	medial /ē/		
Lesson 5	blending with /ē/	*Decodable* 20: We Did It!	be, she
Lesson 6	review /ā/ and /ă/		
Lesson 7	review /ī/ and /ĭ/		
Lesson 8	review /ā/, /ă/, /ī/, and /ĭ/		
Lesson 9	review /ō/ and /ŏ/		
Lesson 10	review /ū/ and /ŭ/		
Lesson 11	review /ō/, /ŏ/, /ū/, and /ŭ/		
Lesson 12	review /ē/ and /ĕ/		
Lesson 13	/ā/, /ī/, /ō/, /ă/, /ŏ/, /ĭ/		
Lesson 14	/ū/, /ē/, /ŭ/, /ĕ/		
Lesson 15	review		

Alphabet Sound Card Stories

Card 2: /b/ Ball

Bobby loves his basketball.

He bounces it all day.

The ball goes /b/ /b/ /b/ /b/ /b/

As it bounces on its way.

Card 4: /d/ Dinosaur

Dinah, the dancing dinosaur,

Had huge and clumsy feet.

They went /d/ /d/ /d/ /d/ /d/

As Dinah kept the beat.

Card 3: /c/ Camera

Carlos clicks his camera

/k/ /k/ /k/ /k/ /k/ /k/ it goes.

The pictures come out crisp and clear.

So give a smile, /k/ /k/ /k/ Carlos is here.

Card 6: /f/ Fan

Franny the fan spins, oh, so fast.

Spreading fresh air with a regular blast.

When Franny the fan goes round and round

/f/ /f/ /f/ /f/ /f/ /f/ is her fast fan sound.

Card 7: /g/ Gopher

Gary is a gopher

Who gulps green grapes all day.

When he gulps and giggles,

/g/ /g/ /g/ /g/ /g/ /g/ is what he'll say.

Card 10: /j/ Jump

Jenny and Jackson like to have fun.

They play jacks, jump rope, and juggle in the sun.

Each time they jump, their feet hit the ground.

/j/ /j/ /j/ /j/ /j/ is the jumping-rope sound.

Card 8: /h/ Hound

Harry the hound dog

Hurries around.

/h/ /h/ /h/ /h/ /h/ /h/

Is his hurrying sound.

Card 11: /k/ Camera

Carlos clicks his camera

/k/ /k/ /k/ /k/ /k/ /k/ it goes.

The pictures come out crisp and clear.

So give a smile, /k/ /k/ /k/ Carlos is here.

Card 12: /l/ Lion

Look! It's Leon the Lion.

Leon loves to lap water from lakes.

This is the lapping sound Leon makes:

/l/ /l/ /l/ /l/ /l/ /l/.

Card 14: /n/ Nest

n/ /n/ /n/ /n/

What is in that noisy nest?

A nervous night owl crying?

A nosy nuthatch chatting?

A nightingale that's sighing?

No! It's a bluebird napping!

/n/ /n/ /n/ /n/

Card 13: /m/ Monkey

For Muzzy, the Monkey,

Bananas are yummy.

She munches so many,

They fill up her tummy.

She says /m/ /m/ /m/ /m/ /m/!

Card 16: /p/ Popcorn

Popcorn! Popcorn! Ping and Pong shouted,

Let's pop some in a pot, because we like it hot!

/p/ /p/ /p/ /p/ /p/ was the sound it made.

Card 17: /kw/ Quacking ducks

Quincy the duck couldn't quite quack.

He said /kw/ /kw/ /kw/.

Quincy kept trying, but all he could say was:

/kw/ /kw/ /kw/ /kw/ /kw/.

Card 19: /s/ Sausages

Sue buys sausages on Saturday.

Sam cooks sausages on Sunday.

The sausages sizzle /s/ /s/ /s/ /s/ /s/ /s/ when hot.

Sam eats sausages, but Sue does not.

Card 18: /r/ Robot

Rosie the Robot just runs and runs: /r/ /r/ /r/,

Racing around to get her chores done /r/ /r/ /r/.

Running here, running there,

Running almost everywhere: /r/ /r/ /r/.

Card 20: /t/ Timer

Tom Tuttle's timer ticks like this:

/t/ /t/ /t/ /t/ /t/.

Tonight Tom Tuttle wants tomatoes on toast.

He sets his timer. Listen carefully:

/t/ /t/ /t/ /t/ /t/.

What sound would the timer make if you set it?

/t/ /t/ /t/ /t/ /t/.

Card 22: /v/ Vacuum

Vinny the Vacuum is cleaning again.

Before visitors visit, he always begins.

This is the sound of his very loud voice:

/v/ /v/ /v/ /v/ /v/ /v/

As he vacuums and vacuums all over the place:

/v/ /v/ /v/ /v/ /v/ /v/.

Card 24: /ks/ Exit

Rex is called the Exiting X.

He runs to guard the door.

To get past Rex,

Make the sound of the x:

/ks/ /ks/ /ks/ /ks/ /ks/.

Card 23: /w/ Washer

Willie the Washer washed white clothes all week.

When he washed he went
/w/ /w/ /w/ /w/ /w/ /w/.

Willie the Washer was tired; he sprang a leak.

He washed and washed and he went:
/w/ /w/ /w/ /w/.

Card 25: /y/ Yaks

Yolanda and Yoshiko are yaks.

They don't yell.

They just yak: /y/ /y/ /y/ /y/ /y/.

Yakety-yak! Yakety-yak!

What is the sound of the curious yaks?

/y/ /y/ /y/ /y/ /y/.

Card 26: /z/ Zipper

Zack's jacket has a zipper.

Zack zips it up and it makes this sound:

/z/ /z/ /z/ /z/ /z/ /z/.

Zack zips it down and it makes this sound:

/z/ /z/ /z/ /z/ /z/ /z/.

Card 28: /e/ Hen

Jen's pet hen likes to peck, peck, peck: /e/ /e/ /e/.

She pecks at a speck on the new red deck: /e/ /e/ /e/.

This is how her pecking sounds:

/e/ /e/ /e/ /e/ /e/ /e/

When she pecks at a speck on the hen house deck.

Card 27: /a/ Lamb

I'm Pam the lamb, I am.

This is how I tell the farmer where I am:

/a/ /a/ /a/ /a/ /a/.

I'm Pam the lamb, I am.

This is how I tell my friends where I am:

/a/ /a/ /a/ /a/ /a/.

Card 29: /i/ Pig

Here sits Pickles the Pig.

Tickle Pickles, and she'll get the giggles.

This is the sound of Pickles' giggles:

/i/ /i/ /i/ /i/ /i/ /i/.

Card 30: /o/ Fox

Bob the fox did not feel well at all.

He jogged to the doctor's office.

"Say /o/, Mr. Fox. /o/ /o/ /o/."

"My head is hot, and my throat hurts a lot."

"Say /o/, Mr. Fox, /o/ /o/ /o/."

Card 31: /u/ Tug

Tubby the Tugboat can huff and puff

And push and pull to move big stuff.

/u/ /u/ /u/ /u/ /u/

That's the sound of Tubby the Tug.

He works all day from dawn till dusk.

/u/ /u/ / u/ /u/ /u/.

High-Frequency Word List

Level Pre-K High-Frequency Words

a	go	in	the
and	had	is	up
at	have	on	was
can	he	see	with
down	I	she	you

Level K High-Frequency Words

all	for	look	there
am	girl	of	they
as	has	out	to
be	her	said	we
boy	him	some	were
but	his	that	what
did	it	then	when
do	little		

Supplemental Word List

You can use the following word list in a number of ways to extend the lessons. Words are listed by beginning sounds, ending sounds, and medial vowel sounds.

Beginning Sounds

Beginning /ā/
acorn
ape
apron

Beginning /a/
acrobat
alligator
apple
apple juice
astronaut

Beginning /b/
bag
bait
ball
balloon
banana
baseball
basketball
bat
beans
bed
bee
bell
bird
boat
book
bow
bowl
bowling ball
box
bread

broom
bug
bus

Beginning /k/
cake
can
cane
cap
cat
clam
coat
cook
core
cup
cut

Beginning /d/
dad
deer
dice
dime
dish
dog
doll
dollar
donkey
door
dress
drum
duck

Beginning /ē/
eagle
ear
earphones
easel
eel

Beginning /e/
Eggplant
elephant
elk

envelope

Beginning /f/
falcon
fan
feet
fern
fir
fish
five
fly
food
football
fork
four
fox
Frisbee
frog

Beginning /g/
game
gate
glue
goat
goose
grass
green
guitar

Beginning /h/
ham
hand
hat
hawk
heaven
hen
hive
hog
hole
hook
horse
hot

house
hug

Beginning /ī/
ice
ice cream
icicles
iron
island
ivy

Beginning /i/
igloo
ill
inch
infant
insect

Beginning /j/
jam
jar
jeans
jellybean
jellyfish
judge
juice

Beginning /k/
kangaroo
kettle
keys
kitchen
kittens
koala

Beginning /l/
ladybug
lake
lamp
lion
lock
lockers

Beginning /m/
magnet

mailbox
man
map
mask
mat
meal
meat
milk
mittens
monkey
moon
moose
mop
mouse
mug

Beginning /n/
nails
necklace
needle
nest
newspaper
nickle
nine
noodle
nurse

Beginning /ō/
oak tree
oasis
oatmeal
oboe
ocean
overalls

Beginning /o/
octopus
olive
ostrich
otter
ox

Beginning /p/
pail
pan
panda
pants
pear
peas
pen
penny
pickle
pickled pears
pie
pig
pineapple
pink
pizza pies
plum bun
popcorn
post
pot
potatoes
pumpkins
purple
Beginning /kw/
quail
quart
queen
quill
quilt
Beginning /r/
raccoon
racer
radio
rake
rat
red
rice
road
robot
rock

rocket
rug
ruler
Beginning /s/
sack
sad
sail
Sam
sand
sandals
seal
seven
silk
six
skate
soccer ball
sock
spoon
star
stew
sticks
stir
store
storm
sun
Beginning /t/
table
tail
tap
tape
target
tear
telephone
television
ten
tie
toad
toast
toe
tomatoes

top
tree
turkey
turtle
two
Beginning /ū/
ukulele
unicorn
uniform
United States
utensil
Beginning /u/
umbrella
umpire
uncle
under
usher
Beginning /v/
van
vase
vegetables
veil
vine
violin
volcano
Beginning /w/
wagon
wallet
walrus
watch
well
wig
wing
Beginning /y/
yam
yard
yarn
yell
yellow

yo-yo
yolk
Beginning /z/
zebra
zero
zinnia
zither
zoo

Ending Sounds
Ending /ā/
away
bay
day
gray
hay
Jay
may
Monday
play
ray
say
today
Ending /b/
Bob
cab
cob
cub
cube
jab
job
mob
rob
robe
rub
scrub
tab
tub
web

Ending /d/
bad
bed
bread
did
feed
had
lid
mad
mud
red
rid
sad
seed
weed
yard
Ending /ē/
bee
Frisbee
he
key
knee
me
monkey
see
she
three
tree
turkey
we
Ending /f/
calf
cough
cuff
deaf
elf
half
laugh
off
rough

stiff
stuff
tough
Ending /g/
bag
big
dog
egg
hog
hug
jog
ladybug
leg
log
pig
rag
rug
tag
twig
wig
Ending /ī/
by
cry
die
dry
fly
high
my
pie
sigh
tie
why
Ending /k/
bike
black
clock
cook
dock
duck

elk
fork
hook
lake
like
lock
milk
pack
pink
poke
rack
rake
rock
sock
take
Ending /l/
basketball
bell
bill
eel
feel
football
oatmeal
pail
quail
rail
seal
snail
tail
Ending /m/
broom
dime
drum
game
hum
jam
room
seem
uniform
yam

Ending /n/
can
fern
green
hen
kitchen
lion
moon
ocean
queen
raccoon
spoon
sun
ten
unicorn
van
vine
violin
wagon
yarn
Ending /ō/
blow
bow
doe
flow
go
low
mow
no
radio
row
slow
so
toe
volcano
yellow
yo-yo
zero

Ending /p/
cap
cape
cup
deep
hip
hop
keep
lip
map
pup
skip
sleep
tap
tip
top
trap
Ending /r/
alligator
bar
car
core
deer
door
fur
four
guitar
jar
more
newspaper
otter
pour
roar
ruler
stir
usher
Ending /s/
bus
class
dress

goose
grass
horse
house
miss
moss
mouse
octopus
pass
toss
walrus
yes
Ending /t/
astronaut
bat
cat
coat
feet
gate
goat
hat
hot
infant
kite
knot
meat
pot
quilt
wallet
white
Ending /ū/
cue
few
hue
menu
nephew
preview
rescue
review
view

Ending /v/
brave
cave
dive
dove
eve
five
gave
give
glove
have
hive
live
love
save
shave
stove

Ending /ks/
ax
box
fix
flax
fox
mix
ox
relax
six
wax

Ending /z/
breeze
buzz
daze
fizz
freeze
fuzz
haze
jazz
maze
peas
quiz

size
sneeze
squeeze
trees

Medial Sounds

Medial /ā/
date
face
fade
game
gate
gave
lake
lane
late
made
make
mate
race
rake
table
wave

Medial /a/
bat
black
can
cap
hat
jam
ham
lamp
pants
sad
van
yam

Medial /ē/
beam
bean
feet

heap
keep
mean
meat
neat
seal
seed
seen
sneeze
team
weed

Medial /e/
bed
bet
head
hen
let
men
met
nest
net
pen
pet
red
set
ten

Medial /ī/
five
hide
hive
kite
life
line
mine
nice
nine
rice
ride
right

side
sight
time
vine

Medial /i/
bib
dish
fib
fin
fish
him
kittens
lip
milk
mittens
pig
pin
pink
rip
tin
tip
wig
win

Medial /ō/
boat
bowl
coal
coat
goat
hole
home
joke
mole
nose
poem
poke
post
roll
rose
toes

Medial /o/
dot
hot
knot
lock
lot
mop
not
pot
rock
sock
top

Medial /ū/
cube
cute
feud
fuel
fuse
huge
mule

Medial /u/
bug
bun
cup
cut
duck
dust
fun
hug
must
nut
rub
rug
run
sun
tub
tug

Index

Q

Question Marks, Unit 3: T109; **Unit 4:** T68, T118, T146, T156, T177, T188; **Unit 5:** T115, T193; **Unit 6:** T185, T189; **Unit 7:** T53, T195, T199; **Unit 8:** T49, T55, T117; **Unit 9:** T171; **Unit 10:** T68, T78, T115, T177, T197; *see also* End Marks

Quotation Marks, Unit 4: T111; **Unit 5:** T115; **Unit 6:** T185; **Unit 7:** T195; **Unit 8:** T117; **Unit 10:** T49, T197

R

Read Aloud Collection

Amelia's Show-and-Tell Fiesta (Mimi Chapra), **Unit 1:** T40–T45, T90, T250

America Is . . . (Louise Borden), **Unit 9:** T36–T41

Big Al (Andrew Clements), **Unit 3:** T36–T39, T55, T76

Bunny Cakes (Rosemary Wells), **Unit 5:** T36–T39

Can You See the Wind? (Allan Fowler), **Unit 10:** T36–T39

Lots and Lots of Zebra Stripes: Patterns in Nature (Stephen R. Swinburne), **Unit 2:** T40–T43

Mr. McGill Goes to Town (Jim Aylesworth), **Unit 7:** T36–T39

What Makes a Shadow? (Clyde Robert Bulla), **Unit 6:** T36–T39

What's Alive? (Kathleen Weidner Zoehfeld), **Unit 8:** T36–T39

Where Land Meets Sea (Allan Fowler), **Unit 4:** T36–T39

Reading Recommendations, Unit 1: T122, T154, T200; **Unit 2:** T38, T66, T116, T148, T194, T226; **Unit 3:** T74, T144, T186, T220; **Unit 4:** T74, T152, T226; **Unit 5:** T148, T222; **Unit 6:** T70, T140, T214; **Unit 7:** T74, T226; **Unit 8:** T78, T152, T226; **Unit 9:** T76, T146, T220; **Unit 10:** T74

Read the Selection, Unit 1: T55, T113, T125, T157, T191, T215; **Unit 2:** T53, T69, T107, T119, T135, T151, T185, T197, T209, T229; **Unit 3:** T47, T97, T107, T121, T135, T167, T177, T189, T205; **Unit 4:** T47, T61, T97, T107, T125, T143, T175, T195, T211; **Unit 5:** T47, T63, T101, T111, T125, T139, T171, T181, T191, T207; **Unit 6:** T47, T59, T93, T103, T117, T131, T163, T183, T199; **Unit 7:** T47, T97, T107, T123, T139, T171, T181, T191, T209; **Unit 8:** T47, T63, T101, T111, T127, T143, T175, T185, T195, T211; **Unit 9:** T49, T63, T99, T109, T123, T137, T169, T179, T189, T205; **Unit 10:** T47, T61, T99, T111, T127, T143, T175, T185, T195, T211

Reading with a Writer's Eye, Unit 3: T61, T63, T65, T67, T121, T123, T125, T127, T177, T179, T205, T207, T209, T211, T213; **Unit 4:** T61, T63, T65, T67, T125, T127, T129, T131, T133, T185, T187, T211, T213, T215, T217, T219; **Unit 5:** T63, T65, T67, T69, T71, T125, T127, T129, T131, T181, T183, T207, T209, T211, T213, T215; **Unit 6:** T59, T61, T63, T117, T119, T121, T123, T173, T175, T199, T201, T203, T205, T207; **Unit 7:** T61, T63, T65, T67, T123, T125, T127, T129, T131, T181, T183, T209, T211, T213, T215, T217, T219; **Unit 8:** T63, T65, T67, T69, T71, T127, T129, T131, T133, T135, T185, T187, T211, T213, T215, T217, T219; **Unit 9:** T63, T65, T67, T123, T125, T127,

T129, T179, T181, T205, T207, T209, T211, T213; **Unit 10:** T61, T63, T65, T67, T127, T129, T131, T133, T185, T187, T211, T213, T215, T217, T219

Reality and Fantasy, Unit 2: T229, T231, T233, T235, T237, T239; **Unit 3:** T205, T207, T209, T211; **Unit 6:** T201, T203, T205; **Unit 10:** T211, T213, T215, T217; *see also* Comprehension Skills: Reality and Fantasy

Research in Action, Unit 1: T32, T55, T65, T132, T154, T215; **Unit 2:** T43, T85, T101, T142; **Unit 3:** T29, T39, T50, T54, T217, T226; **Unit 4:** T39, T152; **Unit 5:** T56, T78, T83, T103, T188; **Unit 6:** T39, T53, T96, T199; **Unit 7:** T77, T100, T202; **Unit 8:** T29, T39, T56, T81, T82; **Unit 9:** T56, T79, T99, T123, T172; **Unit 10:** T29, T68

Reteach, Unit 1: T171, T225, T229; **Unit 2:** T28, T87, T114, T225; **Unit 3:** T34, T45, T58, T73, T93, T95, T104, T119, T132, T165, T174, T218; **Unit 4:** T27, T58, T95, T104, T119, T123, T140, T151, T173, T182, T193, T208; **Unit 5:** T27, T34, T61, T77, T83, T99, T108, T123, T136, T147, T169, T189; **Unit 6:** T27, T45, T56, T69, T89, T100, T115, T161, T170, T181, T196, T209, T213; **Unit 7:** T25, T27, T34, T45, T58, T73, T79, T95, T104, T121, T136, T147, T169, T178, T185, T220, T224; **Unit 8:** T26, T59, T73, T77, T108, T121, T123, T140, T151, T182, T225; **Unit 9:** T26, T43, T46, T71, T73, T75, T96, T120, T141, T144, T167, T187, T215, T219; **Unit 10:** T26, T41, T69, T72, T73, T94, T125, T147, T153, T173, T189, T193, T221, T225, T227; *see also* Differentiating Instruction: Reteach

Reviewing Letter Names, *see* Alphabetic Knowledge

Reviewing Letter Shapes, *see* Alphabetic Knowledge

Rhyme Posters

"Baa, Baa, Black Sheep," **Unit 1:** GS27; **Unit 2:** T179, T243

"Cobbler, Cobbler, Mend My Shoe," **Unit 1:** GS57

"Hickory Dickory Dock," **Unit 1:** GS21

"Higglety, Pigglety, Pop," **Unit 1:** GS33

"Mary Had a Little Lamb," **Unit 1:** GS15, GS24; **Unit 2:** T129, T145; **Unit 3:** T32–T33

"Pat-a-Cake," **Unit 1:** GS45

"Teddy Bear, Teddy Bear," **Unit 1:** GS51; **Unit 3:** T24–T25

"The Mulberry Bush," **Unit 1:** GS9

"Twinkle, Twinkle, Little Star," **Unit 1:** GS39

"Wee Willie Winkie," **Unit 1:** GS63

Rhymes and Rhyming

"One Potato, Two Potato," **Unit 1:** T67; **Unit 2:** T178–T179

"Polly Put the Kettle On," **Unit 1:** T25, T35

"Ten Little Ducklings," **Unit 1:** T48

Rhyming Words, Unit 1: T89, T111, T139, T151, T163, T167, T197, T209, T227, T245, T249; **Unit 2:** T112–T113, T128, T144, T156, T161, T191, T200, T201, T240–T241, T242–T243, T249; **Unit 3:** T24–T25, T92; **Unit 4:** T24–T25, T120, T178; **Unit 5:** T32–T33, T202; **Unit 6:** T126–T127, T136–T137, T210–T211; **Unit 9:** T111, T113, T142–T143, T200–T201, T216–T217

Routines

Discussing the Selection, Unit 1: T33, T63, T81, T131, T147, T205, T223, T241; **Unit 2:** T59, T75, T109, T125, T141, T153,

Science Lap Book

Selections

Index

Notes

Use this page to record lessons or elements that work well or need to be adjusted for future reference.

Lessons that work well.

Lessons that need adjustments.

Notes

Use this page to record lessons or elements that work well or need to be adjusted for future reference.

Lessons that work well.

Lessons that need adjustments.

Notes

Use this page to record lessons or elements that work well or need to be adjusted for future reference.

Lessons that work well.

Lessons that need adjustments.

Notes

Use this page to record lessons or elements that work well or need to be adjusted for future reference.

Lessons that work well.

Lessons that need adjustments.

Notes

Use this page to record lessons or elements that work well or need to be adjusted for future reference.

Lessons that work well.

Lessons that need adjustments.

Notes

Use this page to record lessons or elements that work well or need to be adjusted for future reference.

Lessons that work well.

Lessons that need adjustments.

Notes

Use this page to record lessons or elements that work well or need to be adjusted for future reference.

Lessons that work well.

Lessons that need adjustments.

Notes

Use this page to record lessons or elements that work well or need to be adjusted for future reference.

Lessons that work well.

Lessons that need adjustments.